GREAT
AMERICAN
POETRY

GREAT AMERICAN POETRY

Authors include

EDGAR ALLAN POE
HENRY WADSWORTH LONGFELLOW
WALT WHITMAN
EMILY DICKINSON
ROBERT FROST
WALLACE STEVENS
E. E. CUMMINGS
MARIANNE MOORE

GALLERY BOOKS

This edition published in Great Britain in 1990 by

The Octopus Group Limited
Michelin House, 81 Fulham Road, London SW3 6RB

This edition published in 1990 by Gallery Books
An imprint of W. H. Smith Publishers Inc.
112 Madison Avenue, New York, New York 10016

ISBN   0 8317 3956 8

Printed and bound in Great Britain by
William Clowes Limited, Beccles and London

CONTENTS

William Cullen Bryant

Ralph Waldo Emerson

Henry Wadsworth Longfellow

John Greenleaf Whittier

Edgar Allan Poe

Jones Very

Henry David Thoreau

James Russell Lowell

Walt Whitman

Emily Dickinson

Marianne Moore

e. e. cummings

Langston Hughes

ANNE BRADSTREET
c. 1612-1672

Daughter of Thomas Dudley, Governor of the
Massachusetts Bay Colony, Anne Bradstreet was born
in England but moved to America, aged 18, with her
husband Simon Bradstreet. The first edition of her
poems was published in England as *The Tenth Muse
Lately Sprung Up in England* and followed by prose
meditations and a spiritual autobiography, *Religious
Experiences*.

   She is now best known for later short poems
dealing with the New England she saw about her and
her own feelings, such as 'To my Dear and Loving
Husband' and 'Upon the Burning of our House'.

To my Dear and Loving Husband

If ever two were one, then surely we.
If ever man were lov'd by wife, then thee.
If ever wife was happy in a man,
Compare with me, ye women, if you can.
I prize thy love more than whole Mines of gold,
Or all the riches that the East doth hold.
My love is such that Rivers cannot quench,
Nor ought but love from thee give recompence.
Thy love is such I can no way repay;
The heavens reward thee manifold I pray.
Then while we live, in love lets so persever,
That when we live no more, we may live ever.

A Letter to her Husband, absent upon Publick Employment

As loving Hind that (Hartless) wants her Deer,
Scuds through the woods and fern with harkning ear,
Perplext, in every bush & nook doth pry
Her dearest Deer might answer ear or eye:
So doth my anxious soul, which now doth miss
A dearer Dear (far dearer Heart) than this,
Still wait with doubts, & hopes, and failing eye,
His voice to hear or person to discry.
Or as the pensive Dove doth all alone
On withered bough most uncouthly bemoan
The absence of her Love and loving Mate,
Whose loss hath made her so unfortunate:
Ev'n thus doe I, with many a deep sad groan,
Bewail my turtle true, who now is gone,
His presence and his safe return still woo
With thousand dolefull sighs & mournfull Coo.
Or as the loving Mullet, that true Fish,
Her fellow lost, nor joy nor life doth wish,

But lanches on that shore, there for to dye
Where she her captive husband doth espy.
Mine being gone, I lead a joyless life,
I have a loving fere, yet seem no wife:
But worst of all, to him can't steer my course,
I here, he there, alas, both kept by force.
Return my Dear, my joy, my only Love,
Unto thy Hinde, thy Mullet and thy Dove,
Who neither joyes in pasture, house nor streams;
The substance gone, O me, these are but dreams.
Together at one Tree, oh let us brouze,
And like two Turtles roost within one house,
And like the Mullets in one River glide,
Let's still remain but one, till death divide.

> *Thy loving Love and Dearest Dear,*
> *At home, abroad, and every where,*
>
> *A.B.*

Upon the Burning of our House

July 10th, 1666

In silent night when rest I took,
For sorrow near I did not look,
I waken'd was with thundring noise
And piteous shreiks of dreadfull voice.
That fearfull sound of 'Fire!' and 'Fire!'
Let no man know is my Desire.

I, starting up, the light did spye,
And to my God my heart did cry
To strengthen me in my Distresse,
And not to leave me succourlesse.
Then coming out, beheld apace
The flame consume my dwelling place.

And when I could no longer look,
I blest his Name that gave and took,
That layd my goods now in the dust:
Yea so it was, and so 'twas just.
It was his own: it was not mine;
Far be it that I should repine.

He might of All justly bereft,
But yet sufficient for us left.
When by the Ruines oft I past,
My sorrowing eyes aside did cast,
And here and there the places spye
Where oft I sate, and long did lye.

Here stood that Trunk, and there that chest;
There lay that store I counted best:
My pleasant things in ashes lye,
And them behold no more shall I.
Under thy roof no guest shall sitt,
Nor at thy Table eat a bitt.

No pleasant tale shall e'er be told,
Nor things recounted done of old.
No Candle e'er shall shine in Thee,
Nor bridegroom's voice e'er heard shall bee.
In silence ever shalt thou lye;
Adieu, Adieu; All's vanity.

Then streight I 'gan my heart to chide:
And did thy wealth on earth abide?
Didst fix thy hope on mouldring dust,
The arm of flesh didst make thy trust?
Raise up thy thoughts above the skye,
That dunghill mists away may flie.

Thou hast an house on high erect,
Fram'd by that mighty Architect,
With glory richly furnished,
Stands permanent though this bee fled.
It's purchaséd, and paid for, too,
By Him who hath enough to doe.

A Prise so vast as is unknown,
Yet, by his Gift, is made thine own.
There's wealth enough, I need no more;
Farewell my Pelf, farewell my Store.
The world no longer let me Love,
My Hope and Treasure lyes Above.

Contemplations

Some time now past in the Autumnal Tide,
   When Phoebus wanted but one hour to bed,
The trees all richly clad, yet void of pride,
   Were gilded o'er by his rich golden head;
Their leaves and fruits seem'd painted, but was true
Of green, of red, of yellow, mixed hew;
Rapt were my senses at this delectable view.

Then on a stately Oak I cast mine Eye,
   Whose ruffling top the Clouds seem'd to aspire:
'How long since thou wast in thine Infancy?
   Thy strength and stature, more thy years admire.
Hath hundred winters past since thou wast born,
Or thousand since thou brakest thy shell of horn?
If so, all these as nought, Eternity doth scorn.'

Then higher on the glistering Sun I gaz'd,
   Whose beams was shaded by the leafy Tree.
The more I look'd the more I grew amaz'd,

And softly said: 'What glory's like to thee,
Soul of this world, this Universe's Eye?
No wonder some made thee a Deity;
Had I not better known, alas! the same had I.

'Thou as a Bridegroom from thy Chamber rushest,
  And as a strong man joys to run a race;
The morn doth usher thee with smiles and blushes,
  The Earth reflects her glances in thy face;
Birds, insects, animals, with vegative,
Thy heart from death and dulness doth revive,
And in the darksome womb of fruitful nature dive.

'Thy swift Annual and diurnal Course,
  Thy daily straight and yearly oblique path,
Thy pleasing fervor and thy scorching force,
  All mortals here the feeling knowledge hath.
Thy presence makes it day, thy absence night;
Quaternal Seasons caused by thy might.
Hail, Creature full of sweetness, beauty, and delight!

'Art thou so full of glory that no Eye
  Hath strength thy shining Rays once to behold?
And is thy splendid Throne erect so high
  As to approach it can no earthly mould?
How full of glory, then, must thy Creator be
Who gave this bright light luster unto thee!
Admir'd, ador'd for ever be that Majesty!'

I heard the merry grashopper then sing,
  The black-clad Cricket bear a second part;
They kept one tune and played on the same string,
  Seeming to glory in their little Art.
Shall Creatures abject thus their voices raise,
And in their kind resound their makers praise,
Whilst I as mute can warble forth no higher lays?

Who thinks not oft upon the Fathers' ages?
   Their long descent; how nephews' sons they saw;
The starry observations of those Sages,
   And how their precepts to their sons were law;
How Adam sigh'd to see his Progeny
Clothed all in his black sinful Livery,
Who neither guilt nor yet the punishment could fly.

Our Life compare we with their length of days;
   Who to the tenth of theirs doth now arrive?
And though thus short, we shorten many ways,
   Living so little while we are alive:
In eating, drinking, sleeping, vain delight,
So unawares comes on perpetual night,
And puts all pleasures vain unto eternal flight.

By birth more noble then those creatures all,
   Yet seems by nature and by custom curs'd:
No sooner born, but grief and care makes fall,
   That state obliterate he had at first;
Nor youth, nor strength, nor wisdom spring again,
Nor habitations long their names retain,
But in oblivion to the final day remain.

Under the cooling shadow of a stately Elm,
   Close sate I by a goodly Rivers side,
Where gliding streams the Rocks did overwhelm;
   A lonely place, with pleasures dignified.
I once that lov'd the shady woods so well
Now thought the rivers did the trees excel;
And if the sun would ever shine, there would I dwell.

While on the stealing stream I fixt mine eye,
   Which to the long'd-for Ocean held its course,
I markt nor crooks nor rubs that there did lie
   Could hinder aught, but still augment its force:

'Oh happy Flood,' quoth I, 'that holds thy race
Till thou arrive at thy beloved place,
Nor is it rocks or shoals that can obstruct thy pace.

'Nor is't enough that thou alone may'st slide,
    But hundred brooks in thy clear waves do meet;
So hand in hand along with thee they glide
    To Thetis' house, where all embrace and greet:
Thou Emblem true of what I count the best,
O could I lead my Rivulets to rest,
So may we press to that vast mansion ever blest!

'Ye Fish which in this liquid Region 'bide,
    That for each season have your habitation,
Now salt, now fresh, where you think best to glide
    To unknown coasts to give a visitation,
In Lakes and ponds you leave your numerous fry;
So nature taught, and yet you know not why,
You wat'ry folk that know not your felicity.

'Look how the wantons frisk to taste the air,
    Then to the colder bottom straight they dive;
Eftsoon to Neptune's glassy Hall repair,
    To see what trade the great ones there do drive,
Who forage o'er the spacious sea-green field
And take the trembling prey before it yield,
Whose armour is their scales, their spreading fins their
    shield.'

While musing thus, with contemplation fed,
    And thousand fancies buzzing in my brain,
The sweet-tongu'd Philomel percht o'er my head,
    And chanted forth a most melodious strain;
Which rapt me so with wonder and delight
I judg'd my hearing better then my sight,
And wisht me wings with her a while to take my flight.

'O merry Bird,' said I, 'that fears no snares,
    That neither toils nor hoards up in thy barn,
Feels no sad thoughts, not 'cruciating cares
    To gain more good or shun what might thee harm;
Thy clothes ne'er wear, thy meat is everywhere,
Thy bed a bough, thy drink the water clear;
Reminds not what is past, nor what's to come dost fear.

'The dawning morn with songs thou dost prevent,
    Sets hundred notes unto thy feathered crew,
So each one tunes his pretty instrument
    And, warbling out the old, begins anew;
And thus they pass their youth in summer season,
Then follow thee into a better Region,
Where winter's never felt by that sweet airy legion.'

Man's at the best a creature frail and vain,
    In knowledge ignorant, in strength but weak;
Subject to sorrows, losses, sickness, pain.
    Each storm his state, his mind, his body break;
From some of these he never finds cessation,
But day or night, within, without, vexation,
Troubles from foes, from friends, from dear'st near'st
        relation.

The Mariner that on smooth waves doth glide
    Sings merrily and steers his Barque with ease,
As if he had command of wind and tide,
    And now become great Master of the seas;
But suddenly a storm spoils all the sport,
And makes him long for a more quiet port,
Which 'gainst all adverse winds may serve for fort.

So he that saileth in this world of pleasure,
    Feeding on sweets, that never bit of th' sour,
That's full of friends, of honour, and of treasure,

Fond fool, he takes this earth ev'n for heav'ns bower.
But sad affliction comes and makes him see
Here's neither honour, wealth, nor safety:
Only above is found all with security.

The Author to Her Book

Thou ill-formed offspring of my feeble brain,
Who after birth didst by my side remain,
Till snatched from thence by friends, less wise than true,
Who thee abroad, expos'd to publick view,
Made thee in raggs, halting to th' press to trudg,
Where errors were not lessened (all may judge).
At thy return my blushing was not small,
My rambling brat (in print) should mother call,
I cast thee by as one unfit for light,
Thy Visage was so irksome in my sight;
Yet being mine own, at length affection would
Thy blemishes amend, if so I could:
I wash'd thy face, but more defects I saw,
And rubbing off a spot still made a flaw.
I stretched thy joynts to make thee even feet,
Yet still thou run'st more hobling than is meet;
In better dress to trim thee was my mind,
But nought save homespun Cloth i' th' house I find[.]
In this array 'mongst Vulgars may'st thou roam[.]
In Criticks hands, beware thou dost not come;
And take thy way where yet thou art not known;
If for thy Father asked, say thou hadst none;
And for thy Mother, she alas is poor,
Which caus'd her thus to send thee out of door.

Before the Birth of One of Her Children

All things within this fading world hath end,
Adversity doth still our joys attend;
No ties so strong, no friends so dear and sweet,
But with death's parting blow is sure to meet.
The sentence past is most irrevocable,
A common thing, yet oh inevitable.
How soon, my Dear, death may my steps attend,
How soon't may be thy Lot to lose thy friend,
We are both ignorant, yet love bids me
These farewell lines to recommend to thee,
That when that knot's untied that made us one,
I may seem thine, who in effect am none.
And if I see not half my dayes that's due,
What nature would, God grant to yours and you;
The many faults that well you know I have
Let be interr'd in my oblivious grave;
If any worth or virtue were in me,
Let that live freshly in thy memory
And when thou feel'st no grief, as I no harms,
Yet love thy dead, who long lay in thine arms.
And when thy loss shall be repaid with gains
Look to my little babes[,] my dear remains.
And if thou love thyself, or loved'st me[,]
These o protect from step Dames injury.
And if chance to thine eyes shall bring this verse,
With some sad sighs honour my absent Herse;
And kiss this paper for thy loves dear sake,
Who with salt tears this last Farewel did take.

2

I wist not what to wish, yet sure thought I,
If so much excellence abide below;
How excellent is he that dwells on high?
Whose power and beauty by his works we know.
Sure he is goodness, wisdome, glory, light,
That hath this under world so richly dight:
More Heaven than Earth was here no winter and no
    night.

8

Silent alone, where none or saw, or heard,
In pathless paths I lead my wandring feet,
My humble Eyes to lofty Skyes I rear'd
To sing some Song, my mazed Muse thought meet.
My great Creator I would magnifie,
That nature had, thus decked liberally:
But Ah, and Ah, again, my imbecility!

18

When I behold the heavens as in their prime,
And then the earth (though old) stil clad in green,
The stones and trees, insensible of time,
Nor age nor wrinkle on their front are seen;
If winter comes, and greeness then do fade,
A Spring returns, and they more youthfull made;
But Man grows old, lies down, remains where once he's
    laid.

20

Shall I then praise the heavens, the trees, the earth
Because their beauty and their strength last longer

Shall I wish there, or never to had birth,
Because they're bigger, and their bodyes stronger?
Nay, they shall darken, perish, fade and dye,
And when unmade, so ever shall they lye,
But man was made for endless immortality.

35

O Time the fatal wrack of mortal things,
That draws oblivions curtains over kings,
Their sumptuous monuments, men know them not,
Their names without a Record are forgot,
Their parts, their ports, their pomp's all laid in th' dust
Nor wit nor gold, nor buildings scape times rust;
But he whose name is grav'd in the white stone
Shall last and shine when all of these are gone.

The Flesh and the Spirit

In secret place where once I stood,
Close by the banks of lacrym flood,
I heard two sisters reason on
Things that are past and things to come.
One Flesh was called, who had her eye
On worldly wealth and vanity;
The other Spirit, who did rear
Her thoughts unto a higher sphere.

Longing for Heaven

As weary pilgrim now at rest
 hugs with delight his silent nest,
His wasted limbs now lie full soft
 that miry steps have trodden oft,

Blesses himself to think upon
   his dangers past and travails done;
The burning sun no more shall heat,
   nor stormy rains on him shall beat;
The briars and thorns no more shall scratch,
   nor hungry wolves at him shall catch;
He erring pathes no more shall tread,
   nor wild fruits eat instead of bread;
For waters cold he doth not long,
   for thirst no more shall parch his tongue;
No rugged stones his feet shall gaul,
   nor stumps nor rocks cause him to fall;
All cares and fears he bids farewell,
   and means in safety now to dwell:
A pilgrim I on earth perplext,
   with sins, with cares and sorrows vext,
By age and pains brought to decay,
   and my clay house mould'ring away,
Oh how I long to be at rest
   and soar on high among the blest!
This body shall in silence sleep,
   mine eyes no more shall ever weep,
No fainting fits shall me assail,
   nor grinding pains my body frail,
With cares and fears ne'er cumbered be,
   nor losses know nor sorrows see.
What tho my flesh shall there consume?
   it is the bed Christ did perfume;
And when a few years shall be gone,
   this mortal shall be cloth'd upon:
A corrupt carcasse down it lies,
   a glorious body it shall rise;
In weakness and dishonour sown,
   in power 'tis rais'd by Christ alone.
Then soul and body shall unite,
   and of their maker have the sight.

Such lasting joys shall there behold
  as ear ne'er heard nor tongue e'er told.
Lord, make me ready for that day:
  then come, dear bridegroom, Come away!

EDWARD TAYLOR
c. 1645-1729

Edward Taylor was born in England but emigrated to
Boston in 1668, and after graduating from Harvard
became the pastor and physician of Westfield, Mass.
where he remained until his death. His work
languished unknown until 1937 but he is now
recognized as a major Puritan sacred poet.

The following poems reflect Taylor's debt to the
English devotional metaphysical poets such as Herbert
and Crashaw, and were originally written between
1680 and 1703.

Upon a Spider Catching a Fly

Thou sorrow, venom Elfe:
  Is this thy play,
To spin a web out of thyselfe
  To Catch a Fly?
    For why?

I saw a pettish wasp
  Fall foule therein:
Whom yet thy whorle pins did not hasp
  Lest he should fling
    His sting.

But as afraid, remote
  Didst stand hereat,
And with thy little fingers stroke
  And gently tap
    His back.

Thus gently him didst treate
  Lest he should pet,
And in a froppish, aspish heate
  Should greatly fret
    Thy net.

Whereas the silly Fly,
  Caught by its leg,
Thou by the throate took'st hastily,
  And 'hinde the head
    Bite Dead.

This goes to pot, that not
  Nature doth call.
Strive not above what strength hath got,
  Lest in the brawle
    Thou fall.

This Fray seems thus to us:
  Hells Spider gets
His intrails spun to whip Cords thus,
  And wove to nets,
    And sets.

To tangle Adams race
  In's stratagems
To their Destructions, Spoil'd, made base
  By venom things,
    Damn'd Sins.

But mighty, Gracious Lord,
  Communicate
Thy Grace to break the Cord; afford
  Us Glorys Gate
    And State.

We'll Nightingaile sing like,
  When pearcht on high
In Glories Cage, thy glory, bright:
  Yea, thankfully,
    For joy.

Huswifery

Make me, O Lord, thy Spinning Wheele compleat;
  Thy Holy Worde my Distaff make for mee.
Make mine Affections thy Swift Flyers neate,
  And make my Soule thy holy Spoole to bee.
  My Conversation make to be thy Reele,
  And reele the yarn thereon spun of thy Wheele.

Make me thy Loome then, knit therein this Twine:
  And make thy Holy Spirit, Lord, winde quills:

Then weave the Web thyselfe. The yarn is fine.
   Thine Ordinances make my Fulling Mills.
   Then dy the same in Heavenly Colours Choice,
      All pinkt with Varnish't Flowers of Paradise.

Then cloath therewith mine Understanding, Will,
   Affections, Judgment, Conscience, Memory;
My Words and Actions, that their shine may fill
   My wayes with glory and thee glorify.
   Then mine apparell shall display before yee
   That I am Cloathd in Holy robes for glory.

112. Meditation. 2 Cor. 5.14.

If one died for all then are all Dead

Oh! Good, Good, Good, my Lord. What more Love yet.
   Thou dy for mee! What, am I dead in thee?
What did Deaths arrow shot at me thee hit?
   Didst slip between that flying shaft and mee?
   Didst make thyselfe Deaths marke shot at for mee?
   So that her Shaft shall fly no far than thee?

Di'dst dy for mee indeed, and in thy Death
   Take in thy Dying thus my death the Cause?
And lay I dying in thy Dying breath,
   According to Graces Redemption Laws?
   If one did dy for all, it needs must bee
   That all did dy in one, and from death free.

Infinities fierce firy arrow red
   Shot from the splendid Bow of Justice bright
Did smite thee down, for thine. Thou art their head.
   They di'de in thee. Their death did on thee light.
   They di'de their Death in thee, thy Death is theirs.
   Hence thine is mine, thy death my trespass clears.

How sweet is this: my Death lies buried
  Within thy Grave, my Lord, deep under ground,
It is unskin'd, as Carrion rotten Dead.
  For Grace's hand gave Death its deadly wound.
  Deaths no such terrour on th'Saints blesst Coast.
  Its but a harmless Shade: No walking Ghost.

The Painter lies: the Bellfrey Pillars weare
  A false Effigies now of Death, alas!
With empty Eyeholes, Butter teeth, bones bare
  And spraggling arms, having an Hour Glass
  In one grim paw. Th'other a Spade doth hold
  To shew deaths frightfull region under mould.

Whereas its Sting is gone: its life is lost.
  Though unto Christless ones it is most Grim
Its but a Shade to Saints whose path it Crosst,
  Or Shell or Washen face, in which she sings
  Their Bodies in her lap a Lollaboy
  And sends their Souls to sing their Masters joy.

Lord let me finde Sin, Curse and Death that doe
  Belong to me ly slain too in thy Grave.
And let thy law my clearing hence bestow
  And from these things let me acquittance have.
  The Law suffic'de: and I discharg'd, Hence sing
  Thy praise I will over Deaths Death, and Sin.

Upon a Wasp Child with Cold

The Bare that breaths the Northern blast
Did numb, Torpedo like, a Wasp
Whose stiffend limbs encrampt, lay bathing
In Sol's warm breath and shine as saving,
Which with her hands she chafes and stands

Rubbing her Legs, Shanks, Thighs, and hands.
Her petty toes, and fingers ends
Nipt with this breath, she out extends
Unto the Sun, in greate desire
To warm her digits at that fire.
Doth hold her Temples in this state
Where pulse doth beate, and head doth ake.
Doth turn, and stretch her body small,
Doth Comb her velvet Capitall.
As if her little brain pan were
A Volume of Choice precepts cleare.
As if her sattin jacket hot
Contained Apothecaries Shop
Of Natures recepts, that prevails
To remedy all her sad ailes,
As if her velvet helmet high
Did turret rationality.
She fans her wing up to the Winde
As if her Pettycoate were lin'de,
With reasons fleece, and hoises sails
And hu'ming flies in thankfull gails
Unto her dun Curld palace Hall
Her warm thanks offering for all.
  Lord cleare my misted sight that I
May hence view thy Divinity.
Some sparkes whereof thou up dost hasp
Within this little downy Wasp
In whose small Corporation wee
A school and a schoolmaster see
Where we may learn, and easily finde
A nimble Spirit bravely minde
Her worke in e'ry limb: and lace
It up neate with a vitall grace,
Acting each part though ne'er so small
Here of this Fustian animall.
Till I enravisht Climb into

The Godhead on this Lather doe.
Where all my pipes inspir'de upraise
An Heavenly musick furrd with praise.

[When] Let by Rain

Ye Flippering Soule,
　Why dost between the Nippers dwell?
Not stay, nor goe. Not yea, nor yet Controle.
　Doth this doe well?
　　Rise journy'ng when the skies fall weeping Showers.
　　Not o're nor under th'Clouds and Cloudy Powers.

Not yea, nor noe:
　On tiptoes thus? Why sit on thorns?
Resolve the matter: Stay thyselfe or goe.
　Be n't both wayes born.
　　Wager thyselfe against thy surplice, see,
　　And win thy Coate: or let thy Coate Win thee.

Is this th'Effect,
　To leaven thus my Spirits all?
To make my heart a Crabtree Cask direct?
　A Verjuicte Hall?
　　As Bottle Ale, whose Spirits prisond nurst
　　When jog'd, the bung with Violence doth burst?

Shall I be made
　A sparkling Wildfire Shop
Where my dull Spirits at the Fireball trade
　Do frisk and hop?
　　And while the Hammer doth the Anvill pay,
　　The fireball matter sparkles ery way.
One sorry fret,
　An anvill Sparke, rose higher

And in thy Temple falling almost set
  The house on fire.
    Such fireballs droping in the Temple Flame
    Burns up the building: Lord forbid the same.

Meditation. Joh. 6.51.

I am the Living Bread

I kening through Astronomy Divine
  The Worlds bright Battlement, wherein I spy
A Golden Path my Pensill cannot line,
  From that bright Throne unto my Threshold ly.
  And while my puzzled thoughts about it pore
  I finde the Bread of Life in't at my doore.

When that this Bird of Paradise put in
  This Wicker Cage (my Corps) to tweedle praise
Had peckt the Fruite forbad: and so did fling
  Away its Food; and lost its golden dayes;
  It fell into Celestiall Famine sore:
  And never could attain a morsell more.

Alas! alas! Poore Bird, what wilt thou doe?
  The Creatures field no food for Souls e're gave.
And if thou knock at Angells dores they show
  An Empty Barrell: they no soul bread have.
  Alas! Poore Bird, the Worlds White Loafe is done.
  And cannot yield thee here the smallest Crumb.

In this sad state, God Tender Bowells run
  Out streams of Grace: And he to end all strife
The Purest Wheate in Heaven, his deare-dear Son
  Grinds, and kneads up into this Bread of Life.
  Which Bread of Life from Heaven down came and
    stands
  Disht on thy Table up by Angells Hands.

Did God mould up this Bread in Heaven, and bake,
  Which from his Table came, and to thine goeth?
Doth he bespeake thee thus, This Soule Bread take.
  Come Eate thy fill of this thy Gods White Loafe?
  Its Food too fine for Angells, yet come, take
  And Eate thy fill. Its Heavens Sugar Cake.

What Grace is this knead in this Loafe? This thing
  Souls are but petty things it to admire.
Yee Angells, help: This fill would to the brim
  Heav'ns whelm'd-down Chrystall meele Bowle, yea and
    higher.
  This Bread of Life dropt in thy mouth, doth Cry.
  Eate, Eate me, Soul, and thou shalt never dy.

Meditation. 1 Joh. 2.1.

An Advocate with the Father

Oh! What a thing is Man? Lord, Who am I?
  That thou shouldst give him Law (Oh! golden Line)
To regulate his Thoughts, Words, Life thereby.
  And judge him Wilt thereby too in thy time.
  A Court of Justice thou in heaven holdst
  To try his Case while he's here housd on mould.

How do thy Angells lay before thine eye
  My Deeds both White, and Black I dayly doe?
How doth thy Court thou Pannellst there them try?
  But flesh complains. What right for this? let's know.
  For right, or wrong I can't appeare unto't.
  And shall a sentence Pass on such a suite?

Soft; blemish not this golden Bench, or place.
  Here is no Bribe, nor Colourings to hide

Nor Pettifogger to befog the Case
  But Justice hath her Glory here well tri'de.
  Her spotless Law all spotted Cases tends.
  Without Respect or Disrespect them ends.

God's Judge himselfe: and Christ Atturny is,
  The Holy Ghost Regesterer is founde.
Angells the sergeants are, all Creatures kiss
  The booke, and doe as Evidences abounde.
  All Cases pass according to pure Law
  And in the sentence is no Fret, nor flaw.

What saist, my soule? Here all thy Deeds are tri'de.
  Is Christ thy Advocate to pleade thy Cause?
Art thou his Client? Such shall never slide.
  He never lost his Case: he pleads such Laws
  As Carry do the same, nor doth refuse
  The Vilest sinners Case that doth him Choose.

This is his Honour, not Dishonour: nay
  No Habeas-Corpus gainst his Clients came
For all their Fines his Purse doth make down pay.
  He Non-Suites Satan's Suite or Casts the Same.
  He'l plead thy Case, and not accept a Fee.
  He'll plead Sub Forma Pauperis for thee.

My Case is bad. Lord, be my Advocate.
  My sin is red: I'me under Gods Arrest.
Thou hast the Hint of Pleading; plead my State.
  Although it's bad thy Plea will make it best.
  If thou wilt plead my Case before the King:
  I'le Waggon Loads of Love, and Glory bring.

The Preface
[*to* God's Determinations]

Infinity, when all things it beheld
In Nothing, and of Nothing all did build,
Upon what Base was fixt the Lath, wherein
He turn'd this Globe, and riggalld it so trim?
Who blew the Bellows of his Furnace Vast?
Or held the Mould wherein the world was Cast?
Who laid its Corner Stone? Or whose Command?
Where stand the Pillars upon which it stands?
Who Lac'de and Fillitted the earth so fine,
With Rivers like green Ribbons Smaragdine?
Who made the Sea's its Selvedge, and it locks
Like a Quilt Ball within a Silver Box?
Who Spread its Canopy? Or Curtains Spun?
Who in this Bowling Alley bowld the Sun?
Who made it always when it rises set
To go at once both down, and up to get?
Who th'Curtain rods made for this Tapistry?
Who hung the twinckling Lanthorns in the Sky?
Who? who did this? or who is he? Why, know
Its Onely Might Almighty this did doe.
His hand hath made this noble worke which Stands
His Glorious Handywork not made by hands.
Who spake all things from nothing; and with ease
Can speake all things to nothing, if he please.
Whose Little finger at his pleasure Can
Out mete ten thousand worlds with halfe a Span:
Whose Might Almighty can by half a looks
Root up the rocks and rock the hills by th'roots.
Can take this mighty World up in his hande,
And shake it like a Squitchen or a Wand.
Whose single Frown will make the Heavens shake
Like as an aspen leafe the Winde makes quake.
Oh! what a might is this Whose single frown
Doth shake the world as it would shake it down?

Which All from Nothing fet, from Nothing, All:
Hath All on Nothing set, lets Nothing fall.
Gave All to nothing Man indeed, whereby
Through nothing man all might him Glorify.
In Nothing then imbosst the brightest Gem
More pretious than all pretiousness in them.
But Nothing man did throw down all by Sin:
And darkened that lightsom Gem in him.
    That now his Brightest Diamond is grown
    Darker by far than any Coalpit Stone.

JOEL
BARLOW
1754-1812

Joel Barlow began life as a conservative Connecticut Puritan and ended it as a cosmopolitan Democrat and Minister to France. In between he taught school, ran a business, preached, joined the army, was admitted to the bar and became the Consul for Algiers. He also wrote poetry.

Barlow's great desire was to write the major American epic and his attempt, *The Columbiad*, was completed in 1807 but it is for charming short poems such as 'The Hasty Pudding' that he is now best remembered.

From *The Hasty Pudding*
The Hasty Pudding Described

Ye Alps audacious, thro' the Heavens that rise,
To cramp the day and hide me from the skies;
Ye Gallic flags, that o'er their heights unfurl'd,
Bear death to kings, and freedom to the world,
I sing not you. A softer theme I chuse,
A virgin theme, unconscious of the Muse,
But fruitful, rich, well suited to inspire
The purest frenzy of poetic fire.

   Despise it not, ye Bards to terror steel'd,
Who hurl'd your thunders round the epic field;
Nor ye who strain your midnight throats to sing
Joys that the vineyard and the still-house bring;
Or on some distant fair your notes employ,
And speak of raptures that you ne'er enjoy.
I sing the sweets I know, the charms I feel,
My morning incense, and my evening meal,
The sweets of Hasty-Pudding. Come, dear bowl,
Glide o'er my palate, and inspire my soul.
The milk beside thee, smoking from the kine,
Its substance mingled, married in with thine,
Shall cool and temper thy superior heat,
And save the pains of blowing while I eat.

   Oh! could the smooth, the emblematic song
Flow like thy genial juices o'er my tongue,
Could those mild morsels in my numbers chime,
And, as they roll in substance, roll in rhyme,
No more thy aukward unpoetic name
Should shun the Muse, or prejudice thy fame;
But rising grateful to th' accustom'd ear,
All Bards should catch it, and all realms revere!

Assist me first with pious toil to trace
Thro' wrecks of time thy lineage and thy race;
Declare what lovely squaw, in days of yore,
(Ere great Columbus sought thy native shore)
First gave thee to the world; her works of fame
Have liv'd indeed, but liv'd without a name.
Some tawny Ceres, goddess of her days,
First learn'd with stones to crack the well-dry'd maize,
Thro' the rough sieve to shake the golden show'r,
In boiling water stir the yellow flour:
The yellow flour, bestrew'd and stir'd with haste,
Swells in the flood and thickens to a paste,
Then puffs and wallops, rises to the brim,
Drinks the dry knobs that on the surface swim:
The knobs at last the busy ladle breaks,
And the whole mass its true consistence takes.

Could but her sacred name, unknown so long,
Rise like her labors, to the song of song,
To her, to them, I'd consecrate my lays,
And blow her pudding with the breath of praise.
If 'twas Oella, whom I sang before,
I here ascribe her one great virtue more.
Not thro' the rich Peruvian realms alone
The fame of Sol's sweet daughter should be known,
But o'er the world's wide climes should live secure,
Far as his rays extend, as long as they endure.

Dear Hasty-Pudding, what unpromis'd joy
Expands my heart, to meet thee in Savoy!
Doom'd o'er the world thro' devious paths to roam,
Each clime my country, and each house my home,
My soul is sooth'd, my cares have found an end,
I greet my long-lost, unforgotten friend.

For thee thro' Paris, that corrupted town,
How long in vain I wandered up and down,
Where shameless Bacchus, with his drenching hoard
Cold from his cave usurps the morning board.
London is lost in smoke and steep'd in tea;
No Yankee there can lisp the name of thee;
The uncouth word, a libel on the town,
Would call a proclamation from the crown.
For climes oblique, that fear the sun's full rays,
Chill'd in their fogs, exclude the generous maize;
A grain whose rich luxurient growth requires
Short gentle showers, and bright etherial fires.

But here tho' distant from our native shore,
With mutual glee we meet and laugh once more,
The same! I know thee by that yellow face,
That strong complexion of true Indian race,
Which time can never change, nor soil impair,
Nor Alpine snows, nor Turkey's morbid air;
For endless years, thro' every mild domain,
Where grows the maize, there thou art sure to reign.

But man, more fickle, the bold licence claims,
In different realms to give thee different names.
Thee the soft nations round the warm Levant
Polanta call, the French of course *Polante*;
Ev'n in thy native regions, how I blush
To hear the Pennsylvanians call thee *Mush*!
On Hudson's banks, while men of Belgic spawn
Insult and eat thee by the name *Suppawn*.
All spurious appellations, void of truth:
I've better known thee from my earliest youth,
Thy name is *Hasty-Pudding*! thus our sires
Were wont to greet thee fuming from their fires;
And while they argu'd in thy just defence
With logic clear, they thus explain'd the sense:—

'In *haste* the boiling cauldron o'er the blaze,
'Receives and cooks the ready-powder'd maize;
'In *haste* 'tis serv'd, and then in equal *haste*,
'With cooling milk, we make the sweet repast.
'No carving to be done, no knife to grate
'The tender ear, and wound the stony plate;
'But the smooth spoon, just fitted to the lip,
'And taught with art the yielding mass to dip,
'By frequent journies to the bowl well stor'd,
'Performs the hasty honors of the board.'
Such is thy name, significant and clear,
A name, a sound to every Yankey dear,
But most to me, whose heart and palate chaste
Preserve my pure hereditary taste.

There are who strive to stamp with disrepute
The luscious food, because it feeds the brute;
In tropes of high-strain'd wit, while gaudy prigs
Compare thy nursling man to pamper'd pigs;
With sovereign scorn I treat the vulgar jest,
Nor fear to share thy bounties with the beast.
What though the generous cow gives me to quaff
The milk nutritious; am I then a calf?
Or can the genius of the noisy swine,
Tho' nurs'd on pudding, thence lay claim to mine?
Sure the sweet song, I fashion to thy praise,
Runs more melodious than the notes they raise.

My song resounding in its grateful glee,
No merit claims; I praise myself in thee.
My father lov'd thee thro' his length of days:
For thee his fields were shaded o'er with maize;
From thee what health, what vigour he possest,
Ten sturdy freemen from his loins attest:
Thy constellation rul'd my natal morn,
And all my bones were made of Indian corn.

Delicious grain! whatever form it take,
To roast or boil, to smother or to bake,
In every dish 'tis welcome still to me,
But most, my Hasty-Pudding, most in thee.

  Let the green Succatash with thee contend,
Let beans and corn their sweetest juices blend,
Let butter drench them in its yellow tide,
And a long slice of bacon grace their side;
Not all the plate, how fam'd soe'er it be,
Can please my palate like a bowl of thee.

  Some talk of Hoe-cake, fair Virginia's pride,
Rich Johnny-cake this mouth has often tri'd;
Both please me well, their virtues much the same;
Alike their fabric, as allied their fame,
Except in dear New-England, where the last
Receives a dash of pumpkin in the paste,
To give it sweetness and improve the taste.
But place them all before me, smoking hot,
The big round dumpling rolling from the pot;
The pudding of the bag, whose quivering breast,
With suet lin'd leads on the Yankey feast;
The Charlotte brown, within whose crusty sides
A belly soft the pulpy apple hides;
The yellow bread, whose face like amber glows,
And all of Indian that the bake-pan knows—
You tempt me not – my fav'rite greets my eyes,
To that lov'd bowl my spoon by instinct flies.

The Husking

The days grow short; but though the falling sun
To the glad swain proclaims his day's work done,
Night's pleasing shades his various tasks prolong,
And yield new subjects to my various song.
For now, the corn-house filled, the harvest home,
The invited neighbours to the *Husking* come;
A frolic scene, where work, and mirth, and play,
Unite their charms to chase the hours away.

Where the huge heap lies centred in the hall,
The lamp suspended from the cheerful wall,
Brown corn-fed nymphs and strong hard-handed beaus,
Alternate ranged, extend in circling rows,
Assume their seats, the solid mass attack;
The dry husks rustle, and the corn-cobs crack;
The song, the laugh, alternate notes resound
And the sweet cider trips in silence round.

The laws of husking every wight can tell—
And sure no laws he ever keeps so well:
For each red ear a general kiss he gains,
With each smut ear she smuts the luckless swains;
But when to some sweet maid a prize is cast,
Red as her lips and taper as her waist,
She walks the round, and culls one favored beau,
Who leaps, the luscious tribute to bestow.
Various the sports are as the wit and brains
Of well-pleased lasses and contending swains;
Till the vast mound of corn is swept away,
And he that gets the last ear wins the day.

Meanwhile the housewife urges all her care,
The well-earned feast to hasten and prepare.
The sifted meal already waits her hand,
The milk is strained, the bowls in order stand,

54

The fire flames high; and, as a pool that takes
The headlong stream that o'er the mill-dam breaks,
Foams, roars, and rages, with incessant toils,
So the vexed cauldron rages, roars, and boils.

First with clean salt she seasons well the food,
Then strews the flour and thickens all the flood.
Long o'er the simmering fire she lets it stand—
To stir it well demands a stronger hand:
The husband takes his turn, and round and round
The ladle flies, at last the toil is crown'd;
When to their boards the thronging huskers pour,
And take their seats as at the corn before.

I leave them to their feast. There still belong
More useful matters to my faithful song;
For rules there are, though ne'er unfolded yet,
Nice rules and wise, how pudding should be eat.

The Eating of the Pudding

Some with molasses grace the luscious treat,
And mix, like bards, the useful and the sweet.
A wholesome dish, and well deserving praise,
A great resource in those bleak wintry days
When the chilled earth lies buried in the snow
And raging Boreas dries the shivering cow.

Blest cow! thy praise shall still my notes employ,
Great source of health, the only source of joy,
Mother of Egypt's god; – but sure for me,
Were I to leave my God I'd worship thee.
How oft thy teats these pious hands have pressed!
How oft thy bounties proved my only feast!
How oft I've fed thee with my favorite grain!
And roared like thee to see thy children slain!

Ye swains who know her various worth to prize,
Ah! house her well from Winter's angry skies.
Potatoes, pumpkins, should her sadness cheer,
Corn from your crib and mashes from your beer;
When spring returns, she'll well acquit the loan,
And nurse at once her infants and your own.

Milk then with pudding, I should always choose;
To this in future I confine my Muse,
Till she, in haste, some further hints unfold,
Good for the young, nor useless to the old.
First in your bowl the milk abundant take,
Then drop with care along the silver lake
Your flakes of pudding. These, at first, will hide
Their little bulk beneath the swelling tide;
But when their growing mass no more can sink,
When the soft island looms above the brink,
Then check your hand; you've got the portion due.
So taught my Sire, and what he taught is true.

There is a choice in spoons. Though small appear
The nice distinction, yet to me 'tis clear.
The deep-bowled Gallic spoon, contrived to scoop
In ample draughts the thin diluted soup,
Performs not well in those substantial things,
Whose mass adhesive to the metal clings;
Where the strong labial muscles must embrace,
The gentle curve, and sweep the hollow space,
With ease to enter and discharge the freight,
A bowl less concave, but still more dilate,
Becomes the pudding best. The shape, the size,
A secret rests, unknown to vulgar eyes;
Experienced feeders can alone impart
A rule so much above the lore of art.
These tuneful lips, that thousand spoons have tried,
With just precision could the point decide.

Though not in song; the Muse but poorly shines
In cones and cubes and geometric lines,
Yet the true form, as near as she can tell,
Is that small section of a goose-egg shell
Which in two equal portions shall divide
The distance from the center to the side.

   Fear not to slaver; 'tis no deadly sin.—
Like the free Frenchman, from your joyous chin
Suspend the ready napkin; or, like me,
Poise with one hand your bowl upon your knee;
Just in the zenith your wise head project,
Your full spoon, rising in a line direct,
Bold as a bucket, heed no drops that fall,
The wide-mouthed bowl will surely catch them all!

Advice to a Raven in Russia
December, 1812

Black fool, why winter here? These frozen skies,
Worn by your wings and deafen'd by your cries,
Should warn you hence, where milder suns invite,
And day alternates with his mother night.
   You fear perhaps your food will fail you there,
Your human carnage, that delicious fare
That lured you hither, following still your friend,
The great Napoleon, to the world's bleak end.
You fear, because the southern climes pour'd forth
Their clustering nations to infest the north,
Bavarians, Austrians, those who Drink the Po
And those who skirt the Tuscan seas below,
With all Germania, Neustria, Belgia, Gaul,
Doom'd here to wade through slaughter to their fall,
You fear he left behind no wars, to feed
His feather'd canibals and nurse the breed.

Fear not, my screamer, call your greedy train,
Sweep over Europe, hurry back to Spain,
You'll find his legions there; the valliant crew
Please best their master when they toil for you.
Abundant there they spread the country o'er
And taint the breeze with every nation's gore,
Iberian, Lusian, British widely strown,
But still more wide and copious flows their own.
Go where you will; Calabria, Malta, Greece,
Egypt and Syria still his fame increase,
Domingo's fatten'd isle and India's plains
Glow deep with purple drawn from Gallic veins.
No Raven's wing can stretch the flight so far
As the torn bandrols of Napoleon's war.
Choose then your climate, fix your best abode,
He'll make you deserts and he'll bring you blood.
How could you fear a dearth? have not mankind,
Though slain by millions, millions left behind?
Has not CONSCRIPTION still the power to wield
Her annual falchion o'er the human field?
A faithful harvester; or if a man
Escape that gleaner, shall he scape the BAN?
The triple BAN, that like the hound of hell
Gripes with three jowls, to hold his victim well.
Fear nothing then, hatch fast your ravenous brood,
Teach them to cry to Bonaparte for food;
They'll be like you, of all his suppliant train,
The only class that never cries in vain.
For see what mutual benefits you lend!
(The surest way to fix the mutual friend)
While on his slaughter'd troops your tribes are fed,
You cleanse his camp and carry off his dead.
Imperial Scavenger! but now you know
Your work is vain amid these hills of snow.
His tentless troops are marbled through with frost
And change to crystal when the breath is lost.

Mere trunks of ice, though limb'd like human frames
And lately warm'd with life's endearing flames,
They cannot taint the air, the world impest,
Nor can you tear one fiber from their breast.
No! from their visual sockets, as they lie,
With beak and claws you cannot pluck an eye.
The frozen orb, preserving still its form,
Defies your talons as it braves the storm,
But stands and stares to God, as if to know
In what curst hands he leaves his world below.
  Fly then, or starve; though all the dreadful road
From Minsk to Moskow with their bodies strow'd
May count some myriads, yet they can't suffice
To feed you more beneath these dreary skies.
Go back, and winter in the wilds of Spain;
Feast there awhile, and in the next campaign
Rejoin your master; for you'll find him then,
With his new million of the race of men,
Clothed in his thunders, all his flags unfurl'd,
Raging and storming o'er the prostrate world.
  War after war his hungry soul requires,
State after State shall sink beneath his fires,
Yet other Spains in victim smoke shall rise
And other Moskows suffocate the skies,
Each land lie reeking with its people's slain
And not a stream run bloodless to the main.
Till men resume their souls, and dare to shed
Earth's total vengeance on the monster's head,
Hurl from his blood-built throne this king of woes,
Dash him to dust, and let the world repose.

Hymn to Peace

Hail, sacred Peace, who claim'st thy bright abode
'Mid circling saints that grace the throne of God,
Before his arm, around this shapeless earth,
Stretch'd the wide heav'ns and gave to nature birth;
Ere morning stars his glowing chambers hung,
Or songs of gladness woke an angel's tongue;
Veiled in the brightness of th' Almighty's mind,
In blessed repose thy placid form reclined;
Borne through the heaven, with his creating voice,
Thy presence bade the unfolding worlds rejoice;
Gave to seraphic hearts their sounding lays,
Their joy to angels and to men their praise.

From scenes of blood, these beauteous shoes that stain,
From gasping friends that press the sanguine plain,
From fields, long taught in vain thy flight to mourn,
I rise, delightful power, and greet thy glad return.
Too long the groans of death and battle's bray
Have rung discordant through the unpleasing lay:
Let pity's tear its balmy fragrance shed,
O'er heroes' wounds and patriot warriors dead:
Accept, departed shades, these grateful sighs,
Your fond attendants to the approving skies.
But now the untuneful trump shall grate no more,
Ye silver streams, no longer swell with gore;
Bear from your beauteous banks the crimson stain,
With yon retiring navies to the main;
While other views unfolding on my eyes,
And happier themes bid bolder numbers rise.
Bring, bounteous Peace, in thy celestial throng,
Life to my soul, and rapture to my song;
Give me to trace, with pure unclouded ray,
The arts and virtues that attend thy sway;
To see thy blissful charms that here descend,
Thro' distant realms and endless years extend.

Psalm CXXXVII

The Babylonian Captivity

Along the banks where Babel's current flows
  Our captive bands in deep despondence stray'd,
While Zion's fall in sad remembrance rose,
  Her friends, her children mingled with the dead.

The tuneless harp, that once with joy we strung,
  When praise employ'd and mirth inspir'd the lay,
In mournful silence on the willows hung;
  And growing grief prolong'd the tedious day.

The barbarous tyrants, to increase the woe,
  With taunting smiles a song of Zion claim;
Bid sacred praise in strains melodious flow,
  While they blaspheme the great Jehovah's name.

But how, in heathen chains and lands unknown,
  Shall Israel's sons a song of Zion raise?
O hapless Salem, God's terrestrial throne,
  Thou land of glory, sacred mount of praise.

If e'er my memory lose thy lovely name,
  If my cold heart neglect my kindred race,
Let dire destruction seize this guilty frame;
  My hand shall perish and my voice shall cease.

Yet shall the Lord, who hears when Zion calls,
  O'ertake her foes with terror and dismay,
His arm avenge her desolated walls,
  And raise her children to eternal day.

To Freedom

Sun of the moral world! effulgent source
Of man's best wisdom and his steadiest force,
Soul-searching Freedom! here assume thy stand,
And radiate hence to every distant land;
Point out and prove how all the scenes of strife,
The shock of states, the impassion'd broils of life,
Spring from unequal sway; and how they fly
Before the splendour of thy peaceful eye;
Unfold at last the genuine social plan,
The mind's full scope, the dignity of man,
Bold nature bursting through her long disguise,
And nations daring to be just and wise.
Yes! righteous Freedom, heaven and earth and sea
Yield or withhold their various gifts for thee;
Protected Industry beneath thy reign
Leads all the virtues in her filial train;
Courageous Probity, with brow serene,
And Temperance calm presents her placid mien;
Contentment, Moderation, Labour, Art,
Mould the new man and humanize his heart;
To public plenty private ease dilates,
Domestic peace to harmony of states.
Protected Industry, careering far,
Detects the cause and cures the rage of war,
And sweeps, with forceful arm, to their last graves,
Kings from the earth and pirates from the waves.

From the *Columbiad*

The Zones of America

Where Spring's coy steps in cold Canadia stray,
And joyless seasons hold unequal sway,
He saw the pine its daring mantle rear,
Break the rude blast, and mock the brumal year,

Shag the green zone that bounds the boreal skies,
And bid all southern vegetation rise.
Wild o'er the vast, impenetrable round
The untrod bowers of shadowy nature frown'd;
Millennial cedars wave their honours wide,
The fir's tall boughs, the oak's umbrageous pride,
The branching beach, the aspen's trembling shade
Veil the dim heaven, and brown the dusky glade.
For in dense crowds these sturdy sons of earth,
In frosty regions, claim a stronger birth;
Where heavy beams the sheltering dome requires,
And copious trunks to feed its wintry fires.
But warmer suns, that southern zones emblaze,
A cool, thin umbrage o'er their woodland raise;
Floridia's shores their blooms around him spread,
And Georgian hills erect their shady head;
Whose flowery shrubs regale the passing air
With all the untasted fragrance of the year.
Beneath tall trees, dispersed in loose array,
The rice-grown lawns their humble garb display;
The infant maize, unconscious of its worth,
Points the green spire and bends the foliage forth;
In various forms unbidden harvests rise,
And blooming life repays the genial skies.
Where Mexic hills the breezy gulf defend,
Spontaneous groves with richer burdens bend:
Anana's stalk its shaggy honours yields;
Acassia's flowers perfume a thousand fields;
Their cluster'd dates the mast-like palms unfold;
The spreading orange waves a load of gold;
Connubial vines o'ertop the larch they climb;
The long-lived olive mocks the moth of time;
Pomona's pride, that old Grenada claims,
Here smiles and reddens in diviner flames;
Pimento, citron scent the sky serene;
White, woolly clusters fringe the cotton's green;

The sturdy fig, the frail, deciduous cane,
And foodful cocoa fan the sultry plain.
Here, in one view, the same glad branches bring
The fruits of autumn and the flowers of spring;
No wintry blasts the unchanging year deform,
Nor beasts unshelter'd fear the pinching storm;
But vernal breezes o'er the blossoms rove,
And breathe the ripen'd juices through the grove.

Burning of the New England Villages

Through solid curls of smoke, the bursting fires
Climb in tall pyramids above the spires,
Concentring all the winds; whose forces, driven
With equal rage from every point of heaven,
Whirl into conflict, round the scantling pour
The twisting flames, and through the rafters roar;
Suck up the cinders, send them sailing far,
To warn the nations of the raging war;
Bend high the blazing vortex, swell'd and curl'd,
Careering, brightening o'er the lustred world:
Seas catch the splendour, kindling skies resound,
And falling structures shake the smouldering ground.
Crowds of wild fugitives, with frantic tread,
Flit through the flames that pierce the midnight shade,
Back on the burning domes revert their eyes,
Where some lost friend, some perish'd infant lies.
Their maim'd, their sick, their age-enfeebled sires
Have sunk sad victims to the sateless fires;
They greet with one last look their tottering walls,
See the blaze thicken, as the ruin falls,
Then o'er the country train their dumb despair,
And far behind them leave the dancing glare;
Their own crush'd roofs still lend a trembling light,
Point their long shadows and direct their flight.

Till, wandering wide, they seek some cottage door,
Ask the vile pittance due the vagrant poor;
Or, faint and faltering on the devious road,
They sink at last and yield their mortal load.

WILLIAM CULLEN BRYANT
1794-1878

William Cullen Bryant was born at Cummington, Mass.
His literary career began at the early age of 14 when
he wrote a political satire entitled, *The Embargo*, but he
left his other work unpublished until 1825 while he
pursued a legal career. He was later a leading
Democratic Editor of the *New York Review and Athenaeum
Magazine* then the *New York Evening Post* until his
vigorous opposition to slavery brought him into the
new Republican Party.

Bryant was primarily a poet of nature whose debt
to Wordsworth is clear but whose ideas are expressed
with simple dignity in poems such as 'Thanatopsis',
The Prairies' and 'Green River'.

Thanatopsis

To him who in the love of Nature holds
Communion with her visible forms, she speaks
A various language; for his gayer hours
She has a voice of gladness, and a smile
And eloquence of beauty, and she glides
Into his darker musings, with a mild
And healing sympathy, that steals away
Their sharpness, ere he is aware. When thoughts
Of the last bitter hour come like a blight
Over thy spirit, and sad images
Of the stern agony, and shroud, and pall,
And breathless darkness, and the narrow house,
Make thee to shudder, and grow sick at heart;—
Go forth, under the open sky, and list
To Nature's teachings, while from all around—
Earth and her waters, and the depths of air—
Comes a still voice – Yet a few days, and thee
The all-beholding sun shall see no more
In all his course; nor yet in the cold ground,
Where thy pale form was laid, with many tears,
Nor in the embrace of ocean, shall exist
Thy image. Earth, that nourished thee, shall claim
Thy growth, to be resolved to earth again,
And, lost each human trace, surrendering up
Thine individual being, shalt thou go
To mix for ever with the elements,
To be a brother to the insensible rock
And to the sluggish clod, which the rude swain
Turns with his share, and treads upon. The oak
Shall send his roots abroad, and pierce thy mould.

Yet not to thine eternal resting-place
Shalt thou retire alone, nor couldst thou wish
Couch more magnificent. Thou shalt lie down
With patriarchs of the infant world – with kings,

The powerful of the earth – the wise, the good,
Fair forms, and hoary seers of ages past,
All in one mighty sepulchre. The hills
Rock-ribbed and ancient as the sun, – the vales
Stretching in pensive quietness between;
The venerable woods – rivers that move
In majesty, and the complaining brooks
That make the meadows green; and, poured round all,
Old Ocean's gray and melancholy waste,—
Are but the solemn decorations all
Of the great tomb of man. The golden sun,
The planets, all the infinite host of heaven,
Are shining on the sad abodes of death,
Through the still lapse of ages. All that tread
The globe are but a handful to the tribes
That slumber in its bosom. – Take the wings
Of morning, pierce the Barcan wilderness,
Or lose thyself in the continuous woods
Where rolls the Oregon, and hears no sound,
Save his own dashings – yet the dead are there:
And millions in those solitudes, since first
The flight of years began, have laid them down
In their last sleep – the dead reign there alone.
So shalt thou rest, and what if thou withdraw
In silence from the living, and no friend
Take note of thy departure? All that breathe
Will share thy destiny. The gay will laugh
When thou art gone, the solemn brood of care
Plod on, and each one as before will chase
His favorite phantom; yet all these shall leave
Their mirth and their employments, and shall come
And make their bed with thee. As the long train
Of ages glide away, the sons of men,
The youth in life's green spring, and he who goes
In the full strength of years, matron and maid,

The speechless babe, and the gray-headed man—
Shall one by one be gathered to thy side,
By those, who in their turn shall follow them.

  So live, that when thy summons comes to join
The innumerable caravan, which moves
To that mysterious realm, where each shall take
His chamber in the silent hall of death,
Thou go not, like the quarry-slave at night,
Scourged to his dungeon, but, sustained and soothed
By an unfaltering trust, approach thy grave,
Like one who wraps the drapery of his couch
About him, and lies down to pleasant dreams.

Green River

When breezes are soft and skies are fair,
I steal an hour from study and care,
And hie me away to the woodland scene,
Where wanders the stream with waters of green,
As if the bright fringe of herbs on its brink
Had given their stain to the waves they drink;
And they, whose meadows it murmurs through,
Have named the stream from its own fair hue.

  Yet pure its waters – its shallows are bright
With colored pebbles and sparkles of light,
And clear the depths where its eddies play,
And dimples deepen and whirl away,
And the plane-tree's speckled arms o'ershoot
The swifter current that mines its root,
Through whose shifting leaves, as you walk the hill,
The quivering glimmer of sun and rill
With a sudden flash on the eye is thrown,
Like the ray that streams from the diamond-stone.

Oh, loveliest there the spring days come,
With blossoms, and birds, and wild-bees' hum;
The flowers of summer are fairest there,
And freshest the breath of the summer air;
And sweetest the golden autumn day
In silence and sunshine glides away.

Yet, fair as thou art, thou shunnest to glide,
Beautiful stream! by the village side;
But windest away from haunts of men,
To quiet valley and shaded glen;
And forest, and meadow, and slope of hill,
Around thee, are lonely, lovely, and still,
Lonely – save when, by thy rippling tides,
From thicket to thicket the angler glides;
Or the simpler comes, with basket and book,
For herbs of power on thy banks to look;
Or haply, some idle dreamer, like me,
To wander, and muse, and gaze on thee,
Still – save the chirp of birds that feed
On the river cherry and seedy reed,
And thy own wild music gushing out
With mellow murmur of fairy shout,
From dawn to the blush of another day,
Like traveller singing along his way.

That fairy music I never hear,
Nor gaze on those waters so green and clear,
And mark them winding away from sight,
Darkened with shade or flashing with light,
While o'er them the vine to its thicket clings,
And the zephyr stoops to freshen his wings,
But I wish that fate had left me free
To wander these quiet haunts with thee,
Till the eating cares of earth should depart,
And the peace of the scene pass into my heart;

And I envy thy stream, as it glides along
Through its beautiful banks in a trance of song.

Though forced to drudge for the dregs of men,
And scrawl strange words with the barbarous pen,
And mingle among the jostling crowd,
Where the sons of strife are subtle and loud—
I often come to this quiet place,
To breathe the airs that ruffle thy face,
And gaze upon thee in silent dream,
For in thy lonely and lovely stream
An image of that calm life appears
That won my heart in my greener years.

Lines on Revisiting the Country

I stand upon my native hills again,
  Broad, round, and green, that in the summer sky,
With garniture of waving grass and grain,
  Orchards, and beechen forests, basking lie,
While deep the sunless glens are scoop'd between,
Where brawl o'er shallow beds the streams unseen.

A lisping voice and glancing eyes are near,
  And ever restless feet of one, who, now,
Gathers the blossoms of her fourth bright year;
  There plays a gladness o'er her fair young brow,
As breaks the varied scene upon her sight,
Upheaved and spread in verdure and in light.

For I have taught her, with delighted eye,
  To gaze upon the mountains, to behold,
With deep affection, the pure, ample sky,
  And clouds along its blue abysses roll'd,

To love the song of waters, and to hear
The melody of winds with charmed ear.

Here, I have 'scaped the city's stifling heat,
   Its horrid sounds, and its polluted air;
And where the season's milder fervours beat,
   And gales, that sweep the forest borders, bear
The song of bird, and sound of running stream,
Am come a while to wander and to dream.

Ay, flame thy fiercest, sun! thou canst not wake,
   In this pure air, the plague that walks unseen.
The maize leaf and the maple bough but take,
   From thy strong heats, a deeper, glossier green.
The mountain wind, that faints not in thy ray,
Sweeps the blue streams of pestilence away.

The mountain wind! most spiritual thing of all
   The wide earth knows – when, in the sultry time,
He stoops him from his vast, cerulean hall,
   He seems the breath of a celestial clime;
As if from heaven's wide-open gates did flow,
Health and refreshment on the world below.

The Rivulet

   This little rill that, from the springs
Of yonder grove, its current brings,
Plays on the slope a while, and then
Goes prattling into groves again,
Oft to its warbling waters drew
My little feet, when life was new.
When woods in early green were dress'd,
And from the chambers of the west

The warmer breezes, travelling out,
Breathed the new scent of flowers about,
My truant steps from home would stray,
Upon its grassy side to play,
List the brown thrasher's vernal hymn,
And crop the violet on its brim,
With blooming cheek and open brow,
As young and gay, sweet rill, as thou.
    And when the days of boyhood came,
And I had grown in love with fame,
Duly I sought thy banks, and tried
My first rude numbers by thy side.
Words cannot tell how bright and gay
The scenes of life before me lay.
Then glorious hopes, that now to speak
Would bring the blood into my cheek,
Pass'd o'er me; and I wrote, on high,
A name I deem'd should never die.
    Years change thee not. Upon yon hill
The tall old maples, verdant still,
Yet tell, in grandeur of decay,
How swift the years have pass'd away,
Since first, a child, and half-afraid,
I wander'd in the forest shade.
Thou, ever-joyous rivulet,
Dost dimple, leap, and prattle yet;
And sporting with the sands that pave
The windings of thy silver wave,
And dancing to thy own wild chime,
Thou laughest at the lapse of time.
The same sweet sounds are in my ear
My early childhood loved to hear;
As pure thy limpid waters run,
As bright they sparkle to the sun;
As fresh and thick the bending ranks
Of herbs that line thy oozy banks;

The violet there, in soft May dew,
Comes up, as modest and as blue;
As green amid thy current's stress,
Floats the scarce-rooted water-cress;
And the brown ground-bird, in thy glen,
Still chirps as merrily as then.
    Thou changest not – but I am changed,
Since first thy pleasant banks I ranged;
And the grave stranger, come to see
The play-place of his infancy,
Has scarce a single trace of him
Who sported once upon thy brim.
The visions of my youth are past—
Too bright, too beautiful to last.
I've tried the world – it wears no more
The colouring of romance it wore.
Yet well has Nature kept the truth
She promised to my earliest youth:
The radiant beauty, shed abroad
On all the glorious works of God,
Shows freshly, to my sober'd eye,
Each charm it wore in days gone by.
    A few brief years shall pass away,
And I, all trembling, weak, and gray,
Bow'd to the earth, which waits to fold
My ashes in the embracing mould,
(If haply the dark will of fate
Indulge my life so long a date,)
May come for the last time to look
Upon my childhood's favourite brook.
Then dimly on my eye shall gleam
The sparkle of thy dancing stream;
And faintly on my ear shall fall
Thy prattling current's merry call;
Yet shalt thou flow as glad and bright
As when thou met'st my infant sight.

And I shall sleep – and on thy side,
As ages after ages glide,
Children their early sports shall try,
And pass to hoary age, and die.
But thou, unchanged from year to year,
Gayly shalt play and glitter here;
Amid young flowers and tender grass
Thy endless infancy shalt pass;
And, singing down thy narrow glen,
Shalt mock the fading race of men.

Hymn of the City

Not in the solitude
Alone, may man commune with Heaven, or see
Only in savage wood
And sunny vale, the present Deity;
Or only hear his voice
Where the winds whisper and the waves rejoice.

Even here do I behold
Thy steps, Almighty! – here, amidst the crowd
Through the great city roll'd,
With everlasting murmur, deep and loud
Choking the ways that wind
'Mongst the proud piles, the work of human kind.

Thy golden sunshine comes
From the round heaven, and on their dwellings lies,
And lights their inner homes—
For them thou fill'st with air the unbounded skies,
And givest them the stores
Of ocean, and the harvests of its shores.

Thy spirit is around,
Quickening the restless mass that sweeps along;
    And this eternal sound—
Voices and footfalls of the numberless throng—
    Like the resounding sea,
Or like the rainy tempest, speaks of thee.

    And when the hours of rest
Come, like a calm upon the mid-sea brine,
    Hushing its billowy breast—
The quiet of that moment, too, is thine;
    It breathes of Him who keeps
The vast and helpless city while it sleeps.

The Prairies

These are the gardens of the Desert, these
The unshorn fields, boundless and beautiful,
For which the speech of England has no name—
The Prairies. I behold them for the first,
And my heart swells, while the dilated sight
Takes in the encircling vastness. Lo! they stretch,
In airy undulations, far away,
As if the ocean, in his gentlest swell,
Stood still, with all his rounded billows fixed,
And motionless forever. – Motionless?—
No – they are all unchained again. The clouds
Sweep over with their shadows, and, beneath,
The surface rolls and fluctuates to the eye;
Dark hollows seem to glide along and chase
The sunny ridges. Breezes of the South!
Who toss the golden and the flame-like flowers,
And pass the prairie-hawk that, poised on high,
Flaps his broad wings, yet moves not – ye have played
Among the palms of Mexico and vines

Of Texas, and have crisped the limpid brooks
That from the fountains of Sonora glide
Into the calm Pacific – have ye fanned
A nobler or a lovelier scene than this?
Man hath no power in all this glorious work:
The hand that built the firmament hath heaved
And smoothed these verdant swells, and sown their
    slopes
With herbage, planted them with island groves,
And hedged them round with forests. Fitting floor
For this magnificent temple of the sky—
With flowers whose glory and whose multitude
Rival the constellations! The great heavens
Seem to stoop down upon the scene in love,—
A nearer vault, and of a tenderer blue,
Than that which bends above our eastern hills.

   As o'er the verdant waste I guide my steed,
Among the high rank grass that sweeps his sides
The hollow beating of his footstep seems
A sacrilegious sound. I think of those
Upon whose rest he tramples. Are they here—
The dead of other days? – and did the dust
Of these fair solitudes once stir with life
And burn with passion? Let the mighty mounds
That overlook the rivers, or that rise
In the dim forest crowded with old oaks,
Answer. A race, that long has passed away,
Built them; – a disciplined and populous race
Heaped, with long toil, the earth, while yet the Greek
Was hewing the Pentelicus to forms
Of symmetry, and rearing on its rock
The glittering Parthenon. These ample fields
Nourished their harvests, here their herds were fed,
When haply by their stalls the bison lowed,
And bowed his manèd shoulder to the yoke.

All day this desert murmured with their toils,
Till twilight blushed, and lovers walked, and wooed
In a forgotten language, and old tunes,
From instruments of unremembered form,
Gave the soft winds a voice. The red man came—
The roaming hunter tribes, warlike and fierce,
And the mound-builders vanished from the earth.
The solitude of centuries untold
Has settled where they dwelt. The prairie-wolf
Hunts in their meadows, and his fresh-dug den
Yawns by my path. The gopher mines the ground
Where stood their swarming cities. All is gone;
All – save the piles of earth that hold their bones,
The platforms where they worshipped unknown gods,
The barriers which they builded from the soil
To keep the foe at bay – till o'er the walls
The wild beleaguerers broke, and, one by one,
The strongholds of the plain were forced, and heaped
With corpses. The brown vultures of the wood
Flocked to those vast uncovered sepulchres,
And sat unscared and silent at their feast.
Haply some solitary fugitive,
Lurking in marsh and forest, till the sense
Of desolation and of fear became
Bitterer than death, yielded himself to die.
Man's better nature triumphed then. Kind words
Welcomed and soothed him; the rude conquerors
Seated the captive with their chiefs; he chose
A bride among their maidens, and at length
Seemed to forget – yet ne'er forgot – the wife
Of his first love, and her sweet little ones,
Butchered, amid their shrieks, with all his race.

　　Thus change the forms of being. Thus arise
Races of living things, glorious in strength,

And perish, as the quickening breath of God
Fills them, or is withdrawn. The red man, too,
Has left the blooming wilds he ranged so long,
And, nearer to the Rocky Mountains, sought
A wilder hunting-ground. The beaver builds
No longer by these streams, but far away,
On waters whose blue surface ne'er gave back
The white man's face – among Missouri's springs,
And pools whose issues swell the Oregon—
He rears his little Venice. In these plains
The bison feeds no more. Twice twenty leagues
Beyond remotest smoke of hunter's camp,
Roams the majestic brute, in herds that shake
The earth with thundering steps – yet here I meet
His ancient footprints stamped beside the pool.

   Still this great solitude is quick with life.
Myriads of insects, gaudy as the flowers
They flutter over, gentle quadrupeds,
And birds, that scarce have learned the fear of man,
Are here, and sliding reptiles of the ground,
Startlingly beautiful. The graceful deer
Bounds to the wood at my approach. The bee,
A more adventurous colonist than man,
With whom he came across the eastern deep,
Fills the savannas with his murmurings,
And hides his sweets, as in the golden age,
Within the hollow oak. I listen long
To his domestic hum, and think I hear
The sound of that advancing multitude
Which soon shall fill these deserts. From the ground
Comes up the laugh of children, the soft voice
Of maidens, and the sweet and solemn hymn
Of Sabbath worshippers. The low of herds
Blends with the rustling of the heavy grain
Over the dark brown furrows. All at once

A fresher wind sweeps by, and breaks my dream,
And I am in the wilderness alone.

To a Waterfowl

Whither, 'midst falling dew,
While glow the heavens with the last steps of day,
Far, through their rosy depths, dost thou pursue
    Thy solitary way!

Vainly the fowler's eye
Might mark thy distant flight to do thee wrong,
As, darkly painted on the crimson sky,
    Thy figure floats along.

Seek'st thou the plashy brink
Of weedy lake, or marge of river wide,
Or where the rocking billows rise and sink
    On the chafed ocean side?

There is a power whose care
Teaches thy way along that pathless coast,—
The desert and illimitable air,—
    Lone wandering, but not lost.

All day thy wings have fanned,
At that far height, the cold, thin atmosphere,
Yet stoop not, weary, to the welcome land,
    Though the dark night is near.

And soon that toil shall end;
Soon shalt thou find a summer home, and rest,
And scream among thy fellows; reeds shall bend,
    Soon, o'er thy sheltered nest.

Thou'rt gone, the abyss of heaven
Hath swallowed up thy form; yet, on my heart
Deeply hath sunk the lesson thou hast given,
    And shall not soon depart.

    He who, from zone to zone,
Guides through the boundless sky thy certain flight,
In the long way that I must tread alone,
    Will lead my steps aright.

The Snow-Shower

Stand here by my side and turn, I pray,
  On the lake below thy gentle eyes;
The clouds hang over it, heavy and gray,
  And dark and silent the water lies;
And out of that frozen mist the snow
In wavering flakes begins to flow;
          Flake after flake
They sink in the dark and silent lake.

See how in a living swarm they come
  From the chambers beyond that misty veil;
Some hover awhile in air, and some
  Rush prone from the sky like summer hail.
All, dropping swiftly or settling slow;
Meet, and are still in the depths below;
          Flake after flake
Dissolved in the dark and silent lake.

Here delicate snow-stars, out of the cloud,
  Come floating downward in airy play,
Like spangles dropped from the glistening crowd
  That whiten by night the milky way;
There broader and burlier masses fall;

The sullen water buries them all—
           Flake after flake
All drowned in the dark and silent lake.

Lo! while we are gazing, in swifter haste
   Stream down the snows, till the air is white,
As, myriads by myriads madly chased,
   They fling themselves from their shadowy height.
The fair, frail creatures of middle sky,
What speed they make, with their grave so nigh;
           Flake after flake,
To lie in the dark and silent lake!

I see in thy gentle eyes a tear;
   They turn to me in sorrowful thought;
Thou thinkest of friends, the good and dear,
   Who were for a time, and now are not;
Like these fair children of cloud and frost,
That glisten a moment and then are lost,
           Flake after flake—
All lost in the dark and silent lake.

Yet look again, for the clouds divide;
   A gleam of blue on the water lies;
And far away, on the mountain-side,
   A sunbeam falls from the opening skies,
But the hurrying host that flew between
The cloud and the water, no more is seen;
           Flake after flake,
At rest in the dark and silent lake.

The Evening Wind

Spirit that breathest through my lattice, thou
   That coolest the twilight of the sultry day,
Gratefully flows thy freshness round my brow:
   Thou hast been out upon the deep at play,
Riding all day the wild blue waves till now,
   Roughening their crests, and scattering high their
      spray,
And swelling the white sail. I welcome thee
To the scorched land, thou wanderer of the sea!

Nor I alone – a thousand bosoms round
   Inhale thee in the fulness of delight;
And languid forms rise up, and pulses bound
   Livelier, at coming of the wind at night;
And, languishing to hear thy grateful sound,
   Lies the vast inland stretched beyond the sight.
Go forth into the gathering shade; go forth,
God's blessing breathed upon the fainting earth!

Go, rock the little wood-bird in his nest;
   Curl the still waters, bright with stars, and rouse,
The wide old wood from his majestic rest,
   Summoning, from the innumerable boughs,
The strange, deep harmonies that haunt his breast:
   Pleasant shall be thy way where meekly bows
The shutting flower, and darkling waters pass,
And where the o'ershadowing branches sweep the grass.

Go – but the circle of eternal change,
   Which is the life of nature, shall restore,
With sounds and scents from all thy mighty range,
   Thee to thy birthplace of the deep once more;
Sweet odors in the sea-air, sweet and strange,
   Shall tell the home-sick mariner of the shore;
And, listening to thy murmur, he shall deem
He hears the rustling leaf and running stream.

Spring in Town

The country ever has a lagging Spring,
   Waiting for May to call its violets forth,
And June its roses, – showers and sunshine bring,
   Slowly, the deepening verdure o'er the earth;
To put their foliage out, the woods are slack,
As one by one the singing-birds come back.

Within the city's bounds the time of flowers
   Comes earlier. Let a mild and sunny day,
Such as full often, for a few bright hours,
   Breathes through the sky of March the airs of May,
Shine on our roofs and chase the wintry gloom
And lo! our borders glow with sudden bloom.

For the wide sidewalks of Broadway are then
   Gorgeous as are a rivulet's banks in June,
That overhung with blossoms, through its glen,
   Slides soft away beneath the sunny noon,
And they who search the untrodden wood for flowers
Meet in its depths no lovelier ones than ours.

For here are eyes that shame the violet,
   Or the dark drop that on the pansy lies,
And foreheads white, as when in clusters set,
   The anemones by forest mountains rise;
And the spring-beauty boasts no tenderer streak
Than the soft red on many a youthful cheek.

The Antiquity of Freedom

Here are old trees, tall oaks, and gnarled pines,
That stream with gray-green mosses; here the ground
Was never touched by spade, and flowers spring up
Unsown, and die ungathered. It is sweet
To linger here, among the flitting birds
And leaping squirrels, wandering brooks and winds
That shake the leaves, and scatter as they pass
A fragrance from the cedars thickly set
With pale blue berries. In these peaceful shades—
Peaceful, unpruned, immeasurably old—
My thoughts go up the long dim path of years,
Back to the earliest days of Liberty.

O Freedom! thou art not, as poets dream,
A fair young girl, with light and delicate limbs,
And wavy tresses gushing from the cap
With which the Roman master crowned his slave,
When he took off the gyves. A bearded man,
Armed to the teeth, art thou: one mailed hand
Grasps the broad shield, and one the sword; thy brow,
Glorious in beauty though it be, is scarred
With tokens of old wars; thy massive limbs
Are strong and struggling. Power at thee has launched
His bolts, and with his lightnings smitten thee;
They could not quench the life thou hast from Heaven.
Merciless Power has dug thy dungeon deep,
And his swart armourers, by a thousand fires,
Have forged thy chain. Yet while he deems thee bound,
The links are shivered, and the prison walls
Fall outward; terribly thou springeth forth,
As springs the flame above a burning pile,
And shoutest to the nations, who return
Thy shoutings, while the pale oppressor flies.

Thy birth-right was not given by human hands:
Thou wert twin-born with man. In pleasant fields,
While yet our race was few, thou sat'st with him,
To tend the quiet flock and watch the stars,
And teach the reed to utter simple airs.
Thou by his side, amid the tangled wood,
Didst war upon the panther and the wolf,
His only foes: and thou with him didst draw
The earliest furrows on the mountain side,
Soft with the Deluge. Tyranny himself,
The enemy, though of reverend look,
Hoary with many years, and far obeyed,
Is later born than thou; and as he meets
The grave defiance of thine elder eye,
The usurper trembles in his fastnesses.
   Thou shalt wax stronger with the lapse of years,
But he shall fade into a feebler age;
Feebler, yet subtler; he shall weave his snares,
And spring them on thy careless steps, and clap
His withered hands, and from their ambush call
His hordes to fall upon thee. He shall send
Quaint maskers, forms of fair and gallant mien,
To catch thy gaze, and uttering graceful words
To charm thy ear; while his sly imps, by stealth,
Twine round thee threads of steel, light thread on thread,
That grow to fetters; or bind down thy arms
With chains concealed in chaplets. Oh! not yet
Mayst thou unbrace thy corslet, nor lay by
Thy sword, nor yet, O Freedom! close thy lids
In slumber; for thine enemy never sleeps.
And thou must watch and combat, till the day
Of the new Earth and Heaven. But wouldst thou rest
Awhile from tumult and the frauds of men,
These old and friendly solitudes invite
Thy visit. They, while yet the forest trees
Were young upon the unviolated earth,

And yet the moss-stains on the rock were new,
Beheld thy glorious childhood, and rejoiced.

Seventy-Six

What heroes from the woodland sprung,
  When, through the fresh-awakened land,
The thrilling cry of freedom rung,
And to the work of warfare strung
  The yeoman's iron hand!

Hills flung the cry to hills around,
  And ocean-mart replied to mart,
And streams, whose springs were yet unfound,
Pealed far away the startling sound
  Into the forest's heart.

Then marched the brave from rocky steep,
  From mountain-river swift and cold;
The borders of the stormy deep,
The vales where gathered waters sleep,
  Sent up the strong and bold,—

As if the very earth again
  Grew quick with God's creating breath,
And, from the sods of grove and glen,
Rose ranks of lion-hearted men
  To battle to the death.

The wife, whose babe first smiled that day,
  The fair fond bride of yestereve,
And aged sire and matron gray,
Saw the loved warriors haste away,
  And deemed it sin to grieve.

Already had the strife begun;
　Already blood, on Concord's plain,
Along the springing grass had run,
And blood had flowed at Lexington,
　Like brooks of April rain.

That death-stain on the vernal sward
　Hallowed to freedom all the shore;
In fragments fell the yoke abhorred—
The footstep of a foreign lord
　Profaned the soil no more.

The Waning Moon

I've watched too late; the morn is near;
　One look at God's broad silent sky!
Oh, hopes and wishes vainly dear,
　How in your very strength ye die!

Even while your glow is on the cheek,
　And scarce the high pursuit begun,
The heart grows faint, the hand grows weak,
　The task of life is left undone.

See where, upon the horizon's brim,
　Lies the still cloud in gloomy bars;
The waning moon, all pale and dim,
　Goes up amid the eternal stars.

Late in a flood of tender light,
　She floated through the ethereal blue,
A softer sun, that shone all night
　Upon the gathering beads of dew.

And still thou wanest, pallid moon!
　The encroaching shadow grows apace;
Heaven's everlasting watchers soon
　Shall see thee blotted from thy place.

Oh, Night's dethroned and crownless queen!
　Well may thy sad, expiring ray
Be shed on those whose eyes have seen
　Hope's glorious visions fade away.
Shine thou for forms that once were bright,
　For sages in the mind's eclipse,
For those whose words were spells of might
　But falter now on stammering lips!

In thy decaying beam there lies
　Full many a grave on hill and plain,
Of those who closed their dying eyes
　In grief that they had lived in vain.

Another night, and thou among
　The spheres of heaven shalt cease to shine,
All rayless in the glittering throng
　Whose lustre late was quenched in thine.

Yet soon a new and tender light
　From out thy darkened orb shall beam,
And broaden till it shines all night
　On glistening dew and glimmering stream.

The Wind and Stream

A brook came stealing from the ground;
  You scarcely saw its silvery gleam
Among the herbs that hung around
  The borders of that winding stream,
The pretty stream, the placid stream,
The softly-gliding, bashful stream.

A breeze came wandering from the sky,
  Light as the whispers of a dream;
He put the o'erhanging grasses by,
  And softly stooped to kiss the stream,
The pretty stream, the flattered stream,
The shy, yet unreluctant stream.

The water, as the wind passed o'er,
  Shot upward many a glancing beam,
Dimpled and quivered more and more,
  And tripped along, a livelier stream,
The flattered stream, the simpering stream,
The fond, delighted, silly stream.

Away the airy wanderer flew
  To where the fields with blossoms teem,
To sparkling springs and rivers blue,
  And left alone that little stream,
The flattered stream, the cheated stream,
The sad, forsaken, lonely stream.

That careless wind came never back;
  He wanders yet the fields, I deem,
But, on its melancholy track,
  Complaining went that little stream,
The cheated stream, the hopeless stream,
The ever-murmuring, mourning stream.

Waiting by the Gate

Beside a massive gateway built up in years gone by,
Upon whose top the clouds in eternal shadow lie,
While streams the evening sunshine on quiet wood and
    lea,
I stand and calmly wait till the hinges turn for me.

The tree-tops faintly rustle beneath the breeze's flight,
A soft and soothing sound, yet it whispers of the night;
I hear the wood-thrush piping one mellow descant more,
And scent the flowers that blow when the heat of day is
    o'er.

Behold, the portals open, and o'er the threshold, now,
There steps a weary one with a pale and furrowed brow;
His count of years is full, his allotted task is wrought;
He passes to his rest from a place that needs him not.

In sadness then I ponder how quickly fleets the hour
Of human strength and action, man's courage and his
    power.
I muse while still the wood-thrush sings down the golden
    day,
And as I look and listen the sadness wears away.

Again the hinges turn, and a youth, departing, throws
A look of longing backward, and sorrowfully goes;
A blooming maid, unbinding the roses from her hair,
Moves mournfully away from amid the young and fair.

O glory of our race that so suddenly decays!
O crimson flush of morning that darkens as we gaze!
O breath of summer blossoms that on the restless air
Scatters a moment's sweetness, and flies we know not
    where!

I grieve for life's bright promise, just shown and then
    withdrawn;
But still the sun shines round me: the evening bird sings
    on,
And I again am soothed, and, beside the ancient gate,
In this soft evening sunlight, I calmly stand and wait.

Once more the gates are opened; an infant group go out,
The sweet smile quenched forever, and stilled the
    sprightly shout.
O frail, frail tree of Life, that upon the greensward
    strows
Its fair young buds unopened, with every wind that
    blows!

So come from every region, so enter, side by side,
The strong and faint of spirit, the meek and men of pride.
Steps of earth's great and mighty, between those pillars
    gray,
And prints of little feet, mark the dust along the way.

And some approach the threshold whose looks are blank
    with fear,
And some whose temples brighten with joy in drawing
    near,
As if they saw dear faces, and caught the gracious eye
Of Him, the Sinless Teacher, who came for us to die.

I mark the joy, the terror; yet these, within my heart,
Can neither wake the dread nor the longing to depart;
And, in the sunshine streaming on quiet wood and lea,
I stand and calmly wait till the hinges turn for me.

The Path

The path we planned beneath October's sky,
    Along the hill-side, through the woodland shade,
Is finished; thanks to thee, whose kindly eye
    Has watched me, as I plied the busy spade;
Else had I wearied, ere this path of ours
Had pierced the woodland to its inner bowers.

Yet, 'twas a pleasant toil to trace and beat,
    Among the glowing trees, this winding way,
While the sweet autumn sunshine, doubly sweet,
    Flushed with the ruddy foliage, round us lay,
As if some gorgeous cloud of morning stood,
In glory, mid the arches of the wood.

A path! what beauty does a path bestow
    Even on the dreariest wild! its savage nooks
Seem homelike where accustomed footsteps go,
    And the grim rock puts on familiar looks.
The tangled swamp, through which a pathway strays,
Becomes a garden with strange flowers and sprays.

See, from the weedy earth a rivulet break
And purl along the untrodden wilderness;
There the shy cuckoo comes his thirst to slake,
    There the shrill jay alights his plumes to dress;
And there the stealthy fox, when morn is gray,
Laps the clear stream and lightly moves away.

But let a path approach that fountain's brink,
    And nobler forms of life. behold! are there:
Boys kneeling with protruded lips to drink,
    And slender maids that homeward slowly bear
The brimming pail, and busy dames that lay
Their webs to whiten in the summer ray.

Then know we that for herd and flock are poured
  Those pleasant streams that o'er the pebbles slip;
Those pure sweet waters sparkle on the board;
  Those fresh cool waters wet the sick man's lip;
Those clear bright waters from the font are shed,
In dews of baptism, on the infant's head.

What different steps the rural footway trace!
  The laborer afield at early day;
The schoolboy sauntering with uneven pace;
  The Sunday worshipper in fresh array;
And mourner in the weeds of sorrow drest;
And, smiling to himself, the wedding guest.

There he who cons a speech and he who hums
  His yet unfinished verses, musing walk.
There, with her little brood, the matron comes,
  To break the spring flower from its juicy stalk;
And lovers, loitering, wonder that the moon
Has risen upon their pleasant stroll so soon.

Bewildered in vast woods, the traveller feels
  His heavy heart grow lighter, if he meet
The traces of a path, and straight he kneels,
  And kisses the dear print of human feet,
And thanks his God, and journeys without fear,
For now he knows the abodes of men are near.

Pursue the slenderest path across a lawn:
  Lo! on the broad highway it issues forth,
And, blended with the greater track, goes on,
  Over the surface of the mighty earth,
Climbs hills and crosses vales, and stretches far,
Through silent forests, toward the evening star—

And enters cities murmuring with the feet
  Of multitudes, and wanders forth again,
And joins the climes of frost to climes of heat,
  Binds East to West, and marries main to main,
Nor stays till at the long-resounding shore
Of the great deep, where paths are known no more.

Oh, mighty instinct, that dost thus unite
  Earth's neighborhoods and tribes with friendly bands,
What guilt is theirs who, in their greed or spite,
  Undo thy holy work with violent hands!
And post their squadrons, nursed in war's grim trade,
To bar the ways for mutual succor made.

The Death of Lincoln

Oh, slow to smite and swift to spare,
  Gentle and merciful and just!
Who, in the fear of God, didst bear
  The sword of power, a nation's trust!

In sorrow by thy bier we stand,
  Amid the awe that hushes all,
And speak the anguish of a land
  That shook with horror at thy fall.

Thy task is done; the bond are free:
  We bear thee to an honored grave,
Whose proudest monument shall be
  The broken fetters of the slave.

Pure was thy life; its bloody close
  Hath placed thee with the sons of light,
Among the noble host of those
  Who perished in the cause of Right.

The Death of the Flowers

The melancholy days are come,
 The saddest of the year,
Of wailing winds, and naked woods,
 And meadows brown and sear.
Heaped in the hollows of the grove,
 The withered leaves lie dead;
They rustle to the eddying gust,
 And to the rabbit's tread.
The robin and the wren are flown,
 And from the shrubs the jay,
And from the wood-top calls the crow
 Through all the gloomy day.
Where are the flowers, the fair young flowers,
 That lately sprang and stood
In brighter light and softer airs,
 A beauteous sisterhood?
Alas! they all are in their graves;
 The gentle race of flowers
Are lying in their lowly beds,
 With the fair and good of ours.
The rain is falling where they lie,
 But the cold November rain
Calls not, from out the gloomy earth,
 The lovely ones again.

The wind-flower and the violet,
 They perished long ago,
And the brier-rose and the orchis died,
 Amid the summer glow;
But on the hill the golden-rod,
 And the aster in the wood,
And the yellow sun-flower by the brook
 In autumn beauty stood,

Till fell the frost from the clear, cold heaven,
  As falls the plague on men,
And the brightness of their smile was gone,
  From upland, glade, and glen.

And now, when comes the calm, mild day,
  As still such days will come,
To call the squirrel and the bee
  From out their winter home;
When the sound of dropping nuts is heard,
  Though all the trees are still,
And twinkle in the smoky light
  The waters of the rill,
The south wind searches for the flowers
  Whose fragrance late he bore,
And sighs to find them in the wood
  And by the stream no more.

And then I think of one who in
  Her youthful beauty died,
The fair, meek blossom that grew up
  And faded by my side;
In the cold, moist earth we laid her,
  When the forest cast the leaf,
And we wept that one so lovely
  Should have a life so brief:
Yet not unmeet it was that one,
  Like that young friend of ours,
So gentle and so beautiful,
  Should perish with the flowers.

A Scene on the Banks of the Hudson

Cool shades and dews are round my way,
And silence of the early day;
Mid the dark rocks that watch his bed,
Glitters the mighty Hudson spread,
Unrippled, save by drops that fall
From shrubs that fringe his mountain wall;
And o'er the clear still water swells
The music of the Sabbath bells.

All, save this little nook of land,
Circled with trees, on which I stand;
All, save that line of hills which lie
Suspended in the mimic sky,—
Seems a blue void, above, below,
Through which the white clouds come and go;
And from the green world's farthest steep
I gaze into the airy deep.

Loveliest of lovely things are they,
On earth, that soonest pass away.
The rose that lives its little hour
Is prized beyond the sculptured flower.
Even love, long tried and cherished long,
Becomes more tender and more strong,
At thought of that insatiate grave
From which its yearnings cannot save.

River! in this still hour thou hast
Too much of heaven on earth to last;
Nor long may thy still waters lie,
An image of the glorious sky.
Thy fate and mine are not repose,
And ere another evening close,
Thou to thy tides shall turn again,
And I to seek the haunts of men.

To the Fringed Gentian

Thou blossom, bright with autumn dew,
And coloured with the heaven's own blue,
That openest, when the quiet light
Succeeds the keen and frosty night.

Thou comest not when violets lean
O'er wandering brooks and springs unseen,
Or columbines in purple dress'd,
Nod o'er the ground-bird's hidden nest.

Thou waitest late, and com'st alone,
When woods are bare and birds are flown,
And frosts and shortening days portend
The aged year is near his end.
Then doth thy sweet and quiet eye
Look through its fringes to the sky,
Blue – blue – as if that sky let fall
A flower from its cerulean wall.

I would that thus, when I shall see
The hour of death draw near to me,
Hope, blossoming within my heart,
May look to heaven as I depart.

Forest Hymn

The groves were God's first temples. Ere man learned
To hew the shaft, and lay the architrave,
And spread the roof above them, ere he framed
The lofty vault, to gather and roll back
The sound of anthems; in the darkling wood,
Amid the cool and silence, he knelt down,
And offered to the Mightiest solemn thanks,

And supplication. For his simple heart
Might not resist the sacred influences,
Which, from the stilly twilight of the place,
And from the gray old trunks, that high in heaven
Mingled their mossy boughs, and from the sound
Of the invisible breath, that swayed at once
All their green tops, stole over him, and bowed
His spirit with the thought of boundless power,
And inaccessible majesty. Ah, why
Should we, in the world's riper years, neglect
God's ancient sanctuaries, and adore
Only among the crowd, and under roofs
That our frail hands have raised? Let me, at least,
Here, in the shadow of this aged wood,
Offer one hymn – thrice happy, if it find
Acceptance in his ear.
     Father, thy hand
Hath reared these venerable columns, thou
Didst weave this verdant roof. Thou didst look down
Upon the naked earth, and, forthwith, rose
All these fair ranks of trees. They, in thy sun,
Budded, and shook their green leaves in thy breeze,
And shot towards heaven. The century-living crow,
Whose birth was in their tops, grew old and died
Among their branches; till, at last, they stood,
As now they stand, massy, and tall, and dark,
Fit shrine for humble worshipper to hold
Communion with his Maker. These dim vaults,
These winding aisles, of human pomp or pride
Report not. No fantastic carvings show,
The boast of our vain race, to change the form
Of thy fair works. But thou art here – thou fill'st
The solitude. Thou art in the soft winds,
That run along the summit of these trees
In music; thou art in the cooler breath,
That, from the inmost darkness of the place,

Comes, scarcely felt. The barky trunks, the ground,
The fresh, moist ground, are all instinct with thee.
Here is continual worship, – Nature, here,
In the tranquillity that thou dost love,
Enjoys thy presence. Noiselessly around,
From perch to perch, the solitary bird
Passes; and yon clear spring, that, midst its herbs,
Wells softly forth, and visits the strong roots
Of half the mighty forest, tells no tale
Of all the good it does. Thou hast not left
Thyself without a witness, in these shades,
Of thy perfections. Grandeur, strength, and grace,
Are here to speak of thee. This mighty oak,
By whose immovable stem I stand, and seem
Almost annihilated, – not a prince,
In all that proud old world beyond the deep,
E'er wore his crown as loftily as he
Wears the green coronal of leaves with which
Thy hand has graced him. Nestled at his root
Is beauty, such as blooms not in the glare
Of the broad sun. That delicate forest flower,
With delicate breath, and look so like a smile,
Seems, as it issues from the shapeless mould,
An emanation of the indwelling Life,
A visible token of the upholding Love,
That are the soul of this wide universe.
   My heart is awed within me, when I think
Of the great miracle that still goes on
In silence, round me – the perpetual work
Of thy creation, finished, yet renewed
Forever. Written on thy works, I read
The lesson of thy own eternity.
Lo! all grow old and die; but see, again,
How on the faltering footsteps of decay
Youth presses, ever gay and beautiful youth,
In all its beautiful forms. These lofty trees

Wave not less proudly that their ancestors
Moulder beneath them. O, there is not lost
One of earth's charms: upon her bosom yet,
After the flight of untold centuries,
The freshness of her far beginning lies,
And yet shall lie. Life mocks the idle hate
Of his arch-enemy, Death – yea, seats himself
Upon the tyrant's throne – the sepulchre,
And of the triumphs of his ghastly foe
Makes his own nourishment. For he came forth
From thine own bosom, and shall have no end.
   There have been holy men who hid themselves
Deep in the woody wilderness, and gave
Their lives to thought and prayer, till they outlived
The generation born with them, nor seemed
Less aged than the hoary trees and rocks
Around them; – and there have been holy men
Who deemed it were not well to pass life thus.
But let me often to these solitudes
Retire, and in thy presence reassure
My feeble virtue. Here its enemies,
The passions, at thy plainer footsteps shrink,
And tremble and are still. O, God! when thou
Dost scare the world with tempests, set on fire
The heavens with falling thunderbolts, or fill,
With all the waters of the firmament,
The swift, dark whirlwind that uproots the woods
And drowns the villages; when, at thy call,
Uprises the great deep and throws himself
Upon the continent, and overwhelms
Its cities – who forgets not, at the sight
Of these tremendous tokens of thy power,
His pride, and lays his strifes and follies by?
O, from these sterner aspects of thy face
Spare me and mine, nor let us need the wrath
Of the mad, unchained elements to teach

Who rules them. Be it ours to meditate
In these calm shades thy milder majesty,
And to the beautiful order of thy works
Learn to conform the order of our lives.

To the Past

Thou unrelenting Past!
Strong are the barriers round thy dark domain,
    And fetters, sure and fast,
Hold all that enter thy unbreathing reign.

    Far in thy realm withdrawn,
Old empires sit in sullenness and gloom;
    And glorious ages gone
Lie deep within the shadow of thy womb.

    Childhood, with all its mirth,
Youth, manhood, age, that draws us to the ground.
    And last, man's life on earth,
Glide to thy dim dominions, and are bound.

    Thou hast my better years,
Thou hast my earlier friends – the good – the kind,
    Yielded to thee with tears—
The venerable form – the exalted mind.

    My spirit yearns to bring
The lost ones back – yearns with desire intense,
    And struggles hard to wring
Thy bolts apart, and pluck thy captives thence.

In vain – thy gates deny
All passage, save to those who hence depart;
   Nor to the streaming eye
Thou givest them back – nor to the broken heart.

   In thy abysses hide
Beauty and excellence unknown – to thee
   Earth's wonder and her pride
Are gather'd, as the waters to the sea.

   Labours of good to man,
Unpublish'd charity – unbroken faith—
   Love, that midst grief began,
And grew with years, and falter'd not in death.

   Full many a mighty name
Lurks in thy depths, unutter'd, unrevered;
   With thee are silent fame,
Forgotten arts, and wisdom disappear'd.

   Thine, for a space, are they—
Yet shalt thou yield thy treasures up at last;
   Thy gates shall yet give way,
Thy bolts shall fall, inexorable Past!

   All that of good and fair
Has gone into thy womb, from earliest time,
   Shall then come forth, to wear
The glory and the beauty of its prime.

   They have not perish'd – no!
Kind words, remember'd voices, once so sweet,
   Smiles, radiant long ago,
And features, the great soul's apparent seat;

All shall come back, each tie
Of pure affection shall be knit again;
    Alone shall evil die,
And sorrow dwell a prisoner in thy reign.

    And then shall I behold
Him, by whose kind paternal side I sprung,
    And her, who, still and cold,
Fills the next grave – the beautiful and young.

After a Tempest

The day had been a day of wind and storm;—
    The wind was laid, the storm was overpast,—
And, stooping from the zenith, bright and warm
    Shone the great sun on the wide earth at last.
    I stood upon the upland slope, and cast
My eye upon a broad and beauteous scene,
    Where the vast plain lay girt by mountains vast
And hills o'er hills lifted their heads of green,
With pleasant vales scoop'd out and villages between.

The rain-drops glisten'd on the trees around,
    Whose shadows on the tall grass were not stirr'd
Save when a shower of diamonds to the ground
    Was shaken by the flight of startled bird;
    For birds were warbling round, and bees were heard
About the flowers; the cheerful rivulet sung
    And gossip'd, as he hasten'd ocean-ward;
To the gray oak the squirrel, chiding, clung,
And chirping from the ground the grasshopper upsprung.

And from beneath the leaves that kept them dry
   Flew many a glittering insect here and there,
And darted up and down the butterfly,
   That seem'd a living blossom of the air.
   The flocks came scattering from the thicket, where
The violent rain had pent them; in the way
   Stroll'd groups of damsels frolicsome and fair;
The farmer swung the scythe or turn'd the hay,
And 'twixt the heavy swaths his children were at play.

It was a scene of peace – and, like a spell,
   Did that serene and golden sunlight fall
Upon the motionless wood that clothed the fell,
   And precipice upspringing like a wall,
   And glassy river and white waterfall,
And happy living things that trod the bright
   And beauteous scene; while far beyond them all,
On many a lovely valley, out of sight,
Was pour'd from the blue heavens the same soft, golden
     light.

I look'd, and thought the quiet of the scene
   An emblem of the peace that yet shall be,
When, o'er earth's continents and isles between,
   The noise of war shall cease from sea to sea,
   And married nations dwell in harmony;
When millions, crouching in the dust to one,
   No more shall beg their lives on bended knee,
Nor the black stake be dress'd, nor in the sun
The o'erlabour'd captive toil, and wish his life were done.

Too long, at clash of arms amid her bowers
   And pools of blood, the earth has stood aghast,
The fair earth, that should only blush with flowers
   And ruddy fruits; but not for aye can last
   The storm, and sweet the sunshine when 't is past.

Lo, the clouds roll away – they break – they fly,
  And, like the glorious light of summer, cast
O'er the wide landscape from the embracing sky,
On all the peaceful world the smile of heaven shall lie.

Our Country's Call

Lay down the axe, fling by the spade:
  Leave in its track the toiling plough;
The rifle and the bayonet-blade
  For arms like yours were fitter now;
And let the hands that ply the pen
  Quit the light task, and learn to wield
The horseman's crooked brand, and rein
  The charger on the battle-field.

Our country calls; away! away!
  To where the blood-stream blots the green.
Strike to defend the gentlest sway
  That Time in all his course has seen.
See, from a thousand coverts – see
  Spring the armed foes that haunt her track;
They rush to smite her down, and we
  Must beat the banded traitors back.

Ho! sturdy as the oaks ye cleave,
  And moved as soon to fear and flight,
Men of the glade and forest! leave
  Your woodcraft for the field of fight.
The arms that wield the axe must pour
  An iron tempest on the foe;
His serried ranks shall reel before
  The arm that lays the panther low.

And ye who breast the mountain storm
  By grassy steep or highland lake,
Come, for the land ye love, to form
  A bulwark that no foe can break.
Stand, like your own gray cliffs that mock
  The whirlwind; stand in her defence:
The blast as soon shall move the rock,
  As rushing squadrons bear ye thence.

And ye, whose homes are by her grand
  Swift rivers, rising far away,
Come from the depth of her green land
  As mighty in your march as they;
As terrible as when the rains
  Have swelled them over bank and bourne,
With sudden floods to drown the plains
  And sweep along the woods uptorn.

And ye who throng beside the deep,
  Her ports and hamlets of the strand,
In number like the waves that leap
  On his long murmuring marge of sand,
Come, like that deep, when o'er his brim
  He rises, all his floods to pour,
And flings the proudest barks that swim
  A helpless wreck against his shore.

Few, few were they whose swords of old
  Won the fair land in which we dwell;
But we are many, we who hold
  The grim resolve to guard it well.
Strike for that broad and goodly land
  Blow after blow, till men shall see
That Might and Right move hand in hand,
  And glorious must their triumph be.

An Evening Revery

The summer day is closed – the sun is set:
Well they have done their office, those bright hours,
The latest of whose train goes softly out
In the red west. The green blade of the ground
Has risen, and herds have cropped it; the young twig
Has spread its plaited tissues to the sun;
Flowers of the garden and the waste have blown
And withered; seeds have fallen upon the soil,
From bursting cells, and in their graves await
Their resurrection. Insects from the pools
Have filled the air awhile with humming wings,
That now are stilled for ever; painted moths
Have wandered the blue sky, and died again;
The mother-bird hath broken for her brood
Their prison shell, or shoved them from the nest,
Plumed for their earliest flight. In bright alcoves,
In woodland cottages with barky walls,
In noisome cells of the tumultuous town,
Mothers have clasped with joy the new-born babe.
Graves by the lonely forest, by the shore
Of rivers and of ocean, by the ways
Of the thronged city, have been hollowed out
And filled, and closed. This day hath parted friends
That ne'er before were parted; it hath knit
New friendships; it hath seen the maiden plight
Her faith, and trust her peace to him who long
Had wooed; and it hath heard, from lips which late
Were eloquent of love, the first harsh word,
That told the wedded one her peace was flown.
Farewell to the sweet sunshine! One glad day
Is added now to Childhood's merry days,
And one calm day to those of quiet Age.
Still the fleet hours run on; and as I lean,
Amid the thickening darkness, lamps are lit,

By those who watch the dead, and those who twine
Flowers for the bride. The mother from the eyes
Of her sick infant shades the painful light,
And sadly listens to his quick-drawn breath.

   O Thou great Movement of the Universe,
Or Change, or Flight of Time – for ye are one!
That bearest, silently, this visible scene
Into night's shadow and the streaming rays
Of starlight, whither art thou bearing me?
I feel the mighty current sweep me on,
Yet know not whither. Man foretells afar
The courses of the stars; the very hour
He knows when they shall darken or grow bright;
Yet doth the eclipse of Sorrow and of Death
Come unforewarned. Who next, of those I love,
Shall pass from life, or, sadder yet, shall fall
From virtue? Strife with foes, or bitterer strife
With friends, or shame and general scorn of men—
Which who can bear? – or the fierce rack of pain—
Lie they within my path? Or shall the years
Push me, with soft and inoffensive pace,
Into the stilly twilight of my age?
Or do the portals of another life
Even now, while I am glorying in my strength,
Impend around me? Oh! Beyond that bourne,
In the vast cycle of being which begins
At that dread threshold, with what fairer forms
Shall the great law of change and progress clothe
Its workings? Gently – so have good men taught—
Gently, and without grief, the old shall glide
Into the new; the eternal flow of things,
Like a bright river of the fields of heaven,
Shall journey onward in perpetual peace.

America

Oh, mother of a mighty race,
Yet lovely in thy youthful grace!
The elder dames, thy haughty peers,
Admire and hate thy blooming years.
    With words of shame
And taunts of scorn they join thy name.

For on thy cheeks the glow is spread
That tints the morning hills with red:
Thy step – the wild deer's rustling feet
Within thy woods, are not more fleet;
    Thy hopeful eye
Is bright as thine own sunny sky.

Ay, let them rail – those haughty ones—
While safe thou dwellest with thy sons.
They do not know how loved thou art—
How many a fond and fearless heart
    Would rise to throw
Its life between thee and the foe!

They know not, in their hate and pride,
What virtues with thy children bide;
How true, how good, thy graceful maids
Make bright, like flowers, the valley shades;
    What generous men
Spring, like thine oaks, by hill and glen:

What cordial welcomes greet the guest
By the lone rivers of the west;
How faith is kept, and truth revered,
And man is loved, and God is feared,
    In woodland homes,
And where the solemn ocean foams!

There's freedom at thy gates, and rest
For earth's down-trodden and oppressed,
A shelter for the hunted head,
For the starved labourer toil and bread,
    Power, at thy bounds,
Stops and calls back his baffled hounds.

Oh, fair young mother; on thy brow
Shall sit a nobler grace than now.
Deep in the brightness of thy skies
The thronging years in glory rise,
    And, as they fleet,
Drop strength and riches at thy feet.

Thine eye, with every coming hour,
Shall brighten, and thy form shall tower;
And when thy sisters, elder born,
Would brand thy name with words of scorn,
    Before thine eye,
Upon their lips the taunt shall die!

The Planting of the Apple-Tree

  Come, let us plant the apple-tree.
Cleave the tough greensward with the spade;
Wide let its hollow bed be made;
There gently lay the roots, and there
Sift the dark mould with kindly care,
    And press it o'er them tenderly,
As, round the sleeping infant's feet,
We softly fold the cradle sheet;
    So plant we the apple-tree.

What plant we in this apple-tree?
Buds, which the breath of summer days
Shall lengthen into leafy sprays;
Boughs where the thrush, with crimson breast,
Shall haunt and sing and hide her nest;
   We plant, upon the sunny lea,
A shadow for the noontide hour,
A shelter from the summer shower,
   When we plant the apple-tree.

What plant we in this apple-tree?
Sweets for a hundred flowery springs
To load the May-wind's restless wings,
When, from the orchard row, he pours
Its fragrance through our open doors;
   A world of blossoms for the bee,
Flowers for the sick girl's silent room,
For the glad infant sprigs of bloom,
   We plant with the apple-tree.

What plant we in this apple-tree!
Fruits that shall swell in sunny June,
And redden in the August noon,
And drop, when gentle airs come by,
That fan the blue September sky,
   While children come, with cries of glee,
And seek them where the fragrant grass
Betrays their bed to those who pass,
   At the foot of the apple-tree.

And when, above this apple-tree,
The winter stars are quivering bright,
And winds go howling through the night,
Girls, whose young eyes o'erflow with mirth,
Shall peel its fruit by cottage-hearth,
   And guests in prouder homes shall see,

Heaped with the grape of Cintra's vine
And golden orange of the line,
  The fruit of the apple-tree.

  The fruitage of this apple-tree
Winds and our flag of stripe and star
Shall bear to coasts that lie afar,
Where men shall wonder at the view,
And ask in what fair groves they grew;
  And sojourners beyond the sea
Shall think of childhood's careless day
And long, long hours of summer play,
  In the shade of the apple-tree.

  Each year shall give this apple-tree
A broader flush of roseate bloom,
A deeper maze of verdurous gloom,
And loosen, when the frost-clouds lower,
The crisp brown leaves in thicker shower;
  The years shall come and pass, but we
Shall hear no longer, where we lie,
The summer's songs, the autumn's sigh,
  In the boughs of the apple-tree.

  And time shall waste this apple-tree.
Oh, when its aged branches throw
Thin shadows on the ground below,
Shall fraud and force and iron will
Oppress the weak and helpless still?
  What shall the tasks of mercy be,
Amid the toils, the strifes, the tears
Of those who live when length of years
  Is wasting this little apple-tree?

'Who planted this old apple-tree?'
The children of that distant day
Thus to some aged man shall say;
And, gazing on its mossy stem,
The gray-haired man shall answer them:
  'A poet of the land was he,
Born in the rude but good old times;
'T is said he made some quaint old rhymes
  On planting the apple-tree.'

The Crowded Street

Let me move slowly through the street,
  Filled with an ever-shifting train,
Amid the sound of steps that beat
  The murmuring walks like autumn rain.

How fast the flitting figures come!
  The mild, the fierce, the stony face;
Some bright with thoughtless smiles, and some
  Where secret tears have left their trace.

They pass – to toil, to strife, to rest;
  To halls in which the feast is spread;
To chambers where the funeral guest
  In silence sits beside the dead.

And some to happy homes repair,
  Where children, pressing cheek to cheek,
With mute caresses shall declare
  The tenderness they cannot speak.

And some, who walk in calmness here,
   Shall shudder as they reach the door
Where one who made their dwelling dear,
   Its flower, its light, is seen no more.

Youth, with pale cheek and slender frame,
   And dreams of greatness in thine eye!
Go'st thou to build an early name,
   Or early in the task to die?

Keen son of trade, with eager brow!
   Who is now fluttering in thy snare?
Thy golden fortunes, tower they now,
   Or melt the glittering spires in air?

Who of this crowd tonight shall tread
   The dance till daylight gleam again?
Who sorrow o'er the untimely dead?
   Who writhe in throes of mortal pain?

Some, famine-struck, shall think how long
   The cold dark hours, how slow the light;
And some, who flaunt amid the throng,
   Shall hide in dens of shame to-night.

Each, where his tasks or pleasures call,
   They pass, and heed each other not.
There is who heeds, who holds them all,
   In His large love and boundless thought.

These struggling tides of life that seem
   In wayward, aimless course to tend,
Are eddies of the mighty stream
   That rolls to its appointed end.

The Future Life

How shall I know thee in the sphere which keeps
  The disembodied spirits of the dead,
When all of thee that time could wither sleeps
  And perishes among the dust we tread?

For I shall feel the sting of ceaseless pain
  If there I meet thy gentle presence not;
Nor hear the voice I love, nor read again
  In thy serenest eyes the tender thought.

Will not thy own meek heart demand me there?
  That heart whose fondest throbs to me were given—
My name on earth was ever in thy prayer,
  And wilt thou never utter it in heaven?

In meadows fanned by heaven's life-breathing wind,
  In the resplendence of that glorious sphere,
And larger movements of the unfettered mind,
  Wilt thou forget the love that joined us here?

The love that lived through all the stormy past,
  And meekly with my harsher nature bore,
And deeper grew, and tenderer to the last,
  Shall it expire with life, and be no more?

A happier lot than mine, and larger light,
  Await thee there, for thou hast bowed thy will
In cheerful homage to the rule of right,
  And lovest all, and renderest good for ill.

For me, the sordid cares in which I dwell
  Shrink and consume my heart as heat the scroll;
And wrath has left its scar — that fire of hell
  Has left its frightful scar upon my soul.

Yet, though thou wear'st the glory of the sky,
  Wilt thou not keep the same belovèd name,
The same fair thoughtful brow, and gentle eye,
  Lovelier in heaven's sweet climate, yet the same?
Shalt thou not teach me, in that calmer home,
  The wisdom that I learned so ill in this—
The wisdom which is love – till I become
  Thy fit companion in that land of bliss?

June

I gazed upon the glorious sky
  And the green mountains round,
And thought that when I came to lie
  At rest within the ground,
'T were pleasant, that in flowery June,
When brooks send up a cheerful tune,
  And groves a joyous sound,
The sexton's hand, my grave to make,
The rich, green mountain-turf should break.

A cell within the frozen mould,
  A coffin borne through sleet,
And icy clods above it rolled,
  While fierce the tempests beat—
Away! – I will not think of these—
Blue be the sky and soft the breeze,
  Earth green beneath the feet,
And be the damp mould gently pressed
Into my narrow place of rest.

There through the long, long summer hours
  The golden light should lie,
And thick young herbs and groups of flowers
  Stand in their beauty by.

The oriole should build and tell
His love-tale close beside my cell;
  The idle butterfly
Should rest him there, and there be heard
The housewife bee and humming-bird.

And what if cheerful shouts at noon
  Come, from the village sent,
Or song of maids, beneath the moon
  With fairy laughter blent?
And what if, in the evening light,
Betrothèd lovers walk in sight
  Of my low monument?
I would the lovely scene around
Might know no sadder sight nor sound.

I know that I no more should see
  The season's glorious show,
Nor would its brightness shine for me,
  Nor its wild music flow;
But if, around my place of sleep,
The friends I love should come to weep,
  They might not haste to go.
Soft airs, and song, and light, and bloom
Should keep them lingering by my tomb.

These to their softened hearts should bear
  The thought of what has been,
And speak of one who cannot share
  The gladness of the scene;
Whose part, in all the pomp that fills
The circuit of the summer hills,
  Is that his grave is green;
And deeply would their hearts rejoice
To hear again his living voice.

O Fairest of the Rural Maids

O fairest of the rural maids!
Thy birth was in the forest shades;
Green boughs and glimpses of the sky
Were all that met thine infant eye.

Thy sports, thy wanderings when a child,
Were ever in the sylvan wild;
And all the beauty of the place
Is in thy heart and on thy face.

The twilight of the trees and rocks
Is in the light shade of thy locks;
Thy step is as the wind that weaves
Its playful way among the leaves.

Thine eyes are springs, in whose serene
And silent waters Heaven is seen;
Their lashes are the herbs that look
On their young figures in the brook.

The forest depths by foot impressed
Are not more sinless than thy breast;
The holy peace that fills the air
Of those calm solitudes, is there.

'I Broke the Spell that Held Me Long'

I broke the spell that held me long,
The dear, dear witchery of song.
I said, the poet's idle lore
Shall waste my prime of years no more,
For Poetry, though heavenly born,
Consorts with poverty and scorn.

I broke the spell – nor deemed its power
Could fetter me another hour.
Ah, thoughtless! how could I forget
Its causes were around me yet?
For whereso'er I looked, the while,
Was Nature's everlasting smile.

Still came and lingered on my sight
Of flowers and streams the bloom and light,
And glory of the stars and sun;—
And these and poetry are one.
They, ere the world had held me long,
Recalled me to the love of song.

RALPH WALDO EMERSON
1803-1882

Ralph Waldo Emerson was America's foremost
Transcendentalist combining Romanticism, as it
developed in America, with a Puritan-based
philosophy. Born in Boston, he became a Unitarian
minister like his father but resigned his pastorate in
1832 because he had turned from formal religion to
intuitive spiritual experience.

Emerson's philosophy of the mystical unity of
nature and his deep love of the countryside around
him are clearly reflected in his poetry. 'Rhodora', 'The
Humble Bee' and 'Concord Hymn' are all taken from
Poems of 1847.

The Rhodora:

On being asked, whence is the flower?

In May, when sea-winds pierced our solitudes,
I found the fresh Rhodora in the woods,
Spreading its leafless blooms in a damp nook,
To please the desert and the sluggish brook.
The purple petals, fallen in the pool,
Made the black water with their beauty gay;
Here might the red-bird come his plumes to cool,
And court the flower that cheapens his array.
Rhodora! if the sages ask thee why
This charm is wasted on the earth and sky,
Tell them, dear, that if eyes were made for seeing,
Then Beauty is its own excuse for being:
Why thou wert there, O rival of the rose!
I never thought to ask, I never knew:
But, in my simple ignorance, suppose
The self-same Power that brought me there brought you.

The Humble-Bee

Burly, dozing humble-bee,
Where thou art is clime for me.
Let them sail for Porto Rique,
Far-off heats through seas to seek;
I will follow thee alone,
Thou animated torrid-zone!
Zigzag steerer, desert cheerer,
Let me chase thy waving lines;
Keep me nearer, me thy hearer,
Singing over shrubs and vines.

Insect lover of the sun,
Joy of thy dominion!
Sailor of the atmosphere;
Swimmer through the waves of air;
Voyager of light and noon;
Epicurean of June;
Wait, I prithee, till I come
Within earshot of thy hum,—
All without is martyrdom.

When the south wind, in May days,
With a net of shining haze
Silvers the horizon wall,
And with softness touching all,
Tints the human countenance
With a color of romance,
And infusing subtle heats,
Turns the sod to violets,
Thou, in sunny solitudes,
Rover of the underwoods,
The green silence dost displace
With thy mellow, breezy bass.

Hot midsummer's petted crone,
Sweet to me thy drowsy tone
Tells of countless sunny hours,
Long days, and solid banks of flowers;
Of gulfs of sweetness without bound
In Indian wildernesses found;
Of Syrian peace, immortal leisure,
Firmest cheer, and bird-like pleasure.

Aught unsavory or unclean
Hath my insect never seen;
But violets and bilberry bells,
Maple-sap and daffodels,

Grass with green flag half-mast high,
Succory to match the sky,
Columbine with horn of honey,
Scented fern, and agrimony,
Clover, catchfly, adder's-tongue
And brier-roses, dwelt among;
All beside was unknown waste,
All was picture as he passed.

Wiser far than human seer,
Yellow-breeched philosopher!
Seeing only what is fair,
Sipping only what is sweet,
Thou dost mock at fate and care,
Leave the chaff, and take the wheat.
When the fierce northwestern blast
Cools sea and land so far and fast,
Thou already slumberest deep;
Woe and want thou canst outsleep;
Want and woe, which torture us,
Thy sleep makes ridiculous.

Concord Hymn

*Sung at the Completion of the Battle Monument,
July 4, 1837*

By the rude bridge that arched the flood,
  Their flag to April's breeze unfurled,
Here once the embattled farmers stood
  And fired the shot heard round the world.

The foe long since in silence slept;
  Alike the conqueror silent sleeps;
And Time the ruined bridge has swept
  Down the dark stream which seaward creeps.

On this green bank, by this soft stream,
    We set to-day a votive stone;
That memory may their deed redeem,
    When, like our sires, our sons are gone.

Give All to Love

Give all to love;
Obey thy heart;
Friends, kindred, days,
Estate, good-fame,
Plans, credit and the Muse,—
Nothing refuse.

'T is a brave master;
Let it have scope:
Follow it utterly,
Hope beyond hope:
High and more high
It dives into noon,
With wing unspent,
Untold intent;
But it is a god,
Knows its own path
And the outlets of the sky.

It was never for the mean;
It requireth courage stout.
Souls above doubt,
Valor unbending,
It will reward,—
They shall return
More than they were,
And ever ascending.

Leave all for love;
Yet, hear me, yet,
One word more thy heart behoved,
One pulse more of firm endeavor,—
Keep thee to-day,
To-morrow, forever,
Free as an Arab
Of thy beloved.

Cling with life to the maid;
But when the surprise,
First vague shadow of surmise
Flits across her bosom young,
Of a joy apart from thee,
Free be she, fancy-free;
Nor thou detain her vesture's hem,
Nor the palest rose she flung
From her summer diadem.

Though thou loved her as thyself,
As a self of purer clay,
Though her parting dims the day,
Stealing grace from all alive;
Heartily know,
When half-gods go,
The gods arrive.

Days

Daughters of Time, the hypocritic Days,
Muffled and dumb like barefoot dervishes,
And marching single in an endless file,
Bring diadems and fagots in their hands.
To each they offer gifts after his will,
Bread, kingdoms, stars, and sky that holds them all.

I, in my pleached garden, watched the pomp,
Forgot my morning wishes, hastily
Took a few herbs and apples, and the Day
Turned and departed silent. I, too late,
Under her solemn fillet saw the scorn.

The Problem

I like a church; I like a cowl;
I love a prophet of the soul;
And on my heart monastic aisles
Fall like sweet strains, or pensive smiles;
Yet not for all his faith can see
Would I that cowlèd churchman be.

Why should the vest on him allure,
Which I could not on me endure?

Not from a vain or shallow thought
His awful Jove young Phidias brought;
Never from lips of cunning fell
The thrilling Delphic oracle;
Out from the heart of nature rolled
The burdens of the Bible old;
The litanies of nations came,
Like the volcano's tongue of flame,
Up from the burning core below,—
The canticles of love and woe:
The hand that rounded Peter's dome
And groined the aisles of Christian Rome
Wrought in a sad sincerity;
Himself from God he could not free;
He builded better than he knew;—
The conscious stone to beauty grew.

Know'st thou what wove yon woodbird's nest
Of leaves, and feathers from her breast?
Or how the fish outbuilt her shell,
Painting with morn each annual cell?
Or how the sacred pine-tree adds
To her old leaves new myriads?
Such and so grew these holy piles,
Whilst love and terror laid the tiles.
Earth proudly wears the Parthenon,
As the best gem upon her zone,
And Morning opes with haste her lids
To gaze upon the Pyramids;
O'er England's abbeys bends the sky,
As on its friends, with kindred eye;
For out of Thought's interior sphere
These wonders rose to upper air;
And Nature gladly gave them place,
Adopted them into her race,
And granted them an equal date
With Andes and with Ararat.

These temples grew as grows the grass;
Art might obey, but not surpass.
The passive Master lent his hand
To the vast soul that o'er him planned;
And the same power that reared the shrine
Bestrode the tribes that knelt within.
Ever the fiery Pentecost
Girds with one flame the countless host,
Trances the heart through chanting choirs,
And through the priest the mind inspires.
The word unto the prophet spoken
Was writ on tables yet unbroken;
The word by seers or sibyls told,
In groves of oak, or fanes of gold,
Still floats upon the morning wind,

Still whispers to the willing mind.
One accent of the Holy Ghost
The heedless world hath never lost.
I know what say the fathers wise,—
The Book itself before me lies,
Old *Chrysostom*, best Augustine,
And he who blent both in his line,
The younger *Golden Lips* or mines,
Taylor, the Shakspeare of divines.
His words are music in my ear,
I see his cowlèd portrait dear;
And yet, for all his faith could see,
I would not the good bishop be.

Each and All

Little thinks, in the field, yon red-cloaked clown,
Of thee from the hill-top looking down;
The heifer that lows in the upland farm,
Far-heard, lows not thine ear to charm;
The sexton, tolling his bell at noon,
Deems not that great Napoleon
Stops his horse, and lists with delight,
Whilst his files sweep round yon Alpine height;
Nor knowest thou what argument
Thy life to thy neighbour's creed has lent.
All are needed by each one;
Nothing is fair or good alone.
I thought the sparrow's note from heaven,
Singing at dawn on the alder bough;
I brought him home, in his nest, at even;
He sings the song, but it pleases not now,
For I did not bring home the river and sky;—
He sang to my ear, – they sang to my eye.
The delicate shells lay on the shore;

The bubbles of the latest wave
Fresh pearls to their enamel gave;
And the bellowing of the savage sea
Greeted their safe escape to me.
I wiped away the weeds and foam,
I fetched my sea-born treasures home;
But the poor, unsightly, noisome things
Had left their beauty on the shore,
With the sun and the sand and the wild uproar.
The lover watched his graceful maid,
As 'mid the virgin train she strayed,
Nor knew her beauty's best attire
Was woven still by the snow-white choir.
At last she came to his hermitage,
Like the bird from the woodlands to the cage;—
The gay enchantment was undone,
A gentle wife, but fairy none.
Then I said, 'I covet truth;
Beauty is unripe childhood's cheat;
I leave it behind with the games of youth.'—
As I spoke, beneath my feet
The ground-pine curled its pretty wreath,
Running over the club-moss burrs;
I inhaled the violet's breath;
Around me stood the oaks and firs;
Pine-cones and acorns lay on the ground;
Over me soared the eternal sky,
Full of light and of deity;
Again I saw, again I heard,
The rolling river, the morning bird;—
Beauty through my senses stole;
I yielded myself to the perfect whole.

Bacchus

Bring me wine, but wine which never grew
In the belly of the grape,
Or grew on vine whose tap-roots, reaching through,
Under the Andes to the Cape,
Suffer no savor of the earth to 'scape.

Let its grapes the morn salute
From a nocturnal root,
Which feels the acrid juice
Of Styx and Erebus;
And turns the woe of Night,
By its own craft, to a more rich delight.

We buy ashes for bread;
We buy diluted wine;
Give me of the true,—
Whose ample leaves and tendrils curled
Among the silver hills of heaven
Draw everlasting dew;
Wine of wine,
Blood of the world,
Form of forms, and mould of statures,
That I intoxicated,
And by the draught assimilated,
May float at pleasure through all natures;
The bird-language rightly spell,
And that which roses say so well.

Wine that is shed
Like the torrents of the sun
Up the horizon walls,
Or like the Atlantic streams, which run
When the South Sea calls.

Water and bread,
Food which needs no transmuting,
Rainbow-flowering, wisdom-fruiting,
Wine which is already man,
Food which teach and reason can.

Wine which Music is,—
Music and wine are one,—
That I, drinking this,
Shall hear far Chaos talk with me;
Kings unborn shall walk with me;
And the poor grass shall plot and plan
What it will do when it is man.
Quickened so, will I unlock
Every crypt of every rock.

I thank the joyful juice
For all I know;—
Winds of remembering
Of the ancient being blow,
And seeming-solid walls of use
Open and flow.

Pour, Bacchus! the remembering wine;
Retrieve the loss of me and mine!
Vine for vine be antidote,
And the grape requite the lote!
Haste to cure the old despair,—
Reason in Nature's lotus drenched,
The memory of ages quenched;
Give them again to shine;
Let wine repair what this undid;
And where the infection slid,
A dazzling memory revive;
Refresh the faded tints,
Recut the aged prints,

And write my old adventures with the pen
Which on the first day drew,
Upon the tablets blue,
The dancing Pleiads and eternal men.

The Bohemian Hymn

In many forms we try
To utter God's infinity,
But the boundless hath no form,
And the Universal Friend
Doth as far transcend
An angel as a worm.

The great Idea baffles wit,
Language falters under it,
It leaves the learned in the lurch;
Nor art, nor power, nor toil can find
The measure of the eternal Mind,
Nor hymn, nor prayer, nor church.

Two Rivers

Thy summer voice, Musketaquit,
Repeats the music of the rain;
But sweeter rivers pulsing flit
Through thee, as thou through Concord Plain.

Thou in thy narrow banks art pent:
The stream I love unbounded goes
Through flood and sea and firmament;
Through light, through life, it forward flows.

I see the inundation sweet,
I hear the spending of the stream
Through years, through men, through Nature fleet,
Through love and thought, through power and dream.

Musketaquit, a goblin strong,
Of shard and flint makes jewels gay;
They lose their grief who hear his song,
And where he winds is the day of day.

So forth and brighter fares my stream,—
Who drink it shall not thirst again;
No darkness stains its equal gleam
And ages drop in it like rain.

Brahma

If the red slayer think he slays,
  Or if the slain think he is slain,
They know not well the subtle ways
  I keep, and pass, and turn again.

Far or forgot to me is near;
  Shadow and sunlight are the same;
The vanished gods to me appear;
  And one to me are shame and fame.

They reckon ill who leave me out;
  When me they fly, I am the wings;
I am the doubter and the doubt,
  And I the hymn the Brahmin sings.

The strong gods pine for my abode,
    And pine in vain the sacred Seven;
But thou, meek lover of the good!
    Find me, and turn thy back on heaven.

Unity

Space is ample, east and west,
But two cannot go abreast,
Cannot travel in it two:
Yonder masterful cuckoo
Crowds every egg out of the nest,
Quick or dead, except its own;
A spell is laid on sod and stone,
Night and Day were tampered with,
Every quality and pith
Surcharged and sultry with a power
That works its will on age and hour.

Fable

The mountain and the squirrel
Had a quarrel;
And the former called the latter 'Little Prig.'
Bun replied,
'You are doubtless very big;
But all sorts of things and weather
Must be taken in together,
To make up a year
And a sphere.
And I think it no disgrace
To occupy my place.
If I'm not as large as you,

You are not so small as I,
And not half so spry.
I'll not deny you make
A very pretty squirrel track;
Talents differ; all is well and wisely put;
If I cannot carry forests on my back,
Neither can you crack a nut.'

Ode

(Inscribed to W. H. Channing)

Though loath to grieve
The evil time's sole patriot,
I cannot leave
My honied thought
For the priest's cant,
Or statesman's rant.

If I refuse
My study for their politique,
Which at the best is trick,
The angry Muse
Puts confusion in my brain
But who is he that prates
Of the culture of mankind,
Of better arts and life?
Go, blindworm, go,
Behold the famous States
Harrying Mexico
With rifle and with knife!

Or who, with accent bolder,
Dare praise the freedom-loving mountaineer?
I found by thee, O rushing Contoocook!
And in thy valleys, Agiochook!
The jackals of the negro-holder.

The God who made New Hampshire
Taunted the lofty land
With little men;—
Small bat and wren
House in the oak:—
If earth-fire cleave
The upheaved land, and bury the folk,
The southern crocodile would grieve.
Virtue palters; Right is hence;
Freedom praised, but hid;
Funeral eloquence
Rattles the coffin-lid.

What boots thy zeal,
O glowing friend,
That would indignant rend
The northland from the south?
Wherefore? to what good end?
Boston Bay and Bunker Hill
Would serve things still;—
Things are of the snake.

The horseman serves the horse,
The neatherd serves the neat,
The merchant serves the purse,
The eater serves his meat;
'Tis the day of the chattel,
Web to weave, and corn to grind;
Things are in the saddle,
And ride mankind.

There are two laws discrete,
Not reconciled,—
Law for man, and law for thing;
The last builds town and fleet,
But it runs wild,
And doth the man unking.

'Tis fit the forest fall,
The steep be graded,
The mountain tunnelled,
The sand shaded,
The orchard planted,
The glebe tilled,
The prairie granted,
The steamer built.

Let man serve law for man;
Live for friendship, live for love,
For truth's and harmony's behoof;
The state may follow how it can,
As Olympus follows Jove.

Yet do not I implore
The wrinkled shopman to my sounding woods,
Nor bid the unwilling senator
Ask votes of thrushes in the solitudes.
Every one to his chosen work;—
Foolish hands may mix and mar;
Wise and sure the issues are.
Round they roll till dark is light,
Sex to sex, and even to odd;—
The over-god
Who marries Right to Might,
Who peoples, unpeoples,—
He who exterminates

Races by stronger races,
Black by white faces,—
Knows to bring honey
Out of the lion;
Grafts gentlest scion
On pirate and Turk.

The Cossack eats Poland,
Like stolen fruit;
Her last noble is ruined,
Her last poet mute:
Straight, into double band
The victors divide;
Half for freedom strike and stand;—
The astonished Muse finds thousands at her side.

Uriel

It fell in the ancient periods
  Which the brooding soul surveys,
Or ever the wild Time coined itself
  Into calendar months and days.

This was the lapse of Uriel,
Which in Paradise befell.
Once, among the Pleiads walking,
Seyd overheard the young gods talking;
And the treason, too long pent,
To his ears was evident.
The young deities discussed
Laws of form, and metre just,
Orb, quintessence, and sunbeams,
What subsisteth, and what seems.
One, with low tones that decide,
And doubt and reverend use defied,

With a look that solved the sphere,
And stirred the devils everywhere,
Gave his sentiment divine
Against the being of a line.
'Line in nature is not found;
Unit and universe are round;
In vain produced, all rays return;
Evil will bless, and ice will burn.'
As Uriel spoke with piercing eye,
A shudder ran around the sky;
The stern old war-gods shook their heads,
The seraphs frowned from myrtle-beds;
Seemed to the holy festival
The rash word boded ill to all;
The balance-beam of Fate was bent;
The bounds of good and ill were rent;
Strong Hades could not keep his own,
But all slid to confusion.
A sad self-knowledge, withering, fell
On the beauty of Uriel;
In heaven once eminent, the god
Withdrew, that hour, into his cloud;
Whether doomed to long gyration
In the sea of generation,
Or by knowledge grown too bright
To hit the nerve of feebler sight.
Straightway, a forgetting wind
Stole over the celestial kind,
And their lips the secret kept,
If in ashes the fire-seed slept.
But now and then, truth-speaking things
Shamed the angels' veiling wings;
And, shrilling from the solar course,
Or from fruit of chemic force,
Procession of a soul in matter,
Or the speeding change of water,

Or out of the good of evil born,
Came Uriel's voice of cherub scorn,
And a blush tinged the upper sky,
And the gods shook, they knew not why.

Blight

Give me truths;
For I am weary of the surfaces,
And die of inanition. If I knew
Only the herbs and simples of the wood,
Rue, cinquefoil, gill, vervain and agrimony,
Blue-vetch and trillium, hawkweed, sassafras,
Milkweeds and murky brakes, quaint pipes and sundew,
And rare and virtuous roots, which in these woods
Draw untold juices from the common earth,
Untold, unknown, and I could surely spell
Their fragrance, and their chemistry apply
By sweet affinities to human flesh,
Driving the foe and stablishing the friend,—
O, that were much, and I could be a part
Of the round day, related to the sun
And planted world, and full executor
Of their imperfect functions.
But these young scholars, who invade our hills,
Bold as the engineer who fells the wood,
And travelling often in the cut he makes,
Love not the flower they pluck, and know it not,
And all their botany is Latin names.
The old men studied magic in the flowers,
And human fortunes in astronomy,
And an omnipotence in chemistry,
Preferring things to names, for these were men,
Were unitarians of the united world,
And, wheresoever their clear eye-beams fell,

They caught the footsteps of the Same. Our eyes
Are armed, but we are strangers to the stars,
And strangers to the mystic beast and bird,
And strangers to the plant and to the mine.
The injured elements say, 'Not in us;'
And night and day, ocean and continent,
Fire, plant and mineral say, 'Not in us;'
And haughtily return us stare for stare.
For we invade them impiously for gain;
We devastate them unreligiously,
And coldly ask their pottage, not their love.
Therefore they shove us from them, yield to us
Only what to our griping toil is due;
But the sweet affluence of love and song,
The rich results of the divine consents
Of man and earth, of world beloved and lover,
The nectar and ambrosia, are withheld;
And in the midst of spoils and slaves, we thieves
And pirates of the universe, shut out
Daily to a more thin and outward rind,
Turn pale and starve. Therefore, to our sick eyes,
The stunted trees look sick, the summer short,
Clouds shade the sun, which will not tan our hay,
And nothing thrives to reach its natural term;
And life, shorn of its venerable length,
Even at its greatest space is a defeat,
And dies in anger that it was a dupe;
And, in its highest noon and wantonness,
Is early frugal, like a beggar's child;
Even in the hot pursuit of the best aims
And prizes of ambition, checks its hand,
Like Alpine cataracts frozen as they leaped,
Chilled with a miserly comparison
Of the toy's purchase with the length of life.

Hamatreya

Bulkeley, Hunt, Willard, Hosmer, Meriam, Flint,
Possessed the land which rendered to their toil
Hay, corn, roots, hemp, flax, apples, wool and wood.
Each of these landlords walked amidst his farm,
Saying, ''T is mine, my children's and my name's.
How sweet the west wind sounds in my own trees!
How graceful climb those shadows on my hill!
I fancy these pure waters and the flags
Know me, as does my dog: we sympathize;
And, I affirm, my actions smack of the soil.'

Where are these men? Asleep beneath their grounds:
And strangers, fond as they, their furrows plough.
Earth laughs in flowers, to see her boastful boys
Earth-proud, proud of the earth which is not theirs;
Who steer the plough, but cannot steer their feet
Clear of the grave.
They added ridge to valley, brook to pond,
And sighed for all that bounded their domain;
'This suits me for a pasture; that's my park;
We must have clay, lime, gravel, granite-ledge,
And misty lowland, where to go for peat.
The land is well, – lies fairly to the south.
'T is good, when you have crossed the sea and back,
To find the sitfast acres where you left them.'
Ah! the hot owner sees not Death, who adds
Him to his land, a lump of mould the more.
Hear what the Earth says:—

Woodnotes I

1

When the pine tosses its cones
To the song of its waterfall tones,
Who speeds to the woodland walks?
To birds and trees who talks?
Cæsar of his leafy Rome,
There the poet is at home.
He goes to the river-side,—
Not hook nor line hath he;
He stands in the meadows wide,—
Nor gun nor scythe to see.
Sure some god his eye enchants:
What he knows nobody wants.
In the wood he travels glad,
Without better fortune had,
Melancholy without bad.
Knowledge this man prizes best
Seems fantastic to the rest:
Pondering shadows, colors, clouds,
Grass-buds and caterpillar-shrouds,
Boughs on which the wild bees settle,
Tints that spot the violet's petal,
Why Nature loves the number five,
And why the star-form she repeats:
Lover of all things alive,
Wonderer at all he meets,
Wonderer chiefly at himself,
Who can tell him what he is?
Or how meet in human elf
Coming and past eternities?

2

And such I knew, a forest seer,
A minstrel of the natural year,

Foreteller of the vernal ides,
Wise harbinger of spheres and tides,
A lover true, who knew by heart
Each joy the mountain dales impart;
It seemed that Nature could not raise
A plant in any secret place,
In quaking bog, on snowy hill,
Beneath the grass that shades the rill,
Under the snow, between the rocks,
In damp fields known to bird and fox.
But he would come in the very hour
It opened in its virgin bower,
As if a sunbeam showed the lace,
And tell its long-descended race.
It seemed as if the breezes brought him,
It seemed as if the sparrows taught him;
As if by secret sight he knew
Where, in far fields, the orchis grew.
Many haps fall in the field
Seldom seen by wishful eyes,
But all her shows did Nature yield,
To please and win this pilgrim wise.
He saw the partridge drum in the woods;
He heard the woodcock's evening hymn;
He found the tawny thrushes' broods;
And the shy hawk did wait for him;
What others did at distance hear,
And guessed within the thicket's gloom,
Was shown to this philosopher,
And at his bidding seemed to come.

3

In unploughed Maine he sought the lumberers' gang
Where from a hundred lakes young rivers sprang;
He trode the unplanted forest floor, whereon
The all-seeing sun for ages hath not shone;

Where feeds the moose, and walks the surly bear,
And up the tall mast runs the woodpecker.
He saw beneath dim aisles, in odorous beds,
The slight Linnæa hang its twin-born heads,
And blessed the monument of the man of flowers,
Which breathes his sweet fame through the northern
    bowers.
He heard, when in the grove, at intervals,
With sudden roar the aged pine-tree falls,—
One crash, the death-hymn of the perfect tree,
Declares the close of its green century.
Low lies the plant to whose creation went
Sweet influence from every element;
Whose living towers the years conspired to build,
Whose giddy top the morning loved to gild.
Through these green tents, by eldest Nature dressed,
He roamed, content alike with man and beast.
Where darkness found him he lay glad at night;
There the red morning touched him with its light.
Three moons his great heart him a hermit made,
So long he roved at will the boundless shade.
The timid it concerns to ask their way,
And fear what foe in caves and swamps can stray,
To make no step until the event is known,
And ills to come as evils past bemoan.
Not so the wise; no coward watch he keeps
To spy what danger on his pathway creeps;
Go where he will, the wise man is at home,
His hearth the earth, – his hall the azure dome;
Where his clear spirit leads him, there's his road,
By God's own light illumined and foreshowed.

4

'Twas one of the charmèd days
When the genius of God doth flow,
The wind may alter twenty ways,
A tempest cannot blow;
It may blow north, it still is warm;
Or south, it still is clear;
Or east, it smells like a clover-farm;
Or west, no thunder fear.
The musing peasant lowly great
Beside the forest water sate;
The rope-like pine roots crosswise grown
Composed the network of his throne;
The wide lake, edged with sand and grass,
Was burnished to a floor of glass,
Painted with shadows green and proud
Of the tree and of the cloud.
He was the heart of all the scene;
On him the sun looked more serene;
To hill and cloud his face was known,—
It seemed the likeness of their own;
They knew by secret sympathy
The public child of earth and sky.
'You ask,' he said, 'what guide
Me through trackless thickets led,
Through thick-stemmed woodlands rough and wide.
I found the water's bed.
The watercourses were my guide;
I travelled grateful by their side,
Or through their channel dry;
They led me through the thicket damp,
Through brake and fern, the beavers' camp,
Through beds of granite cut my road,
And their resistless friendship showed:
The falling waters led me,
The foodful waters fed me,

And brought me to the lowest land,
Unerring to the ocean sand.
The moss upon the forest bark
Was pole-star when the night was dark;
The purple berries in the wood
Supplied me necessary food;
For Nature ever faithful is
To such as trust her faithfulness.
When the forest shall mislead me,
When the night and morning lie,
When sea and land refuse to feed me,
'T will be time enough to die;
Then will yet my mother yield
A pillow in her greenest field,
Nor the June flowers scorn to cover
The clay of their departed lover.'

Woodnotes II

As sunbeams stream through liberal space
And nothing jostle or displace,
So waved the pine-tree through my thought
And fanned the dreams it never brought.

'Whether is better, the gift or the donor?
Come to me,'
Quoth the pine-tree,
'I am the giver of honor.
My garden is the cloven rock,
And my manure the snow;
And drifting sand-heaps feed my stock,
In summer's scorching glow.
He is great who can live by me:
The rough and bearded forester
Is better than the lord;

God fills the scrip and canister,
Sin piles the loaded board.
The lord is the peasant that was,
The peasant the lord that shall be;
The lord is hay, the peasant grass,
One dry, and one the living tree.
Who liveth by the ragged pine
Foundeth a heroic line;
Who liveth in the palace hall
Waneth fast and spendeth all.
He goes to my savage haunts,
With his chariot and his care;
My twilight realm he disenchants,
And finds his prison there.

'What prizes the town and the tower?
Only what the pine-tree yields;
Sinew that subdued the fields;
The wild-eyed boy, who in the woods
Chants his hymn to hills and floods,
Whom the city's poisoning spleen
Made not pale, or fat, or lean;
Whom the rain and the wind purgeth,
Whom the dawn and the day-star urgeth,
In whose cheek the rose-leaf blusheth,
In whose feet the lion rusheth,
Iron arms, and iron mould,
That know not fear, fatigue, or cold.
I give my rafters to his boat,
My billets to his boiler's throat,
And I will swim the ancient sea
To float my child to victory,
And grant to dwellers with the pine
Dominion o'er the palm and vine.
Who leaves the pine-tree, leaves his friend,
Unnerves his strength, invites his end.

Cut a bough from my parent stem,
And dip it in thy porcelain vase;
A little while each russet gem
Will swell and rise with wonted grace;
But when it seeks enlarged supplies,
The orphan of the forest dies.
Whoso walks in solitude
And inhabiteth the wood,
Choosing light, wave, rock and bird,
Before the money-loving herd,
Into that forester shall pass,
From these companions, power and grace.
Clean shall he be, without, within,
From the old adhering sin,
All ill dissolving in the light
Of his triumphant piercing sight:
Not vain, sour, nor frivolous;
Not mad, athirst, nor garrulous;
Grave, chaste, contented, though retired,
And of all other men desired.
On him the light of star and moon
Shall fall with purer radiance down;
All constellations of the sky
Shed their virtue through his eye.
Him Nature giveth for defence
His formidable innocence;
The mounting sap, the shells, the sea,
All spheres, all stones, his helpers be;
He shall meet the speeding year,
Without wailing, without fear;
He shall be happy in his love,
Like to like shall joyful prove;
He shall be happy whilst he wooes,
Muse-born, a daughter of the Muse.
But if with gold she bind her hair,
And deck her breast with diamond,

Take off thine eyes, thy heart forbear,
Though thou lie alone on the ground.

'Heed the old oracles,
Ponder my spells;
Song wakes in my pinnacles
When the wind swells.
Soundeth the prophetic wind,
The shadows shake on the rock behind,
And the countless leaves of the pine are strings
Tuned to the lay the wood-god sings.
    Hearken! Hearken!
If thou wouldst know the mystic song
Chanted when the sphere was young.
Aloft, abroad, the pæan swells;
O wise man! hear'st thou half it tells?
O wise man! hear'st thou the least part?
'T is the chronicle of art.
To the open ear it sings
Sweet the genesis of things,
Of tendency through endless ages,
Of star-dust, and star-pilgrimages,
Of rounded worlds, of space and time,
Of the old flood's subsiding slime,
Of chemic matter, force and form,
Of poles and powers, cold, wet, and warm:
The rushing metamorphosis
Dissolving all that fixture is,
Melts things that be to things that seem,
And solid nature to a dream.
O, listen to the undersong,
The ever old, the ever young;
And, far within those cadent pauses,
The chorus of the ancient Causes!
Delights the dreadful Destiny
To fling his voice into the tree,

And shock thy weak ear with a note
Breathed from the everlasting throat.
In music he repeats the pang
Whence the fair flock of Nature sprang.
O mortal! thy ears are stones;
These echoes are laden with tones
Which only the pure can hear;
Thou canst not catch what they recite
Of Fate and Will, of Want and Right,
Of man to come, of human life,
Of Death and Fortune, Growth and Strife.'

Once again the pine-tree sung:—
'Speak not thy speech my boughs among:
Put off thy years, wash in the breeze;
My hours are peaceful centuries.
Talk no more with feeble tongue;
No more the fool of space and time,
Come weave with mine a nobler rhyme.
Only thy Americans
Can read thy line, can meet thy glance,
But the runes that I rehearse
Understands the universe;
The least breath my boughs which tossed
Brings again the Pentecost;
To every soul resounding clear
In a voice of solemn cheer,—
'Am I not thine? Are not these thine?'
And they reply, 'Forever mine!'
My branches speak Italian,
English, German, Basque, Castilian,
Mountain speech to Highlanders,
Ocean tongues to islanders,
To Fin and Lap and swart Malay,
To each his bosom-secret say.

'Come learn with me the fatal song
Which knits the world in music strong,
Come lift thine eyes to lofty rhymes,
Of things with things, of times with times,
Primal chimes of sun and shade,
Of sound and echo, man and maid,
The land reflected in the flood,
Body with shadow still pursued.
For Nature beats in perfect tune,
And sounds with rhyme her every rune,
Whether she work in land or sea,
Or hide underground her alchemy.
Thou canst not wave thy staff in air,
Or dip thy paddle in the lake,
But it carves the bow of beauty there,
And the ripples in rhymes the oar forsake.
The wood is wiser far than thou;
The wood and wave each other know
Not unrelated, unaffied.
But to each thought and thing allied,
Is perfect Nature's every part,
Rooted in the mighty Heart.
But thou, poor child! unbound, unrhymed,
Whence camest thou, misplaced, mistimed,
Whence, O thou orphan and defrauded?
Is thy land peeled, thy realm marauded?
Who thee divorced, deceived and left?
Thee of thy faith who hath bereft,
And torn the ensigns from thy brow,
And sunk the immortal eye so low?
Thy cheek too white, thy form too slender,
Thy gait too slow, thy habits tender
For royal man; —they thee confess
An exile from the wilderness,—
The hills where health with health agrees,
And the wise soul expels disease.

Hark! in thy ear I will tell the sign
By which thy hurt thou may'st divine.
When thou shalt climb the mountain cliff,
Or see the wide shore from thy skiff,
To thee the horizon shall express
But emptiness on emptiness;
There lives no man of Nature's worth
In the circle of the earth;
And to thine eye the vast skies fall,
Dire and satirical,
On clucking hens and prating fools,
On thieves, on drudges and on dolls.
And thou shalt say to the Most High,
'Godhead! all this astronomy,
And fate and practice and invention,
Strong art and beautiful pretension,
This radiant pomp of sun and star,
Throes that were, and worlds that are,
Behold! were in vain and in vain;—
It cannot be, –I will look again.
Surely now will the curtain rise,
And earth's fit tenant me surprise;—
But the curtain doth *not* rise,
And Nature has miscarried wholly
Into failure, into folly.'

'Alas! thine is the bankruptcy,
Blessed Nature so to see.
Come, lay thee in my soothing shade,
And heal the hurts which sin has made.
I see thee in the crowd alone;
I will be thy companion.
Quit thy friends as the dead in doom,
And build to them a final tomb;
Let the starred shade that nightly falls
Still celebrate their funerals,

And the bell of beetle and of bee
Knell their melodious memory.
Behind thee leave thy merchandise,
Thy churches and thy charities;
And leave thy peacock wit behind;
Enough for thee the primal mind
That flows in streams, that breathes in wind:
Leave all thy pedant lore apart;
God hid the whole world in thy heart.
Love shuns the sage, the child it crowns,
Gives all to them who all renounce.
The rain comes when the wind calls;
The river knows the way to the sea;
Without a pilot it runs and falls,
Blessing all lands with its charity;
The sea tosses and foams to find
Its way up to the cloud and wind;
The shadow sits close to the flying ball;
The date fails not on the palm-tree tall;
And thou, –go burn thy wormy pages,—
Shalt outsee seers, and outwit sages.
Oft didst thou thread the woods in vain
To find what bird had piped the strain:—
Seek not, and the little eremite
Flies gayly forth and sings in sight.

'Hearken once more!
I will tell thee the mundane lore.
Older am I than thy numbers wot,
Change I may, but I pass not.
Hitherto all things fast abide,
And anchored in the tempest ride.
Trenchant time behoves to hurry
All to yean and all to bury:
All the forms are fugitive,
But the substances survive.

160

Ever fresh the broad creation,
A divine improvisation,
From the heart of God proceeds,
A single will, a million deeds.
Once slept the world an egg of stone,
And pulse, and sound, and light was none;
And God said, 'Throb!' and there was motion
And the vast mass became vast ocean.
Onward and on, the eternal Pan,
Who layeth the world's incessant plan,
Halteth never in one shape,
But forever doth escape,
Like wave or flame, into new forms
Of gem, and air, of plants, and worms.
I, that today am a pine,
Yesterday was a bundle of grass.
He is free and libertine,
Pouring of his power the wine
To every age, to every race;
Unto every race and age
He emptieth the beverage;
Unto each, and unto all,
Maker and original.
The world is the ring of his spells,
And the play of his miracles.
As he giveth to all to drink,
Thus or thus they are and think.
With one drop sheds form and feature;
With the next a special nature;
The third adds heat's indulgent spark;
The fourth gives light which eats the dark;
Into the fifth himself he flings,
And conscious Law is King of kings.
As the bee through the garden ranges,
From world to world the godhead changes;

As the sheep go feeding in the waste,
From form to form He maketh haste;
This vault which glows immense with light
Is the inn where he lodges for a night.
What recks such Traveller if the bowers
Which bloom and fade like meadow flowers.
A bunch of fragrant lilies be,
Or the stars of eternity?
Alike to him the better, the worse,—
The glowing angel, the outcast corse.
Thou metest him by centuries,
And lo! he passes like the breeze;
Thou seek'st in globe and galaxy,
He hides in pure transparency;
Thou askest in fountains and in fires,
He is the essence that inquires.
He is the axis of the star;
He is the sparkle of the spar;
He is the heart of every creature;
He is the meaning of each feature;
And his mind is the sky,
Than all it holds more deep, more high.'

The Sphinx

The Sphinx is drowsy,
   Her wings are furled:
Her ear is heavy,
   She broods on the world.
'Who'll tell me my secret,
   The ages have kept?—
I awaited the seer
   While they slumbered and slept:—

'The fate of the man-child,
  The meaning of man;
Known fruit of the unknown;
  Dædalian plan;
Out of sleeping a waking,
  Out of waking a sleep;
Life death overtaking;
  Deep underneath deep?

'Erect as a sunbeam,
  Upspringeth the palm;
The elephant browses,
  Undaunted and calm;
In beautiful motion
  The thrush plies his wings;
Kind leaves of his covert,
  Your silence he sings.

'The waves, unashamèd,
  In difference sweet,
Play glad with the breezes,
  Old playfellows meet;
The journeying atoms,
  Primordial wholes,
Firmly draw, firmly drive,
  By their animate poles.

'Sea, earth, air, sound, silence,
  Plant, quadruped, bird,
By one music enchanted,
  One deity stirred,—
Each the other adorning,
  Accompany still;
Night veileth the morning,
  The vapor the hill.

'The babe by its mother
    Lies bathèd in joy;
Glide its hours uncounted,—
    The sun is its toy;
Shines the peace of all being,
    Without cloud, in its eyes;
And the sum of the world
    In soft miniature lies.

'But man crouches and blushes,
    Absconds and conceals;
He creepeth and peepeth,
    He palters and steals;
Infirm, melancholy,
    Jealous glancing around,
An oaf, an accomplice,
    He poisons the ground.

'Out spoke the great mother,
    Beholding his fear;—
At the sound of her accents
    Cold shuddered the sphere:—
"Who has drugged my boy's cup?
    Who has mixed my boy's bread?
Who, with sadness and madness,
    Has turned my child's head?"'

I heard a poet answer
    Aloud and cheerfully,
'Say on, sweet Sphinx! thy dirges
    Are pleasant songs to me.
Deep love lieth under
    These pictures of time;
They fade in the light of
    Their meaning sublime.

'The fiend that man harries
   Is love of the Best;
Yawns the pit of the Dragon,
   Lit by rays from the Blest.
The Lethe of Nature
   Can't trance him again,
Whose soul sees the perfect,
   Which his eyes seek in vain.

'To vision profounder,
   Man's spirit must dive;
His aye-rolling orb
   At no goal will arrive;
The heavens that now draw him
   With sweetness untold,
Once found, – for new heavens
   He spurneth the old.

'Pride ruined the angels,
   Their shame them restores;
Lurks the joy that is sweetest
   In stings of remorse.
Have I a lover
   Who is noble and free?—
I would he were nobler
   Than to love me.

'Eterne alternation
   Now follows, now flies;
And under pain, pleasure,—
   Under pleasure, pain lies.
Love works at the centre,
   Heart-heaving alway;
Forth speed the strong pulses
   To the borders of day.

'Dull Sphinx, Jove keep thy five wits;
    Thy sight is growing blear;
Rue, myrrh and cummin for the Sphinx,
    Her muddy eyes to clear!'
The old Sphinx bit her thick lip,—
Said, 'Who taught thee me to name?
I am thy spirit, yoke-fellow;
    Of thine eye I am eyebeam.

'Thou art the unanswered question;
    Couldst see thy proper eye,
Alway it asketh, asketh;
    And each answer is a lie.
So take thy quest through nature,
    It through thousand natures ply;
Ask on, thou clothed eternity;
    Time is the false reply.'

Uprose the merry Sphinx,
    And crouched no more in stone;
She melted into purple cloud,
    She silvered in the moon;
She spired into a yellow flame;
    She flowered in blossoms red;
She flowed into a foaming wave:
    She stood Monadnoc's head.

Thorough a thousand voices
    Spoke the universal dame;
'Who telleth one of my meanings
    Is master of all I am.'

Terminus

It is time to be old,
To take in sail:—
The god of bounds,
Who sets to seas a shore,
Came to me in his fatal rounds,
And said: 'No more!
No farther shoot
Thy broad ambitious branches, and thy root.
Fancy departs: no more invent;
Contract thy firmament
To compass of a tent.
There's not enough for this and that,
Make thy option which of two;
Economize the failing river,
Not the less revere the Giver,
Leave the many and hold the few.
Timely wise accept the terms,
Soften the fall with wary foot;
A little while
Still plan and smile,
And, – fault of novel germs, –
Mature the unfallen fruit.
Curse, if thou wilt, thy sire,
Bad husbands of their fires,
Who, when they gave thee breath,
Failed to bequeath
The needful sinew stark as once,
The Baresark marrow to thy bones,
But left a legacy of ebbing veins,
Inconstant heat and nerveless reins,—
Amid the Muses, left thee deaf and dumb,
Amid the gladiators, halt and numb.'

As the bird trims her to the gale,
I trim myself to the storm of time,
I man the rudder, reef the sail,
Obey the voice at eve obeyed at prime:
'Lowly faithful, banish fear,
Right onward drive unharmed;
The port, well worth the cruise, is near,
And every wave is charmed.'

My Garden

If I could put my woods in song,
And tell what's there enjoyed,
All men would to my gardens throng,
And leave the cities void.

In my plot no tulips blow,—
Snow-loving pines and oaks instead;
And rank the savage maples grow
From spring's faint flush to autumn red.

My garden is a forest ledge
Which older forests bound;
The banks slope down to the blue lake-edge,
Then plunge to depths profound.

Here once the Deluge ploughed,
Laid the terraces, one by one;
Ebbing later whence it flowed,
They bleach and dry in the sun.

The sowers made haste to depart,—
The wind and the birds which sowed it;
Not for fame, nor by rules of art,
Planted these, and tempests flowed it.

Waters that wash my garden side
Play not in Nature's lawful web,
They heed not moon or solar tide,—
Five years elapse from flood to ebb.

Hither hasted, in old time, Jove,
And every god,—none did refuse;
And be sure at last came Love,
And after Love, the Muse.

Keen ears can catch a syllable,
As if one spake to another,
In the hemlocks tall, untamable,
And what the whispering grasses smother.

Aeolian harps in the pine
Ring with the song of the Fates;
Infant Bacchus in the vine,—
Far distant yet his chorus waits.

Canst thou copy in verse one chime
Of the wood-bell's peal and cry,
Write in a book the morning's prime,
Or match with words that tender sky?

Wonderful verse of the gods,
Of one import, of varied tone;
They chant the bliss of their abodes
To man imprisoned in his own.

Ever the words of the gods resound;
But the porches of man's ear
Seldom in this low life's round
Are unsealed, that he may hear.

Wandering voices in the air,
And murmurs in the wold,
Speak what I cannot declare,
Yet cannot all withhold.

When the shadow fell on the lake,
The whirlwind in ripples wrote
Air-bells of fortune that shine and break,
And omens above thought.

But the meanings cleave to the lake,
Cannot be carried in book or urn;
Go thy ways now, come later back,
On waves and hedges still they burn.

These the fates of men forecast,
Of better men than live to-day;
If who can read them comes at last,
He will spell in the sculpture, "Stay!"

Threnody

The South-wind brings
Life, sunshine, and desire,
And on every mount and meadow
Breathes aromatic fire;
But over the dead he has no power,
The lost, the lost, he cannot restore;
And, looking over the hills, I mourn
The darling who shall not return.

I see my empty house,
I see my trees repair their boughs;
And he, the wondrous child,
Whose silver warble wild

Outvalued every pulsing sound
Within the air's cerulean round,—
The hyacinthine boy, for whom
Morn well might break and April bloom,—
The gracious boy, who did adorn
The world whereinto he was born,
And by his countenance repay
The favour of the loving Day,—
Has disappeared from the Day's eye;
Far and wide she cannot find him;
My hopes pursue, they cannot bind him.
Returned this day, the south-wind searches,
And finds young pines and budding birches;
But finds not the budding man;
Nature, who lost, cannot remake him;
Fate let him fall, Fate can't retake him;
Nature, Fate, men, him seek in vain.

And whither now, my truant wise and sweet,
O, whither tend thy feet?
I had the right, few days ago,
Thy steps to watch, thy place to know;
How have I forfeited the right?
Hast thou forgot me in a new delight?
I hearken for thy household cheer,
O eloquent child!
Whose voice, an equal messenger,
Conveyed thy meaning mild.
What though the pains and joys
Whereof it spoke were toys
Fitting his age and ken,
Yet fairest dames and bearded men,
Who heard the sweet request,
So gentle, wise, and grave,
Bended with joy to his behest,
And let the world's affairs go by,

Awhile to share his cordial game,
Or mend his wicker wagon-frame,
Still plotting how their hungry ear
That winsome voice again might hear;
For his lips could well pronounce
Words that were persuasions.

Gentlest guardians marked serene
His early hope, his liberal mien;
Took counsel from his guiding eyes
To make this wisdom earthly wise.
Ah, vainly do these eyes recall
The school-march, each day's festival,
When every morn my bosom glowed
To watch the convoy on the road;
The babe in willow wagon closed,
With rolling eyes and face composed;
With children forward and behind,
Like Cupids studiously inclined;
And he the chieftain paced beside,
The centre of the troop allied,
With sunny face of sweet repose,
To guard the babe from fancied foes.
The little captain innocent
Took the eye with him as he went;
Each village senior paused to scan
And speak the lovely caravan.
From the window I look out
To mark thy beautiful parade,
Stately marching in cap and coat
To some tune by fairies played;—
A music heard by thee alone
To works as noble led thee on.

Now Love and Pride, alas! in vain,
Up and down their glances strain.

The painted sled stands where it stood;
The kennel by the corded wood;
The gathered sticks to stanch the wall
Of the snow-tower, when snow should fall;
The ominous hole he dug in the sand,
And childhood's castles built or planned;
His daily haunts I well discern,—
The poultry-yard, the shed, the barn,—
And every inch of garden ground
Paced by the blessed feet around,
From the roadside to the brook
Whereinto he loved to look.
Step the meek birds where erst they ranged;
The wintry garden lies unchanged;
The brook into the stream runs on;
But the deep-eyed boy is gone.

On that shaded day,
Dark with more clouds than tempests are,
When thou didst yield thy innocent breath
In birdlike heavings unto death,
Night came, and Nature had not thee;
I said, 'We are mates in misery.'
The morrow dawned with needless glow;
Each snowbird chirped, each fowl must crow;
Each tramper started; but the feet
Of the most beautiful and sweet
Of human youth had left the hill
And garden,—they were bound and still.
There's not a sparrow or a wren,
There's not a blade of autumn grain,
Which the four seasons do not tend,
And tides of life and increase lend;
And every chick of every bird,
And weed and rock-moss is preferred.

O ostrich-like forgetfulness!
O loss of larger in the less!
Was there no star that could be sent,
No watcher in the firmament,
No angel from the countless host
That loiters round the crystal coast,
Could stoop to heal that only child,
Nature's sweet marvel undefiled,
And keep the blossom of the earth,
Which all her harvests were not worth?
Not mine,—I never called thee mine,
But Nature's heir,—if I repine,
And seeing rashly torn and moved
Not what I made, but what I loved,
Grow early old with grief that thou
Must to the wastes of Nature go,—
'Tis because a general hope
Was quenched, and all must doubt and grope.
For flattering planets seemed to say
This child should ills of ages stay,
By wondrous tongue, and guided pen,
Bring the flown Muses back to men.
Perchance not he but Nature ailed,
The world and not the infant failed.
It was not ripe yet to sustain
A genius of so fine a strain,
Who gazed upon the sun and moon
As if he came unto his own,
And, pregnant with his grander thought,
Brought the old order into doubt.
His beauty once their beauty tried;
They could not feed him, and he died,
And wandered backward as in scorn,
To wait an aeon to be born.

Ill day which made this beauty waste,
Plight broken, this high face defaced!
Some went and came about the dead;
And some in books of solace read;
Some to their friends the tidings say;
Some went to write, some went to pray;
One tarried here, there hurried one;
But their heart abode with none.
Covetous death bereaved us all,
To aggrandize one funeral.
The eager fate which carried thee
Took the largest part of me:
For this losing is true dying;
This is lordly man's down-lying,
This his slow but sure reclining,
Star by star his world resigning.

O child of paradise,
Boy who made dear his father's home,
In whose deep eyes
Men read the welfare of the times to come,
I am too much bereft.
The world dishonoured thou has left.
O truth's and nature's costly lie!
O trusted broken prophecy!
O richest fortune sourly crossed!
Born for the future, to the future lost!

The deep Heart answered, 'Weepest thou?
Worthier cause for passion wild
If I had not taken the child.
And deemest thou as those who pore,
With aged eyes, short way before,—
Think'st Beauty vanished from the coast
Of matter, and thy darling lost?
Taught he not thee—the man of eld,
Whose eyes within his eyes beheld

Heaven's numerous hierarchy span
The mystic gulf from God to man?
To be alone wilt thou begin
When worlds of lovers hem thee in?
Tomorrow, when the masks shall fall
That dizen Nature's carnival,
The pure shall see by their own will,
Which overflowing Love shall fill,
'Tis not within the force of fate
The fate-conjoined to separate.
But thou, my votary, weepest thou?
I gave thee sight—where is it now?
I taught thy heart beyond the reach
Of ritual, bible, or of speech;
Wrote in thy mind's transparent table,
As far as the incommunicable;
Taught thee each private sign to raise,
Lit by the supersolar blaze.
Past utterance, and past belief,
And past the blasphemy of grief,
The mysteries of Nature's heart;
And though no Muse can these impart,
Throb thine with Nature's throbbing breast,
And all is clear from east to west.

'I came to thee as to a friend;
Dearest, to thee I did not send
Tutors, but a joyful eye,
Innocence that matched the sky,
Lovely locks, a form of wonder,
Laughter rich as woodland thunder,
That thou might'st entertain apart
The richest flowering of all art:
And, as the great all-loving Day
Through smallest chambers takes its way,

That thou might'st break thy daily bread
With prophet, saviour, and head;
That thou might'st cherish for thine own
The riches of sweet Mary's Son,
Boy-Rabbi, Israel's paragon.
And thoughtest thou such guest
Would in thy hall take up his rest?
Would rushing life forget her laws,
Fate's glowing revolution pause?
High omens ask diviner guess;
Not to be conned to tediousness.
And know my higher gifts unbind
The zone that girds the incarnate mind.
When the scanty shores are full
With Thought's perilous, whirling pool;
When frail Nature can no more,
Then the Spirit strikes the hour:
My servant Death, with solving rite,
Pours finite into infinite.

'Wilt thou freeze love's tidal flow,
Whose streams through nature circling go?
Nail the wild star to its track
On the half-climbed zodiac?
Light is light which radiates,
Blood is blood which circulates,
Life is life which generates,
And many-seeming life is one,—
Wilt thou transfix and make it none?
Its onward force too starkly pent
In figure, bone, and lineament?
Wilt thou, uncalled, interrogate,
Talker! the unreplying Fate?
Nor see the genius of the whole
Ascendant in the private soul,
Beckon it when to go and come,

Self-announced its hour of doom?
Fair the soul's recess and shrine,
Magic-built to last a season;
Masterpiece of love benign,
Fairer that expansive reason
Whose omen 't is, and sign.
Wilt thou not ope thy heart to know
What rainbows teach, and sunsets show?
Verdict which accumulates
From lengthening scroll of human fates,
Voice of earth to earth returned,
Prayers of saints that inly burned,—
Saying, *What is excellent,*
As God lives, is permanent;
Hearts are dust, hearts' loves remain;
Heart's love will meet thee again.
Revere the Maker; fetch thine eye
Up to his style, and manners of the sky.
Not of adamant and gold
Built he heaven stark and cold;
No, but a nest of bending reeds,
Flowering grass, and scented weeds;
Or like a traveller's fleeing tent,
Or bow above the tempest bent;
Built of tears and sacred flames,
And virtue reaching to its aims;
Built of furtherance and pursuing,
Not of spent deeds, but of doing.
Silent rushes the swift Lord
Through ruined systems still restored,
Broadsowing, bleak and void to bless,
Plants with worlds the wilderness;
Waters with tears of ancient sorrow
Apples of Eden ripe tomorrow.
House and tenant go to ground,
Lost in God, in Godhead found.'

The Apology

Think me not unkind and rude
  That I walk alone in grove and glen;
I go to the god of the wood
  To fetch his word to men.

Tax not my sloth that I
  Fold my arms beside the brook;
Each cloud that floated in the sky
  Writes a letter in my book.

Chide me not, laborious band,
  For the idle flowers I brought;
Every aster in my hand
  Goes home loaded with a thought.

There was never mystery
  But 't is figured in the flowers;
Was never secret history
  But birds tell it in the bowers.

One harvest from thy field
  Homeward brought the oxen strong;
A second crop thine acres yield,
  Which I gather in a song.

Thine Eyes Still Shined

Thine eyes still shined for me, though far
  I lonely roved the land or sea:
As I behold yon evening star,
  Which yet beholds not me.

This morn I climbed the misty hill,
    And roamed the pastures through;
How danced thy form before my path
    Amidst the deep-eyed dew!

When the redbird spread his sable wing,
    And showed his side of flame;
When the rosebud ripened to the rose,
    In both I read thy name.

Compensation

Why should I keep holiday
    When other men have none?
Why but because, when these are gay,
    I sit and mourn alone?

And why, when mirth unseals all tongues,
    Should mine alone be dumb?
Ah! late I spoke to silent throngs,
    And now their hour is come.

Suum Cuique

The rain has spoiled the farmer's day;
Shall sorrow put my books away?
    Thereby are two days lost:
Nature shall mind her own affairs;
I will attend my proper cares,
    In rain, or sun, or frost.

Tact

What boots it, thy virtue,
  What profit thy parts,
While one thing thou lackest,—
  The art of all arts?

The only credentials,
  Passport to success;
Opens castle and parlour,—
  Address, man, Address.

The maiden in danger
  Was saved by the swain;
His stout arm restored her
  To Broadway again.

The maid would reward him,—
  Gay company come,—
They laugh, she laughs with them:
  He is moonstruck and dumb.

This clinches the bargain;
  Sails out of the bay;
Gets the vote in the senate,
  Spite of Webster and Clay.

Has for genius no mercy,
  For speeches no heed;
It lurks in the eyebeam,
  It leaps to its deed.

Church, market, and tavern,
  Bed and board, it will sway.
It has no tomorrow;
  It ends with today.

To J.W.

Set not thy foot on graves;
Hear what wine and roses say;
The mountain chase, the summer waves,
The crowded town, thy feet may well delay.

Set not thy foot on graves;
Nor seek to unwind the shroud
Which charitable Time
And Nature have allowed
To wrap the errors of a sage sublime.

Set not thy foot on graves:
Care not to strip the dead
Of his sad ornament,
His myrrh, and wine, and rings,

His sheet of lead,
And trophies buried:
Go, get them where he earned them when alive;
As resolutely dig or dive.

Life is too short to waste
In critic peep or cynic bark,
Quarrel or reprimand:
'T will soon be dark;
Up! mind thine own aim, and
God speed the mark!

Mithridates

I cannot spare water or wine,
 Tobacco-leaf, or poppy, or rose;
From the earth-poles to the line,
 All between that works or grows,
Everything is kin of mine.

Give me agates for my meat;
Give me cantharids to eat;
From air and ocean bring me foods,
From all zones and altitudes:—

From all natures, sharp and slimy,
  Salt and basalt, wild and tame:
Tree and lichen, ape, sea-lion,
  Bird, and reptile, be my game.

Ivy for my fillet band;
Blinding dog-wood in my hand;
Hemlock for my sherbet cull me,
And the prussic juice to lull me;
Swing me in the upas boughs,
Vampyre-fanned, when I carouse.

Too long shut in strait and few,
Thinly dieted on dew,
I will use the world, and sift it,
To a thousand humours shift it,
As you spin a cherry.
O doleful ghosts, and goblins merry!

O all you virtues, methods, mights,
Means, appliances, delights,
Reputed wrongs and braggart rights,
Smug routine, and things allowed,
Minorities, things under cloud!
Hither! take me, use me, fill me,
Vein and artery, though ye kill me!
God! I will not be an owl,
But sun me in the Capitol.

The Visit

Askest, 'How long thou shalt stay?'
Devastator of the day!
Know, each substance, and relation,
Thorough nature's operation,
Hath its unit, bound, and metre;
And every new compound
Is some product and repeater,—
Product of the earlier found.
But the unit of the visit,
The encounter of the wise,—
Say, what other metre is it
Than the meeting of the eyes?
Nature poureth into nature
Through the channels of that feature.
Riding on the ray of sight,
Fleeter far than whirlwinds go,
Or for service, or delight,
Hearts to hearts their meaning show,
Sum their long experience,
And import intelligence.
Single look has drained the breast;
Single moment years confessed.
The duration of a glance
Is the term of convenance,
And, though thy rede be church or state,
Frugal multiples of that.
Speeding Saturn cannot halt;
Linger,—thou shalt rue the fault;
If Love his moment overstay,
Hatred's swift repulsions play.

Goodbye

Goodbye, proud world! I'm going home;
 Thou art not my friend, and I'm not thine.
Long through thy weary crowds I roam;
 A river-ark on the ocean brine,
Long I've been toss'd like the driven foam,
But now, proud world, I'm going home.

Goodbye to flattery's fawning face,
To grandeur, with his wise grimace,
To upstart wealth's averted eye,
To supple office, low and high,
To crowded halls, to court and street,
To frozen hearts and hasting feet,
To those who go and those who come—
Goodbye, proud world! I'm going home.
I am going to my own hearthstone,
Bossom'd in yon green hills alone—
A secret nook in a pleasant land,
Whose groves the frolic fairies plann'd,
Where arches green, the livelong day,
Echo the blackbird's roundelay,
And vulgar feet have never trod—
A spot that is sacred to thought and God.

Oh, when I am safe in my sylvan home,
I tread on the pride of Greece and Rome,
And when I am stretch'd beneath the pines,
Where the evening star so holy shines,
I laugh at the lore and pride of man
At the sophist schools, and the learnèd clan;
For what are they all, in their high conceit,
When man in the bush with God may meet?

Ode: Sung in the Town Hall, Concord, July 4th, 1857

O tenderly the haughty day
  Fills his blue urn with fire;
One morn is in the mighty heaven,
  And one in our desire.

The cannon booms from town to town,
  Our pulses beat not less,
The joy-bells chime their tidings down,
  Which children's voices bless.

For He that flung the broad blue fold
  O'er-mantling land and sea,
One third part of the sky unrolled
  For the banner of the free.

The men are ripe of Saxon kind
  To build an equal state—
To take the statute from the mind
  And make of duty fate.

United States! the ages plead—
  Present and Past in under-song—
Go put your creed into your deed,
  Nor speak with double tongue.

For sea and land don't understand,
  Nor skies without a frown
See rights for which the one hand fights
  By the other cloven down.

Be just at home; then write your scroll
  Of honor o'er the sea,
And bid the broad Atlantic roll,
  A ferry of the free.

And henceforth there shall be no chain,
   Save underneath the sea
The wires shall murmur through the main
   Sweet songs of liberty.

The conscious stars accord above,
   The waters wild below,
And under, through the cable wove,
   Her fiery errands go.

For He that worketh high and wise,
   Nor pauses in his plan,
Will take the sun out of the skies
   Ere freedom out of man.

The Test

I hung my verses in the wind,
Time and tide their faults may find.
All were winnowed through and through,
Five lines lasted sound and true;
Five were smelted in a pot
Than the South more fierce and hot;
These the siroc could not melt,
Fire their fiercer flaming felt,
And the meaning was more white
Than July's meridian light.
Sunshine cannot bleach the snow,
Nor time unmake what poets know.
Have you eyes to find the five
Which five hundred did survive?

Forbearance

Hast thou named all the birds without a gun?
Loved the wood-rose, and left it on its stalk?
At rich men's tables eaten bread and pulse?
Unarmed, faced danger with a heart of trust?
And loved so well a high behavior,
In man or maid, that thou from speech refrained,
Nobility more nobly to repay?
O, be my friend, and teach me to be thine!

Heroism

So nigh is grandeur to our dust,
So near is God to man,
When Duty whispers low, *Thou must*,
The youth replies, *I can.*

HENRY WADSWORTH LONGFELLOW
1807-1882

Henry Wadsworth Longfellow was born at Portland, Maine and became Professor of modern languages at Harvard. He contributed many successful essays and sketches to magazines before embarking on his career as a poet with *Voices of the Night*. Having become a successful and admired writer throughout Europe and America, Longfellow gave up the academic life in 1854 to concentrate on writing. He is the only American to be honored with a bust in the Poet's Corner of Westminster Abbey.

'The Village Blacksmith', 'The Wreck of the Hesperus' and 'Excelsior' are taken from *Ballads and Other Poems* (1841); 'The Jewish Cemetery at Newport' is taken from *The Courtship of Miles Standish* (1858) and 'Paul Revere's Ride' comes from *Tales of a Wayside Inn*.

The Jewish Cemetery at Newport

How strange it seems! These Hebrews in their graves,
   Close by the street of this fair seaport town,
Silent beside the never-silent waves,
   At rest in all this moving up and down!

The trees are white with dust, that o'er their sleep
   Wave their broad curtains in the southwind's breath,
While underneath these leafy tents they keep
   The long, mysterious Exodus of Death.

And these sepulchral stones, so old and brown,
   That pave with level flags their burial-place,
Seem like the tablets of the Law, thrown down
   And broken by Moses at the mountain's base.

The very names recorded here are strange,
   Of foreign accent, and of different climes;
Alvares and Rivera interchange
   With Abraham and Jacob of old times.

'Blessed be God, for he created Death!'
   The mourners said, 'and Death is rest and peace';
Then added, in the certainty of faith,
   'And giveth Life that nevermore shall cease.'

Closed are the portals of their Synagogue,
   No Psalms of David now the silence break,
No Rabbi reads the ancient Decalogue
   In the grand dialect the Prophets spake.

Gone are the living, but the dead remain,
   And not neglected; for a hand unseen,
Scattering its bounty, like a summer rain,
   Still keeps their graves and their remembrance green.

How came they here? What burst of Christian hate,
  What persecution, merciless and blind,
Drove o'er the sea – that desert desolate—
  These Ishmaels and Hagars of mankind?

They lived in narrow streets and lanes obscure,
  Ghetto and Judenstrass, in mirk and mire;
Taught in the school of patience to endure
  The life of anguish and the death of fire.

All their lives long, with the unleavened bread
  And bitter herbs of exile and its fears,
The wasting famine of the heart they fed,
  And slaked its thirst with marah of their tears.

Anathema maranatha! was the cry
  That rang from town to town, from street to street:
At every gate the accursed Mordecai
  Was mocked and jeered, and spurned by Christian feet.

Pride and humiliation hand in hand
  Walked with them through the world where'er they
    went;
Trampled and beaten were they as the sand,
  And yet unshaken as the continent.

For in the background figures vague and vast
  Of patriarchs and of prophets rose sublime,
And all the great traditions of the Past
  They saw reflected in the coming time.

And thus forever with reverted look
  The mystic volume of the world they read,
Spelling it backward, like a Hebrew book,
  Till life became a Legend of the Dead.

But ah! what once has been shall be no more!
  The groaning earth in travail and in pain
Brings forth its races, but does not restore,
  And the dead nations never rise again.

The Wreck of the Hesperus

It was the schooner *Hesperus*,
  That sailed the wintry sea;
And the skipper had taken his little daughtèr,
  To bear him company.

Blue were her eyes as the fairy-flax,
  Her cheeks like the dawn of day,
And her bosom white as the hawthorn buds,
  That ope in the month of May.

The skipper he stood beside the helm,
  His pipe was in his mouth,
And he watched how the veering flaw did blow
  The smoke now West, now South.

Then up and spake an old Sailòr,
  Had sailed the Spanish Main,
'I pray thee, put into yonder port,
  For I fear a hurricane.

'Last night the moon had a golden ring,
  And to-night no moon we see!'
The skipper he blew a whiff from his pipe,
  And a scornful laugh laughed he.

Colder and louder blew the wind,
  A gale from the North-east;
The snow fell hissing in the brine,
  And the billows frothed like yeast.

Down came the storm, and smote amain
  The vessel in its strength;
She shuddered and paused, like a frighted steed,
  Then leaped her cable's length.

'Come hither! come hither! my little daughtèr,
  And do not tremble so;
For I can weather the roughest gale
  That ever wind did blow.'

He wrapped her warm in his seaman's coat,
  Against the stinging blast;
He cut a rope from a broken spar,
  And bound her to the mast.

'O father! I hear the church-bells ring,
  O say what may it be?'
''Tis a fog-bell on a rock-bound coast!'—
  And he steered for the open sea.

'O father! I hear the sound of guns,
  O say, what may it be?'
'Some ship in distress, that cannot live
  In such an angry sea!'

'O father, I see a gleaming light,
  O say, what may it be?'
But the father answered never a word,
  A frozen corpse was he.

Lashed to the helm, all stiff and stark,
  With his face turned to the skies,
The lantern gleamed through the gleaming snow
  On his fixed and glassy eyes.

Then the maiden clasped her hands and prayed
    That savèd she might be;
And she thought of Christ, who stilled the wave,
    On the Lake of Galilee.

And fast through the midnight dark and drear,
    Through the whistling sleet and snow,
Like a sheeted ghost the vessel swept
    Towards the reef of Norman's Woe.

And ever the fitful gusts between
    A sound came from the land;
It was the sound of the trampling surf,
    On the rocks and the hard sea-sand.

The breakers were right beneath her bows,
    She drifted a dreary wreck,
And a whooping billow swept the crew
    Like icicles from her deck.

She struck where the white and fleecy waves
    Look soft as carded wool,
But the cruel rocks, they gored her side
    Like the horns of an angry bull.

Her rattling shrouds, all sheathed in ice,
    With the masts went by the board;
Like a vessel of glass, she stove and sank,
    Ho! ho! the breakers roared!

At daybreak, on a bleak sea-beach,
    A fisherman stood aghast,
To see the form of a maiden fair,
    Lashed close to a drifting mast.

The salt sea was frozen on her breast,
 The salt tears in her eyes;
And he saw her hair, like the brown sea-weed,
 On the billows fall and rise.

Such was the wreck of the *Hesperus*,
 In the midnight and the snow;
Christ save us all from a death like this,
 On the reef of Norman's Woe!

Excelsior

The shades of night were falling fast,
As through an Alpine village passed
A youth, who bore, 'mid snow and ice,
A banner, with the strange device,
   Excelsior!

His brow was sad; his eye beneath
Flashed like a falchion from its sheath,
And like a silver clarion rung
The accents of that unknown tongue,
   Excelsior!

In happy homes he saw the light
Of household fires gleam warm and bright;
Above, the spectral glaciers shone,
And from his lips escaped a groan,
   Excelsior!

'Try not the Pass!' the old man said;
'Dark lowers the tempest overhead,
The roaring torrent is deep and wide!'
And loud that clarion voice replied,
   Excelsior!

'O stay,' the maiden said, 'and rest
Thy weary head upon this breast!'
A tear stood in his bright blue eye,
But still he answered, with a sigh,
      Excelsior!

'Beware the pine-tree's withered branch!
Beware the awful avalanche!'
This was the peasant's last Good-night,
A voice replied, far up the height,
      Excelsior!

At break of day, as heavenward
The pious monks of Saint Bernard
Uttered the oft-repeated prayer,
A voice cried through the startled air,
      Excelsior!

A traveller, by the faithful hound,
Half-buried in the snow was found,
Still grasping in his hand of ice
That banner with the strange device,
      Excelsior!

There in the twilight cold and grey,
Lifeless, but beautiful, he lay,
And from the sky, serene and far,
A voice fell, like a falling star,
      Excelsior!

The Village Blacksmith

Under a spreading chestnut-tree
  The village smithy stands;
The smith, a mighty man is he,
  With large and sinewy hands;

And the muscles of his brawny arms
   Are strong as iron bands.

His hair is crisp, and black, and long,
   His face is like the tan;
His brow is wet with honest sweat,
   He earns whate'er he can,
And looks the whole world in the face,
   For he owes not any man.

Week in, week out, from morn till night,
   You can hear his bellows blow;
You can hear him swing his heavy sledge,
   With measured beat and slow,
Like a sexton ringing the village bell,
   When the evening sun is low.

And children coming home from school
   Look in at the open door;
They love to see the flaming forge,
   And hear the bellows roar,
And catch the burning sparks that fly
   Like chaff from a threshing-floor.

He goes on Sunday to the church,
   And sits among his boys;
He hears the parson pray and preach,
   He hears his daughter's voice,
Singing in the village choir,
   And it makes his heart rejoice.

It sounds to him like her mother's voice,
   Singing in Paradise!
He needs must think of her once more,
   How in the grave she lies;
And with his hard, rough hand he wipes
   A tear out of his eyes.

Toiling – rejoicing – sorrowing,
  Onward through life he goes;
Each morning sees some task begin,
  Each evening sees it close;
Something attempted, something done,
  Has earned a night's repose.

Thanks, thanks to thee, my worthy friend,
  For the lesson thou hast taught!
Thus at the flaming forge of life
  Our fortunes must be wrought;
Thus on its sounding anvil shaped
  Each burning deed and thought.

The Landlord's Tale

Paul Revere's Ride

Listen, my children, and you shall hear
Of the midnight ride of Paul Revere,
On the eighteenth of April, in Seventy-five;
Hardly a man is now alive
Who remembers that famous day and year.

He said to his friend, 'If the British march
By land or sea from the town to-night,
Hang a lantern aloft in the belfry-arch
Of the North Church tower as a signal light,—
One, if by land, and two, if by sea;
And I on the opposite shore will be,
Ready to ride and spread the alarm
Through every Middlesex village and farm,
For the country-folk to be up and to arm.'
Then he said, 'Good night!' and with muffled oar
Silently rowed to the Charlestown shore,

Just as the moon rose over the bay,
Where swinging wide at her moorings lay
The *Somerset*, British man-of-war;
A phantom-ship, with each mast and spar
Across the moon like a prison-bar,
And a huge black hulk, that was magnified
By its own reflection in the tide.

Meanwhile, his friend, through alley and street,
Wanders and watches with eager ears,
Till in the silence around him he hears
The muster of men at the barrack-door,
The sound of arms, and the tramp of feet,
And the measured tread of the grenadiers,
Marching down to their boats on the shore.

Then he climbed to the tower of the Old North Church,
Up the wooden stairs, with stealthy tread,
To the belfry-chamber overhead,
And startled the pigeons from their perch
On the sombre rafters, that round him made
Masses and moving shapes of shade,—
Up the trembling ladder, steep and tall,
To the highest window in the wall,
Where he paused to listen and look down
A moment on the roofs of the town,
And the moonlight flowing over all.

Beneath, in the churchyard, lay the dead,
In their night-encampment on the hill,
Wrapped in silence so deep and still
That he could hear, like a sentinel's tread,
The watchful night-wind, as it went,
Creeping along from tent to tent,
And seeming to whisper, 'All is well!'
A moment only he feels the spell

Of the place and the hour, and the secret dread
Of the lonely belfry and the dead;
For suddenly all his thoughts are bent
On a shadowy something far away,
Where the river widens to meet the bay,—
A line of black that bends and floats
On the rising tide, like a bridge of boats.

Meanwhile, impatient to mount and ride,
Booted and spurred, with a heavy stride
On the opposite shore walked Paul Revere.
Now he patted his horse's side,
Now gazed at the landscape far and near,
Then, impetuous, stamped the earth,
And turned and tightened his saddle-girth;
But mostly he watched with eager search
The belfry tower of the Old North Church,
As it rose above the graves on the hill,
Lonely and spectral, and sombre and still.
And lo! as he looks, on the belfry's height
A glimmer, and then a gleam of light!
He springs to the saddle, the bridle he turns,
But lingers and gazes, till full on his sight
A second lamp in the belfry burns!
A hurry of hoofs in a village street,
A shape in the moonlight, a bulk in the dark,
And beneath, from the pebbles, in passing, a spark
Struck out by a steed flying fearless and fleet;
That was all! And yet, through the gloom and the light,
The fate of a nation was riding that night;
And the spark struck out by that steed in his flight,
Kindled the land into flame with its heat.

He has left the village and mounted the steep,
And beneath him, tranquil and broad and deep,
Is the Mystic, meeting the ocean tides;

And under the alders, that skirt its edge,
Now soft on the sand, now loud on the ledge,
Is heard the tramp of his steed as he rides.

It was twelve by the village clock,
When he crossed the bridge into Medford town.
He heard the crowing of the cock,
And the barking of the farmer's dog,
And felt the damp of the river fog,
That rises after the sun goes down.

It was one by the village clock,
When he galloped into Lexington.
He saw the gilded weathercock
Swim in the moonlight as he passed,
And the meeting-house windows, blank and bare,
Gaze at him with a spectral glare,
As if they already stood aghast
At the bloody work they would look upon.

It was two by the village clock,
When he came to the bridge in Concord town.
He heard the bleating of the flock,
And the twitter of birds among the trees,
And felt the breath of the morning breeze
Blowing over the meadows brown.
And one was safe and asleep in his bed
Who at the bridge would be first to fall,
Who that day would be lying dead,
Pierced by a British musket-ball.

You know the rest. In the books you have read,
How the British Regulars fired and fled,—
How the farmers gave them ball for ball,
From behind each fence and farmyard wall,

Chasing the red-coats down the lane,
Then crossing the field to emerge again
Under the trees at the turn of the road,
And only pausing to fire and load.

So through the night rode Paul Revere;
And so through the night went his cry of alarm
To every Middlesex village and farm,—
A cry of defiance and not of fear,
A voice in the darkness, a knock at the door,
And a word that shall echo for evermore!
For, borne on the night-wind of the Past,
Through all our history, to the last,
In the hour of darkness and peril and need
The people will waken and listen to hear
The hurrying hoof-beats of that steed,
And the midnight message of Paul Revere.

The Tide Rises, the Tide Falls

The tide rises, the tide falls,
The twilight darkens, the curlew calls;
Along the sea-sands damp and brown
The traveller hastens towards the town,
    And the tide rises, the tide falls.

Darkness settles on roofs and walls,
But the sea, the sea in the darkness calls;
The little waves, with their soft, white hands,
Efface the footprints in the sands,
    And the tide rises, the tide falls.

The morning breaks; the steeds in their stalls
Stamp and neigh, as the hostler calls;

The day returns, but nevermore
Returns the traveller to the shore,
  And the tide rises, the tide falls.

Ultima Thule

To G. W. G.

With favoring winds, o'er sunlit seas,
We sailed for the Hesperides,
The land where golden apples grow;
But that, ah! that was long ago.

How far, since then, the ocean streams
Have swept us from that land of dreams,
That land of fiction and of truth,
The lost Atlantis of our youth!

Whither, ah, whither? Are not these
The tempest-haunted Orcades,
Where sea-gulls scream, and breakers roar,
And wreck and sea-weed line the shore?

Ultima Thule! Utmost Isle!
Here in thy harbors for a while
We lower our sails; a while we rest
From the unending, endless quest.

The Children's Hour

Between the dark and the daylight,
  When the night is beginning to lower,
Comes a pause in the day's occupations,
  That is known as the Children's Hour.

I hear in the chamber above me
  The patter of little feet,
The sound of a door that is opened,
  And voices soft and sweet.

From my study I see in the lamplight,
  Descending the broad hall stair,
Grave Alice, and laughing Allegra,
  And Edith with golden hair.

A whisper, and then a silence:
  Yet I know by their merry eyes
They are plotting and planning together
  To take me by surprise.

A sudden rush from the stairway,
  A sudden raid from the hall!
By three doors left unguarded
  They enter my castle wall!

They climb up into my turret
  O'er the arms and back of my chair;
If I try to escape, they surround me;
  They seem to be everywhere.

They almost devour me with kisses,
  Their arms about me entwine,
Till I think of the Bishop of Bingen
  In his Mouse-Tower on the Rhine!

Do you think, O blue-eyed banditti,
  Because you have scaled the wall,
Such an old mustache as I am
  Is not a match for you all!

I have you fast in my fortress,
  And will not let you depart,
But put you down into the dungeon
  In the round-tower of my heart.

And there will I keep you forever,
  Yes, forever and a day.
Till the walls shall crumble to ruin,
  And moulder in dust away!

The Cross of Snow

In the long, sleepless watches of the night,
  A gentle face – the face of one long dead—
  Looks at me from the wall, where round its head
  The night-lamp casts a halo of pale light.
Here in this room she died; and soul more white
  Never through martyrdom of fire was led
  To its repose; nor can in books be read
  The legend of a life more benedight.
There is a mountain in the distant West
  That, sun-defying, in its deep ravines
  Displays a cross of snow upon its side.
Such is the cross I wear upon my breast
  These eighteen years, through all the changing
  scenes
  And seasons, changeless since the day she died.

Seaweed

When descends on the Atlantic
    The gigantic
Storm-wind of the equinox,
Landward in his wrath he scourges
    The toiling surges,
Laden with seaweed from the rocks:

From Bermuda's reefs; from edges
    Of sunken ledges,
In some far-off, bright Azore;
From Bahama, and the dashing,
    Silver-flashing
Surges of San Salvador;

From the tumbling surf, that buries
    The Orkneyan skerries,
Answering the hoarse Hebrides;
And from wrecks of ships, and drifting
    Spars, uplifting
On the desolate, rainy seas;—

Ever drifting, drifting, drifting
    On the shifting
Currents of the restless main;
Till in sheltered coves, and reaches
    Of sandy beaches,
All have found repose again.

From The Building of the Ship

The Republic

Thou, too, sail on, O Ship of State!
Sail on, O UNION, strong and great!
Humanity with all its fears,
With all the hopes of future years,
Is hanging breathless on thy fate!
We know what Master laid thy keel,
What Workmen wrought thy ribs of steel,
Who made each mast, and sail, and rope,
What anvils rang, what hammers beat,
In what a forge and what a heat
Were shaped the anchors of thy hope!
Fear not each sudden sound and shock,
'Tis of the wave, and not the rock;
'Tis but the flapping of the sail,
And not a rent made by the gale!
In spite of rock and tempest's roar,
In spite of false lights on the shore,
Sail on, nor fear to breast the sea!
Our hearts, our hopes, are all with thee,
Our hearts, our hopes, our prayers, our tears,
Our faith triumphant o'er our fears,
Are all with thee, – are all with thee!

The Day is Done

The day is done, and the darkness
   Falls from the wings of Night,
As a feather is wafted downward
   From an eagle in his flight.

I see the lights of the village
  Gleam through the rain and the mist,
And a feeling of sadness comes o'er me
  That my soul cannot resist:

A feeling of sadness and longing,
  That is not akin to pain,
And resembles sorrow only
  As the mist resembles the rain.

Come, read to me some poem,
  Some simple and heartfelt lay,
That shall soothe this restless feeling,
  And banish the thoughts of day.

Not from the grand old masters,
  Not from the bards sublime,
Whose distant footsteps echo
  Through the corridors of Time.

For, like strains of martial music,
  Their mighty thoughts suggest
Life's endless toil and endeavor;
  And to-night I long for rest.

Read from some humbler poet,
  Whose songs gushed from his heart,
As showers from the clouds of summer,
  Or tears from the eyelids start;

Who, through long days of labor,
  And nights devoid of ease,
Still heard in his soul the music
  Of wonderful melodies.

Such songs have power to quiet
  The restless pulse of care,
And come like the benediction
  That follows after prayer.

Then read from the treasured volume
  The poem of thy choice,
And lend to the rhyme of the poet
  The beauty of thy voice.

And the night shall be filled with music,
  And the cares that infest the day
Shall fold their tents, like the Arabs,
  And as silently steal away.

Nature

As a fond mother, when the day is o'er,
  Leads by the hand her little child to bed,
  Half willing, half reluctant to be led,
And leave his broken playthings on the floor,
Still gazing at them through the open door,
  Nor wholly reassured and comforted
  By promises of others in their stead,
Which, though more splendid, may not please him
    more,—
So Nature deals with us, and takes away
  Our playthings one by one, and by the hand
    Leads us to rest so gently, that we go
Scarce knowing if we wish to go or stay,
  Being too full of sleep to understand
    How far the unknown transcends the what we know.

Serenade

Stars of the summer night!
  Far in yon azure deeps,
Hide, hide your golden light!
  She sleeps!
My lady sleeps!
  Sleeps!

Moon of the summer night!
  Far down yon western steeps,
Sink, sink in silver light!
  She sleeps!
My lady sleeps!
  Sleeps!

Wind of the summer night!
  Where yonder woodbine creeps,
Fold, fold thy pinions light!
  She sleeps!
My lady sleeps!
  Sleeps!

Dreams of the summer night!
  Tell her, her lover keeps
Watch! while in slumbers light
  She sleeps!
My lady sleeps!
  Sleeps!

My Lost Youth

Often I think of the beautiful town
  That is seated by the sea;
Often in thought go up and down
The pleasant streets of that dear old town,

And my youth comes back to me.
   And a verse of a Lapland song
   Is haunting my memory still:
   'A boy's will is the wind's will,
And the thoughts of youth are long, long thoughts.'

I can see the shadowy lines of its trees,
   And catch, in sudden gleams,
The sheen of the far-surrounding seas,
And islands that were the Hesperides
   Of all my boyish dreams.
     And the burden of that old song,
     It murmurs and whispers still:
     'A boy's will is the wind's will,
And the thoughts of youth are long, long thoughts.'

I remember the black wharves and the slips,
   And the sea-tides tossing free;
And Spanish sailors with bearded lips,
And the beauty and mystery of the ships,
   And the magic of the sea.
     And the voice of that wayward song
     Is singing and saying still:
     'A boy's will is the wind's will,
And the thoughts of youth are long, long thoughts.'

I remember the bulwarks by the shore,
   And the fort upon the hill;
The sunrise gun, with its hollow roar,
The drum-beat repeated o'er and o'er,
   And the bugle wild and shrill.
     And the music of that old song
     Throbs in my memory still:
     'A boy's will is the wind's will,
And the thoughts of youth are long, long thoughts.'

I remember the sea-fight far away,
 How it thundered o'er the tide!
And the dead captains, as they lay
In their graves, o'erlooking the tranquil bay,
 Where they in battle died.
  And the sound of that mournful song
  Goes through me with a thrill:
  'A boy's will is the wind's will,
And the thoughts of youth are long, long thoughts.'

I can see the breezy dome of groves,
 The shadows of Deering's Woods;
And the friendships old and the early loves
Come back with a Sabbath sound, as of doves
 In quiet neighborhoods.
  And the verse of that sweet old song,
  It flutters and murmurs still:
  'A boy's will is the wind's will,
And the thoughts of youth are long, long thoughts.'

I remember the gleams and glooms that dart
 Across the school-boy's brain;
The song and the silence in the heart,
That in part are prophecies, and in part
 Are longings wild and vain.
  And the voice of that fitful song
  Sings on, and is never still:
  'A boy's will is the wind's will,
And the thoughts of youth are long, long thoughts.'

There are things of which I may not speak;
 There are dreams that cannot die;
There are thoughts that make the strong heart weak,
And bring a pallor into the cheek,
 And a mist before the eye.

And the words of that fatal song
Come over me like a chill:
'A boy's will is the wind's will,
And the thoughts of youth are long, long thoughts.'

Strange to me now are the forms I meet
    When I visit the dear old town;
But the native air is pure and sweet,
And the trees that o'ershadow each well-known street,
    As they balance up and down,
        Are singing the beautiful song,
        Are sighing and whispering still:
        'A boy's will is the wind's will,
And the thoughts of youth are long, long thoughts.'

And Deering's Woods are fresh and fair,
    And with joy that is almost pain
My heart goes back to wander there,
And among the dreams of the days that were,
    I find my lost youth again.
        And the strange and beautiful song,
        The groves are repeating it still:
        'A boy's will is the wind's will,
And the thoughts of youth are long, long thoughts.'

The Arrow and the Song

I shot an arrow into the air,
It fell to earth, I knew not where;
For, so swiftly it flew, the sight
Could not follow it in its flight.

I breathed a song into the air,
It fell to earth, I knew not where;
For who has sight so keen and strong
That it can follow the flight of song?

Long, long afterward, in an oak
I found the arrow, still unbroke;
And the song, from beginning to end,
I found again in the heart of a friend.

JOHN GREENLEAF WHITTIER
1807-1892

John Greenleaf Whittier was a Massachusetts poet of Quaker stock whose poetry and newspaper work reflected his commitment to the anti-slavery movement and other human rights causes. He fought for these during the Civil War and then retired to his beloved New England, his poetic feelings transformed by a comprehensive religious faith.

'Proem' reflects the early romantic influence of Burns on Whittier's work; 'Dedication' to *Songs of Labor*, his interest in political causes, and 'Skipper Ireson's Ride' and 'Telling the Bees' his abiding love for the history and beauty of the New England countryside.

Proem

I love the old melodious lays
Which softly melt the ages through,
    The songs of Spenser's golden days,
    Arcadian Sidney's silvery phrase,
Sprinkling our noon of time with freshest morning dew.

    Yet, vainly in my quiet hours
To breathe their marvellous notes I try;
    I feel them, as the leaves and flowers
    In silence feel the dewy showers,
And drink with glad, still lips the blessing of the sky.

    The rigor of a frozen clime,
The harshness of an untaught ear,
    The jarring words of one whose rhyme
    Beat often Labor's hurried time,
Or Duty's rugged march through storm and strife, are
    here.

    Of mystic beauty, dreamy grace,
No rounded art the lack supplies;
    Unskilled the subtle lines to trace,
    Or softer shades of Nature's face,
I view her common forms with unanointed eyes.

    Nor mine the seer-like power to show
The secrets of the heart and mind;
    To drop the plummet-line below
    Our common world of joy and woe,
A more intense despair or brighter hope to find.

Yet here at least an earnest sense
Of human right and weal is shown;
A hate of tyranny intense,
And hearty in its vehemence,
As if my brother's pain and sorrow were my own.

O Freedom! if to me belong
Nor mighty Milton's gift divine,
Nor Marvell's wit and graceful song,
Still with a love as deep and strong
As theirs, I lay, like them, my best gifts on thy shrine.

From *Songs of Labor*

Dedication

I would the gift I offer here
Might graces from thy favor take,
And, seen through Friendship's atmosphere,
On softened lines and coloring, wear
The unaccustomed light of beauty, for thy sake.

Few leaves of Fancy's spring remain:
But what I have I give to thee,
The o'er-sunned bloom of summer's plain,
And paler flowers, the latter rain
Calls from the westering slope of life's autumnal lea.

Above the fallen groves of green,
Where youth's enchanted forest stood,
Dry root and mossèd trunk between,
A sober after-growth is seen,
As springs the pine where falls the gay-leafed maple
wood!

Yet birds will sing, and breezes play
    Their leaf-harps in the sombre tree;
And through the bleak and wintry day
It keeps its steady green alway,—
So, even my after-thoughts may have a charm for thee.

Art's perfect forms no moral need,
    And beauty is its own excuse;
But for the dull and flowerless weed
Some healing virtue still must plead,
And the rough ore must find its honors in its use.

So haply these, my simple lays
    Of homely toil, may serve to show
The orchard bloom and tasselled maize
That skirt and gladden duty's ways,
The unsung beauty hid life's common things below.

Haply from them the toiler, bent
    Above his forge or plough, may gain
A manlier spirit of content,
And feel that life is wisest spent
Where the strong working hand makes strong the
        working brain.

The doom which to the guilty pair
    Without the walls of Eden came,
Transforming sinless ease to care
And rugged toil, no more shall bear
The burden of old crime, or mark of primal shame.

A blessing now, a curse no more;
    Since He, whose name we breathe with awe,
The coarse mechanic vesture wore,
A poor man toiling with the poor,
In labor, as in prayer, fulfilling the same law.

Skipper Ireson's Ride

Of all the rides since the birth of time,
Told in story or sung in rhyme,—
On Apuleius's Golden Ass,
Or one-eyed Calender's horse of brass,
Witch astride of a human back,
Islam's prophet on Al-Borák,—
The strangest ride that ever was sped
Was Ireson's, out from Marblehead!
  Old Floyd Ireson, for his hard heart,
    Tarred and feathered and carried in a cart
      By the women of Marblehead!

Body of turkey, head of owl,
Wings a-droop like a rained-on fowl,
Feathered and ruffled in every part,
Skipper Ireson stood in the cart.
Scores of women, old and young,
Strong of muscle, and glib of tongue,
Pushed and pulled up the rocky lane,
Shouting and singing the shrill refrain:
  'Here's Flud Oirson, fur his horrd horrt,
    Torr'd an' futherr'd an' corr'd in a corrt
      By the women o' Morble'ead!'

Wrinkled scolds with hands on hips,
Girls in bloom of cheek and lips,
Wild-eyed, free-limbed, such as chase
Bacchus round some antique vase,
Brief of skirt, with ankles bare,
Loose of kerchief and loose of hair,
With conch-shells blowing and fish-horns' twang,
Over and over the Mænads sang:
  'Here's Flud Oirson, fur his horrd horrt,
    Torr'd an' futherr'd an' corr'd in a corrt
      By the women o' Morble'ead!'

Small pity for him! – He sailed away
From a leaking ship in Chaleur Bay,—
Sailed away from a sinking wreck,
With his own town's-people on her deck!
'Lay by! lay by!' they called to him.
Back he answered, 'Sink or swim!
Brag of your catch of fish again!'
And off he sailed through the fog and rain!
   Old Floyd Ireson, for his hard heart,
    Tarred and feathered and carried in a cart
      By the women of Marblehead!

Fathoms deep in dark Chaleur
That wreck shall lie forevermore.
Mother and sister, wife and maid,
Looked from the rocks of Marblehead
Over the moaning and rainy sea,—
Looked for the coming that might not be!
What did the winds and the sea-birds say
Of the cruel captain who sailed away?—
   Old Floyd Ireson, for his hard heart,
    Tarred and feathered and carried in a cart
      By the women of Marblehead!

Through the street, on either side,
Up flew windows, doors swung wide;
Sharp-tongued spinsters, old wives gray,
Treble lent the fish-horn's bray.
Sea-worn grandsires, cripple-bound,
Hulks of old sailors, run aground,
Shook head, and fist, and hat, and cane,
And cracked with curses the hoarse refrain:
   'Here's Flud Oirson, fur his horrd horrt,
    Torr'd an' futherr'd an' corr'd in a corrt
      By the women o' Morble'head!'

Sweetly along the Salem road
Bloom of orchard and lilac showed.
Little the wicked skipper knew
Of the fields so green and the sky so blue.
Riding there in his sorry trim,
Like an Indian idol glum and grim,
Scarcely he seemed the sound to hear
Of voices shouting, far and near:
   'Here's Flud Oirson, fur his horrd horrt,
   Torr'd an' futherr'd an' corr'd in a corrt
     By the women o' Morble'head!'

'Hear me, neighbors!' at last he cried,—
'What to me is this noisy ride?
What is the shame that clothes the skin
To the nameless horror that lives within?
Waking or sleeping, I see a wreck,
And hear a cry from a reeling deck!
Hate me and curse me, – I only dread
The hand of God and the face of the dead!'
   Said old Floyd Ireson, for his hard heart,
   Tarred and feathered and carried in a cart
     By the women of Marblehead!

Then the wife of the skipper lost at sea
Said, 'God has touched him! why should we!'
Said an old wife mourning her only son,
'Cut the rogue's tether and let him run!'
So with soft relentings and rude excuse,
Half scorn, half pity, they cut him loose,
And gave him a cloak to hide him in,
And left him alone with his shame and sin.
   Poor Floyd Ireson, for his hard heart,
   Tarred and feathered and carried in a cart
     By the women of Marblehead!

Telling the Bees

Here is the place; right over the hill
  Runs the path I took;
You can see the gap in the old wall still,
  And the stepping-stones in the shallow brook.

There is the house, with a gate red-barred,
  And the poplars tall;
And the barn's brown length, and the cattle-yard,
  And the white horns tossing above the wall.

There are the beehives ranged in the sun;
  And down by the brink
Of the brook are her poor flowers, weed-o'errun,
  Pansy and daffodil, rose and pink.

A year has gone, as the tortoise goes,
  Heavy and slow;
And the same rose blows, and the same sun glows,
  And the same brook sings of a year ago.

There's the same sweet clover-smell in the breeze;
  And the June sun warm
Tangles his wings of fire in the trees,
  Setting, as then, over Fernside farm.

I mind me how with a lover's care
  From my Sunday coat
I brushed off the burrs, and smoothed my hair,
  And cooled at the brookside my brow and throat.

Since we parted, a month had passed,—
  To love, a year;
Down through the beeches I looked at last
  On the little red gate and the well-sweep near.

I can see it all now, – the slantwise rain
   Of light through the leaves,
The sundown's blaze on her window-pane,
   The bloom of her roses under the eaves.

Just the same as a month before,—
   The house and the trees,
The barn's brown gable, the vine by the door,—
   Nothing changed but the hives of bees.

Before them, under the garden wall,
   Forward and back,
Went drearily singing the chore-girl small,
   Draping each hive with a shred of black.

Trembling, I listened: the summer sun
   Had the chill of snow;
For I knew she was telling the bees of one
   Gone on the journey we all must go!

Then I said to myself, 'My Mary weeps
   For the dead to-day:
Haply her blind old grandsire sleeps
   The fret and the pain of his age away.'

But her dog whined low; on the doorway sill,
   With his cane to his chin,
The old man sat; and the chore-girl still
   Sung to the bees stealing out and in.

And the song she was singing ever since
   In my ear sounds on:—
'Stay at home, pretty bees, fly not hence!
   Mistress Mary is dead and gone!'

Snow-Bound
A winter idyl

The sun that brief December day
Rose cheerless over hills of gray,
And, darkly circled, gave at noon
A sadder light than waning moon.
Slow tracing down the thickening sky
Its mute and ominous prophecy,
A portent seeming less than threat,
It sank from sight before it set.
A chill no coat, however stout,
Of homespun stuff could quite shut out,
A hard, dull bitterness of cold,
That checked, mid-vein, the circling race
Of life-blood in the sharpened face,
The coming of the snow-storm told.
The wind blew east; we heard the roar
Of Ocean on his wintry shore,
And felt the strong pulse throbbing there
Beat with low rhythm our inland air.

Meanwhile we did our nightly chores,—
Brought in the wood from out of doors,
Littered the stalls, and from the mows
Raked down the herd's-grass for the cows:
Heard the horse whinnying for his corn;
And, sharply clashing horn on horn,
Impatient down the stanchion rows
The cattle shake their walnut bows;
While, peering from his early perch
Upon the scaffold's pole of birch,
The cock his crested helmet bent
And down his querulous challenge sent.

Unwarmed by any sunset light
The gray day darkened into night,

A night made hoary with the swarm
And whirl-dance of the blinding storm,
As zigzag, wavering to and fro,
Crossed and recrossed the wingèd snow:
And ere the early bedtime came
The white drift piled the window-frame,
And through the glass the clothes-line posts
Looked in like tall and sheeted ghosts.

So all night long the storm roared on:
The morning broke without a sun;
In tiny spherule traced with lines
Of Nature's geometric signs,
In starry flake, and pellicle,
All day the hoary meteor fell;
And, when the second morning shone,
We looked upon a world unknown,
On nothing we could call our own.
Around the glistening wonder bent
The blue walls of the firmament,
No cloud above, no earth below,—
A universe of sky and snow!
The old familiar sights of ours
Took marvellous shapes; strange domes and towers
Rose up where sty or corn-crib stood,
Or garden-wall, or belt of wood;
A smooth white mound the brush-pile showed,
A fenceless drift what once was road;
The bridle-post an old man sat
With loose-flung coat and high cocked hat;
The well-curb had a Chinese roof;
And even the long sweep, high aloof,
In its slant splendor, seemed to tell
Of Pisa's leaning miracle.

A prompt, decisive man, no breath
Our father wasted: 'Boys, a path!'
Well pleased, (for when did farmer boy
Count such a summons less than joy?)
Our buskins on our feet we drew;
With mittened hands, and caps drawn low,
To guard our necks and ears from snow,
We cut the solid whiteness through.
And, where the drift was deepest, made
A tunnel walled and overlaid
With dazzling crystal: we had read
Of rare Aladdin's wondrous cave,
And to our own his name we gave,
With many a wish the luck were ours
To test his lamp's supernal powers.
We reached the barn with merry din,
And roused the prisoned brutes within.
The old horse thrust his long head out,
And grave with wonder gazed about;
The cock his lusty greeting said,
And forth his speckled harem led;
The oxen lashed their tails, and hooked,
And mild reproach of hunger looked;
The hornèd patriarch of the sheep,
Like Egypt's Amun roused from sleep,
Shook his sage head with gesture mute,
And emphasized with stamp of foot.

All day the gusty north-wind bore
The loosening drift its breath before;
Low circling round its southern zone,
The sun through dazzling snow-mist shone.
No church-bell lent its Christian tone
To the savage air, no social smoke
Curled over woods of snow-hung oak.

A solitude made more intense
By dreary-voicëd elements,
The shrieking of the mindless wind,
The moaning tree-boughs swaying blind,
And on the glass the unmeaning beat
Of ghostly finger-tips of sleet.
Beyond the circle of our hearth
No welcome sound of toil or mirth
Unbound the spell, and testified
Of human life and thought outside.
We minded that the sharpest ear
The buried brooklet could not hear,
The music of whose liquid lip
Had been to us companionship,
And, in our lonely life, had grown
To have an almost human tone.

As night drew on, and, from the crest
Of wooded knolls that ridged the west,
The sun, a snow-blown traveller, sank
From sight beneath the smothering bank,
We piled, with care, our nightly stack
Of wood against the chimney-back,—
The oaken log, green, huge, and thick,
And on its top the stout back-stick;
The knotty forestick laid apart,
And filled between with curious art
The ragged brush; then, hovering near,
We watched the first red blaze appear,
Heard the sharp crackle, caught the gleam
On whitewashed wall and sagging beam,
Until the old, rude-furnished room
Burst, flower-like, into rosy bloom;
While radiant with a mimic flame
Outside the sparkling drift became,

And through the bare-boughed lilac-tree
Our own warm hearth seemed blazing free.
The crane and pendent trammels showed,
The Turks' heads on the andirons glowed;
While childish fancy, prompt to tell
The meaning of the miracle,
Whispered the old rhyme: *'Under the tree,*
When fire outdoors burns merrily,
There the witches are making tea.'

The moon above the eastern wood
Shone at its full; the hill-range stood
Transfigured in the silver flood,
Its blown snows flashing cold and keen,
Dead white, save where some sharp ravine
Took shadow, or the sombre green
Of hemlocks turned to pitchy black
Against the whiteness at their back.
For such a world and such a night
Most fitting that unwarming light,
Which only seemed where'er it fell
To make the coldness visible.

Shut in from all the world without,
We sat the clean-winged hearth about,
Content to let the north-wind roar
In baffled rage at pane and door,
While the red logs before us beat
The frost-line back with tropic heat;
And ever, when a louder blast
Shook beam and rafter as it passed,
The merrier up its roaring draught
The great throat of the chimney laughed;
The house-dog on his paws outspread
Laid to the fire his drowsy head,

The cat's dark silhouette on the wall
A couchant tiger's seemed to fall;
And, for the winter fireside meet,
Between the andirons' straddling feet,
The mug of cider simmered slow,
The apples sputtered in a row,
And, close at hand, the basket stood
With nuts from brown October's wood.

What matter how the night behaved?
What matter how the north-wind raved?
Blow high, blow low, not all its snow
Could quench our hearth-fire's ruddy glow.
O Time and Change! – with hair as gray
As was my sire's that winter day,
How strange it seems, with so much gone
Of life and love, to still live on!
Ah, brother! only I and thou
Are left of all that circle now,—
The dear home faces whereupon
That fitful firelight paled and shone.
Henceforward, listen as we will,
The voices of that hearth are still;
Look where we may, the wide earth o'er,
Those lighted faces smile no more.
We tread the paths their feet have worn,
  We sit beneath their orchard trees,
  We hear, like them, the hum of bees
And rustle of the bladed corn;
We turn the pages that they read,
  Their written words we linger o'er,
But in the sun they cast no shade,
No voice is heard, no sign is made,
  No step is on the conscious floor!

Yet Love will dream, and Faith will trust,
(Since He who knows our need is just,)
That somehow, somewhere, meet we must.

Alas for him who never sees
The stars shine through his cypress-trees!
Who, hopeless, lays his dead away,
Nor looks to see the breaking day
Across the mournful marbles play!
Who hath not learned, in hours of faith,
   The truth to flesh and sense unknown,
That Life is ever lord of Death,
    And Love can never lose its own!

We sped the time with stories old,
Wrought puzzles out, and riddles told,
Or stammered from our school-book lore
'The Chief of Gambia's golden shore.'
How often since, when all the land
Was clay in Slavery's shaping hand,
As if a far-blown trumpet stirred
The languorous sin-sick air, I heard:
'Does not the voice of reason cry,
   Claim the first right which Nature gave,
From the red scourge of bondage fly,
   Nor deign to live a burdened slave!'
Our father rode again his ride
On Memphremagog's wooded side;
Sat down again to moose and samp
In trapper's hut and Indian camp;
Lived o'er the old idyllic ease
Beneath St François' hemlock-trees;
Again for him the moonlight shone
On Norman cap and bodiced zone;
Again he heard the violin play
Which led the village dance away.

And mingled in its merry whirl
The grandam and the laughing girl.
Or, nearer home, our steps he led
Where Salisbury's level marshes spread
  Mile-wide as flies the laden bee;
Where merry mowers, hale and strong,
Swept, scythe on scythe, their swaths along
  The low green prairies of the sea.
We share the fishing off Boar's Head,
  And round the rocky Isles of Shoals
  The hake-broil on the drift-wood coals;
The chowder on the sand-beach made,
Dipped by the hungry, steaming hot,
With spoons of clam-shell from the pot.
We heard the tales of witchcraft old,
And dream and sign and marvel told
To sleepy listeners as they lay
Stretched idly on the salted hay,
Adrift along the winding shores,
When favoring breezes deigned to blow
The square sail of the gundelow
And idle lay the useless oars.

Our mother, while she turned her wheel
Or run the new-knit stocking-heel,
Told how the Indian hordes came down
At midnight on Cocheco town,
And how her own great-uncle bore
His cruel scalp-mark to fourscore.
Recalling, in her fitting phrase,
  So rich and picturesque and free,
  (The common unrhymed poetry
Of simple life and country ways,)
The story of her early days,—
She made us welcome to her home;
Old hearths grew wide to give us room;

We stole with her a frightened look
At the gray wizard's conjuring-book,
The fame whereof went far and wide
Through all the simple country side;
We heard the hawks at twilight play,
The boat-horn on Piscataqua,
The loon's weird laughter far away;
We fished her little trout-brook, knew
What flowers in wood and meadow grew,
What sunny hillsides autumn-brown
She climbed to shake the ripe nuts down,
Saw where in sheltered cove and bay
The ducks' black squadron anchored lay,
And heard the wild-geese calling loud
Beneath the gray November cloud.

Then, haply, with a look more grave,
And soberer tone, some tale she gave
From painful Sewel's ancient tome,
Beloved in every Quaker home,
Of faith fire-winged by martyrdom,
Or Chalkley's Journal, old and quaint,—
Gentlest of skippers, rare sea-saint!—
Who, when the dreary calms prevailed,
And water-butt and bread-cask failed,
And cruel, hungry eyes pursued
His portly presence mad for food,
With dark hints muttered under breath
Of casting lots for life or death,
Offered, if Heaven withheld supplies,
To be himself the sacrifice.
Then, suddenly, as if to save
The good man from his living grave,
A ripple on the water grew,
A school of porpoise flashed in view.

'Take, eat,' he said, 'and be content;
These fishes in my stead are sent
By Him who gave the tangled ram
To spare the child of Abraham.'

Our uncle, innocent of books,
Was rich in lore of fields and brooks,
The ancient teachers never dumb
Of Nature's unhoused lyceum.
In moons and tides and weather wise,
He read the clouds as prophecies,
And foul or fair could well divine,
By many an occult hint and sign,
Holding the cunning-warded keys
To all the woodcraft mysteries;
Himself to Nature's heart so near
That all her voices in his ear
Of beast or bird had meanings clear,
Like Apollonius of old,
Who knew the tales the sparrows told,
Or Hermes who interpreted
What the sage cranes of Nilus said;
A simple, guileless, childlike man,
Content to live where life began;
Strong only on his native grounds,
The little world of sights and sounds
Whose girdle was the parish bounds,
Whereof his fondly partial pride
The common features magnified,
As Surrey hills to mountains grew
In White of Selborne's loving view,—
He told how teal and loon he shot,
And how the eagle's eggs he got,
The feats on pond and river done,
The prodigies of rod and gun;
Till, warming with the tales he told,

Forgotten was the outside cold,
The bitter wind unheeded blew,
From ripening corn the pigeons flew,
The partridge drummed i' the wood, the mink
Went fishing down the river-brink.
In fields with bean or clover gay,
The woodchuck, like a hermit gray,
   Peered from the doorway of his cell:
The muskrat plied the mason's trade,
And tier by tier his mud-walls laid;
And from the shagbark overhead
   The grizzled squirrel dropped his shell.

Next, the dear aunt, whose smile of cheer
And voice in dreams I see and hear,—
The sweetest woman ever Fate
Perverse denied a household mate,
Who, lonely, homeless, not the less
Found peace in love's unselfishness,
And welcome wheresoe'er she went,
A calm and gracious element,
Whose presence seemed the sweet income
And womanly atmosphere of home,—
Called up her girlhood memories,
The huskings and the apple-bees,
The sleigh-rides and the summer sails.
Weaving through all the poor details
And homespun warp of circumstance
A golden woof-thread of romance.
For well she kept her genial mood
And simple faith of maidenhood;
Before her still a cloud-land lay,
The mirage loomed across her way;
The morning dew, that dries so soon
With others, glistened at her noon;
Through years of toil and soil and care,

From glossy tress to thin gray hair,
All unprofaned she held apart
The virgin fancies of the heart.
Be shame to him of woman born
Who hath for such but thought of scorn.

There, too, our elder sister plied
Her evening task the stand beside;
A full, rich nature, free to trust,
Truthful and almost sternly just,
Impulsive, earnest, prompt to act,
And make her generous thought a fact,
Keeping with many a light disguise
The secret of self-sacrifice.
O heart sore-tried! thou hast the best
That Heaven itself could give thee, – rest,
Rest from all bitter thoughts and things!
    How many a poor one's blessing went
    With thee beneath the low green tent
Whose curtain never outward swings!

As one who held herself a part
Of all she saw, and let her heart
    Against the household bosom lean,
Upon the motley-braided mat
Our youngest and our dearest sat,
Lifting her large, sweet, asking eyes,
    Now bathed in the unfading green
And holy peace of Paradise.
Oh, looking from some heavenly hill,
    Or from the shade of saintly palms,
    Or silver reach of river calms,
Do those large eyes behold me still?
With me one little year ago:—
The chill weight of the winter snow
    For months upon her grave has lain;

And now, when summer south-winds blow
  And brier and harebell bloom again,
I tread the pleasant paths we trod,
I see the violet-sprinkled sod
Whereon she leaned, too frail and weak
The hillside flowers she loved to seek,
Yet following me where'er I went
With dark eyes full of love's content.
The birds are glad; the brier-rose fills
The air with sweetness; all the hills
Stretch green to June's unclouded sky;
But still I wait with ear and eye
For something gone which should be nigh,
A loss in all familiar things,
In flower that blooms, and bird that sings.
And yet, dear heart! remembering thee,
  Am I not richer than of old?
Safe in thy immortality,
  What change can reach the wealth I hold?
  What chance can mar the pearl and gold
Thy love hath left in trust with me?
And while in life's late afternoon,
  Where cool and long the shadows grow,
I walk to meet the night that soon
  Shall shape and shadow overflow,
I cannot feel that thou art far,
Since near at need the angels are;
And when the sunset gates unbar,
  Shall I not see thee waiting stand,
And, white against the evening star,
  The welcome of thy beckoning hand?

Brisk wielder of the birch and rule,
The master of the district school
Held at the fire his favored place,
Its warm glow lit a laughing face

Fresh-hued and fair, where scarce appeared
The uncertain prophecy of beard.
He teased the mitten-blinded cat,
Played cross-pins on my uncle's hat,
Sang songs, and told us what befalls
In classic Dartmouth's college halls.
Born the wild Northern hills among,
From whence his yeoman father wrung
By patient toil subsistence scant,
Not competence and yet not want,
He early gained the power to pay
His cheerful, self-reliant way;
Could doff at ease his scholar's gown
To peddle wares from town to town:
Or through the long vacation's reach
In lonely lowland districts teach,
Where all the droll experience found
At stranger hearths in boarding round,
The moonlit skater's keen delight,
The sleigh-drive through the frosty night,
The rustic-party, with its rough
Accompaniment of blind-man's-buff,
And whirling-plate, and forfeits paid,
His winter task a pastime made.
Happy the snow-locked homes wherein
He tuned his merry violin,
Or played the athlete in the barn,
Or held the good dame's winding-yarn,
Or mirth-provoking versions told
Of classic legends rare and old,
Wherein the scenes of Greece and Rome
Had all the commonplace of home,
And little seemed at best the odds
'Twixt Yankee pedlers and old gods;
Where Pindus-born Arachthus took
The guise of any grist-mill brook,

And dread Olympus at his will
Became a huckleberry hill.

A careless boy that night he seemed;
  But at his desk he had the look
And air of one who wisely schemed,
  And hostage from the future took
  In trainëd thought and lore of book.
Large-brained, clear-eyed, of such as he
Shall Freedom's young apostles be,
Who, following in War's bloody trail,
Shall every lingering wrong assail;
All chains from limb and spirit strike,
Uplift the black and white alike;
Scatter before their swift advance
The darkness and the ignorance,
The pride, the lust, the squalid sloth,
Which nurtured Treason's monstrous growth,
Made murder pastime, and the hell
Of prison-torture possible;
The cruel lie of caste refute,
Old forms remould, and substitute
For Slavery's lash the freeman's will,
For blind routine, wise-handed skill;
A school-house plant on every hill,
Stretching in radiate nerve-lines thence
The quick wires of intelligence;
Till North and South together brought
Shall own the same electric thought,
In peace a common flag salute,
And, side by side in labor's free
And unresentful rivalry,
Harvest the fields wherein they fought.

Another guest that winter night
Flashed back from lustrous eyes the light.

Unmarked by time, and yet not young,
The honeyed music of her tongue
And words of meekness scarcely told
A nature passionate and bold,
Strong, self-concentred, spurning guide,
Its milder features dwarfed beside
Her unbent will's majestic pride.
She sat among us, at the best,
A not unfeared, half-welcome guest,
Rebuking with her cultured phrase
Our homeliness of words and ways.
A certain pard-like, treacherous grace
Swayed the lithe limbs and drooped the lash,
Lent the white teeth their dazzling flash;
And under low brows, black with night,
Rayed out at times a dangerous light;
The sharp heat-lightnings of her face
Presaging ill to him whom Fate
Condemned to share her love or hate.
A woman tropical, intense
In thought and act, in soul and sense,
She blended in a like degree
The vixen and the devotee,
Revealing with each freak or feint
  The temper of Petruchio's Kate,
The raptures of Siena's saint.
Her tapering hand and rounded wrist
Had facile power to form a fist;
The warm, dark languish of her eyes
Was never safe from wrath's surprise.
Brows saintly calm and lips devout
Knew every change of scowl and pout;
And the sweet voice had notes more high
And shrill for social battle-cry.

Since then what old cathedral town

Has missed her pilgrim staff and gown,
What convent-gate has held its lock
Against the challenge of her knock!
Through Smyrna's plague-hushed thoroughfares,
Up sea-set Malta's rocky stairs,
Gray olive slopes of ills that hem
Thy tombs and shrines, Jerusalem,
Or startling on her desert throne
The crazy Queen of Lebanon
With claims fantastic as her own,
Her tireless feet have held their way;
And still, unrestful, bowed, and gray,
She watches under Eastern skies,
  With hope each day renewed and fresh,
  The Lord's quick coming in the flesh,
Whereof she dreams and prophesies!

Where'er her troubled path may be,
  The Lord's sweet pity with her go!
The outward wayward life we see,
  The hidden springs we may not know.
Nor is it given us to discern
  What threads the fatal sisters spun,
  Through what ancestral years has run
The sorrow with the woman born,
What forged her cruel chain of moods,
What set her feet in solitudes,
  And held the love within her mute,
What mingled madness in the blood,
  A life-long discord and annoy,
  Water of tears with oil of joy,
And hid within the folded bud
  Perversities of flower and fruit.
It is not ours to separate
The tangled skein of will and fate,
To show what metes and bounds should stand

Upon the soul's debatable land,
And between choice and Providence
Divide the circle of events;
But He who knows our frame is just,
Merciful and compassionate,
And full of sweet assurances
And hope for all the language is,
That He remembereth we are dust!

At last the great logs, crumbling low,
Sent out a dull and duller glow,
The bull's-eye watch that hung in view,
Ticking its weary circuit through,
Pointed with mutely warning sign
Its black hand to the hour of nine.
That sign the pleasant circle broke:
My uncle ceased his pipe to smoke,
Knocked from its bowl the refuse gray,
And laid it tenderly away;
Then roused himself to safely cover
The dull red brands with ashes over.
And while, with care, our mother laid
The work aside, her steps she stayed
One moment, seeking to express
Her grateful sense of happiness
For food and shelter, warmth and health,
And love's contentment more than wealth,
With simple wishes (not the weak,
Vain prayers which no fulfilment seek,
O'er-prompt to do with Heaven its part)
That none might lack, that bitter night,
For bread and clothing, warmth and light.

Within our beds awhile we heard
The wind that round the gables roared,
With now and then a ruder shock,

Which made our very bedsteads rock.
We heard the loosened clapboards tost,
The board-nails snapping in the frost;
And on us, through the unplastered wall,
Felt the light sifted snow-flakes fall.
But sleep stole on, as sleep will do
When hearts are light and life is new;
Faint and more faint the murmurs grew,
Till in the summer-land of dreams
They softened to the sound of streams,
Low stir of leaves, and dip of oars,
And lapsing waves on quiet shores.

Next morn we wakened with the shout
Of merry voices high and clear;
And saw the teamsters drawing near
To break the drifted highways out.
Down the long hillside treading slow
We saw the half-buried oxen go,
Shaking the snow from heads uptost,
Their straining nostrils white with frost.
Before our door the straggling train
Drew up, an added team to gain.
The elders threshed their hands a-cold,
    Passed, with the cider-mug, their jokes
    From lip to lip; the younger folks
Down the loose snow-banks, wrestling, rolled,
Then toiled again the cavalcade
    O'er windy hill, through clogged ravine,
    And woodland paths that wound between
Low drooping pine-boughs winter-weighed.
From every barn a team afoot,
At every house a new recruit,
Where, drawn by Nature's subtlest law,
Haply the watchful young men saw
Sweet doorway pictures of the curls

And curious eyes of merry girls,
Lifting their hands in mock defence
Again the snow-ball's compliments,
And reading in each missive tost
The charm with Eden never lost.

We heard once more the sleigh-bells' sound;
   And, following where the teamsters led,
The wise old Doctor went his round,
Just pausing at our door to say,
In the brief autocratic way
Of one who, prompt at Duty's call,
Was free to urge her claim on all,
   That some poor neighbor sick abed
At night our mother's aid would need.
For, one in generous thought and deed,
   What mattered in the sufferer's sight
   The Quaker matron's inward light,
The Doctor's mail of Calvin's creed?
All hearts confess the saints elect
   Who, twain in faith, in love agree,
And melt not in an acid sect
   The Christian pearl of charity!

So days went on: a week had passed
Since the great world was heard from last.
The Almanac we studied o'er,
Read and reread our little store
Of books and pamphlets, scarce a score;
One harmless novel, mostly hid
From younger eyes, a book forbid,
And poetry, (or good or bad,
A single book was all we had,)
Where Ellwood's meek, drab-skirted Muse,
   A stranger to the heathen Nine,
   Sang, with a somewhat nasal whine,

The wars of David and the Jews.
At last the floundering carrier bore
The village paper to our door.
Lo! broadening outward as we read,
To warmer zones the horizon spread
In panoramic length unrolled
We saw the marvels that it told.
Before us passed the painted Creeks,
    And daft McGregor on his raids
    In Costa Rica's everglades.
And up Taygetos winding slow
Rode Ypsilanti's Mainote Greeks,
A Turk's head at each saddle-bow!
Welcome to us its week-old news,
Its corner for the rustic Muse,
    Its monthly gauge of snow and rain,
Its record, mingling in a breath
The wedding bell and dirge of death:
Jest, anecdote, and love-lorn tale,
The latest culprit sent to jail;
Its hue and cry of stolen and lost,
Its vendue sales and goods at cost,
    And traffic calling loud for gain.
We felt the stir of hall and street,
The pulse of life that round us beat;
The chill embargo of the snow
Was melted in the genial glow;
Wide swung again our ice-locked door,
And all the world was ours once more!
Clasp, Angel of the backward look
    And folded wings of ashen gray
    And voice of echoes far away,
The brazen covers of thy book;
The weird palimpsest old and vast,
Wherein thou hid'st the spectral past;
Where, closely mingling, pale and glow

The characters of joy and woe;
The monographs of outlived years,
Or smile-illumed or dim with tears,
 Green hills of life that slope to death,
And haunts of home, whose vistaed trees
Shade off to mournful cypresses
 With the white amaranths underneath
Even while I look, I can but heed
 The restless sands' incessant fall,
Importunate hours that hours succeed,
Each clamorous with its own sharp need,
 And duty keeping pace with all.
Shut down and clasp the heavy lids;
I hear again the voice that bids
The dreamer leave his dream midway
For larger hopes and graver fears:
Life greatens in these later years,
The century's aloe flowers to-day!

Yet, haply, in some lull of life,
Some Truce of God which breaks its strife,
The worldling's eyes shall gather dew,
 Dreaming in throngful city ways
Of winter joys his boyhood knew;
And dear and early friends – the few
Who yet remain – shall pause to view
 These Flemish pictures of old days;
Sit with me by the homestead hearth,
And stretch the hands of memory forth
 To warm them at the wood-fire's blaze!
And thanks untraced to lips unknown
Shall greet me like the odors blown
From unseen meadows newly mown,
Or lilies floating in some pond,
Wood-fringed, the wayside gaze beyond;
The traveller owns the grateful sense

Of sweetness near, he knows not whence,
And, pausing, takes with forehead bare
The benediction of the air.

My Playmate

The pines were dark on Ramoth hill,
　Their song was soft and low;
The blossoms in the sweet May wind
　Were falling like the snow.

The blossoms drifted at our feet,
　The orchard birds sang clear;
The sweetest and the saddest day
　It seemed of all the year.

For, more to me than birds or flowers,
　My playmate left her home,
And took with her the laughing spring,
　The music and the bloom.

She kissed the lips of kith and kin,
　She laid her hand in mine:
What more could ask the bashful boy
　Who fed her father's kine?

She left us in the bloom of May:
　The constant years told o'er
Their seasons with as sweet May morns,
　But she came back no more.

I walk, with noiseless feet, the round
　Of uneventful years;
Still o'er and o'er I sow the spring
　And reap the autumn ears.

She lives where all the golden year
   Her summer roses blow;
The dusky children of the sun
   Before her come and go.

There haply with her jewelled hands
   She smooths her silken gown,—
No more the homespun lap wherein
   I shook the walnuts down.

The wild grapes wait us by the brook,
   The brown nuts on the hill,
And still the May-day flowers make sweet
   The woods of Follymill.

The lilies blossom in the pond,
   The bird builds in the tree,
The dark pines sing on Ramoth hill
   The slow song of the sea.

I wonder if she thinks of them,
   And how the old time seems,—
If ever the pines of Ramoth wood
   Are sounding in her dreams.

I see her face, I hear her voice:
   Does she remember mine?
And what to her is now the boy
   Who fed her father's kine?

What cares she that the orioles build
   For other eyes than ours,—
That other hands with nuts are filled,
   And other laps with flowers?

O playmate in the golden time!
　Our mossy seat is green,
Its fringing violets blossom yet,
　The old trees o'er it lean.

The winds so sweet with birch and fern
　A sweeter memory blow;
And there in spring the veeries sing
　The song of long ago.

And still the pines of Ramoth wood
　Are moaning like the sea,—
The moaning of the sea of change
　Between myself and thee!

The Haschish

Of all that Orient lands can vaunt
　Of marvels with our own competing,
The strangest is the Haschish plant,
　And what will follow on its eating.

What pictures to the taster rise,
　Of Dervish or of Almeh dances!
Of Eblis, or of Paradise,
　Set all aglow with Houri glances!

The poppy visions of Cathay,
　The heavy beer-trance of the Suabian;
The wizard lights and demon play
　Of nights Walpurgis and Arabian!

The Mollah and the Christian dog
   Change places in mad metempsychosis;
The Muezzin climbs the synagogue,
   The Rabbi shakes his beard at Moses!

The Arab by his desert well
   Sits choosing from some Caliph's daughters,
And hears his single camel's bell
   Sound welcome to his regal quarters.

The Koran's reader makes complaint
   Of Shitan dancing on and off it;
The robber offers alms, the saint
   Drinks Tokay and blasphemes the Prophet.

Such scenes that Eastern plant awakes;
   But we have one ordained to beat it.
The Haschish of the West, which makes
   Or fools or knaves of all who eat it.

The preacher eats, and straight appears
   His Bible in a new translation;
Its angels negro overseers,
   And Heaven itself a snug plantation!

The man of peace, about whose dreams
   The sweet millennial angels cluster,
Tastes the mad weed, and plots and schemes,
   A raving Cuban filibuster!

The noisiest Democrat, with ease,
   It turns to Slavery's parish beadle;
The shrewdest statesman eats and sees
   Due southward point the polar needle.

The Judge partakes, and sits erelong
  Upon his bench a railing blackguard;
Decides off-hand that right is wrong,
  And reads the ten commandments backward.

O potent plant! so rare a taste
  Has never Turk or Gentoo gotten;
The hempen Haschish of the East
  Is powerless to our Western Cotton!

Barbara Frietchie

This poem was written in strict conformity to the account of the incident
as I had it from respectable and trustworthy sources. It has since been
the subject of a good deal of conflicting testimony, and the story was
probably incorrect in some of its details. It is admitted by all that
Barbara Frietchie was no myth, but a worthy and highly esteemed
gentlewoman, intensely loyal and a hater of the Slavery Rebellion,
holding her Union flag sacred and keeping it with her Bible; that when
the Confederates halted before her house, and entered her dooryard, she
denounced them in vigorous language, shook her cane in their faces, and
drove them out; and when General Burnside's troops followed close upon
Jackson's, she waved her flag and cheered them. It is stated that May
Quantrell, a brave and loyal lady in another part of the city, did wave her
flag in sight of the Confederates. It is possible that there has been a
blending of the two incidents.

Up from the meadows rich with corn,
Clear in the cool September morn.

The clustered spires of Frederick stand
Green-walled by the hills of Maryland.

Round about them orchards seep,
Apple and peach tree fruited deep.

Fair as the garden of the Lord
To the eyes of the famished rebel horde,

On that pleasant morn of the early fall
When Lee marched over the mountain-wall;

Over the mountains winding down,
Horse and foot, into Frederick town.

Forty flags with their silver stars,
Forty flags with their crimson bars,

Flapped in the morning wind: the sun
Of noon looked down, and saw not one.

Up rose old Barbara Frietchie then,
Bowed with her fourscore years and ten;

Bravest of all in Frederick town,
She took up the flag the men hauled down;

In her attic window the staff she set,
To show that one heart was loyal yet.

Up the street came the rebel tread,
Stonewall Jackson riding ahead.

Under his slouched hat left and right
He glanced; the old flag met his sight.

'Halt!' – the dust-brown ranks stood fast.
'Fire!' – out blazed the rifle-blast.

It shivered the window, pane and sash;
It rent the banner with seam and gash.

Quick, as it fell, from the broken staff
Dame Barbara snatched the silken scarf,

She leaned far out on the window-sill,
And shook it forth with a royal will.

'Shoot, if you must, this old gray head,
But spare your country's flag,' she said.

A shade of sadness, a blush of shame,
Over the face of the leader came;

The nobler nature within him stirred
To life at that woman's deed and word;

'Who touches a hair of yon gray head
Dies like a dog! March on!' he said.

All day long through Frederick street
Sounded the tread of marching feet:

All day long that free flag tost
Over the heads of the rebel host.

Ever its torn folds rose and fell
On the loyal winds that loved it well;

And through the hill-gaps sunset light
Shone over it with a warm good-night.

Barbara Frietchie's work is o'er,
And the Rebel rides on his raids no more.

Honor to her! and let a tear
Fall, for her sake, on Stonewall's bier.

Over Barbara Frietchie's grave,
Flag of Freedom and Union, wave!

Peace and order and beauty draw
Round thy symbol of light and law;

And ever the stars above look down
On thy stars below in Frederick town!

In the 'Old South'

She came and stood in the Old South Church,
    A wonder and a sign,
With a look the old-time sibyls wore,
    Half-crazed and half-divine.

Save the mournful sackcloth about her wound,
    Unclothed as the primal mother,
With limbs that trembled and eyes that blazed
    With a fire she dare not smother.

Loose on her shoulders fell her hair,
    With sprinkled ashes gray;
She stood in the broad aisle strange and weird
    As a soul at the judgment day.

And the minister paused in his sermon's midst,
    And the people held their breath,
For these were the words the maiden spoke
    Through lips as the lips of death:

'Thus saith the Lord, with equal feet
    All men my courts shall tread,
And priest and ruler no more shall eat
    My people up like bread!

'Repent! repent! ere the Lord shall speak
  In thunder and breaking seals!
Let all souls worship Him in the way
  His light within reveals.'

She shook the dust from her naked feet,
  And her sackcloth closer drew,
And into the porch of the awe-hushed church
  She passed like a ghost from view.

They whipped her away at the tail o' the cart
  Through half the streets of the town,
But the words she uttered that day nor fire
  Could burn nor water drown.

And now the aisles of the ancient church
  By equal feet are trod,
And the bell that swings in its belfry rings
  Freedom to worship God!

And now whenever a wrong is done
  It thrills the conscious walls;
The stone from the basement cries aloud
  And the beam from the timber calls.

There are steeple-houses on every hand,
  And pulpits that bless and ban,
And the Lord will not grudge the single church
  That is set apart for man.

For in two commandments are all the law
  And the prophets under the sun,
And the first is last and the last is first,
  And the twain are verily one.

So long as Boston shall Boston be,
  And her bay-tides rise and fall,
Shall freedom stand in the Old South Church
  And plead for the rights of all!

First-Day Thoughts

In calm and cool and silence, once again
  I find my old accustomed place among
  My brethren, where, perchance, no human tongue
  Shall utter words; where never hymn is sung,
  Nor deep-toned organ blown, nor censer swung,
Nor dim light falling through the pictured pane!
There, syllabled by silence, let me hear
The still small voice which reached the prophet's ear;
Read in my heart a still diviner law
Than Israel's leader on his table saw!
There let me strive with each besetting sin
  Recall my wandering fancies, and restrain
  The sore disquiet of a restless brain;
  And, as the path of duty is made plain,
May grace be given that I may walk therein,
  Not like the hireling, for his selfish gain,
With backward glances and reluctant tread,
Making a merit of his coward dread,
  But, cheerful, in the light around me thrown,
  Walking as one to pleasant service led;
  Doing God's will as if it were my own,
Yet trusting not in mine, but in His strength alone!

Maud Muller

Maud Muller on a summer's day
Raked the meadow sweet with hay.

Beneath her torn hat glowed the wealth
Of simple beauty and rustic health.

Singing, she wrought, and her merry glee
The mock-bird echoed from his tree.

But when she glanced to the far-off town,
White from its hill-slope looking down,

The sweet song died, and a vague unrest
And a nameless longing filled her breast,—

A wish that she hardly dared to own,
For something better than she had known.

The Judge rode slowly down the lane,
Smoothing his horse's chestnut mane.

He drew his bridle in the shade
Of the apple-trees, to greet the maid,

And asked a draught from the spring that flowed
Through the meadow across the road.

She stooped where the cool spring bubbled up,
And filled for him her small tin cup,

And blushed as she gave it, looking down
On her feet so bare, and her tattered gown.

'Thanks!' said the Judge; 'a sweeter draught
From a fairer hand was never quaffed.'

He spoke of the grass and flowers and trees,
Of the singing birds and the humming bees;

Then talked of the haying, and wondered whether
The cloud in the west would bring foul weather.

And Maud forgot her brier-torn gown,
And her graceful ankles bare and brown;

And listened, while a pleased surprise
Looked from her long-lashed hazel eyes.

At last, like one who for delay
Seeks a vain excuse, he rode away.

Maud Muller looked and sighed: 'Ah me!
That I the Judge's bride might be!

'He would dress me up in silks so fine,
And praise and toast me at his wine.

'My father should wear a broadcloth coat;
My brother should sail a painted boat.

'I'd dress my mother so grand and gay,
And the baby should have a new toy each day.

'And I'd feed the hungry and clothe the poor,
And all should bless me who left our door.'

The Judge looked back as he climbed the hill,
And saw Maud Muller standing still.

'A form more fair, a face more sweet,
Ne'er hath it been my lot to meet.

'And her modest answer and graceful air
Show her wise and good as she is fair.

'Would she were mine, and I today,
Like her, a harvester of hay;

'No doubtful balance of right and wrongs,
Nor weary lawyers with endless tongues,

'But low of cattle and song of birds,
And health and quiet and loving words.'

But he thought of his sisters, proud and cold,
And his mother, vain of her rank and gold.

So, closing his heart, the Judge rode on,
And Maud was left in the field alone.

But the lawyers smiled that afternoon,
When he hummed in court an old love-tune;

And the young girl mused beside the well
Till the rain on the unraked clover fell.

He wedded a wife of richest dower,
Who lived for fashion, as he for power.

Yet oft, in his marble hearth's bright glow,
He watched a picture come and go;

And sweet Maud Muller's hazel eyes
Looked out in their innocent surprise.

Oft, when the wine in his glass was red,
He longed for the wayside well instead;

And closed his eyes on his garnished rooms
To dream of meadows and clover-blooms.

And the proud man sighed, with a secret pain,
'Ah, that I were free again!

'Free as when I rode that day,
Where the barefoot maiden raked her hay.'

She wedded a man unlearned and poor,
And many children played round her door.

But care and sorrow, and childbirth pain,
Left their traces on heart and brain.

And oft, when the summer sun shone hot
On the new-mown hay in the meadow lot,

And she heard the little spring brook fall
Over the roadside, through the wall,

In the shade of the apple-tree again
She saw a rider draw his rein;

And, gazing down with timid grace,
She felt his pleased eyes read her face.

Sometimes her narrow kitchen walls
Stretched away into stately halls;

The weary wheel to a spinnet turned,
The tallow candle an astral burned,

And for him who sat by the chimney lug,
Dozing and grumbling o'er pipe and mug,

A manly form at her side she saw,
And joy was duty and love was law.

Then she took up her burden of life again,
Saying only, 'It might have been.'

Alas for maiden, alas for Judge,
For rich repiner and household drudge!

God pity them both! and pity us all,
Who vainly the dreams of youth recall.

For of all sad words of tongue or pen,
The saddest are these: 'It might have been!'

Ah, well! for us all some sweet hope lies
Deeply buried from human eyes;

And, in the hereafter, angels may
Roll the stone from its grave away!

The Homestead

Against the wooded hills it stands,
    Ghosts of a dead home, staring through
Its broken lights on wasted lands
    Where old-time harvests grew.

Unploughed, unsown, by scythe unshorn,
    The poor, forsaken farm-fields lie,
Once rich and rife with golden corn
    And pale green breadths of rye.

Of healthful herb and flower bereft,
    The garden plot no housewife keeps
Through weeds and tangle only left,
    The snake, its tenant, creeps.

A lilac spray, once blossom-clad,
 Sways bare before the empty rooms;
Beside the roofless porch a sad
 Pathetic red rose blooms.

His track, in mould and dust of drouth,
 On floor and hearth the squirrel leaves,
And in the fireless chimney's mouth
 His web the spider weaves.

The leaning barn, about to fall,
 Resounds no more on husking eves;
No cattle low in yard or stall,
 No thresher beats his sheaves.

So sad, so drear! It seems almost
 Some haunting Presence makes its sign;
That down yon shadowy lane some ghost
 Might drive his spectral kine!

O home so desolate and lorn!
 Did all thy memories die with thee?
Were any wed, were any born,
 Beneath this low roof-tree?

Whose axe the wall of forest broke,
 And let the waiting sunshine through?
What good-wife sent the earliest smoke
 Up the great chimney flue?

Did rustic lovers hither come?
 Did maidens, swaying back and forth
In rhythmic grace, at wheel and loom,
 Make light their toil with mirth?

Did child feet patter on the stair?
  Did boyhood frolic in the snow?
Did grey age, in her elbow chair,
  Knit, rocking to and fro?

The murmuring brook, the sighing breeze,
  The pine's slow whisper, cannot tell;
Low mounds beneath the hemlock-trees
  Keep the home-secrets well.

Cease, mother-land, to fondly boast
  Of sons far off who strive and thrive,
Forgetful that each swarming host
  Must leave an emptier hive!

O wanderers from ancestral soil,
  Leave noisome mill and chaffering store;
Gird up your loins for sturdier toil,
  And build the home once more.

Come back to bayberry-scented slopes,
  And fragrant fern, and ground-mat vine;
Breathe airs blown over holt and copse
  Sweet with black birch and pine.

What matter if the gains are small
  That life's essential wants supply?
Your homestead's title gives you all
  That idle wealth can buy.

All that the many-dollared crave,
  The brick-walled slaves of 'Change and mart,
Lawns, trees, fresh air, and flowers you have,
  More dear for lack of art.

Your own sole masters, freedom-willed,
  With none to bid you go or stay,
Till the old fields your fathers tilled,
  As manly men as they!

With skill that spares your toiling hands,
  And chemic aid that science brings,
Reclaim the waste and outworn lands,
  And reign thereon as kings!

The River Path

No bird-song floated down the hill,
The tangled bank below was still;

No rustle from the birchen stem,
No ripple from the water's hem.

The dusk of twilight round us grew,
We felt the falling of the dew;

For, from us, ere the day was done,
The wooded hills shut out the sun.

But on the river's farther side
We saw the hill-tops glorified,—

A tender glow, exceeding fair,
A dream of day without its glare.

With us the damp, the chill, the gloom;
With them the sunset's rosy bloom;

While dark, through willowy vistas seen,
The river rolled in shade between.

From out the darkness where we trod,
We gazed upon those hills of God,

Whose light seemed not of moon or sun.
We spake not, but our thought was one.

We paused, as if from that bright shore
Beckoned our dear ones gone before;

And stilled our beating hearts to hear
The voices lost to mortal ear!

Sudden our pathway turned from night;
The hills swung open to the light;

Through their green gates the sunshine showed,
A long, slant splendour downward flowed.

Down glade and glen and bank it rolled;
It bridged the shaded stream with gold;

And, borne on piers of mist, allied
The shadowy with the sunlit side!

'So,' prayed we, "when our feet draw near
The river dark with mortal fear,

'And the night cometh chill with dew,
O Father! let Thy light break through!

'So let the hills of doubt divide,
So bridge with faith the sunless tide!

'So let the eyes that fail on earth
On Thy eternal hills look forth;

'And in Thy beckoning angels know
The dear ones whom we loved below!'

Abraham Davenport

In the old days (a custom laid aside
With breeches and cocked hats) the people sent
Their wisest men to make the public laws.
And so, from a brown homestead, where the Sound
Drinks the small tribute of the Mianas,
Waved over by the woods of Rippowam,
And hallowed by pure lives and tranquil deaths,
Stamford sent up to the councils of the State
Wisdom and grace in Abraham Davenport.

'Twas on a May-day of the far old year
Seventeen hundred eighty, that there fell
Over the bloom and sweet life of the Spring,
Over the fresh earth and the heaven of noon,
A horror of great darkness, like the night
In day of which the Norland sagas tell,—
The Twilight of the Gods. The low-hung sky
Was black with ominous clouds, save where its rim
Was fringed with a dull glow, like that which climbs
The crater's sides from the red hell below.
Birds ceased to sing, and all the barnyard fowls
Roosted; the cattle at the pasture bars
Lowed, and looked homeward; bats on leathern wings
Flitted abroad; the sounds of labor died;
Men prayed, and women wept; all ears grew sharp
To hear the doom-blast of the trumpet shatter
The black sky, that the dreadful face of Christ
Might look from the rent clouds, not as he looked
A loving guest at Bethany, but stern
As Justice and inexorable Law.

Meanwhile in the old State House, dim as ghosts,
Sat the lawgivers of Connecticut,
Trembling beneath their legislative robes.
'It is the Lord's Great Day! Let us adjourn,'
Some said; and then, as if with one accord,
All eyes were turned to Abraham Davenport.
He rose, slow cleaving with his steady voice
The intolerable hush. 'This well may be
The Day of Judgment which the world awaits;
But be it so or not, I only know
My present duty, and my Lord's command
To occupy till He come. So at the post
Where He hath set me in His providence,
I choose, for one, to meet Him face to face,—
No faithless servant frightened from my task,
But ready when the Lord of the harvest calls;
And therefore, with all reverence, I would say,
Let God do His work, we will see to ours.
Bring in the candles.' And they brought them in.

Then by the flaring lights the Speaker read,
Albeit with husky voice and shaking hands,
An act to amend an act to regulate
The shad and alewive fisheries. Whereupon
Wisely and well spake Abraham Davenport,
Straight to the question, with no figures of speech
Save the ten Arab signs, yet not without
The shrewd dry humor natural to the man:
His awe-struck colleagues listening all the while,
Between the pauses of his argument,
To hear the thunder of the wrath of God
Break from the hollow trumpet of the cloud.

And there he stands in memory to this day,
Against the background of unnatural dark,
Erect, self-poised, a rugged face, half seen
A witness to the ages as they pass,
That simple duty hath no place for fear.

What the Birds Said

The birds against the April wind
   Flew northward, singing as they flew;
They sang, 'The land we leave behind
   Has swords for corn-blades, blood for dew.'

'O wild-birds, flying from the South,
   What saw and heard ye, gazing down?'
'We saw the mortar's upturned mouth,
   The sickened camp, the blazing town!

'Beneath the bivouac's starry lamps,
   We saw your march-worn children die;
In shrouds of moss, in cypress swamps,
   We saw your dead uncoffined lie.

'We heard the starving prisoner's sighs,
   And saw, from line and trench, your sons
Follow our flight with home-sick eyes
   Beyond the battery's smoking guns.'

'And heard and saw ye only wrong
   And pain,' I cried, 'O wing-worn flocks?'
'We heard,' they sang, 'the freedman's song,
   The crash of Slavery's broken locks!

'We saw from new, uprising states
   The treason-nursing mischief spurned,
As, crowding Freedom's ample gates,
   The long-estranged and lost returned.

'O'er dusky faces, seamed and old,
  And hands horn-hard with unpaid toil,
With hope in every rustling fold,
  We saw your star-dropt flag uncoil.

'And struggling up through sounds accursed,
  A grateful murmur clomb the air;
A whisper scarcely heard at first,
  It filled the listening heavens with prayer.

'And sweet and far, as from a star,
  Replied a voice which shall not cease,
Till, drowning all the noise of war,
  It sings the blessed song of peace!'

So to me, in a doubtful day
  Of chill and slowly greening spring,
Low stooping from the cloudy gray,
  The wild-birds sang or seemed to sing.

They vanished in the misty air,
  The song went with them in their flight;
But lo! they left the sunset fair,
  And in the evening there was light.

My Triumph

The autumn-time has come;
On woods that dream of bloom,
And over purpling vines,
The low sun fainter shines.

The aster-flower is failing,
The hazel's gold is paling;
Yet overhead more near
The eternal stars appear!

And present gratitude
Insures the future's good,
And for the things I see
I trust the things to be;

That in the paths untrod,
And the long days of God,
My feet shall still be led,
My heart be comforted.

O living friends who love me!
O dear ones gone above me!
Careless of other fame,
I leave to you my name.

Hide it from idle praises,
Save it from evil phrases:
Why, when dear lips that spake it
Are dumb, should strangers wake it?

Let the thick curtain fall;
I better know than all
How little I have gained,
How vast the unattained.

Not by the page word-painted
Let life be banned or sainted:
Deeper than written scroll
The colors of the soul.

Sweeter than any sung
My songs that found no tongue;
Nobler than any fact
My wish that failed of act.

Others shall sing the song,
Others shall right the wrong,—
Finish what I begin,
And all I fail of win.

What matter, I or they?
Mine or another's day,
So the right word be said
And life the sweeter made?

Hail to the coming singers!
Hail to the brave light-bringers!
Forward I reach and share
All that they sing and dare.

The airs of heaven blow o'er me;
A glory shines before me
Of what mankind shall be,—
Pure, generous, brave, and free.

A dream of man and woman
Diviner but still human,
Solving the riddle old,
Shaping the Age of Gold!

The love of God and neighbor;
An equal-handed labor;
The richer life, where beauty
Walks hand in hand with duty.

Ring, bells in unreared steeples,
The joy of unborn peoples!
Sound, trumpets far off blown,
Your triumph is my own!

Parcel and part of all,
I keep the festival,
Fore-reach the good to be,
And share the victory.

I feel the earth more sunward,
I join the great march onward,
And take, by faith, while living,
My freehold of thanksgiving.

The Lost Occasion

Some die too late and some too soon,
At early morning, heart of noon,
Or the chill evening twilight. Thou,
Whom the rich heavens did so endow
With eyes of power and Jove's own brow,
With all the massive strength that fills
Thy home-horizon's granite hills,
With rarest gifts of heart and head
From manliest stock inherited,
New England's stateliest type of man,
In port and speech Olympian;
Whom no one met, at first, but took
A second awed and wondering look
(As turned, perchance, the eyes of Greece
On Phidias' unveiled masterpiece);
Whose words in simplest homespun clad,
The Saxon strength of Cædmon's had,
With power reserved at need to reach

The Roman forum's loftiest speech,
Sweet with persuasion, eloquent
In passion, cool in argument,
Or, ponderous, falling on thy foes
As fell the Norse god's hammer blows,
Crushing as if with Talus' flail
Through Error's logic-woven mail,
And failing only when they tried
The adamant of the righteous side,—
Thou, foiled in aim and hope, bereaved
Of old friends, by the new deceived,
Too soon for us, too soon for thee,
Beside thy lonely Northern sea,
Where long and low the marsh-lands spread,
Laid wearily down thy august head.

Thou shouldst have lived to feel below
Thy feet Disunion's fierce upthrow;
The late-sprung mine that underlaid
Thy sad concessions vainly made.
Thou shouldst have seen from Sumter's wall
The star-flag of the Union fall,
And armed rebellion pressing on
The broken lines of Washington!
No stronger voice than thine had then
Called out the utmost might of men,
To make the Union's charter free
And strengthen law by liberty.
How had that stern arbitrament
To thy gray age youth's vigor lent,
Shaming ambition's paltry prize
Before thy disillusioned eyes;
Breaking the spell about thee wound
Like the green withes that Samson bound;
Redeeming in one effort grand,
Thyself and thy imperilled land!

Ah, cruel fate, that closed to thee,
O sleeper by the Northern sea,
The gates of opportunity!
God fills the gaps of human need,
Each crisis brings its word and deed.
Wise men and strong we did not lack;
But still, with memory turning back,
In the dark hours we thought of thee,
And thy lone grave beside the sea.

Above that grave the east winds blow,
And from the marsh-lands drifting slow
The sea-fog comes, with evermore
The wave-wash of a lonely shore,
And sea-bird's melancholy cry,
As Nature fain would typify
The sadness of a closing scene,
The loss of that which should have been.
But, where thy native mountains bare
Their foreheads to diviner air,
Fit emblem of enduring fame,
One lofty summit keeps thy name.
For thee the cosmic forces did
The rearing of that pyramid,
The prescient ages shaping with
Fire, flood, and frost thy monolith.
Sunrise and sunset lay thereon
With hands of light their benison,
The stars of midnight pause to set
Their jewels in its coronet.
And evermore that mountain mass
Seems climbing from the shadowy pass
To light, as if to manifest
Thy nobler self, thy life at best!

The Summons

My ear is full of summer sounds,
  Of summer sights my languid eye;
Beyond the dusty village bounds
I loiter in my daily rounds,
  And in the noon-time shadows lie.

I hear the wild bee wind his horn,
  The bird swings on the ripened wheat,
The long green lances of the corn
Are tilting in the winds of morn,
  The locust shrills his song of heat.

Another sound my spirit hears,
  A deeper sound that drowns them all,—
A call of pleading choked with tears,
The call of human hopes and fears,
  The Macedonian cry to Paul!

The storm-bell rings, the trumpet blows;
  I know the word and countersign;
Wherever Freedom's vanguard goes,
Where stand or fall her friends or foes,
  I know the place that should be mine.

Shamed be the hands that idly fold,
  And lips that woo the reeds accord,
When laggard Time the hour has tolled
For true with false and new with old
  To fight the battles of the Lord!

O brothers! blest by partial Fate
  With power to match the will and deed,
To him your summons comes too late
Who sinks beneath his armour's weight,
  And has no answer but God-speed!

The Last Walk in Autumn

I

O'er the bare woods, whose outstretched hands
  Plead with the leaden heavens in vain,
I see, beyond the valley lands,
  The sea's long level dim with rain.
Around me all things, stark and dumb,
  Seem praying for the snows to come,
And, for the summer bloom and greenness gone,
With winter's sunset lights and dazzling morn atone.

II

Along the river's summer walk,
  The withered tufts of asters nod;
And trembles on its arid stalk
  The hoar plume of the golden rod.
And on a ground of sombre fir,
  And azure-studded juniper,
The silver birch its buds of purple shows,
And scarlet berries tell where bloomed the sweet
    wild-rose!

III

With mingled sound of horns and bells,
  A far-heard clang, the wild geese fly,
Storm-sent, from Arctic moors and fells,
  Like a great arrow through the sky,
Two dusky lines converged in one,
  Chasing the southward-flying sun;
While the brave snow-bird and the hardy jay
Call to them from the pines, as if to bid them stay.

IV

I passed this way a year ago:
  The wind blew south; the noon of day
Was warm as June's; and save that snow
  Flecked the low mountains far away,
And that the vernal-seeming breeze
Mocked faded grass and leafless trees,
I might have dreamed of summer as I lay,
Watching the fallen leaves with the soft wind at play.

V

Since then, the winter blasts have piled
  The white pagodas of the snow
On these rough slopes, and strong and wild,
  Yon river, in its overflow
Of spring-time rain and sun, set free,
Crashed with its ices to the sea;
And over these grey fields, then green and gold,
The summer corn has waved, the thunder's organ rolled.

VI

Rich gift of God! A year of time!
  What pomp of rise and shut of day,
What hues wherewith our Northern clime
  Makes autumn's dropping woodlands gay,
What airs outblown from ferny dells,
And clover-bloom and sweetbrier smells,
What songs of brooks and birds, what fruit and flowers,
Green woods and moonlit snows, have in its round been
    ours!

VII

I know not how, in other lands,
  The changing seasons come and go;
What splendours fall on Syrian sands,
  What purple lights on Alpine snow!
Nor how the pomp of sunrise waits
On Venice at her watery gates;
A dream alone to me is Arno's vale,
And the Alhambra's halls are but a traveller's tale.

VIII

Yet, on life's current, he who drifts
  Is one with him who rows or sails;
And he who wanders widest lifts
  No more of beauty's jealous veils
Than he who from his doorway sees
The miracle of flowers and trees,
Feels the warm Orient in the noonday air,
And from cloud minaret hears the sunset call to prayer!

IX

The eye may well be glad, that looks
  Where Pharpar's fountains rise and fall;
But he who sees his native brooks
  Laugh in the sun, has seen them all.
The marble palaces of Ind
Rise round him in the snow and wind;
From his lone sweetbrier Persian Hafiz smiles,
And Rome's cathedral awe is in his woodland aisles.

X

And thus it is my fancy blends
  The near at hand and far and rare;
And while the same horizon bends
  Above the silver-sprinkled hair
Which flashed the light of morning skies
On childhood's wonder-lifted eyes,
Within its round of sea and sky and field,
Earth wheels with all her zones, the Kosmos stands
    revealed.

XI

And thus the sick man on his bed,
  The toiler to his tasks-work bound,
Behold their prison-walls outspread,
  Their clipped horizon widen round!
While freedom-giving fancy waits,
  Like Peter's angel at the gates,
The power is theirs to baffle care and pain,
To bring the lost world back, and make it theirs again!

XII

What lack of goodly company,
  When masters of the ancient lyre
Obey my call, and trace for me
  Their words of mingled tears and fire!
I talk with Bacon, grave and wise,
  I read the world with Pascal's eyes;
And priest and sage, with solemn brows austere,
And poets, garland-bound, the Lords of Thought, draw
    near.

XIII

Methinks, O friend, I hear thee say,
   In vain the human heart we mock;
Bring living guests who love the day,
   Not ghosts who fly at crow of cock!
The herbs we share with flesh and blood
Are better than ambrosial food,
With laurelled shades.' I grant it, nothing loath,
But doubly blest is he who can partake of both.

XIV

He who might Plato's banquet grace,
   Have I not seen before me sit,
And watched his puritanic face,
   With more than Eastern wisdom lit?
Shrewd mystic! who, upon the back
Of his Poor Richard's Almanack,
Writing the Sufi's song, the Gentoo's dream,
Links Menu's age of thought to Fulton's age of steam.

XV

Here too, of answering love secure,
   Have I not welcomed to my hearth
The gentle pilgrim troubadour,
   Whose songs have girdled half the earth;
Whose pages, like the magic mat
Whereon the Eastern lover sat,
Have borne me over Rhineland's purple vines,
And Nubia's tawny sands, and Phrygia's mountain pines!

XVI

And he, who to the lettered wealth
  Of ages adds the lore unpriced,
The wisdom and the moral health,
  The ethics of the school of Christ;
The statesman to his holy trust,
  As the Athenian archon, just,
Struck down, exiled like him for truth alone,
Has he not graced my home with beauty all his own?

XVII

What greetings smile, what farewells wave,
  What loved ones enter and depart!
The good, the beautiful, the brave,
  The Heaven-lent treasures of the heart!
How conscious seems the frozen sod
And beechen slope whereon they trod!
The oak-leaves rustle, and the dry grass bends
Beneath the shadowy feet of lost or absent friends.

XVIII

Then ask not why to these bleak hills
  I cling as clings the tufted moss,
To bear the winter's lingering chills,
  The mocking spring's perpetual loss.
I dream of lands where summer smiles,
  And soft winds blow from spicy isles,
But scarce would Ceylon's breath of flowers be sweet,
Could I not feel thy soil, New England, at my feet!

XIX

At times I long for gentler skies,
    And bathe in dreams of softer air,
But homesick tears would fill the eyes
    That saw the Cross without the Bear.
The pine must whisper to the palm,
    The north-wind break the tropic calm;
And with the dreamy languor of the Line,
The North's keen virtue blend, and strength to beauty
    join.

XX

Better to stem with heart and hand
    The roaring tide of life, than lie,
Unmindful, on its flowery strand,
    Of God's occasions drifting by!
Better with naked nerve to bear
    The needles of this goading air,
Than, in the lap of sensual ease, forgo
The godlike power to do, the godlike aim to know.

XXI

Home of my heart! to me more fair
    Than gay Versailles or Windsor's halls,
The painted, shingly town-house where
    The freeman's vote for Freedom falls!
The simple roof where prayer is made,
    Than Gothic groin and colonnade;
The living temple of the heart of man,
Than Rome's sky-mocking vault, or many-spired Milan!

XXII

More dear thy equal village schools,
  Where rich and poor the Bible read,
Than classic halls where Priestcraft rules,
  And Learning wears the chains of Creed;
Thy glad Thanksgiving, gathering in
The scattered sheaves of home and kin,
Than the mad licence following Lenten pains,
Or holidays of slaves who laugh and dance in chains.

XXIII

And sweet homes nestle in these dales,
  And perch along these wooded swells;
And, blest beyond Arcadian vales,
  They hear the sound of Sabbath bells!
Here dwells no perfect man sublime,
Nor woman winged before her time,
But with the faults and follies of the race,
Old home-bred virtues hold their not unhonoured place.

XXIV

Here manhood struggles for the sake
  Of mother, sister, daughter, wife,
The graces and the loves which make
  The music of the march of life;
And woman, in her daily round
Of duty, walks on holy ground.
No unpaid menial tills the soil, nor here
Is the bad lesson learned at human rights to sneer.

XXV

Then let the icy north-wind blow
   The trumpets of the coming storm,
To arrowy sleet and blinding snow
   Yon slanting lines of rain transform.
Young hearts shall hail the drifted cold,
   As gaily as I did of old;
And I, who watch them through the frosty pane,
Unenvious, live in them my boyhood o'er again.

XXVI

And I will trust that He who heeds
   The life that hides in mead and wold,
Who hangs yon alder's crimson beads,
   And stains these mosses green and gold,
Will still, as He hath done, incline
   His gracious care to me and mine;
Grant what we ask aright, from wrong debar,
And, as the earth grows dark, make brighter every star!

XXVII

I have not seen, I may not see,
   My hopes for man take form in fact,
But God will give the victory
   In due time; in that faith I act.
And he who sees the future sure,
   The baffling present may endure,
And bless, meanwhile, the unseen Hand that leads
The heart's desires beyond the halting step of deeds.

XXVIII

And thou, my song, I send thee forth,
  Where harsher songs of mine have flown;
Go, find a place at home and hearth
  Where'er thy singer's name is known;
Revive for him the kindly thought
Of friends; and they who love him not,
Touched by some strain of thine, perchance may take
The hands he proffers all, and thank him for thy sake.

The Lakeside

The shadows round the inland sea
  Are deepening into night;
Slow up the slopes of Ossipee
  They chase the lessening light.
Tired of the long day's blinding heat,
  I rest my languid eye,
Lake of the Hills! where, cool and sweet,
  Thy sunset waters lie!

Along the sky, in wavy lines,
  O'er isle and reach and bay,
Green-belted with eternal pines,
  The mountains stretch away.
Below, the maple masses sleep
  Where shore with water blends,
While midway on the tranquil deep
  The evening light descends.

So seemed it when yon hill's red crown,
  Of old, the Indian trod,
And, through the sunset air looked down
  Upon the 'Smile of God.'*
* Winnipiseogee: 'Smile of the Great Spirit.'

To him of light and shade the laws
   No forest sceptic taught;
Their living and eternal Cause
   His truer instincts sought.

He saw these mountains in the light
   Which now across them shines;
This lake, in summer sunset bright,
   Walled round with sombering pines.
God near him seemed; from earth and skies
   His loving voice he heard,
As, face to face, in Paradise,
   Man stood before the Lord.

Thanks, O our Father! that, like him,
   Thy tender love I see,
In radiant hill and woodland dim,
   Amd tinted sunset sea.
For not in mockery dost Thou fill
   Our earth with light and grace;
Thou hid'st no dark and cruel will
   Behind Thy smiling face!

Democracy

'All things whatsoever ye would that men should do
to you, do ye even so to them.'—*Matthew* vii. 12.

Breaker of Slavery's chain and rod,
The foe of all which pains the sight,
   Or wounds the generous ear of God!

Beautiful yet thy temples rise,
  Though there profaning gifts are thrown;
And fires unkindled of the skies
  Are glaring round thy altar-stone.

Still sacred,—though thy name be breathed
  By those whose hearts thy truth deride;
And garlands, plucked from thee, are wreathed
  Around the haughty brows of Pride.

Oh, ideal of my boyhood's time!
  The faith in which my father stood,
Even when the sons of Lust and Crime
  Had stained thy peaceful courts with blood!

Still to those courts my footsteps turn,
  For through the mists which darken there,
I see the flame of Freedom burn,—
  The Kebla of the patriot's prayer!

The generous feeling, pure and warm,
  Which owns the rights of *all* divine,—
The pitying heart,—the helping arm,—
  The prompt self-sacrifice,—are thine.

Beneath thy broad, impartial eye,
  How fade the lines of caste and birth!
How equal in their suffering lie
  The groaning multitudes of earth!

Still to a stricken brother true,
  Whatever clime hath nurtured him;
As stooped to heal the wounded Jew
  The worshipper of Gerizim.

By misery unrepelled, unawed
  By pomp or power, thou seest a MAN
In prince or peasant,—slave or lord,—
  Pale priest, or swarthy artisan.

Through all disguise, form, place, or name,
  Beneath the flaunting robes of sin,
Through poverty and squalid shame,
  Thou lookest on *the man* within.

On man, as man, retaining yet,
  Howe'er debased, and soiled, and dim,
The crown upon his forehead set,—
  The immortal gift of God to him.

And there is reverence in thy look;
  For that frail form which mortals wear
The Spirit of the Holiest took,
  And veiled His perfect brightness there.

Not from the shallow babbling fount
  Of vain philosophy thou art;
He who of old on Syria's mount
  Thrilled, warmed, by turns, the listener's heart.

In holy words which cannot die,
  In thoughts which angels leaned to know,
Proclaimed thy message from on high,—
  Thy mission to a world of woe.

That voice's echo hath not died!
  From the blue lake of Galilee,
And Tabor's lonely mountain-side,
  It calls a struggling world to thee.

Thy name and watchword o'er this land
  I hear in every breeze that stirs,
And round a thousand altars stand
  Thy banded party worshippers.

Not to these altars of a day,
  At party's call, my gift I bring:
But on thy olden shrine I lay
  A freeman's dearest offering:

The voiceless utterance of his will,—
  His pledge to Freedom and to Truth,
That manhood's heart remembers still
  The homage of his generous youth.

The Battle Autumn of 1862

The flags of war like storm-birds fly,
  The charging trumpets blow;
Yet rolls no thunder in the sky,
  No earthquake strives below.

And calm and patient, Nature keeps
  Her ancient promise well,
Though o'er her bloom and greenness sweeps
  The battle's breath of hell.

And still she walks in golden hours
  Through harvest-happy farms,
And still she wears her fruits and flowers
  Like jewels on her arms.

What mean the gladness of the plain,
 This joy of eve and morn,
The mirth that shakes the beard of grain
 And yellow locks of corn?

Ah! eyes may well be full of tears,
 And hearts with hate are hot;
But even-paced come round the years,
 And Nature changes not.

She meets with smiles our bitter grief,
 With songs our groans of pain;
She mocks with tint of flower and leaf
 The war-field's crimson stain.

Still, in the cannon's pause, we hear
 Her sweet thanksgiving-psalm;
Too near to God for doubt or fear,
 She shares the eternal calm.

She knows the seed lies safe below
 The fires that blast and burn;
For all the tears of blood we sow
 She waits the rich return.

She sees with clearer eye than ours
 The good of suffering born,—
The hearts that blossosm like her flowers,
 And ripen like her corn.

Oh, give to us, in times like these,
 The vision of her eyes;
And make her fields and fruited trees
 Our golden prophecies!

Oh, give to us her finer ear!
  Above this stormy din,
We too would hear the bells of cheer
  Ring peace and freedom in.

Stanzas for the Times

Is this the land our fathers loved,
  The freedom which they toiled to win?
Is this the soil whereon they moved?
  Are these the graves they slumber in?
Are *we* the sons by whom are borne
The mantles which the dead have worn?

And shall we crouch above these graves,
  With craven soul and fettered lip?
Yoke in with marked and branded slaves,
  And tremble at the driver's whip?
Bend to the earth our pliant knees,
And speak—but as our masters please?

Shall outraged Nature cease to feel?
  Shall Mercy's tears no longer flow?
Shall ruffian threats of cord and steel,—
  The dungeon's gloom,—the assassin's blow,
Turn back the spirit roused to save
The Truth, our Country, and the Slave?

Of human skulls that shrine was made,
  Round which the priests of Mexico
Before their loathsome idol prayed;—
  Is Freedom's altar fashioned so?
And must we yield to Freedom's God,
As offering meet, the negro's blood?

Shall tongues be mute, when deeds are wrought
   Which well might shame extremest hell?
Shall freemen lock the indignant thought?
   Shall Pity's bosom cease to swell?
Shall Honour bleed?—shall Truth succumb?
Shall pen, and press, and soul be dumb?

No;—by each spot of haunted ground,
   Where Freedom weeps her children's fall,—
By Plymouth's rock, and Bunker's mound,—
   By Griswold's stained and shattered wall,—
By Warren's ghost,—by Langdon's shade,—
By all the memories of our dead!

By their enlarging souls, which burst
   The bands and fetters round them set,—
By the free Pilgrim spirit nursed
   Within our inmost bosoms, yet,—
By all above, around, below,
Be ours the indignant answer,—No!

No;—guided by our country's laws,
   For truth, and right, and suffering man,
Be ours to strive in Freedom's cause,
   As Christians *may*,—as freemen *can*!
Still pouring on unwilling ears
That truth oppression only fears.

What! shall we guard our neighbour still,
   While woman shrieks beneath his rod,
And while he tramples down at will
   The image of a common God?
Shall watch and ward be round him set,
Of Northern nerve and bayonet?

And shall we know and share with him
  The danger and the growing shame?
And see our Freedom's light grow dim,
  Which should have filled the world with flame?
And, writhing, feel where'er we turn,
A world's reproach around us burn?

Is't not enough that this is borne?
  And asks our haughty neighbour more
Must fetters which his slaves have worn
  Clank round the Yankee farmer's door?
Must he be told, beside his plough,
What he must speak, and when, and how?

Must he be told his freedom stands
  On Slavery's dark foundations strong,—
On breaking hearts and fettered hands,
  On robbery, and crime, and wrong?
That all his fathers taught is vain,—
That Freedom's emblem is the chain?

Its life, its soul, from Slavery drawn?
  False, foul, profane! Go,—teach a well
Of holy Truth from Falsehood born!
  Of Heaven refreshed by airs from Hell!
Of Virtue in the arms of Vice!
Of Demons planting Paradise!

Rail on, then, 'brethren of the South,'—
  Ye shall not hear the truth the less;—
No seal is on the Yankee's mouth,
  No fetter on the Yankee's press!
From our Green Mountains to the sea,
One voice shall thunder,—WE ARE FREE!

The Old Burying-Ground

Our vales are sweet with fern and rose,
  Our hills are maple-crowned;
But not from them our fathers chose
  The village burying-ground.

The dreariest spot in all the land
  To Death they set apart;
With scanty grace from Nature's hand,
  And none from that of Art.

A winding wall of mossy stone,
  Frost-flung and broken, lines
A lonesome acre thinly grown
  With grass and wandering vines.

Without the wall a birch-tree shows
  Its drooped and tasselled head;
Within, a stag-horned sumach grows,
  Fern-leafed, with spikes of red.

There, sheep that graze the neighboring plain
  Like white ghosts come and go,
The farm-horse drags his fetlock chain,
  The cow-bell tinkles slow.

Low moans the river from its bed,
  The distant pines reply;
Like mourners shrinking from the dead,
  They stand apart and sigh.

Unshaded smites the summer sun,
  Unchecked the winter blast;
The school-girl learns the place to shun,
  With glances backward cast.

For thus our fathers testified,—
   That he might read who ran,—
The emptiness of human pride,
   The nothingness of man.

They dared not plant the grave with flowers,
   Nor dress the funeral sod,
Where, with a love as deep as ours,
   They left their dead with God.

The hard and thorny path they kept
   From beauty turned aside;
Nor missed they over those who slept
   The grace to life denied.

Yet still the wilding flowers would blow,
   The golden leaves would fall,
The seasons come, the seasons go,
   And God be good to all.

Above the graves the blackberry hung
   In bloom and green its wreath,
And harebells swung as if they rung
   The chimes of peace beneath.

The beauty Nature loves to share,
   The gifts she hath for all,
The common light, the common air,
   O'ercrept the graveyard's wall.

It knew the glow of eventide,
   The sunrise and the noon,
And glorified and sanctified
   It slept beneath the moon.

With flowers or snow-flakes for its sod,
  Around the seasons ran,
And evermore the love of God
  Rebuked the fear of man.

We dwell with fears on either hand,
  Within a daily strife,
And spectral problems waiting stand
  Before the gates of life.

The doubts we vainly seek to solve,
  The truths we know, are one;
The known and nameless stars revolve
  Around the Central Sun.

And if we reap as we have sown,
  And take the dole we deal,
The law of pain is love alone,
  The wounding is to heal.

Unharmed from change to change we glide,
  We fall as in our dreams;
The far-off terror at our side
  A smiling angel seems.

Secure on God's all-tender heart
  Alike rest great and small;
Why fear to lose our little part,
  When he is pledged for all?

O fearful heart and troubled brain!
  Take hope and strength from this,—
That Nature never hints in vain,
  Nor prophesies amiss.

Her wild birds sing the same sweet stave,
　Her lights and airs are given
Alike to playground and the grave;
　And over both is Heaven.

Ichabod

So fallen! so lost! the light withdrawn
　Which once he wore!
The glory from his gray hairs gone
　Forevermore!

Revile him not, – the Tempter hath
　A snare for all;
And pitying tears, not scorn and wrath,
　Befit his fall!

Oh, dumb be passion's stormy rage,
　When he who might
Have lighted up and led his age,
　Falls back in night.

Scorn! would the angels laugh, to mark
　A bright soul driven,
Fiend-goaded, down the endless dark,
　From hope and heaven!

Let not the land once proud of him
　Insult him now,
Nor brand with deeper shame his dim,
　Dishonoured brow.

But let its humbled sons, instead,
　From sea to lake,
A long lament, as for the dead,
　In sadness make.

Of all we loved and honored, naught
　Save power remains—
A fallen angel's pride of thought,
　Still strong in chains.

All else is gone; from those great eyes
　The soul has fled:
When faith is lost, when honor dies,
　The man is dead!

Then, pay the reverence of old days
　To his dead fame:
Walk backward, with averted gaze,
　And hide the shame!

To Englishmen

You flung your taunt across the wave,
　We bore it as became us,
Well knowing that the fettered slave
Left friendly lips no option, save
　To pity or to blame us.

You scoffed our plea. 'Mere lack of will,
　Not lack of power,' you told us;
We showed our Free-State records; still
You mocked, confounding good and ill,
　Slave haters and slave holders.

We struck at Slavery; to the verge
    Of power and means we checked it;
Lo! – presto, change! its claims you urge,
Send greetings to it o'er the surge,
    And comfort and protect it.

But yesterday you scarce could shake,
    In slave-abhorring rigor,
Our Northern palms for conscience' sake:
Today you clasp the hands that ache
    With 'walloping the nigger!'

O Englishmen! – in hope and creed,
    In blood and tongue our brothers!
We too are heirs of Runnymede;
And Shakspeare's fame and Cromwell's deed
    Are not alone our mother's.

'Thicker than water,' in one rill
    Through centuries of story
Our Saxon blood has flowed, and still
We share with you its good and ill,
    The shadow and the glory.

Joint heirs and kinfolk, leagues of wave
    Nor length of years can part us;
Your right is ours to shrine and grave
The common freehold of the brave,
    The gift of saints and martyrs.

Our very sins and follies teach
    Our kindred frail and human:
We carp at faults with bitter speech,
The while for one unshared by each
    We have a score in common.

We bow the heart, if not the knee,
    To England's Queen, God bless her!
We praised you when your slaves went free;
We seek to unchain ours. Will ye
    Join hands with the oppressor?

And is it Christian England cheers
    The bruiser, not the bruised?
And must she run, despite the tears
And prayers of eighteen hundred years,
    A-muck in Slavery's crusade?

O black disgrace! O shame and loss
    Too deep for tongue to phrase on!
Tear from your flag its holy cross,
And in your van of battle toss
    The pirate's skull-bone blazon!

The Last Eve of Summer

Summer's last sun nigh unto setting shines
    Through yon columnar pines,
And on the deepening shadows of the lawn
    Its golden lines are drawn.

Dreaming of long gone summer days like this,
    Feeling the wind's soft kiss,
Grateful and glad that failing ear and sight
    Have still their old delight,

I sit alone and watch the warm, sweet day
    Lapse tenderly away;
And, wistful, with a feeling of forecast,
    I ask, 'Is this the last?

'Will nevermore for me the seasons run
    Their round, and will the sun
Of ardent summers yet to come forget
    For me to rise and set?'

Thou shouldst be here, or I should be with thee,
    Wherever thou mayst be,
Lips mute, hands clasped, in silences of speech
    Each answering unto each.

For this still hour, this sense of mystery far
    Beyond the evening star,
No words outworn suffice on lip or scroll:
    The soul would fain with soul

Wait, while these few swift-passing days fulfil
    The wise-disposing Will,
And, in the evening as at morning, trust
    The All-Merciful and Just.

The solemn joy that soul-communion feels
    Immortal life reveals;
And human love, its prophecy and sign,
    Interprets love divine.

Come then, in thought, if that alone may be,
    O friend! and bring with thee
Thy calm assurance of transcendent Spheres,
    And the Eternal Years!

EDGAR ALLAN POE
1809-1849

Edgar Allan Poe was the great American Romantic and an important influence on the French symbolists with his conception of poetic unity through mood or emotion, especially melancholy. An unhappy childhood and dissipated interlude at the University of Virginia set the pattern for Poe's brief, violent and tragic life.

Despite distractions and poverty Poe produced a body of outstanding work including classic stories of horror and detection; fine literary criticism; and lyric poetry including 'A Dream within a Dream', 'To Helen', 'The Raven', 'Ulalume' and 'Annabel Lee'.

A Dream within a Dream

Take this kiss upon the brow!
And, in parting from you now,
Thus much let me avow:
You are not wrong, who deem
That my days have been a dream;
Yet if Hope has flown away
In a night, or in a day,
In a vision, or in none,
Is it therefore the less *gone*?
All that we see or seem
Is but a dream within a dream.

I stand amid the roar
Of a surf-tormented shore,
And I hold within my hand
Grains of the golden sand—
How few! yet how they creep
Through my fingers to the deep,
While I weep – while I weep!
O God! can I not grasp
Them with a tighter clasp?
O God! can I not save
One from the pitiless wave?
Is *all* that we see or seem
But a dream within a dream?

To Helen

Helen, thy beauty is to me
  Like those Nicéan barks of yore,
That gently, o'er a perfumed sea,
  The weary, way-worn wanderer bore
  To his own native shore.

On desperate seas long wont to roam,
  Thy hyacinth hair, thy classic face,
Thy Naiad airs have brought me home
  To the glory that was Greece
And the grandeur that was Rome.

Lo! in yon brilliant window-niche
  How statue-like I see thee stand,
  The agate lamp within thy hand!
Ah, Psyche, from the regions which
  Are Holy Land!

The Raven

Once upon a midnight dreary, while I pondered, weak
    and weary,
Over many a quaint and curious volume of forgotten
    lore—
While I nodded, nearly napping, suddenly there came a
    tapping,
As of some one gently rapping, rapping at my chamber
    door.
''T is some visitor,' I muttered, 'tapping at my chamber
    door—
        Only this and nothing more.'

Ah, distinctly I remember it was in the bleak December;
And each separate dying ember wrought its ghost upon
    the floor.
Eagerly I wished the morrow; – vainly I had sought to
    borrow
From my books surcease of sorrow – sorrow for the lost
    Lenore—

For the rare and radiant maiden whom the angels name
    Lenore—
        Nameless *here* for evermore.

And the silken, sad, uncertain rustling of each purple
    curtain
Thrilled me – filled me with fantastic terrors never felt
    before;
So that now, to still the beating of my heart, I stood
    repeating,
''T is some visitor entreating entrance at my chamber
    door—
Some late visitor entreating entrance at my chamber
    door;—
        This it is and nothing more.'

Presently my soul grew stronger; hesitating then no
    longer,
'Sir,' said I, 'or Madam, truly your forgiveness I implore;
But the fact is I was napping, and so gently you came
    rapping,
And so faintly you came tapping, tapping at my chamber
    door,
That I scarce was sure I heard you' – here I opened wide
    the door;—
        Darkness there and nothing more.

Deep into that darkness peering, long I stood there
    wondering, fearing,
Doubting, dreaming dreams no mortal ever dared to
    dream before;
But the silence was unbroken, and the stillness gave no
    token,
And the only word there spoken was the whispered word,
    'Lenore?'

This I whispered, and an echo murmured back the word,
    'Lenore!'
        Merely this and nothing more.

Back into the chamber turning, all my soul within me
    burning,
Soon again I heard a tapping somewhat louder than before.
'Surely,' said I, 'surely that is something at my window
    lattice;
Let me see, then, what thereat is, and this mystery
    explore—
        'T is the wind and nothing more!'

Open here I flung the shutter, when, with many a flirt
    and flutter,
In there stepped a stately Raven of the saintly days of
    yore;
Not the least obeisance made he; not a minute stopped or
    stayed he;
But, with mien of lord or lady, perched above my
    chamber door—
Perched upon a bust of Pallas just above my chamber
    door—
        Perched, and sat, and nothing more.

Then this ebony bird beguiling my sad fancy into
    smiling,
By the grave and stern decorum of the countenance it
    wore,
'Though thy crest be shorn and shaven, thou,' I said, 'art
    sure no craven,
Ghastly grim and ancient Raven wandering from the
    Nightly shore—
Tell me what thy lordly name is on the Night's Plutonian
    shore!'
        Quoth the Raven, 'Nevermore.'

Much I marvelled this ungainly fowl to hear discourse so
    plainly,
Though its answer little meaning – little relevancy bore;
For we cannot help agreeing that no living human being
Ever yet was blessed with seeing bird above his chamber
    door—
Bird or beast upon the sculptured bust above his chamber
    door,
               With such name as 'Nevermore.'

But the Raven, sitting lonely on the placid bust, spoke
    only
That one word, as if his soul in that one word he did
    outpour.
Nothing farther then he uttered – not a feather then he
    fluttered—
Till I scarcely more than muttered, 'Other friends have
    flown before—
On the morrow *he* will leave me, as my Hopes have flown
    before.'
               Then the bird said, 'Nevermore.'

Startled at the stillness broken by reply so aptly spoken,
'Doubtless,' said I, 'what it utters is its only stock and
    store
Caught from some unhappy master whom unmerciful
    Disaster
Followed fast and followed faster till his songs one
    burden bore—
Till the dirges of his Hope that melancholy burden bore
             Of "Never – nevermore."'

But the Raven still beguiling my sad fancy into smiling,
Straight I wheeled a cushioned seat in front of bird and
    bust and door;
Then, upon the velvet sinking, I betook myself to linking

Fancy unto fancy, thinking what this ominous bird of
    yore—
What this grim, ungainly, ghastly, gaunt, and ominous
    bird of yore
        Meant in croaking 'Nevermore.'

This I sat engaged in guessing, but no syllable expressing
To the fowl whose fiery eyes now burned into my bosom's
    core;
This and more I sat divining, with my head at ease
    reclining
On the cushion's velvet lining that the lamp-light gloated
    o'er,
But whose velvet-violet lining with the lamp-light
    gloating o'er,
        She shall press, ah, nevermore!

Then, methought, the air grew denser, perfumed from an
    unseen censer
Swung by seraphim whose foot-falls tinkled on the tufted
    floor.
'Wretch,' I cried, 'thy God hath lent thee – by these
    angels he hath sent thee
Respite – respite and nepenthe from thy memories of
    Lenore;
Quaff, oh, quaff this kind nepenthe and forget this lost
    Lenore!'
        Quoth the Raven, 'Nevermore.'

'Prophet!' said I, 'thing of evil! – prophet still, if bird or
    devil!—
Whether Tempter sent, or whether tempest tossed thee
    here ashore,
Desolate yet all undaunted, on this desert land
    enchanted—

On this home by Horror haunted – tell me truly, I
    implore—
Is there – *is* there balm in Gilead? – tell me – tell me, I
    implore!'
          Quoth the Raven, 'Nevermore.'

'Prophet!' said I, 'thing of evil! – prophet still, if bird or
    devil!
By that Heaven that bends above us – by that God we
    both adore—
Tell this soul with sorrow laden if, within the distant
    Aidenn,
It shall clasp a sainted maiden whom the angels name
    Lenore—
Clasp a rare and radiant maiden whom the angels name
    Lenore.'
          Quoth the raven, 'Nevermore.'

'Be that word our sign of parting, bird or fiend!' I
    shrieked, upstarting—
'Get thee back into the tempest and the Night's
    Plutonian shore!
Leave no black plume as a token of that lie thy soul hath
    spoken!
Leave my loneliness unbroken! – quit the bust above my
    door!
Take thy beak from out my heart, and take thy form
    from off my door!'
          Quoth the Raven, 'Nevermore.'

And the Raven, never flitting, still is sitting, *still* is
    sitting
On the pallid bust of Pallas just above my chamber door;
And his eyes have all the seeming of a demon's that is
    dreaming,

And the lamp-light o'er him streaming throws his shadow
    on the floor;
And my soul from out that shadow that lies floating on
    the floor
        Shall be lifted – nevermore!

Ulalume – A Ballad

The skies they were ashen and sober;
    The leaves they were crispéd and sere—
    The leaves they were withering and sere:
It was night, in the lonesome October
    Of my most immemorial year:
It was hard by the dim lake of Auber,
    In the misty mid region of Weir—
It was down by the dank tarn of Auber,
    In the ghoul-haunted woodland of Weir.

Here once, through an alley Titanic,
    Of cypress, I roamed with my Soul—
    Of cypress, with Psyche, my Soul.
These were days when my heart was volcanic
    As the scoriac rivers that roll–
    As the lavas that restlessly roll
Their sulphurous currents down Yaanek
    In the ultimate climes of the Pole—
That groan as they roll down Mount Yaanek
    In the realms of the Boreal Pole.

Our talk had been serious and sober,
    But our thoughts they were palsied and sere—
    Our memories were treacherous and sere;
For we knew not the month was October,
    And we marked not the night of the year
    (Ah, night of all nights in the year!)—

We noted not the dim lake of Auber
    (Though once we had journeyed down here)—
We remembered not the dank tarn of Auber,
    Nor the ghoul-haunted woodland of Weir.
And now, as the night was senescent
    And star-dials pointed to morn—
    As the star-dials hinted of morn—
At the end of our path a liquescent
    And nebulous lustre was born,
Out of which a miraculous crescent
    Arose with a duplicate horn—
Astarte's bediamonded crescent
    Distinct with its duplicate horn.

And I said: 'She is warmer than Dian;
    She rolls through an ether of sighs—
    She revels in a region of sighs.
She has seen that the tears are not dry on
    These cheeks, where the worm never dies,
And has come past the stars of the Lion,
    To point us the path to the skies—
    To the Lethean peace of the skies—
Come up, in despite of the Lion,
    To shine on us with her bright eyes—
Come up through the lair of the Lion,
    With love in her luminous eyes.'

But Psyche, uplifting her finger,
    Said: 'Sadly this star I mistrust—
    Her pallor I strangely mistrust:
Ah, hasten! – ah, let us not linger:
    Ah, fly! – let us fly! – for we must.'
In terror she spoke, letting sink her
    Wings till they trailed in the dust—
In agony sobbed, letting sink her

Plumes till they trailed in the dust—
Till they sorrowfully trailed in the dust.

I replied: 'This is nothing but dreaming:
Let us on by this tremulous light!
Let us bathe in this crystalline light!
Its Sibyllic splendor is beaming
With Hope and in Beauty to-night:—
See! – it flickers up the sky through the night!
Ah, we safely may trust to its gleaming,
And be sure it will lead us aright—
We surely may trust to a gleaming,
That cannot but guide us aright,
Since it flickers up to Heaven through the night.'

Thus I pacified Psyche and kissed her,
And tempted her out of her gloom—
And conquered her scruples and gloom;
And we passed to the end of the vista,
But were stopped by the door of a tomb—
By the door of a legended tomb;
And I said: 'What is written, sweet sister,
On the door of this legended tomb?'
She replied: 'Ulalume – Ulalume!—
'T is the vault of thy lost Ulalume!'

Then my heart it grew ashen and sober
As the leaves that were crispéd and sere—
As the leaves that were withering and sere;
And I cried! 'It was surely October
On *this* very night of last year
That I journeyed – I journeyed down here!—
That I brought a dread burden down here—
On this night of all nights in the year,
Ah, what demon hath tempted me here?
Well I know, now, this dim lake of Auber—

This misty mid region of Weir—
Well I know, now, this dank tarn of Auber,
This ghoul-haunted woodland of Weir.'

Said we, then – the two, then: 'Ah, can it
Have been that the woodlandish ghouls—
The pitiful, the merciful ghouls—
To bar up our way and to ban it
From the secret that lies in these wolds—
From the thing that lies hidden in these wolds—
Have drawn up the spectre of a planet
From the limbo of lunary souls—
This sinfully scintillant planet
From the Hell of the planetary souls?'

Annabel Lee

It was many and many a year ago,
In a kingdom by the sea,
That a maiden there lived whom you may know
By the name of Annabel Lee;—
And this maiden she lived with no other thought
Than to love and be loved by me.

She was a child and *I* was a child,
In this kingdom by the sea,
But we loved with a love that was more than love—
I and my Annabel Lee—
With a love that the wingéd seraphs of Heaven
Coveted her and me.

And this was the reason that, long ago,
In this kingdom by the sea,
A wind blew out of a cloud by night
Chilling my Annabel Lee;

So that her highborn kinsmen came
    And bore her away from me,
To shut her up in a sepulchre
    In this kingdom by the sea.

The angels, not half so happy in Heaven,
    Went envying her and me:—
Yes! that was the reason (as all men know,
    In this kingdom by the sea)
That the wind came out of the cloud, chilling
    And killing my Annabel Lee.

But our love it was stronger by far than the love
    Of those who were older than we—
    Of many far wiser than we—
And neither the angels in Heaven above
    Nor the demons down under the sea,
Can ever dissever my soul from the soul
    Of the beautiful Annabel Lee:—

For the moon never beams without bringing me dreams
    Of the beautiful Annabel Lee;
And the stars never rise but I see the bright eyes
    Of the beautiful Annabel Lee;
And so, all the night-tide, I lie down by the side
Of my darling, my darling, my life and my bride,
    In her sepulchre there by the sea—
    In her tomb by the side of the sea.

The Conqueror Worm

Lo! 'tis a gala night
  Within the lonesome latter years!
An angel throng, bewinged, bedight
  In veils, and drowned in tears,

Sit in a theatre, to see
  A play of hopes and fears,
While the orchestra breathes fitfully
  The music of the spheres.

Mimes, in the form of God on high.
  Mutter and mumble low,
And hither and thither fly—
  Mere puppets they, who come and go
At bidding of vast formless things
  That shift the scenery to and fro,
Flapping from out their Condor wings
  Invisible Woe!

That motley drama – oh, be sure
  It shall not be forgot!
With its Phantom chased for evermore,
  By a crowd that seize it not,
Through a circle that ever returneth in
  To the self-same spot.
And much of Madness, and more of Sin,
  And Horror the soul of the plot.

But see, amid the mimic rout
  A crawling shape intrude!
A blood-red thing that writhes from out
  The scenic solitude!
It writhes! – it writhes! – with mortal pangs
  The mimes become its food,
And seraphs sob at vermin fangs
  In human gore imbued.

Out – out are the lights – out all!
  And, over each quivering form,
The curtain, a funeral pall,
  Comes down with the rush of a storm,

While the angels, all pallid and wan,
  Uprising, unveiling, affirm
That the play is the tragedy, 'Man,'
  And its hero the Conqueror Worm.

The Valley of Unrest

Once it smiled a silent dell
Where the people did not dwell;
They had gone unto the wars,
Trusting to the mild-eyed stars,
Nightly, from their azure towers,
To keep watch above the flowers,
In the midst of which all day
The red sunlight lazily lay.
Now each visitor shall confess
The sad valley's restlessness.
Nothing there is motionless,
Nothing save the airs that brood
Over the magic solitude.
Ah, by no wind are stirred those trees
That palpitate like the chill seas
Around the misty Hebrides!
Ah, by no wind those clouds are driven
That rustle through the unquiet Heaven
Uneasily, from morn to even,
Over the violets there that lie
In myriad types of the human eye,
Over the lilies there that wave
And weep above a nameless grave!
They wave: —from out their fragrant tops
Eternal dews come down in drops.
They weep: —from off their delicate stems
Perennial tears descend in gems.

The Haunted Palace

In the greenest of our valleys
  By good angels tenanted,
Once a fair and stately palace—
  Radiant palace – reared its head.
In the monarch thought's dominion,
  It stood there;
Never seraph spread a pinion
  Over fabric half so fair.

Banners yellow, glorious, golden,
  On its roof did float and flow
(This – all this – was in the olden
  Time long ago),
And every gentle air that dallied,
  In that sweet day,
Along the ramparts plumed and pallid,
  A wingèd odor went away.

Wanderers in that happy valley
  Through two luminous windows saw
Spirits moving musically,
  To a lute's well-tunèd law,
Round about a throne where, sitting,
  Porphyrogene,
In state his glory well befitting,
  The ruler of the realm was seen.

And all with pearl and ruby glowing
  Was the fair palace door,
Through which came flowing, flowing, flowing,
  And sparkling evermore,
A troop of Echoes, whose sweet duty
  Was but to sing,
In voices of surpassing beauty,
  The wit and wisdom of their king.

But evil things, in robes of sorrow,
  Assailed the monarch's high estate;
(Ah, let us mourn, for never morrow
  Shall dawn upon him desolate!)
And round about his home the glory
  That blushed and bloomed
Is but a dim-remembered story
  Of the old time entombed.

And travellers now within that valley
  Through the red-litten windows see
Vast forms that move fantastically
  To a discordant melody;
While, like a ghastly rapid river,
  Through the pale door
A hideous throng rush out forever,
  And laugh – but smile no more.

The Bells

I

Hear the sledges with the bells—
  Silver bells!
What a world of merriment their melody foretells!
  How they tinkle, tinkle, tinkle,
    In the icy air of night!
  While the stars that oversprinkle
  All the heavens, seem to twinkle
    With a crystalline delight;
    Keeping time, time, time,
    In a sort of Runic rhyme,
To the tintinnabulation that so musically wells
  From the bells, bells, bells, bells
    Bells, bells, bells—
  From the jingling and the tinkling of the bells.

II

Hear the mellow wedding bells
    Golden bells!
What a world of happiness their harmony foretells!
    Through the balmy air of night
    How they ring out their delight!—
    From the molten-golden notes,
      And all in tune,
    What a liquid ditty floats
To the turtle-dove that listens, while she gloats
    On the moon!
    Oh, from out the sounding cells,
What a gush of euphony voluminously wells!
    How it swells!
    How it dwells
    On the Future! – how it tells
    Of the rapture that impels
    To the swinging and the ringing
    Of the bells, bells, bells—
    Of the bells, bells, bells, bells,
      Bells, bells, bells—
To the rhyming and the chiming of the bells!

III

Hear the loud alarum bells—
    Brazen bells!
What a tale of terror, now their turbulency tells!
    In the startled ear of night
    How they scream out their affright!
    Too much horrified to speak,
    They can only shriek, shriek,
      Out of tune,
In a clamorous appealing to the mercy of the fire,
In a mad expostulation with the deaf and frantic fire,

Leaping higher, higher, higher,
With a desperate desire,
And a resolute endeavour
Now – now to sit, or never,
By the side of the pale-faced moon.
Oh, the bells, bells, bells!
What a tale their terror tells
Of Despair!
How they clang, and clash, and roar!
What a horror they outpour
On the bosom of the palpitating air!
Yet the ear, it fully knows,
By the twanging,
And the clanging,
How the danger ebbs and flows;
Yet the ear distinctly tells,
In the jangling,
And the wrangling,
How the danger sinks and swells,
By the sinking or the swelling in the anger of the bells—
Of the bells—
Of the bells, bells, bells, bells,
Bells, bells, bells—
In the clamor and the clanging of the bells!

IV

Hear the tolling of the bells—
Iron bells!
What a world of solemn thought their monody compels!
In the silence of the night,
How we shiver with affright
At the melancholy menace of their tone!
For every sound that floats
From the rust within their throats
Is a groan.

And the people – ah, the people—
They that dwell up in the steeple,
　　All alone,
And who, tolling, tolling, tolling,
　In that muffled monotone,
Feel a glory in so rolling
　On the human heart a stone—
They are neither man nor woman—
They are neither brute nor human—
　　They are Ghouls:—
And their king it is who tolls:—
And he rolls, rolls, rolls,
　　　Rolls
　　A pæan from the bells;
And his merry bosom swells
　With the pæan of the bells!
And he dances, and he yells;
Keeping time, time, time,
In a sort of runic rhyme,
　To the pæan of the bells:—
　　Of the bells:
Keeping time, time, time
In a sort of Runic rhyme,
　To the throbbing of the bells—
Of the bells, bells, bells—
　To the sobbing of the bells:—
Keeping time, time, time,
　As he knells, knells, knells,
In a happy Runic rhyme,
　To the rolling of the bells—
　Of the bells, bells, bells:—
　To the tolling of the bells—
Of the bells, bells, bells, bells,
　Bells, bells, bells—
To the moaning and the groaning of the bells.

The City in the Sea

Lo! Death has reared himself a throne
In a strange city lying alone
Far down within the dim West,
Where the good and the bad and the worst and the best
Have gone to their eternal rest.
There shrines and palaces and towers
(Time-eaten towers that tremble not!)
Resemble nothing that is ours.
Around, by lifting winds forgot,
Resignedly beneath the sky
The melancholy waters lie.
No rays from the holy heaven come down
On the long night-time of that town;
But light from out the lurid sea
Streams up the turrets silently—
Gleams up the pinnacles far and free—
Up domes – up spires – up kingly halls—
Up fanes – up Babylon-like walls—
Up shadowy long-forgotten bowers
Of sculptured ivy and stone flowers—
Up many and many a marvellous shrine
Whose wreathéd friezes intertwine
The viol, the violet, and the vine.

Resignedly beneath the sky
The melancholy waters lie.
So blend the turrets and shadows there
That all seem pendulous in air,
While from a proud tower in the town
Death looks gigantically down.

There, open fanes and gaping graves
Yawn level with the luminous waves;
But not the riches there that lie

In each idol's diamond eye—
Not the gaily-jewelled dead
Tempt the waters from their bed;
For no ripples curl, alas!
Along that wilderness of glass—
No swellings tell that winds may be
Upon some far-off happier sea—
No heavings hint that winds have been
On seas less hideously serene.

But lo, a stir is in the air!
The wave – there is a movement there!
As if the towers had thrust aside,
In slightly sinking, the dull tide—
As if their tops had feebly given
A void within the filmy Heaven.
The waves have now a redder glow—
The hours are breathing faint and low—
And when, amid no earthly moans,
Down, down that town shall settle hence,
Hell, rising from a thousand thrones,
Shall do it reverence.

To One in Paradise

Thou wast that all to me, love,
    For which my soul did pine—
A green isle in the sea, love,
    A fountain and a shrine,
All wreathed with fairy fruits and flowers,
    And all the flowers were mine.

Ah, dream too bright to last!
    Ah, starry Hope! that didst arise
But to be overcast!

A voice from out the Future cries,
'On! on!' – but o'er the Past
   (Dim, gulf!) my spirit hovering lies
Mute, motionless, aghast!

For, alas! alas! with me
   The light of Life is o'er!
No more – no more – no more—
   (Such language holds the solemn sea
To the sands upon the shore)
   Shall bloom the thunder-blasted tree,
Or the stricken eagle soar!

And all my days are trances,
   And all my nightly dreams
Are where thy grey eye glances,
   And where thy footstep gleams—
In what ethereal dances,
   By what eternal streams.

   For Annie

Thank heaven! the crisis,
   The danger, is past,
And the lingering illness
   Is over at last—
And the fever called 'Living'
   Is conquered at last.

Sadly, I know
   I am shorn of my strength,
And no muscle I move
   As I lie at full length—
But no matter! I feel
   I am better at length.

And I rest so composedly,
  Now, in my bed,
That any beholder
  Might fancy me dead—
Might start at beholding me,
  Thinking me dead.

The moaning and groaning,
  The sighing and sobbing,
Are quieted now,
  With that horrible throbbing
At heart: – ah, that horrible,
  Horrible throbbing!

The sickness – the nausea—
  The pitiless pain—
Have ceased, with the fever
  That maddened my brain—
With the fever called 'Living'
  That burned in my brain.

And oh! of all tortures
  That torture the worst
Has abated – the terrible
  Torture of thirst
For the naphthaline river
  Of Passion accurst:—
I have drank of a water
  That quenches all thirst:—

Of a water that flows,
  With a lullaby sound,
From a spring but a very few
  Feet under ground—
From a cavern not very far
  Down under ground.

And ah! let it never
  Be foolishly said
That my room it is gloomy
  And narrow my bed;
For man never slept
  In a different bed—
And, to *sleep*, you must slumber
  In just such a bed.

My tantalized spirit
  Here blandly reposes,
Forgetting, or never
  Regretting, its roses—
Its old agitations
  Of myrtles and roses:

For now, while so quietly
  Lying, it fancies
A holier odor
  About it, of pansies—
A rosemary odor,
  Commingled with pansies—
With rue and the beautiful
  Puritan pansies.

And so it lies happily,
  Bathing in many
A dream of the truth
  And the beauty of Annie—
Drowned in a bath
  Of the tresses of Annie.

She tenderly kissed me,
  She fondly caressed,
And then I fell gently
  To sleep on her breast—

Deeply to sleep
  From the heaven of her breast.

When the light was extinguished,
  She covered me warm,
And she prayed to the angels
  To keep me from harm—
To the queen of the angels
  To shield me from harm.

And I lie so composedly,
  Now, in my bed,
(Knowing her love),
  That you fancy me dead—
And I rest so contentedly,
  Now, in my bed
(With her love at my breast),
  That you fancy me dead—
That you shudder to look at me,
  Thinking me dead:—

But my heart it is brighter
  Than all of the many
Stars in the sky,
  For it sparkles with Annie—
It glows with the light
  Of the love of my Annie—
With the thought of the light
  Of the eyes of my Annie.

Introduction
[*to* Poems, 1831]

Romance, who loves to nod and sing,
With drowsy head and folded wing,
Among the green leaves as they shake
Far down within some shadowy lake,
To me a painted paroquet
Hath been – a most familiar bird—
Taught me my alphabet to say—
To lisp my very earliest word
While in the wild-wood I did lie
A child – with a most knowing eye.

Succeeding years, too wild for song,
Then roll'd like tropic storms along,
Where, tho' the garish lights that fly
Dying along the troubled sky,
Lay bare, thro' vistas thunder-riven,
The blackness of the general Heaven,
That very blackness yet doth fling
Light on the lightning's silver wing.

For, being an idle boy lang syne,
Who read Anacreon, and drank wine,
I early found Anacreon rhymes
Were almost passionate sometimes—
And by strange alchemy of brain
His pleasures always turn'd to pain—
His naivete to wild desire—
His wit to love – his wine to fire—
And so, being young and dipt in folly
I fell in love with melancholy,
And used to throw my earthy rest
And quiet all away in jest—
I could not love except where Death
Was mingling his with Beauty's breath—

Or Hymen, Time, and Destiny
Were stalking between her and me.

O, then the eternal Condor years
So shook the very Heavens on high,
With tumult as they thunder'd by;
I had no time for idle cares,
Thro' gazing on the unquiet sky!
Or if an hour with calmer wing
Its down did on my spirit fling,
That little hour with lyre and rhyme
To while away – forbidden thing!
My heart half fear'd to be a crime
Unless it trembled with the string.

But *now* my soul hath too much room—
Gone are the glory and the gloom—
The black hath mellow'd into grey,
And all the fires are fading away.

My draught of passion hath been deep—
I revell'd, and I now would sleep—
And after-drunkenness of soul
Succeeds the glories of the bowl—
An idle longing night and day
To dream my very life away.

But dreams –of those who dream as I,
Aspiringly, are damned, and die:
Yet should I swear I mean alone,
By notes so very shrilly blown,
To break upon Time's monotone,
While yet my vapid joy and grief
Are tintless of the yellow leaf—
Why not an imp the greybeard hath,
Will shake his shadow in my path—

And even the greybeard will o'erlook
Connivingly my dreaming-book.

Eldorado

Gaily bedight,
A gallant knight,
In sunshine and in shadow,
Had journeyed long,
Singing a song,
In search of Eldorado.

But he grew old—
This knight so bold—
And o'er his heart a shadow
Fell, as he found
No spot of ground
That looked like Eldorado.

And, as his strength
Failed him at length
He met a pilgrim shadow—
'Shadow,' said he,
'Where can it be—
This land of Eldorado?'

'Over the Mountains
Of the Moon,
Down the Valley of the Shadow,
Ride, boldly ride,'
The shade replied,—
'If you seek for Eldorado!'

Israfel*

I.

In heaven a spirit doth dwell
  'Whose heart strings are a lute;'
None sing so wildly well
As the angel Israfel;
And the giddy stars (so legends tell),
Ceasing their hymns, attend the spell
  Of his voice, all mute.

II.

Tottering above
  In her highest noon,
  The enamoured Moon
Blushes with love;
  While, to listen, the red levin
  (With the rapid Pleiades even
  Which were seven)
  Pauses in heaven.

III.

And they say (the starry choir
  And the other listening things)
That Israfeli's fire
Is owing to that lyre
  By which he sits and sings,—
The trembling living wire
Of those unusual strings.

---

* 'And the angel Israfel, whose heart-strings are a lute, and who has
  the sweetest voice of all God's creatures.'—*Koran.*

IV.

But the skies that angel trod,
Where deep thoughts are a duty—
Where Love's a grown-up god—
　Where the houri glances are
Imbued with all the beauty
　Which we worship in a star.

V.

Therefore thou art not wrong,
　Israfeli, who despisest
An unimpassioned song;
To thee the laurels belong,
　Best bard, because the wisest:
Merrily live and long!

VI.

The ecstasies above
　With thy burning measure suit;
Thy grief, thy joy, thy hate, thy love,
　With the fervour of thy lute:
　Well may the stars be mute!

VII.

Yes, heaven is thine; but this
　Is a world of sweets and sours;
　Our flowers are merely flowers,
And the shadow of thy perfect bliss
　Is the sunshine of ours.

VIII.

If I could dwell
Where Israfel
  Hath dwelt, and he where I,
He might not sing so wildly well
  A mortal melody,
While a bolder note than this might swell
  From my lyre within the sky.

JONES VERY
1813-1880

Jones Very was a mystic who claimed that his religious
sonnets were communicated to him in visions of the
Holy Ghost. His fervor led him to spend a short time
in an insane asylum in 1838 although Emerson
considered him 'profoundly sane' and admired his
work. Very finally retired to life as a recluse under the
care of his sister Lydia.

The following poems of religious experience such
as 'The Garden' and 'The Dead' have led to Very's
comparison with seventeenth century metaphysical
poets such as George Herbert, but they were little read
until their rediscovery in 1938.

In Him We Live

Father! I bless thy name that I do live,
And in each motion am made rich with Thee,
That when a glance is all that I can give,
It is a kingdom's wealth, if I but see;
This stately body cannot move, save I
Will to its nobleness my little bring;
My voice its measured cadence will not try,
Save I with every note consent to sing;
I cannot raise my hands to hurt or bless,
But I with every action must conspire
To show me there how little I possess,
And yet that little more than I desire;
May each new act my new allegiance prove,
Till in thy perfect love I ever live and move.

The Garden

I saw the spot where our first parents dwelt;
And yet it wore to me no face of change,
For while amid its fields and groves, I felt
As if I had not sinned, nor thought it strange;
My eye seemed but a part of every sight,
My ear heard music in each sound that rose;
Each sense forever found a new delight,
Such as the spirit's vision only knows;
Each act some new and ever-varying joy
Did by my Father's love for me prepare;
To dress the spot my ever fresh employ,
And in the glorious whole with Him to share;
No more without the flaming gate to stray,
No more for sin's dark stain the debt of death to pay.

The Latter Rain

The latter rain, – it falls in anxious haste
Upon the sun-dried fields and branches bare,
Loosening with searching drops the rigid waste,
As if it would each root's lost strength repair;
But not a blade grows green as in the spring,
No swelling twig puts forth its thickening leaves;
The robins only mid the harvests sing,
Pecking the grain that scatters from the sheaves:
The rain falls still, – the fruit all ripened drops,
It pierces chestnut burr and walnut shell,
The furrowed fields disclose the yellow crops,
Each bursting pod of talents used can tell,
And all that once received the early rain
Declare to man it was not sent in vain.

The Dead

I see them, – crowd on crowd they walk the earth,
Dry leafless trees no autumn wind laid bare;
And in their nakedness find cause for mirth,
And all unclad would winter's rudeness dare;
No sap doth through their clattering branches flow,
Whence springing leaves and blossoms bright appear;
Their hearts the living God have ceased to know
Who gives the spring-time to th' expectant year.
They mimic life, as if from Him to steal
His glow of health to paint the livid cheek;

They borrow words for thoughts they cannot feel,
That with a seeming heart their tongue may speak;
And in their show of life more dead they live
Than those that to the earth with many tears they give.

The Grave-Yard

My heart grows sick before the wide-spread death
That walks and speaks in seeming life around;
And I would love the corse without a breath,
That sleeps forgotten 'neath the cold, cold ground;
For these do tell the story of decay,
The worm and rotten flesh hide not nor lie;
But this, though dying too from day to day,
With a false show doth cheat the longing eye;
And hide the worm that gnaws the core of life,
With painted cheek and smooth deceitful skin;
Covering a grave with sights of darkness rife,
A secret cavern filled with death and sin;
And men walk o'er these graves and know it not,
For in the body's health the soul's forgot.

Thy Brother's Blood

I have no Brother, – they who meet me now
Offer a hand with their own wills defiled,
And, while they wear a smooth unwrinkled brow,
Know not that Truth can never be beguiled;
Go wash the hand that still betrays thy guilt;—
Before the spirit's gaze what stain can hide?
Abel's red blood upon the earth is spilt,
And by thy tongue it cannot be denied;
I hear not with the ear, – the heart doth tell
Its secret deeds to me untold before;
Go, all its hidden plunder quickly sell,
Then shalt thou cleanse thee from thy brother's gore,
Then will I take thy gift; – that bloody stain
Shall not be seen upon thy hand again.

The Clouded Morning

The morning comes, and thickening clouds prevail,
  Hanging like curtains all the horizon round,
Or overhead in heavy stillness sail;
  So still is day, it seems like night profound;
Scarce by the city's din the air is stirred,
  And dull and deadened comes its every sound;
The cock's shrill, piercing voice subdued is heard,
  By the thick folds of muffling vapors drowned.
Dissolved in mists the hills and trees appear,
  Their outlines lost and blended with the sky;
And well-known objects, that to all are near,
  No longer seem familiar to the eye,
But with fantastic forms they mock the sight,
As when we grope amid the gloom of night.

The Lost

The fairest day that ever yet has shone
Will be when thou the day within shalt see;
The fairest rose that ever yet has blown,
When thou the flower thou lookest on shalt be;
But thou art far away amidst Time's toys;
Thyself the day thou lookest for in them,
Thyself the flower that now thine eye enjoys;
But wilted now thou hang'st upon thy stem;
The bird thou hearest on the budding tree
Thou hast made sing with thy forgotten voice;
But when it swells again to melody,
The song is thine in which thou wilt rejoice;
And thou new risen 'midst these wonders live,
That now to them dost all thy substance give.

Enoch

I look'd to find a man who walk'd with God,
Like the translated patriarch of old;—
Though gladden'd millions on his footstool trod,
Yet none with him did such sweet converse hold;
I heard the wind in low complaint go by,
That none its melodies like him could hear;
Day unto day spoke wisdom from on high,
Yet none with David turn'd a willing ear;
God walk'd alone unhonour'd through the earth;
For him no heart-built temple open stood,
The soul, forgetful of her nobler birth,
Had hewn him lofty shrines of stone and wood,
And left unfinished and in ruins still
The only temple he delights to fill.

The Wind-Flower

Thou lookest up with meek, confiding eye
Upon the clouded smile of April's face,
Unharm'd though Winter stands uncertain by,
Eyeing with jealous glance each opening grace.
Thou trustest wisely! in thy faith array'd,
More glorious thou than Israel's wisest king.
Such faith was His whom men to death betray'd,
As thine who hearest the timid voice of Spring,
While other flowers still hide them from her call
Along the river's brink and meadow bare.
Thee will I seek beside the stony wall,
And in thy trust with childlike heart would share,
O'erjoy'd that in thy early leaves I find
A lesson taught by Him who loved all humankind.

The Tree

I love thee when thy swelling buds appear,
And one by one their tender leaves unfold,
As if they knew that warmer suns were near,
Nor longer sought to hide from winter's cold;
And when with darker growth thy leaves are seen
To veil from view the early robin's nest,
I love to lie beneath thy waving screen,
With limbs by summer's heat and toil oppress'd;
And when the autumn winds have stript thee bare,
And round thee lies the smooth, untrodden snow,
When naught is thine that made thee once so fair,
I love to watch thy shadowy form below,
And through thy leafless arms to look above
On stars that brighter beam when most we need their
    love.

The Prayer

Wilt Thou not visit me?
The plant beside me feels Thy gentle dew;
    And every blade of grass I see,
From Thy deep earth its moisture drew.

Wilt Thou not visit me?
Thy morning calls on me with cheering tone;
    And every hill and tree
Lend but one voice, the voice of Thee alone.

Come, for I need Thy love,
More than the flower the dew or grass the rain;
    Come, gently as Thy holy dove;
And let me in Thy sight rejoice to live again.

I will not hide from them,
When Thy storms come, though fierce may be their
      wrath,
   But bow with leafy stem,
And strengthened follow on Thy chosen path.

   Yes, Thou wilt visit me;
Nor plant nor tree Thy eye delights so well,
   As when from sin set free,
My spirit loves with Thine in peace to dwell.

Not in some future world alone 'twill be,
   Beyond the grave, beyond the bounds of time;
But on the earth Thy glory we shall see,
   And share Thy triumph, peaceful, pure, sublime.

Lord! help me that I faint not, weary grow,
   Nor at Thy Coming slumber too, and sleep;
For Thou hast promised, and full well I know
   Thou wilt to us Thy word of promise keep.

The Strangers

Each care-worn face is but a book
   To tell of houses bought or sold;
Or filled with words that men have took
   From those who lived and spoke of old.

I see none whom I know, for they
   See other things than him they meet;
And though they stop me by the way,
   'Tis still some other one to greet.

There are no words that reach my ear;
  Those speak who tell of other things
Than what they mean for me to hear,
  For in their speech the counter rings.

I would be where each word is true,
  Each eye sees what it looks upon;
For here my eye has seen but few
  Who in each act that act have done.

Yourself

'Tis to yourself I speak; you cannot know
Him whom I call in speaking such a one,
For you beneath the earth lie buried low,
Which he alone as living walks upon:
You may at times have heard him speak to you,
And often wished perchance that you were he;
And I must ever wish that it were true,
For then you could hold fellowship with me:
But now you hear us talk as strangers, met
Above the room wherein you lie abed;
A word perhaps loud spoken you may get,
Or hear our feet when heavily they tread;
But he who speaks, or him who's spoken to,
Must both remain as strangers still to you.

The Created

There is naught for thee by thy haste to gain;
'Tis not the swift with me that win the race;
Through long endurance of delaying pain.
Thine opened eye shall see thy Father's face;
Nor here nor there, where now thy feet would turn,

Thou wilt find Him who ever waits for thee;
But let obedience quench desires that burn,
And where thou art thy Father too will be.
Behold! as day by day the spirit grows,
Thou see'st by inward light things hid before;
Till what God is, thyself, His image shows;
And thou wilt wear the robe that first thou wore,
When bright with radiance from his forming hand,
He saw the lord of all His creatures stand.

The Hand and Foot

The hand and foot that stir not, they shall find
Sooner than all the rightful place to go:
Now in their motion free as roving wind,
Though first no snail so limited and slow;
I mark them full of labor all the day,
Each active motion made in perfect rest;
They cannot from their path mistaken stray,
Though 'tis not theirs, yet in it they are blest;
The bird has not their hidden track found out,
The cunning fox though full of art he be;
It is the way unseen, the certain route,
Where ever bound, yet thou art ever free;
The path of Him, whose perfect law of love
Bids spheres and atoms in just order move.

Nature

The bubbling brook doth leap when I come by,
Because my feet find measure with its call;
The birds know when the friend they love is nigh,
For I am known to them, both great and small;
The flower that on the lovely hill-side grows

Expects me there when spring its bloom has given;
And many a tree and bush my wanderings knows,
And e'en the clouds and silent stars of heaven;
For he who with his Maker walks aright,
Shall be their lord as Adam was before;
His ear shall catch each sound with new delight,
Each object wear the dress that then it wore;
And he, as when erect in soul he stood,
Hear from his Father's lips that all is good.

Morning

The light will never open sightless eyes,
It comes to those who willingly would see;
And every object, – hill, and stream, and skies,
Rejoice within the encircling line to be;
'Tis day, – the field is fill'd with busy hands,
The shop resounds with noisy workmen's din,
The traveller with his staff already stands
His yet unmeasured journey to begin.
The light breaks gently too within the breast,
Yet there no eye awaits the crimson morn,
The forge and noisy anvil are at rest,
Nor men nor oxen tread the fields of corn,
Nor pilgrim lifts his staff, – it is no day
To those who find on earth their place to stay.

I Was Sick and in Prison

Thou hast not left the rough-barked tree to grow
Without a mate upon the river's bank;
Nor dost Thou on one flower the rain bestow,
But many a cup the glittering drops has drank;
The bird must sing to one who sings again,

Else would her note less welcome be to hear;
Nor hast Thou bid thy word descend in vain,
But soon some answering voice shall reach my ear;
Then shall the brotherhood of peace begin,
And the new song be raised that never dies,
That shall the soul from death and darkness win,
And burst the prison where the captive lies;
And one by one new-born shall join the strain,
Till earth restores her sons to heaven again.

The Day of Denial

Are there not twelve whole hours in every day
The sun upon thy dial marks for toil;
How is it some but five, some seven say,
And some among you of the whole make spoil?
Think'st thou to gain by taking from your life,
By dying many hours to live the more?

Dost thou not see the suicidal knife,
Made hour by hour yet redder in thy gore?
The day! the living day! how soon 't is night,
With him who rises not till near its noon;
His candle lit for many hours to light,
Put out ere yet he learned to prize the boon;
How dark his darkness, who till latest eve
Still slumbers on, nor then his couch will leave!

HENRY DAVID THOREAU
1817-1862

Henry David Thoreau, author of *Walden* and *Civil Disobedience* was one of the best known men of his age. A discipline of Emerson, proponent of the simple life, poet and worker for the rights of the individual, he accurately described himself as a 'mystic, a transcendentalist and a natural philosopher to boot'.

Most of Thoreau's poems were written in the early 1840s and scattered through *A Week on the Concord and Merrimack Rivers* (1849) and *Walden* (1854). They were not brought together in a single volume until 1943.

Inspiration

Whate'er we leave to God, God does,
  And blesses us;
The work we choose should be our own,
  God lets alone.

If with light head erect I sing,
  Though all the muses lend their force,
From my poor love of anything,
  The verse is weak and shallow as its source.

But if with bended neck I grope,
  Listening behind me for my wit,
With faith superior to hope,
  More anxious to keep back than forward it,

Making my soul accomplice there
  Unto the flame my heart hath lit,
Then will the verse forever wear,—
  Time cannot bend the line which God hath writ.

Always the general show of things
  Floats in review before my mind,
And such true love and reverence brings,
  That sometimes I forget that I am blind.

But now there comes unsought, unseen,
  Some clear, divine electuary,
And I who had but sensual been,
  Grow sensible, and as God is, am wary.

I hearing get who had but ears,
  And sight, who had but eyes before,
I moments live who lived but years,
  And truth discern who knew but learning's lore.

I hear beyond the range of sound,
  I see beyond the range of sight,
New earths and skies and seas around,
  And in my day the sun doth pale his light.

A clear and ancient harmony
  Pierces my soul through all its din,
As through its utmost melody,—
  Farther behind than they – farther within.

More swift its bolt than lightning is,
  Its voice than thunder is more loud,
It doth expand my privacies
  To all, and leave me single in the crowd.

It speaks with such authority,
  With so serene and lofty tone,
That idle Time runs gadding by,
  And leaves me with Eternity alone.

Then chiefly is my natal hour,
  And only then my prime of life,
Of manhood's strength it is the flower,
  'Tis peace's end and war's beginning strife.

'T 'hath come in summer's broadest noon,
  By a grey wall or some chance place,
Unseasoned time, insulted June,
  And vexed the day with its presuming face.

Such fragrance round my couch it makes,
  More rich than are Arabian drugs,
That my soul scents its life and wakes
  The body up beneath its perfumed rugs.

Such is the Muse – the heavenly maid,
  The star that guides our mortal course,
Which shows where life's true kernel's laid,
  Its wheat's fine flower, and its undying force.

She with one breath attunes the spheres,
  And also my poor human heart,
With one impulse propels the years
  Around, and gives my throbbing pulse its start.

I will not doubt forever more,
  Nor falter from a steadfast faith,
For though the system be turned o'er,
  God takes not back the word which once he saith.

I will then trust the love untold
  Which not my worth nor want has bought,
Which wooed me young and woos me old,
  And to this evening hath me brought.

My memory I'll educate
  To know the one historic truth,
Remembering to the latest date
  The only true and sole immortal youth.

Be but thy inspiration given,
  No matter through what danger sought,
I'll fathom hell or climb to heaven,
  And yet esteem that cheap which love has bought.

    Fame cannot tempt the bard
      Who's famous with his God,
    Nor laurel him reward
      Who hath his Maker's nod.

The Inward Morning

Packed in my mind lie all the clothes
    Which outward nature wears,
And in its fashion's hourly change
    It all things else repairs.

In vain I look for change abroad,
    And can no difference find,
Till some new ray of peace uncalled
    Illumes my inmost mind.

What is it gilds the trees and clouds,
    And paints the heavens so gay,
But yonder fast-abiding light
    With its unchanging ray?

Lo, when the sun streams through the wood,
    Upon a winter's morn,
Where'er his silent beams intrude
    The murky night is gone.

How could the patient pine have known
    The morning breeze would come,
Or humble flowers anticipate
    The insect's noonday hum,—

Till the new light with morning cheer
    From far streamed through the aisles,
And nimbly told the forest trees
    For many stretching miles?

I've heard within my inmost soul
    Such cheerful morning news,
In the horizon of my mind
    Have seen such orient hues,

As in the twilight of the dawn,
    When the first birds awake,
Are heard within some silent wood,
    Where they the small twigs break,

Or in the eastern skies are seen,
    Before the sun appears,
The harbingers of summer heats
    Which from afar he bears.

Smoke

Light-winged Smoke, Icarian bird,
Melting thy pinions in thy upward flight;
Lark without song, and messenger of dawn,
Circling above the hamlets as thy nest;
Or else, departing dream, and shadowy form
Of midnight vision, gathering up thy skirts;
By night star-veiling, and by day
Darkening the light and blotting out the sun;
Go thou, my incense, upward from this hearth,
And ask the gods to pardon this clear flame.

The Respectable Folks

The respectable folks,—
Where dwell they?
They whisper in the oaks,
And they sigh in the hay;
Summer and winter, night and day,
Out on the meadow, there dwell they.
They never die,
Nor snivel, nor cry,
Nor ask our pity

With a wet eye.
A sound estate they ever mend,
To every asker readily lend;
To the ocean wealth,
To the meadow health,
To Time his length,
To the rocks strength,
To the stars light,
To the weary night,
To the busy day,
To the idle play;
And so their good cheer never ends,
For all are their debtors, and all their friends.

My Prayer

Great God, I ask thee for no meaner pelf
Than that I may not disappoint myself;
That in my action I may soar as high
As I can now discern with this clear eye.

And next in value, which thy kindness lends,
That I may greatly disappoint my friends,
Howe'er they think or hope that it may be,
They may not dream how thou'st distinguished me.

That my weak hand may equal my firm faith,
And my life practise more than my tongue saith;
That my low conduct may not show,
Nor my relenting lines,
That I thy purpose did not know,
Or overrated thy designs.

Nature

O Nature! I do not aspire
To be the highest in thy quire,—
To be a meteor in the sky,
Or comet that may range on high;
Only a zephyr that may blow
Among the reeds by the river low;
Give me thy most privy place
Where to run my airy race.

In some withdrawn, unpublic mead
Let me sigh upon a reed,
Or in the woods, with leafy din,
Whisper the still evening in:
Some still work give me to do,—
Only – be it near to you!
For I'd rather be thy child
And pupil, in the forest wild,
Than be the king of men elsewhere,
And most sovereign slave of care.

Sic Vita

I am a parcel of vain strivings tied
   By a chance bond together,
Dangling this way and that, their links
  Were made so loose and wide,
      Methinks,
    For milder weather.

A bunch of violets without their roots,
   And sorrel intermixed,
  Encircled by a wisp of straw
   Once coiled about their shoots,
    The law
    By which I'm fixed.

A nosegay which Time clutched from out
   Those fair Elysian fields,
  With weeds and broken stems, in haste,
   Doth make the rabble rout
    That waste
    The day he yields.

And here I bloom for a short hour unseen
   Drinking my juices up,
  With no root in the land
   To keep my branches green,
    But stand
    In a bare cup.

Some tender buds were left upon my stem
   In mimicry of life,
  But ah! the children will not know,
   Till time has withered them,
    The woe
    With which they're rife.

But now I see I was not plucked for nought,
   And after in life's vase
  Of glass set while I might survive,
   But by a kind hand brought
    Alive
    To a strange place.

That stock thus thinned will soon redeem its hours,
    And by another year,
Such as God knows, with freer air,
    More fruits and fairer flowers
        Will bear,
    While I droop here.

The Fisher's Boy

My life is like a stroll upon the beach,
    As near the ocean's edge as I can go;
My tardy steps its waves sometimes o'erreach,
    Sometimes I stay to let them overflow.

My sole employment is, and scrupulous care,
    To place my gains beyond the reach of tides,—
Each smoother pebble, and each shell more rare,
    Which Ocean kindly to my hand confides.

I have but few companions on the shore:
    They scorn the strand who sail upon the sea;
Yet oft I think the ocean they've sailed o'er
    Is deeper known upon the strand to me.

The middle sea contains no crimson dulse,
    Its deeper waves cast up no pearls to view;
Along the shore my hand is on its pulse,
    And I converse with many a shipwrecked crew.

The River Swelleth More and More

The river swelleth more and more,
Like some sweet influence stealing o'er
The passive town; and for a while
Each tussuck makes a tiny isle,
Where, on some friendly Ararat,
Resteth the weary water-rat.

No ripple shows Musketaquid,
Her very current e'en is hid,
As deepest souls do calmest rest,
When thoughts are swelling in the breast,
And she that in the summer's drought
Doth make a rippling and a rout,
Sleeps from Nahshawtuck to the Cliff,
Unruffled by a single skiff.
But by a thousand distant hills
The louder roar a thousand rills,
And many a spring which now is dumb,
And many a stream with smothered hum,
Doth swifter well and faster glide,
Though buried deep beneath the tide.

Our village shows a rural Venice,
Its broad lagoons where yonder fen is;
As lovely as the Bay of Naples
Yon placid cove amid the maples;
And in my neighbor's field of corn
I recognise the Golden Horn.
Here Nature taught from year to year,
When only red men came to hear,
Methinks 'twas in this school of art
Venice and Naples learned their part,
But still their mistress, to my mind,
Her young disciples leaves behind.

Within the Circuit of this Plodding Life

Within the circuit of this plodding life
There enter moments of an azure hue,
Untarnished fair as is the violet
Or anemone, when the spring strews them
By some meandering rivulet, which make
The best philosophy untrue that aims
But to console man for his grievances.
I have remembered when the winter came,
High in my chamber in the frosty nights,
When in the still light of the cheerful moon,
On every twig and rail and jutting spout,
The icy spears were adding to their length
Against the arrows of the coming sun,
How in the shimmering noon of summer past
Some unrecorded beam slanted across
The upland pastures where the Johnwort grew;
Or heard, amid the verdure of my mind,
The bee's long smothered hum, on the blue flag
Loitering amidst the mead; or busy rill,
Which now through all its course stands still and dumb
Its own memorial, – purling at its play
Along the slopes, and through the meadows next,
Until its youthful sound was hushed at last
In the staid current of the lowland stream;
Or seen the furrows shine but late upturned,
And where the fieldfare followed in the rear,
When all the fields around lay bound and hoar
Beneath a thick integument of snow.
So by God's cheap economy made rich
To go upon my winter's task again.

The Summer Rain

My books I'd fain cast off, I cannot read,
    'Twixt every page my thoughts go stray at large
Down in the meadow, where is richer feed,
    And will not mind to hit their proper targe.

Plutarch was good, and so was Homer too,
    Our Shakespeare's life were rich to live again,
What Plutarch read, that was not good nor true,
    Nor Shakespeare's books, unless his books were men.

Here while I lie beneath this walnut bough,
    What care I for the Greeks or for Troy town,
If juster battles are enacted now
    Between the ants upon this hummock's crown?

Bid Homer wait till I the issue learn,
    If red or black the gods will favor most,
Or yonder Ajax will the phalanx turn,
    Struggling to heave some rock against the host.

Tell Shakespeare to attend some leisure hour,
    For now I've business with this drop of dew,
And see you not, the clouds prepare a shower,—
    I'll meet him shortly when the sky is blue.

This bed of herdsgrass and wild oats was spread
    Last year with nicer skill than monarchs use.
A clover tuft is pillow for my head,
    And violets quite overtop my shoes.

And now the cordial clouds have shut all in,
    And gently swells the wind to say all's well;
The scattered drops are falling fast and thin,
    Some in the pool, some in the flowerbell.

I am well drenched upon my bed of oats;
　But see that globe come rolling down its stem,
Now like a lonely planet there it floats,
　And now it sinks into my garment's hem.

Drip, drip the trees for all the country round,
　And richness rare distills from every bough;
The wind alone it is makes every sound,
　Shaking down crystals on the leaves below.

For shame the sun will never show himself,
　Who could not with his beams e'er melt me so;
My dripping locks, – they would become an elf,
　Who in a beaded coat does gayly go.

Conscience

Conscience is instinct bred in the house,
Feeling and Thinking propagate the sin
By an unnatural breeding in and in.
I say, Turn it out doors,
Into the moors.
I love a life whose plot is simple,
And does not thicken with every pimple,
A soul so sound no sickly conscience binds it,
That makes the universe no worse than't finds it.
I love an earnest soul,
Whose mighty joy and sorrow
Are not drowned in a bowl,
And brought to life tomorrow;
That lives one tragedy,
And not seventy;
A conscience worth keeping,
Laughing not weeping;
A conscience wise and steady,

And for ever ready;
Not changing with events,
Dealing in compliments;
A conscience exercised about
Large things, where one *may* doubt.
I love a soul not all of wood,
Predestinated to be good,
But true to the backbone
Unto itself alone,
And false to none;
Born to its own affairs,
Its own joys and own cares;
By whom the work which God begun
Is finished, and not undone;
Taken up where he left off,
Whether to worship or to scoff;
If not good, why then evil,
If not good god, good devil.
Goodness! – you hypocrite, come out of that,
Live your life, do your work, then take your hat.
I have no patience towards
Such conscientious cowards.
Give me simple laboring folk,
Who love their work,
Whose virtue is a song
To cheer God along.

When Winter Fringes Every Bough

When Winter fringes every bough
  With his fantastic wreath,
And puts the seal of silence now
  Upon the leaves beneath;

When every stream in its pent-house
  Goes gurgling on its way,
And in his gallery the mouse
  Nibbleth the meadow hay;

Methinks the summer still is nigh,
  And lurketh underneath,
As that same meadow mouse doth lie
  Snug in the last year's heath.

And if perchance the chicadee
  Lisp a faint note anon,
The snow in summer's canopy,
  Which she herself put on.

Fair blossoms deck the cheerful trees,
  And dazzling fruits depend,
The north wind sighs a summer breeze,
  The nipping frosts to fend,

Bringing glad tidings unto me,
  The while I stand all ear,
Of a serene eternity,
  Which need not winter fear.

Out on the silent pond straightway
  The restless ice doth crack,
And pond sprites merry gambols play
  Amid the deafening rack.

Eager I hasten to the vale,
  As if I heard brave news,
How nature held high festival,
  Which it were hard to lose.

I gambol with my neighbor ice,
   And sympathizing quake,
As each new crack darts in a trice
   Across the gladsome lake.

One with the cricket in the ground,
   And faggot on the hearth,
Resounds the rare domestic sound
   Along the forest path.

Carpe Diem

Build not on tomorrow,
   But seize on today!
From no future borrow,
   The present to pay.

Wait not any longer
   Thy work to begin;
The worker grows stronger,—
   Be steadfast and win!

Forbode not new sorrow—
   Bear that of today,
   And trust that the morrow
   Shall chase it away.

The task of the present
   Be sure to fulfil;
If sad, or if pleasant,
   Be true to it still.

God sendeth us sorrow
  And cloudeth our day;
  His sun on the morrow
  Shines bright on our way.

Each Summer Sound

Each summer sound
Is a summer round.

The Needles of the Pine

The needles of the pine,
All to the west incline.

In the East Fames are Won

In the East fames are won,
In the West deeds are done.

Love Equals Swift and Slow

Love equals swift and slow,
  And high and low,
Racer and lame,
  The hunter and his game.

Men Say They Know
Many Things

Men say they know many things;
But lo! they have taken wings,—
The arts and sciences,
And a thousand appliances;
The wind that blows
Is all that any body knows.

What's the Railroad to Me

What's the railroad to me?
I never go to see
Where it ends.
It fills a few hollows,
And makes banks for the swallows,
It sets the sand a-blowing.
And the blackberries a-growing.

It is No Dream of Mine

It is no dream of mine,
To ornament a line;
I cannot come nearer to God and Heaven
Than I live to Walden even.
I am its stony shore,
And the breeze that passes o'er;
In the hollow of my hand
Are its water and its sand,
And its deepest resort
Lies high in my thought.

Though All the Fates Should
Prove Unkind

Though all the fates should prove unkind,
Leave not your native land behind.
The ship, becalmed, at length stands still;
The steed must rest beneath the hill;
But swiftly still our fortunes pace
To find us out in every place.

The vessel, though her masts be firm,
Beneath her copper bears a worm;
Around the cape, across the line,
Till fields of ice her course confine;
It matters not how smooth the breeze,
How shallow or how deep the seas,
Whether she bears Manilla twine,
Or in her hold Madeira wine,
Or China teas, or Spanish hides,
In port or quarantine she rides;
Far from New England's blustering shore,
New England's worm her hulk shall bore,
And sink her in the Indian seas,
Twine, wine, and hides, and China teas.

With Frontier Strength Ye Stand
Your Ground

With frontier strength ye stand your ground,
With grand content ye circle round,
Tumultuous silence for all sound,
Ye distant nursery of rills,
Monadnock and the Peterborough Hills;—
Firm argument that never stirs,
Outcircling the philosophers,—
Like some vast fleet,

Sailing through rain and sleet,
Through winter's cold and summer's heat;
Still holding on upon your high emprise,
Until ye find a shore amid the skies;
Not skulking close to land,
With cargo contraband,
For they who sent a venture out by ye
Have set the Sun to see
Their honesty.
Ships of the line, each one,
Ye westward run,
Convoying clouds,
Which cluster in your shrouds,
Always before the gale,
Under a press of sail,
With weight of metal all untold,—
I seem to feel ye in my firm seat here,
Immeasurable depth of hold,
And breadth of beam, and length of running gear.

The Western Wind Came Lumbering In

The western wind came lumbering in,
Bearing a faint Pacific din,
Our evening mail, swift at the call
Of its Postmaster General;
Laden with news from Californ',
What 'er transpired hath since morn,
How wags the world by brier and brake
From hence to Athabasca Lake;—

Where Gleaming Fields
of Haze

Where gleaming fields of haze
Meet the voyageur's gaze,
And above, the heated air
Seems to make a river there,
The pines stand up with pride
By the Souhegan's side,
And the hemlock and the larch
With their triumphal arch
Are waving o'er its march
   To the sea.
No wind stirs its waves,
But the spirits of the braves
   Hov'ring o'er,
Whose antiquated graves
Its still water laves
   On the shore.
With an Indian's stealthy tread,
It goes sleeping in its bed,
Without joy or grief,
Or the rustle of a leaf,
Without a ripple or a billow,
Or the sigh of a willow,
From the Lyndeboro' hills
To the Merrimack mills.
With a louder din
Did its current begin,
When melted the snow
On the far mountain's brow,
And the drops came together
In that rainy weather.
Experienced river,
Hast thou flowed forever?
Souhegan soundeth old,
But the half is not told,

What names has thou borne,
In the ages far gone,
When the Xanthus and Meander
Commenced to wander,
Ere the black bear haunted
   Thy red forest-floor,
Or Nature had planted
   The pines by thy shore?

My Love Must Be
As Free

My love must be as free
   As is the eagle's wing,
Hovering o'er land and sea
   And everything.

I must not dim my eye
   In thy saloon,
I must not leave my sky
   And nightly moon.

Be not the fowler's net
   Which stays my flight,
And craftily is set
   T' allure the sight.

But be the favoring gale
   That bears me on,
And still doth fill my sail
   When thou art gone.

I cannot leave my sky
  For thy caprice,
True love would soar as high
  As heaven is.

The eagle would not brook
  Her mate thus won,
Who trained his eye to look
  Beneath the sun.

The Poet's Delay

In vain I see the morning rise,
  In vain observe the western blaze,
Who idly look to other skies,
  Expecting life by other ways.
Amidst such boundless wealth without,
  I only still am poor within,
The birds have sung their summer out,
  But still my spring does not begin.

Shall I then wait the autumn wind,
  Compelled to seek a milder day,
And leave no curious nest behind,
  No woods still echoing to my lay?

Salmon Brook

  Salmon Brook,
  Penichook,
Ye sweet waters of my brain,
  When shall I look,
  Or cast the hook,
In your waves again?

Silver eels,
Wooden creels,
These the baits that still allure,
And dragon-fly
That floated by,
May they still endure?

I am the Autumnal Sun

I am the autumnal sun,
With autumn gales my race is run;
When will the hazel put forth its flowers,
Or the grape ripen under my bowers?
When will the harvest or the hunter's moon,
Turn my midnight into mid-noon?
I am all sere and yellow,
And to my core mellow.
The mast is dropping within my woods,
The winter is lurking within my moods,
And the rustling of the withered leaf
Is the constant music of my grief.

Friendship

I think awhile of Love, and while I think,
Love is to me a world,
Sole meat and sweetest drink,
And close connecting link
Tween heaven and earth.

I only know it is, not how or why,
My greatest happiness;
However hard I try,
Not if I were to die,
Can I explain.

I fain would ask my friend how it can be,
But when the time arrives,
Then Love is more lovely
Than anything to me,
And so I'm dumb.

For if the truth were known, Love cannot speak,
But only thinks and does;
Though surely out 'twill leak
Without the help of Greek,
Or any tongue.

A man may love the truth and practise it,
Beauty he may admire,
And goodness not omit,
As much as may befit
To reverence.

The Cliffs & Springs

When breathless noon hath paused on hill and vale,
And now no more the woodman plies his axe,
Nor mower whets his scythe,
Somewhat it is, sole sojourner on earth,
To hear the veery on her oaken perch
Ringing her modest trill—
Sole sound of all the din that makes a world,
And I sole ear.
Fondly to nestle me in that sweet melody,

And own a kindred soul, speaking to me
From out the depths of universal being.
O'er birch and hazle, through the sultry air,
Comes that faint sound this way,
On Zephyr borne, straight to my ear.
No longer time or place, nor faintest trace
Of earth, the landscape's shimmer is my only space,
Sole remnant of a world.
Anon that throat has done, and familiar sounds
Swell strangely on the breeze, the low of cattle,
And the novel cries of sturdy swains
That plod the neighboring vale—
And I walk once more confounded a denizen of earth.

May Morning

The school boy loitered on his way to school,
Scorning to live so rare a day by rule.
So mild the air a pleasure 'twas to breathe,
For what seems heaven above was earth beneath.
Soured neighbors chatted by the garden pale,
Nor quarrelled who should drive the needed nail—
The most unsocial made new friends that day,
As when the sun shines husbandmen make hay

How long I slept I know not, but at last
I felt my consciousness returning fast,
For Zephyr rustled past with leafy tread,
And heedlessly with one heel grazed my head.

My eyelids opened on a field of blue,
For close above a nodding violet grew,
A part of heaven it seemed, which one could scent,
Its blue commingling with the firmament.

Walden

—True, our converse a stranger is to speech,
Only the practised ear can catch the surging words,
That break and die upon thy pebbled lips.
Thy flow of thought is noiseless as the lapse of thy
       own waters,
Wafted as is the morning mist up from thy surface,
So that the passive Soul doth breathe it in,
And is infected with the truth thou wouldst express.

E'en the remotest stars have come in troops
And stooped low to catch the benediction
Of thy countenance. Oft as the day came round,
Impartial has the sun exhibited himself
Before thy narrow skylight—nor has the moon
For cycles failed to roll this way
As oft as elsewhither, and tell thee of the night.
No cloud so rare but hitherward it stalked,
And in thy face looked doubly beautiful.
O! tell me what the winds have writ within these
       thousand years,
On the blue vault that spans thy flood—
Or sun transferred and delicately reprinted
For thy own private reading. Somewhat
Within these latter days I've read,
But surely there was much that would have thrilled
       the Soul,
Which human eye saw not
I would give much to read that first bright page,
Wet from a virgin press, when Eurus—Boreas—
And the host of airy quill-drivers
First dipped their pens in mist.

In the Busy Streets, Domains of Trade

In the busy streets, domains of trade,
Man is a surly porter, or a vain and hectoring bully,
Who can claim no nearer kindredship with me
Than brotherhood by law.

I Knew a Man by Sight

I knew a man by sight,
    A blameless wight,
Who, for a year or more,
Had daily passed my door,
Yet converse none had had with him.

I met him in a lane,
    Him and his cane,
About three miles from home,
Where I had chanced to roam,
And volumes stared at him, and he at me.

In a more distant place
    I glimpsed his face,
And bowed instinctively;
Starting he bowed to me,
Bowed simultaneously, and passed along.

Next, in a foreign land
    I grasped his hand,
And had a social chat,
About this thing and that,
As I had known him well a thousand years.

Late in a wilderness
　　I shared his mess,
For he had hardships seen,
　　And I a wanderer been;
He was my bosom friend, and I was his.

And as, methinks, shall all,
　　Both great and small,
That ever lived on earth,
　　Early or late their birth,
Stranger and foe, one day each other know.

Last Night as I Lay Gazing
with Shut Eyes

Last night as I lay gazing with shut eyes
　　Into the golden land of dreams,
I thought I gazed adown a quiet reach
　　Of land and water prospect,
　　　Whose low beach
Was peopled with the now subsiding hum
Of happy industry—whose work is done.

And as I turned me on my pillow o'er,
I heard the lapse of waves upon the shore,
Distinct as it had been at broad noonday,
And I were wandering at Rockaway.

Each More Melodious Note
I Hear

Each more melodious note I hear
Brings this reproach to me,
That I alone afford the ear,
Who would the music be.

I Was Born Upon thy
Bank River

I was born upon thy bank river
My blood flows in thy stream
And thou meanderest forever
    At the bottom of my dream

They Who Prepare My Evening Meal Below

They who prepare my evening meal below
Carelessly hit the kettle as they go
With tongs or shovel,
And ringing round and round,
Out of this hovel
It makes an eastern temple by the sound.

At first I thought a cow-bell right at hand
Mid birches sounded o'er the open land,
Where I plucked flowers
Many years ago,
Spending midsummer hours
With such secure delight they hardly seemed to flow.

Independence

My life more civil is and free
Than any civil polity.

Ye princes keep your realms
And circumscribed power,
Not wide as are my dreams,
Nor rich as is this hour.

What can ye give which I have not?
What can ye take which I have got?
Can ye defend the dangerless?
Can ye inherit nakedness?

To all true wants time's ear is deaf,
Penurious states lend no relief
Out of their pelf—
But a free soul—thank God—
Can help itself.

Be sure your fate
Doth keep apart its state—
Not linked with any band—
Even the nobles of the land

In tented fields with cloth of gold—
No place doth hold
But is more chivalrous than they are.
And sigheth for a nobler war.
A finer strain its trumpet rings—
A brighter gleam its armor flings.

The life that I aspire to live
No man proposeth me—
No trade upon the street
Wears its emblazonry.

I Mark the Summer's Swift Decline

I mark the summer's swift decline
The springing sward its grave clothes weaves
Whose rustling woods the gales confine
The aged year turns on its couch of leaves.

Oh could I catch the sounds remote
Could I but tell to human ear—
The strains which on the breezes float
And sing the requiem of the dying year.

Brother Where Dost Thou Dwell

Brother where dost thou dwell?
  What sun shines for thee now?
Dost thou indeed farewell?
  As we wished here below.

What season didst thou find?
  'Twas winter here.
Are not the fates more kind
  Than they appear?

Is thy brow clear again
  As in thy youthful years?
And was that ugly pain
  The summit of thy fears?

Yet thou wast cheery still,
  They could not quench thy fire,
Thou dids't abide their will,
  And then retire.

Where chiefly shall I look
  To feel thy presence near?
Along the neighboring brook
  May I thy voice still hear?

Dost thou still haunt the brink
  Of yonder river's tide?
And may I ever think
  That thou art at my side?

The Hero

What doth he ask?
Some worthy task.
Never to run
Till that be done,
that never done
Under the sun.
Here to begin
All things to win
By his endeavor
Forever and ever—
Happy and well
On this ground to dwell
This soil subdue
Plant and renew.
By might & main
Hea[l]th & strength gain
So to give nerve
To his slenderness
Yet Some mighty pain
He would sustain.
So to preserve
His tenderness.
Not be deceived

Of suffring bereaved
Not lose his life
By living too well
Nor escape strife
In his lonely cell.

I Seek the Present Time

I seek the Present Time,
No other clime,
Life in today,
Not to sail another way,
To Paris or to Rome,
Or farther still from home.
That man, whoe'er he is,
Lives but a moral death,
Whose life is not coeval
With his breath.
What are deeds done
Away from home?
What the best essay
On the Ruins of Rome?
The dusty highways,
What Scripture says,
This pleasant weather
And all signs together—
The river's meander,
All things, in short,
Forbid me to wander
In deed or in thought.
In cold or in drouth,
seek Not the sunny South,
But make the whole tour
Of the sunny Present Hour.

Th' Ambrosia of the Gods 's
A Weed On Earth

Th' ambrosia of the Gods 's a weed on earth
Their nectar is the morning dew which on
'ly our shoes taste—For they are simple folks
'Tis very fit the ambrosia of the gods
Should be a weed on earth. As nectar is
The morning dew with which we wet our shoes
For the gods are simple folks and we should pine
          upon their humble fare.

I Saw a Delicate Flower Had
Grown Up 2 Feet High

I saw a delicate flower had grown up 2 feet high
Between the horse's paths & the wheel track
Which Dakin's & Maynards wagons had
Passed over many a time
An inch more to right or left had sealed its fate
Or an inch higher. And yet it lived & flourish[e]d
As much as if it had a thousand acres
Of untrodden space around it—and never
Knew the danger it incurred.
It did not borrow trouble nor invite an
Evil fate by apprehending it.
For though the distant market-wagon
Every other day—inevitably rolled
This way—it just as inevitably rolled
In those ruts—And the same
Charioteer who steered the flower
Upward—guided the horse & cart aside from it.
There were other flowers which you would say
Incurred less danger grew more out of the way
Which no cart rattled near, no walker daily passed.
But at length one rambling deviously

For no rut restrained plucked them
And then it appeared that they stood
Directly in his way though he had come
From farther than the market wagon—

JAMES
RUSSELL
LOWELL
1819-1891

James Russell Lowell was a leader among the mid-
nineteenth century authors said to have brought a
renaissance to New England. A natural conservative,
he supported the anti-slavery cause for many years at
the behest of his wife and attacked England's part in
the Civil War. He later became Minister for Spain and
England, finally retiring from public life back to
Cambridge, Mass.

Many of the extracts included here come from
Lowell's amiable verse satire *A Fable for Critics*,
published anonymously in 1848. Each mocks another
of the poets found in this collection, combining wit and
humor with some shrewd analysis.

From *A Fable for Critics*

Emerson

There comes Emerson first, whose rich words, every one,
Are like gold nails in temples to hang trophies on,
Whose prose is grand verse, while his verse, the Lord
    knows,
Is some of it pr— No, 'tis not even prose;
I'm speaking of metres; some poems have welled
From those rare depths of soul that have ne'er been
    excelled;
They're not epics, but that doesn't matter a pin,
In creating, the only hard thing's to begin;
A grass-blade's no easier to make than an oak;
If you've once found the way, you've achieved the grand
    stroke;
In the worst of his poems are mines of rich matter,
But thrown in a heap with a crash and a clatter;
Now it is not one thing nor another alone
Makes a poem, but rather the general tone,
The something pervading, uniting the whole,
The before unconceived, unconceivable soul,
So that just in removing this trifle or that, you
Take away, as it were, a chief limb of the statue;
Roots, wood, bark, and leaves singly perfect may be,
But, clapt hodge-podge together, they don't make a tree.

    But, to come back to Emerson (whom, by the way,
I believe we left waiting), – his is, we may say,
A Greek head on right Yankee shoulders, whose range
Has Olympus for one pole, for t'other the Exchange;
He seems, to my thinking (although I'm afraid
The comparison must, long ere this, have been made),
A Plotinus-Montaigne, where the Egyptian's gold mist
And the Gascon's shrewd wit cheek-by-jowl coexist;
All admire, and yet scarcely six converts he's got
To I don't (nor they either) exactly know what;

For though he builds glorious temples, 't is odd
He leaves never a doorway to get in a god.
'T is refreshing to old-fashioned people like me
To meet such a primitive Pagan as he,
In whose mind all creation is duly respected
As parts of himself – just a little projected;
And who's willing to worship the stars and the sun,
A convert to – nothing but Emerson.
So perfect a balance there is in his head,
That he talks of things sometimes as if they were dead;
Life, nature, love, God, and affairs of that sort,
He looks at as merely ideas; in short,
As if they were fossils stuck round in a cabinet,
Of such vast extent that our earth's a mere dab in it;
Composed just as he is inclined to conjecture her,
Namely, one part pure earth, ninety-nine parts pure
    lecturer;
You are filled with delight at his clear demonstration,
Each figure, word, gesture, just fits the occasion,
With the quiet precision of science he'll sort 'em,
But you can't help suspecting the whole a *post mortem*.

There are persons, mole-blind to the soul's make and
    style,
Who insist on a likeness 'twixt him and Carlyle;
To compare him with Plato would be vastly fairer,
Carlyle's the more burly, but E. is the rarer;
He sees fewer objects, but clearlier, truelier,
If C.'s as original, E.'s more peculiar;
That he's more of a man you might say of the one,
Of the other he's more of an Emerson;
C.'s the Titan, as shaggy of mind as of limb,—
E. the clear-eyed Olympian, rapid and slim;
The one's two thirds Norseman, the other half Greek,
Where the one's most abounding, the other's to seek;

C.'s generals require to be seen in the mass,—
E.'s specialties gain if enlarged by the glass;
C. gives nature and God his own fits of the blues,
And rims common-sense things with mystical hues,—
E. sits in a mystery calm and intense,
And looks coolly around him with sharp common-sense;
C. shows you how every-day matters unite
With the dim transdiurnal recesses of night,—
While E., in a plain, preternatural way,
Makes mysteries matters of mere every day;
C. draws all his characters quite à la Fuseli,—
Not sketching their bundles of muscles and thews illy,
He paints with a brush so untamed and profuse,
They seem nothing but bundles of muscles and thews;
E. is rather like Flaxman, lines strait and severe,
And a colorless outline, but full, round, and clear;—
To the men he thinks worthy he frankly accords
The design of a white marble statue in words.
C. labors to get at the centre, and then
Take a reckoning from there of his actions and men;
E. calmly assumes the said centre as granted,
And, given himself, has whatever is wanted.

    He has imitators in scores, who omit
No part of the man but his wisdom and wit,—
Who go carefully o'er the sky-blue of his brain,
And when he has skimmed it once, skim it again;
If at all they resemble him, you may be sure it is
Because their shoals mirror his mists and obscurities,
As a mud-puddle seems deep as heaven for a minute,
While a cloud that floats o'er is reflected within it.

Bryant

'There is Bryant, as quiet, as cool, and as dignified,
As a smooth, silent iceberg, that never is ignified,
Save when by reflection 't is kindled o' nights
With a semblance of flame by the chill Northern Lights.
He may rank (Griswold says so) first bard of your nation
(There's no doubt that he stands in supreme iceolation),
Your topmost Parnassus he may set his heel on,
But no warm applauses come, peal following peal on,—
He's too smooth and too polished to hang any zeal on:
Unqualified merits, I'll grant, if you choose, he has 'em,
But he lacks the one merit of kindling enthusiasm;
If he stir you at all, it is just, on my soul,
Like being stirred up with the very North Pole.

'He is very nice reading in summer, but *inter
Nos*, we don't want *extra* freezing in winter;
Take him up in the depth of July, my advice is,
When you feel an Egyptian devotion to ices.
But, deduct all you can, there's enough that's right good
    in him,
He has a true soul for field, river, and wood in him;
And his heart, in the midst of brick walls, or where'er it
    is,
Glows, softens, and thrills with the tenderest charities—
To you mortals that delve in this trade-ridden planet?
No, to old Berkshire's hills, with their limestone and
    granite.
If you're one who *in loco* (add *foco* here) *desipis*,
You will get of his outermost heart (as I guess) a piece;
But you'd get deeper down if you came as a precipice,
And would break the last seal of its inwardest fountain,
If you only could palm yourself off for a mountain.
Mr Quivis, or somebody quite as discerning,
Some scholar who's hourly expecting his learning,
Calls B. the American Wordsworth; but Wordsworth

May be rated at more than your whole tuneful herd's
    worth.
No, don't be absurd, he's an excellent Bryant;
But, my friends, you'll endanger the life of your client,
By attempting to stretch him up into a giant:
If you choose to compare him, I think there are two per-
-sons fit for a parallel – Thomson and Cowper;
I don't mean exactly, – there's something of each,
There's T.'s love of nature, C.'s penchant to preach;
Just mix up their minds so that C.'s spice of craziness
Shall balance and neutralize T.'s turn for laziness,
And it gives you a brain cool, quite frictionless, quiet,
Whose internal police nips the buds of all riot,—
A brain like a permanent strait-jacket put on
The heart that strives vainly to burst off a button,—
A brain which, without being slow or mechanic,
Does more than a larger less drilled, more volcanic;
He's a Cowper condensed, with no craziness bitten,
And the advantage that Wordsworth before him had
    written.

   'But, my dear little bardlings, don't prick up your ears
Nor suppose I would rank you and Bryant as peers;
If I call him an iceberg, I don't mean to say
There is nothing in that which is grand in its way;
He is almost the one of your poets that knows
How much grace, strength, and dignity lie in Repose;
If he sometimes fall short, he is too wise to mar
His thought's modest fulness by going too far;
'T would be well if your authors should all make a trial
Of what virtue there is in severe self-denial,
And measure their writings by Hesiod's staff,
Which teaches that all has less value than half.

Whittier

There is Whittier, whose swelling and vehement heart
Strains the strait-breasted drab of the Quaker apart,
And reveals the live Man, still supreme and erect,
Underneath the bemummying wrappers of sect;
There was ne'er a man born who had more of the swing
Of the true lyric bard and all that kind of thing;
And his failures arise (though he seem not to know it)
From the very same cause that has made him a poet,—
A fervor of mind which knows no separation
'Twixt simple excitement and pure inspiration,
As my Pythoness erst sometimes erred from not knowing
If 't were I or mere wind through her tripod was blowing;
Let his mind once get head in its favorite direction
And the torrent of verse bursts the dams of reflection,
While, borne with the rush of the metre along,
The poet may chance to go right or go wrong,
Content with the whirl and delirium of song;
Then his grammar's not always correct, nor his rhymes,
And he's prone to repeat his own lyrics sometimes,
Not his best, though, for those are struck off at
    white-heats
When the heart in his breast like a trip-hammer beats,
And can ne'er be repeated again any more
Than they could have been carefully plotted before:
Like old what's-his-name there at the battle of Hastings
(Who, however, gave more than mere rhythmical
    bastings),
Our Quaker leads off metaphorical fights
For reform and whatever they call human rights,
Both singing and striking in front of the war,
And hitting his foes with the mallet of Thor;
Anne haec, one exclaims, on beholding his knocks,
Vestis filii tui, O leather-clad Fox?
Can that be thy son, in the battle's mid din,
Preaching brotherly love and then driving it in

To the brain of the tough old Goliath of sin,
With the smoothest of pebbles from Castaly's spring
Impressed on his hard moral sense with a sling?
　All honour and praise to the right-hearted bard
Who was true to The Voice when such service was hard,
Who himself was so free he dared sing for the slave
When to look but a protest in silence was brave;
All honor and praise to the women and men
Who spoke out for the dumb and the down-trodden then!

American Literature

　'There are truths you Americans need to be told,
And it never 'll refute them to swagger and scold ...

'The most of you (this is what strikes all beholders)
Have a mental and physical stoop in the shoulders;
Though you ought to be free as the winds and the waves,
You've the gait and the manners of runaway slaves ...

　'You steal Englishmen's books and think Englishmen's
　　thought.
With their salt on her tail your wild eagle is caught:
Your literature suits its each whisper and motion
To what will be thought of it over the ocean;
The cast clothes of Europe your statesmanship tries
And mumbles again the old blarneys and lies;—
Forget Europe wholly, your veins throb with blood,
To which the dull current in hers is but mud ...

'On my friends, thank your God, if you have one, that he
'Twixt the Old World and you set the gulf of a sea;
Be strong-backed, brown-handed, upright as your pines,
By the scale of a hemisphere shape your designs,
Be true to yourselves and this new nineteenth age,

As a statue by Powers, or a picture by Page,
Plough, sail, forge, build, carve, paint, all things make
   new,
To your own New-World instincts contrive to be true,
Keep your ears open wide to the Future's first call,
Be whatever you will, but yourselves first of all,
Stand fronting the dawn on Toil's heaven-scaling peaks,
And become my new race of more practical Greeks.

Poe and Longfellow

There comes Poe, with his raven, like Barnaby Rudge,
Three fifths of him genius and two fifths sheer fudge,
Who talks like a book of iambs and pentameters,
In a way to make people of common sense damn metres,
Who has written some things quite the best of their kind,
But the heart somehow seems all squeezed out by the
   mind,
Who — But hey-day! What's this? Messieurs Mathews and
   Poe,
You mustn't fling mud-balls at Longfellow so,
Does it make a man worse that his character's such
As to make his friends love him (as you think) too much?
Why, there is not a bard at this moment alive
More willing than he that his fellows should thrive;
While you are abusing him thus, even now
He would help either one of you out of a slough;
You may say that he's smooth and all that till you're
   hoarse,
But remember that elegance also is force;
After polishing granite as much as you will,
The heart keeps its tough old persistency still;
Deduct all you can, *that* still keeps you at bay;
Why, he'll live till men weary of Collins and Gray.
I'm not over-fond of Greek metres in English,

To me rhyme's a gain, so it be not too jinglish,
And your modern hexameter verses are no more
Like Greek ones than sleek Mr Pope is like Homer;
As the roar of the sea to the coo of a pigeon is,
So, compared to your moderns, sounds old Melesigenes;
I may be too partial, the reason, perhaps, o't is
That I've heard the old blind man recite his own
    rhapsodies,
And my ear with that music impregnate may be,
Like the poor exiled shell with the soul of the sea,
Or as one can't bear Strauss when his nature is cloven
To its deeps within deeps by the stroke of Beethoven;
But, set that aside, and 'tis truth that I speak,
Had Theocritus written in English, not Greek,
I believe that his exquisite sense would scarce change a
    line
In that rare, tender, virgin-like pastoral Evangeline.
That's not ancient nor modern, its place is apart
Where time has no sway, in the realm of pure Art,
'T is a shrine of retreat from Earth's hubbub and strife
As quiet and chaste as the author's own life.

Lowell

There is Lowell, who's striving Parnassus to climb
With a whole bale of *isms* tied together with rhyme,
He might get on alone, spite of brambles and boulders,
But he can't with that bundle he has on his shoulders,
The top of the hill he will ne'er come nigh reaching
Till he learns the distinction 'twixt singing and
    preaching;
His lyre has some chords that would ring pretty well,
But he'd rather by half make a drum of the shell,
And rattle away till he's old as Methusalem,
At the head of a march to the last new Jerusalem.

Daphne's Embarkation

Phoebus, sitting one day in a laurel-tree's shade,
Was reminded of Daphne, of whom it was made,
For the god being one day too warm in his wooing,
She took to the tree to escape his pursuing;
Be the cause what it might, from his offers she shrunk,
And, Ginevra-like, shut herself up in a trunk;
And, though 'twas a step into which he had driven her,
He somehow or other had never forgiven her;
Her memory he nursed as a kind of a tonic,
Something bitter to chew when he'd play the Byronic,
And I can't count the obstinate nymphs that he brought
    over
By a strange kind of smile he put on when he thought of
    her.
'My case is like Dido's,' he sometimes remarked;
'When I last saw my love, she was fairly embarked
In a laurel, as *she* thought, – but (ah, how Fate mocks!)
She has found it by this time a very bad box;
Let hunters from me take this saw when they need it,—
You're not always sure of your game when you've treed
    it.
Just conceive such a change taking place in one's
    mistress!
What romance would be left? – who can flatter or kiss
    trees?
And, for mercy's sake, how could one keep up a dialogue
With a dull wooden thing that will live and will die a
    log,—
Not to say that the thought would forever intrude
That you've less chance to win her the more she is wood?
Ah! it went to my heart, and the memory still grieves,
To see those loved graces all taking their leaves;
Those charms beyond speech, so enchanting but now,

As they left me forever, each making its bough!
If her tongue *had* a tang sometimes more than was right,
Her new bark is worse than ten times her old bite.'

In an Album

The misspelt scrawl, upon the wall
By some Pompeian idler traced,
In ashes packed (ironic fact!)
Lies eighteen centuries uneffaced,
While many a page of bard and sage,
Deemed once mankind's immortal gain,
Lost from Time's ark, leaves no more mark
Than a keel's furrow through the main.

O Chance and Change! our buzz's range
Is scarcely wider than a fly's;
Then let us play at fame today,
Tomorrow be unknown and wise;
And while the fair beg locks of hair,
And autographs, and Lord knows what,
Quick! let us scratch our moment's match,
Make our brief blaze, and be forgot!

Too pressed to wait, upon her slate
Fame writes a name or two in doubt;
Scarce written, these no longer please,
And her own finger rubs them out:
It may ensue, fair girl, that you
Years hence this yellowing leaf may see,
And put to task, your memory ask
In vain, 'This Lowell, who was he?'

Aladdin

When I was a beggarly boy
  And lived in a cellar damp,
I had not a friend nor a toy,
  But I had Aladdin's lamp;
When I could not sleep for the cold,
  I had fire enough in my brain,
And builded, with roofs of gold,
  My beautiful castles in Spain!

Since then I have toiled day and night,
  I have money and power good store,
But I'd give all my lamps of silver bright
  For the one that is mine no more;
Take, Fortune, whatever you choose,
  You gave, and may snatch again;
I have nothing 'twould pain me to lose,
  For I own no more castles in Spain!

Credidimus Jovem Regnare

O days endeared to every Muse,
When nobody had any Views,
Nor, while the cloudscape of his mind
By every breeze was new designed,
Insisted all the world should see
Camels or whales where none there be!
O happy days, when men received
From sire to son what all believed,
And left the other world in bliss,
Too busy with bedevilling this!

Beset by doubts of every breed
In the last bastion of my creed,
With shot and shell for Sabbath-chime,

I watch the storming-party climb,
Panting (their prey in easy reach),
To pour triumphant through the breach
In wall that shed like snowflakes tons
Of missiles from old-fashioned guns,
But crumble 'neath the storm that pours
All day and night from bigger bores.
There, as I hopeless watch and wait
The last life-crushing coil of Fate,
Despair finds solace in the praise
Of those serene dawn-rosy days
Ere microscopes had made us heirs
To large estates of doubts and snares,
By proving that the title-deeds,
Once all-sufficient for men's needs,
Are palimpsests that scarce disguise
The tracings of still earlier lies,
Themselves as surely written o'er
An older fib erased before.
So from these days I fly to those
That in the landlocked Past repose,
Where no rude wind of doctrine shakes
From bloom-flushed boughs untimely flakes;
Where morning's eyes see nothing strange,
No crude perplexity of change,
And morrows trip along their ways
Secure as happy yesterdays.
Then there were rulers who could trace
Through heroes up to gods their race,
Pledged to fair fame and noble use
By veins from Odin filled or Zeus,
And under bonds to keep divine
The praise of a celestial line.
Then priests could pile the altar's sods,
With whom gods spake as they with gods,
And everywhere from haunted earth

Broke springs of wonder, that had birth
In depths divine beyond the ken
And fatal scrutiny of men;
Then hills and groves and streams and seas
Thrilled with immortal presences,
Not too ethereal for the scope
Of human passion's dream or hope.

Now Pan at last is surely dead,
And King No-Credit reigns instead,
Whose officers, morosely strict,
Poor Fancy's tenantry evict,
Chase the last Genius from the door,
And nothing dances any more.
Nothing? Ah, yes, our tables do,
Drumming the Old One's own tattoo,
And, if the oracles are dumb,
Have we not mediums? Why be glum?

Fly thither? Why, the very air
Is full of hindrance and despair!
Fly thither? But I cannot fly;
My doubts enmesh me if I try,—
Each lilliputian, but, combined,
Potent a giant's limbs to bind.
This world and that are growing dark;
A huge interrogation mark,
The Devil's crook episcopal,
Still borne before him since the Fall,
Blackens with its ill-omened sign
The old blue heaven of faith benign.

Whence ? Whither? Wherefore? How? Which? Why?
All ask at once, all wait reply.
Men feel old systems cracking under 'em;
Life saddens to a mere conundrum

Which once Religion solved, but she
Has lost — has Science found? — the key.

What was snow-bearded Odin, trow,
The mighty hunter long ago,
Whose horn and hounds the peasant hears
Still when the Northlights shake their spears?
Science hath answers twin, I've heard;
Choose which you will, nor hope a third;
Whichever box the truth be stowed in,
There's not a sliver left of Odin.
Either he was a pinchbrowed thing,
With scarcely wit a stone to fling,
A creature both in size and shape
Nearer than we are to the ape,
Who hung sublime with brat and spouse
By tail prehensile from the boughs,
And, happier than his maimed descendants,
The culture-curtailed *in*dependents,
Could pluck his cherries with both paws,
And stuff with both his big-boned jaws;
Or else the core his name enveloped
Was from a solar myth developed,
Which, hunted to its primal shoot,
Takes refuge in a Sanskrit root,
Thereby to instant death explaining
The little poetry remaining.

Try it with Zeus, 't is just the same;
The thing evades, we hug a name;
Nay, scarcely that, — perhaps a vapor
Born of some atmospheric caper.
All Lempriere's fables blur together
In cloudy symbols of the weather,
And Aphrodite rose from frothy seas
But to illustrate such hypotheses.

With years enough behind his back,
Lincoln will take the selfsame track,
And prove, hulled fairly to the cob,
A mere vagary of Old Prob.
Give the right man a solar myth,
And he'll confute the sun therewith.

They make things admirably plain,
But one hard question *will* remain:
If one hypothesis you lose,
Another in its place you choose,
But, your faith gone, O man and brother,
Whose shop shall furnish you another?
One that will wash, I mean, and wear,
And wrap us warmly from despair?
While they are clearing up our puzzles,
And clapping prophylactic muzzles
On the Actæon's hounds that sniff
Our devious track through But and If,
Would they'd explain away the Devil
And other facts that won't keep level,
But rise beneath our feet or fail,
A reeling ship's deck in a gale!
God vanished long ago, iwis,
A mere subjective synthesis;
A doll, stuffed out with hopes and fears,
Too homely for us pretty dears,
Who want one that conviction carries,
Last make of London or of Paris.
He gone, I felt a moment's spasm,
But calmed myself with Protoplasm,
A finer name, and, what is more,
As enigmatic as before;
Greek, too, and sure to fill with ease
Minds caught in the Symplegades
Of soul and sense, life's two conditions,

Each baffled with its own omniscience.
The men who labor to revise
Our Bibles will, I hope, be wise,
And print it without foolish qualms
Instead of God in David's psalms:
Noll had been more effective far
Could he have shouted at Dunbar,
'Rise, Protoplasm!' No dourest Scot
Had waited for another shot.

And yet I frankly must confess
A secret unforgivingness,
And shudder at the saving chrism
Whose best New Birth is Pessimism;
My soul – I mean the bit of phosphorus
That fills the place of what that was for us—
Can't bid its inward bores defiance
With the new nursery-tales of science.
What profits me, though doubt by doubt,
As nail by nail, be driven out,
When every new one, like the last,
Still holds my coffin-lid as fast?
Would I find thought a moment's truce,
Give me the young world's Mother Goose
With life and joy in every limb,
The chimney-corner tales of Grimm!

Our dear and admirable Huxley
Cannot explain to me why ducks lay,
Or, rather, how into their eggs
Blunder potential wings and legs
With will to move them and decide
Whether in air or lymph to glide.
Who gets a hair's-breadth on by showing
That Something Else set all agoing?
Farther and farther back we push

From Moses and his burning bush;
Cry, 'Art Thou there?' Above, below,
All Nature mutters *yes* and *no!*

'T is the old answer: we're agreed
Being from Being must proceed,
Life be Life's source. I might as well
Obey the meeting-house's bell,
And listen while Old Hundred pours
Forth through the summer-opened doors,
From old and young. I hear it yet,
Swelled by bass-viol and clarinet,
While the gray minister, with face
Radiant, let loose his noble bass.

If Heaven it reached not, yet its roll
Waked all the echoes of the soul,
And in it many a life found wings
To soar away from sordid things.
Church gone and singers too, the song
Sings to me voiceless all night long,
Till my soul beckons me afar,
Glowing and trembling like a star.
Will any scientific touch
With my worn strings achieve as much?

I don't object, not I, to know
My sires were monkeys, if 't was so;
I touch my ear's collusive tip
And own the poor-relationship.
That apes of various shapes and sizes
Contained their germs that all the prizes
Of senate, pulpit, camp, and bar win
May give us hopes that sweeten Darwin.
Who knows but from our loins may spring
(Long hence) some winged sweet-throated thing

As much superior to us
As we to Cynocephalus?

This is consoling, but, alas,
It wipes no dimness from the glass
Where I am flattening my poor nose,
In hope to see beyond my toes.
Though I accept my pedigree,
Yet where, pray tell me, is the key
That should unlock a private door
To the Great Mystery, such no more?
Each offers his, but one nor all
Are much persuasive with the wall
That rises now, as long ago,
Between I wonder and I know,
Nor will vouchsafe a pin-hole peep
At the viled Isis in its keep.
Where is no door, I but produce
My key to find it of no use.

Yet better keep it, after all,
Since Nature's economical,
And who can tell but some fine day
(If it occur to her) she may,
In her good-will to you and me,
Make door and lock to match the key?

from *The Biglow Papers*

The Courtin'

God makes sech nights, all white an' still
    Fur'z you can look or listen,
Moonshine an' snow on field an' hill,
    All silence an' all glisten.

Zekle crep' up quite unbeknown
  An' peeked in thru' the winder,
An' there sot Huldy all alone,
  'Ith no one nigh to hender.

A fireplace filled the room's one side
  With half a cord o' wood in—
There warn't no stoves (tell comfort died)
  To bake ye to a puddin'.

The wa'nut logs shot sparkles out
  Towards the pootiest, bless her,
An' leetle flames danced all about
  The chiny on the dresser.

Agin the chimbley crook-necks hung,
  An' in amongst 'em rusted
The ole queen's-arm thet gran'ther Young
  Fetched back f'om Concord busted.

The very room, coz she was in,
  Seemed warm f'om floor to ceilin',
An' she looked full ez rosy agin
  Ez the apples she was peelin'.

'T was kin' o' kingdom-come to look
  On sech a blessed cretur,
A dogrose blushin' to a brook
  Ain't modester nor sweeter.

He was six foot o' man, A1,
  Clear grit an' human natur',
None couldn't quicker pitch a ton
  Nor dror a furrer straighter.

He'd sparked it with full twenty gals,
   He'd squired 'em, danced 'em, druv 'em,
Fust this one, an' then thet, by spells—
   All is, he could n't love 'em.

But long o' her his veins 'ould run
   All crinkly like curled maple,
The side she breshed felt full o' sun
   Ez a south slope in Ap'il.

She thought no v'ice hed sech a swing
   Ez hisn in the choir;
My! when he made Ole Hunderd ring,
   She *knowed* the Lord was nigher.

An' she'd blush scarlit, right in prayer,
   When her new meetin'-bunnet
Felt somehow thru' its crown a pair
   O' blue eyes sot upon it.

Thet night, I tell ye, she looked *some*!
   She seemed to 've gut a new soul,
For she felt sartin-sure he'd come,
   Down to her very shoe-sole.

She heered a foot, an' knowed it tu,
   A-raspin' on the scraper,—
All ways to once her feelins flew
   Like sparks in burnt-up paper.

He kin' o' l'itered on the mat
   Some doubtfle o' the sekle,
His heart kep' goin' pity-pat,
   But hern went pity Zekle.

An' yit she gin her cheer a jerk
  Ez though she wished him furder,
An' on her apples kep' to work,
  Parin' away like murder.

'You want to see my Pa, I s'pose?'
  'Wal ... no ... I come dasignin''—
'To see my Ma? She's sprinklin' clo'es
  Agin tomorrer's i'nin'.'

To say why gals act so or so,
  Or don't, 'ould be persumin';
Mebby to mean *yes* an' say *no*
  Comes nateral to women.

He stood a spell on one foot fust,
  Then stood a spell on t' other,
An' on which one he felt the wust
  He could n't ha' told ye nuther.

Says he, 'I'd better call agin;'
  Says she, 'Think likely, Mister.'
Thet last word pricked im like a pin,
  An' ... Wal, he up an' kist her.

When Ma bimeby upon 'em slips,
  Huldy sot pale ez ashes,
All kin' o' smily roun' the lips
  An' teary roun' the lashes.

For she was jes' the quiet kind
  Whose naturs never vary,
Like streams that keep a summer mind
  Snowhid in Jenooary.

The blood clost roun' her heart felt glued
  Too tight for all expressin',
Tell mother see how metters stood,
  An' gin 'em both her blessin'.

Then her red come back like the tide
  Down to the Bay o' Fundy,
An' all I know is they was cried
  In meetin' come nex' Sunday.

What Mr Robinson Thinks

Guvener B. is a sensible man;
  He stays to his home an' looks arter his folks;
He draws his furrer ez straight ez he can,
  An' into nobody's tater-patch pokes;
      But John P.
      Robinson he
  Sez he wunt vote fer Guvener B.

My! aint it terrible? Wut shall we du?
  We can't never choose him o' course, – thet's flat;
Guess we shall hev to come round, (don't you?)
  An' go in fer thunder an' guns, an' all that;
      Fer John P.
      Robinson he
  Sez he wunt vote fer Guvener B.

Gineral C. is a dreffle smart man:
  He's ben on all sides thet give places or pelf;
But consistency still wuz a part of his plan.—
  He's ben true to *one* party, – an' thet is himself;—
        So John P.
        Robinson he
    Sez he shall vote fer Gineral C.

Gineral C. he goes in fer the war;
  He don't vally principle more'n an old cud;
Wut did God make us raytional creeturs fer,
  But glory an' gunpowder, plunder an' blood?
        So John P.
        Robinson he
    Sez he shall vote fer Gineral C.

We were gittin' on nicely up here to our village,
  With good old idees o' wut's right an' wut aint,
We kind o' thought Christ went agin war an' pillage,
  An' thet eppyletts worn't the best mark of a saint;
        But John P.
        Robinson he
    Sez this kind o' thing's an exploded idee.

Parson Wilbur he calls all these argimunts lies;
  Sez they're nothin' on airth but jest *fee, faw, fum*:
An' thet all this big talk of our destinies
  Is half on it ign'ance, an' t'other half rum;
        But John P.
        Robinson he
    Sez it aint no sech thing; an', of course, so must we.

Parson Wilbur sez *he* never heerd in his life
  Thet th'Apostles rigged out in their swaller-tail coats,
An' marched round in front of a drum an' a fife,
  To git some on 'em office, an' some on 'em votes;
        But John P.
        Robinson he
  Sez they didn't know everythin' down in Judee.

Wal, it's a marcy we've gut folks to tell us
  The rights an' the wrongs o' these matters, I vow,—
God sends country lawyers, an' other wise fellers,
  To start the world's team wen it gits in a slough;
        Fer John P.
        Robinson he
  Sez the world'll go right, ef he hollers out Gee!

An Incident
in a Railroad Car

He spoke of Burns: men rude and rough
  Pressed round to hear the praise of one
Whose heart was made of manly, simple stuff,
  As homespun as their own.

And, when he read, they forward leaned,
  Drinking, with thirsty hearts and ears,
His brook-like songs whom glory never weaned
  From humble smiles and tears.

Slowly there grew a tender awe,
  Sun-like, o'er faces brown and hard,
As if in him who read they felt and saw
  Some presence of the bard.

It was a sight for sin and wrong
And slavish tyranny to see,
A sight to make our faith more pure and strong
    In high humanity.

I thought, these men will carry hence
Promptings their former life above,
And something of a finer reverence
    For beauty, truth and love.

God scatters love on every side
Freely among His children all,
And always hearts are lying open wide,
    Wherein some grains may fall.

There is no wind but soweth seeds
Of a more true and open life,
Which burst, unlooked for, into high-souled deeds,
    With wayside beauty rife.

We find within these souls of ours
Some wild germs of a higher birth,
Which in the poet's tropic heart bear flowers
    Whose fragrance fills the earth.

Within the hearts of all men lie
These promises of wider bliss,
Which blossom into hopes that cannot die,
    In sunny hours like this.

All that hath been majestical
In life or death, since time began,
Is native in the simple heart of all,
    The angel heart of man.

And thus, among the untaught poor,
Great deeds and feelings find a home,
That cast in shadow all the golden lore
    Of classic Greece and Rome.

O mighty brother-soul of man,
    Where'er thou art, in low or high,
Thy skyey arches with exulting span
    O'er-roof infinity!

All thoughts that mould the age begin
Deep down within the primitive soul
And from the many slowly upward win
    To one who grasps the whole:

In his wide brain the feeling deep
That struggled on the many's tongue
Swells to a tide of thought, whose surges leap
    O'er the weak thrones of wrong.

All thought begins in feeling,—wide
In the great mass its base is hid,
And, narrowing up to thought, stands glorified,
    A moveless pyramid.

Nor is he far astray, who deems
That every hope, which rises and grows broad
In the world's heart, by ordered impulse streams
    From the great heart of God.

God wills, man hopes: in common souls
Hope is but vague and undefined,
Till from the poet's tongue the message rolls
    A blessing to his kind.

Never did Poesy appear
So full of heaven to me, as when
I saw how it would pierce through pride and fear
To the lives of coarsest men.

It may be glorious to write
Thoughts that shall glad the two or three
High souls, like those far stars that come in sight
Once in a century;—

But better far it is to speak
One simple word, which now and then
Shall waken their free nature in the weak
And friendless sons of men;

To write some earnest verse or line,
Which, seeking not the praise of art,
Shall make a clearer faith and manhood shine
In the untutored heart.

He who doth this, in verse or prose,
May be forgotten in his day,
But surely shall be crowned at last with those
Who live and speak for aye.

Guvener B. is a sensible man

Guvener B. is a sensible man;
He stays to his home an' looks arter his folks;
He draws his furrer ez straight ez he can,
An' into nobody's tater-patch pokes;
But John P.
Robinson he
Sez he wunt vote fer Guvener B.

My! aint it terrible? Wut shall we du?
  We can't never choose him o' course,—thet's flat;
Guess we shall hev to come round, (don't you?)
  An' go in fer thunder an' guns, an' all that;
        Fer John P.
        Robinson he
      Sez he wunt vote fer Guvener B.

Gineral C. is a dreffle smart man:
  He's ben on all sides thet give places or pelf;
But consistency still wuz a part of his plan,—
  He's ben true to *one* party,—an' thet is himself;—
        So John P.
        Robinson he
      Sez he shall vote fer Gineral C.

Gineral C. he goes in fer the war;
  He don't vally princerple more'n an old cud;
Wut did God make us raytional creeturs fer,
  But glory an' gunpowder, plunder an' blood?
        So John P.
        Robinson he
      Sez he shall vote fer Gineral C.

We were gittin' on nicely up here to our village,
  With good old idees o' wut's right an' wut aint,
We kind o' thought Christ went agin war an' pillage,
  An' thet eppyletts worn't the best mark of a saint;
        But John P.
        Robinson he
      Sez this kind o' thing's an exploded idee.

The side of our country must ollers be took,
  An' Presidunt Polk, you know, *he* is our country.
An' the angel thet writes all our sins in a book
  Puts the *debit* to him, an' to us the *per contry*;
      An' John P.
      Robinson he
  Sez this is his view o' the thing to a T.

Parson Wilbur he calls all these argimunts lies;
  Sez they're nothin' on airth but jest *fee, faw, fum*;
An' thet all this big talk of our destinies
  Is half on it ign'ance, an' t'other half rum;
      But John P.
      Robinson he
  Sez it ain't no sech thing: an', of course, so must we.

Parson Wilbur sez *he* never heerd in his life
  Thet th' Apostles rigged out in their swaller-tail coats,
An' marched round in front of a drum an' a fife,
  To git some on 'em office, an' some on 'em votes;
      But John P.
      Robinson he
  Sez they didn't know everythin' down in Judee.

Wal, it's a marcy we've gut folks to tell us
  The rights an' the wrongs o' these matters, I vow,—
God sends country lawyers, an' other wise fellers,
  To start the world's team wen it gits in a slough;
      Fer John P.
      Robinson he
  Sez the world'll go right, ef he hollers out Gee!

A Letter

Dear Sir,—You wish to know my notions
  On sartin pints thet rile the land;
There's nothin' thet my nature so shuns
  Ez bein' mum or underhand;
I'm a straight-spoken kind o' creetur
  Thet blurts right out wut's in his head,
An' ef I've one pecooler feetur,
  It is a nose thet wunt be led.

So, to begin at the beginnin'
  An' come direcly to the pint,
I think the country's underpinnin'
  Is some consid'ble out o' jint;
I aint agoin' to try your patience
  By tellin' who done this or thet,
I don't make no insinooations,
  I jest let on I smell a rat.

Thet is, I mean, it seems to me so,
  But, ef the public think I'm wrong,
I wunt deny but wut I be so,—
  An', fact, it don't smell very strong;
My mind's tu fair to lose its balance
  An' say wich party hez most sense;
There may be folks o' greater talence
  Thet can't set stiddier on the fence.

I'm an eclectic; ez to choosin'
  'Twixt this an' thet, I'm plaguy lawth;
I leave a side thet looks like losin',
  But (wile there's doubt) I stick to both;
I stan' upon the Constitution,
  Ez predunt statesmun say, who've planned
A way to git the most profusion
  O' chances ez to *ware* they'll stand.

Ez fer the war, I go agin it,—
  I mean to say I kind o' du,—
Thet is, I mean thet, bein' in it,
  The best way wuz to fight it thru;
Not but wut abstract war is horrid,
  I sign to thet with all my heart,—
But civlyzation *doos* git forrid
  Sometimes upon a powder-cart.

About thet darned Proviso matter
  I never hed a grain o' doubt,
Nor I ain't one my sense to scatter
  So'st no one couldn't pick it out;
My love fer North an' South is equil,
  So I'll jest answer plump an' frank,
No matter wut may be the sequil,—
  Yes, Sir, I *am* agin a Bank.

Ez to the answerin' o' questions,
  I'm an off ox at bein' druv,
Though I aint one thet ary test shuns
  'll give our folks a helpin' shove;
Kind o' permiscoous I go it
  Fer the holl country, an' the ground
I take, ez nigh ez I can show it,
  Is pooty gen'ally all round.

I don't appruve o' givin' pledges;
  You'd ough' to leave a feller free,
An' not go knockin' out the wedges
  To ketch his fingers in the tree;
Pledges air awfle breachy cattle
  Thet preudunt farmers don't turn out,—
Ez long'z the people git their rattle,
  Wut is there fer'm to grout about?

Ez to the slaves, there's no confusion
  In *my* idees consarnin' them,—
I think they air an Institution,
  A sort of—yes, jest so,—ahem:
Do *I* own any? Of my merit
  On thet pint you yourself may jedge;
All is, I never drink no sperit,
  Nor I haint never signed no pledge.

Ez to my princerples, I glory
  In hevin' nothing' o' the sort;
I ain't a Wig, I ain't a Tory,
  I'm jest a canderdate, in short;
Thet's fair an' square an' parpendicler,
  But, ef the Public cares a fig
To hev me an' thin' in particler,
  Wy, I'm a kind o' peri-Wig.

WALT WHITMAN
1819-1892

Walt Whitman was born on Long Island and brought up in Brooklyn. He worked at a variety of jobs in his early years and read avidly: Shakespeare, Scott, Homer, The Bible, and Greek and Hindu poetry – all exerted great influence on his writing. While living in New Orleans in 1855 Whitman underwent a spiritual transformation and this, with transcendentalism, science and phrenology, is clearly reflected in his poetry.

The following poems are all taken from Whitman's central achievement *Leaves of Grass*. It was originally published in 1855, with an enlarged second edition in 1856, and a greatly expanded edition of 1860, after which he continued to revise it and add to it for the rest of his life.

There Was a Child Went Forth

There was a child went forth every day,
And the first object he look'd upon, that object he became,
And that object became part of him for the day or a
    certain part of the day,
Or for many years or stretching cycles of years.

The early lilacs became part of this child,
And grass and white and red morning-glories, and white
    and red clover, and the song of the phœbe-bird,
And the Third-month lambs and the sow's pink-faint
    litter, and the mare's foal and the cow's calf,
And the noisy brood of the barnyard or by the mire of the
    pond-side,
And the fish suspending themselves so curiously below
    there, and the beautiful curious liquid,
And the water-plants with their graceful flat heads, all
    became part of him.

The field-sprouts of Fourth-month and Fifth-month
    became part of him,
Winter-grain sprouts and those of the light-yellow corn,
    and the esculent roots of the garden,
And the apple-trees cover'd with blossoms and the fruit
    afterward, and wood-berries, and the commonest
    weeds by the road,
And the old drunkard staggering home from the outhouse
    of the tavern whence he had lately risen,
And the schoolmistress that pass'd on her way to the
    school,
And the friendly boys that pass'd, and the quarrelsome
    boys,
And the tidy and fresh-cheek'd girls, and the barefoot
    negro boy and girl,
And all the changes of city and country wherever he
    went.

His own parents, he that had father'd him and she that
    had conceiv'd him in her womb and birth'd him,
They gave this child more of themselves than that,
They gave him afterward every day, they became part of
    him.

The mother at home quietly placing the dishes on the
    supper-table,
The mother with mild words, clean her cap and gown, a
    wholesome odor falling off her person and clothes as
    she walks by,
The father, strong, self-sufficient, manly, mean, anger'd,
    unjust,
The blow, the quick loud word, the tight bargain, the
    crafty lure,
The family usages, the language, the company, the
    furniture, the yearning and swelling heart,
Affection that will not be gainsay'd, the sense of what is
    real, the thought if after all it should prove unreal,
The doubts of day-time and the doubts of night-time, the
    curious whether and how,
Whether that which appears so is so, or is it all flashes
    and specks?
Men and women crowding fast in the streets, if they are
    not flashes and specks what are they?
The streets themselves and the façades of houses, and
    goods in the windows,
Vehicles, teams, the heavy-plank'd wharves, the huge
    crossing at the ferries,
The village on the highland seen from afar at sunset, the
    river between,
Shadows, aureola and mist, the light falling on roofs and
    gables of white or brown two miles off,
The schooner near by sleepily dropping down the tide, the
    little boat slack-tow'd astern,

The hurrying tumbling waves, quick-broken crests,
    slapping,
The strata of color'd clouds, the long bar of maroon-tint
    away solitary by itself, the spread of purity it lies
    motionless in,
The horizon's edge, the flying sea-crow, the fragrance of
    salt marsh and shore mud,
These became part of that child who went forth every
    day, and who now goes, and will always go forth
    every day.

Song of Myself

1

I celebrate myself, and sing myself,
And what I assume you shall assume,
For every atom belonging to me as good belongs to you.

I loafe and invite my soul,
I lean and loafe at my ease observing a spear of summer
    grass.

My tongue, every atom of my blood, form'd from this soil,
    this air,
Born here of parents born here from parents the same,
    and their parents the same,
I, now thirty-seven years old in perfect health begin,
Hoping to cease not till death.

Creeds and schools in abeyance,
Retiring back a while sufficed at what they are, but
    never forgotten,
I harbor for good or bad, I permit to speak at every
    hazard,
Nature without check with original energy.

2

Houses and rooms are full of perfumes, the shelves are
    crowded with perfumes,
I breathe the fragrance myself and know it and like it,
The distillation would intoxicate me also, but I shall not
    let it.
The atmosphere is not a perfume, it has no taste of the
    distillation, it is odorless,
It is for my mouth forever, I am in love with it,
I will go to the bank by the wood and become undisguised
    and naked,
I am mad for it to be in contact with me.

The smoke of my own breath,
Echoes, ripples, buzz'd whispers, love-root, silk-thread,
    crotch and vine,
My respiration and inspiration, the beating of my heart,
    the passing of blood and air through my lungs,
The sniff of green leaves and dry leaves, and of the shore
    and dark-color'd sea-rocks, and hay in the barn,
The sound of the belch'd words of my voice loos'd to the
    eddies of the wind,
A few light kisses, a few embraces, a reaching around of
    arms,
The play of shine and shade on the trees as the supple
    boughs wag,
The delight alone or in the rush of the streets, or along
    the fields and hill-sides,
The feeling of health, the full-noon trill, the song of me
    rising from bed and meeting the sun.

Have you reckon'd a thousand acres much? have you
    reckon'd the earth much?
Have you practis'd so long to learn to read?
Have you felt so proud to get at the meaning of poems?

Stop this day and night with me and you shall possess
  the origin of all poems,
You shall possess the good of the earth and sun, (there
  are millions of suns left,)
You shall no longer take things at second or third hand,
  nor look through the eyes of the dead, nor feed on the
  spectres in books,
You shall not look through my eyes either, nor take
  things from me,
You shall listen to all sides and filter them from your
  self.

3

I have heard what the talkers were talking, the talk of
  the beginning and the end,
But I do not talk of the beginning or the end.

There was never any more inception than there is now,
Nor any more youth or age than there is now,
And will never be any more perfection than there is now,
Nor any more heaven or hell than there is now.

Urge and urge and urge,
Always the procreant urge of the world.
Out of the dimness opposite equals advance, always
  substance and increase, always sex,
Always a knit of identity, always distinction, always a
  breed of life.

To elaborate is no avail, learn'd and unlearn'd feel that it
  is so.

Sure as the most certain sure, plumb in the uprights,
  well entretied, braced in the beams,
Stout as a horse, affectionate, haughty, electrical,
I and this mystery here we stand.

Clear and sweet is my soul, and clear and sweet is all
that is not my soul.
Lack one lacks both, and the unseen is proved by the
seen,
Till that becomes unseen and receives proof in its turn.

Showing the best and dividing it from the worst age
vexes age,
Knowing the perfect fitness and equanimity of things,
while they discuss I am silent, and go bathe and
admire myself.
Welcome is every organ and attribute of me, and of any
man hearty and clean,
Not an inch nor a particle of an inch is vile, and none
shall be less familiar than the rest.

I am satisfied – I see, dance, laugh, sing;
As the hugging and loving bed-fellow sleeps at my side
through the night, and withdraws at the peep of the
day with stealthy tread,
Leaving me baskets cover'd with white towels swelling
the house with their plenty,
Shall I postpone my acceptation and realization and
scream at my eyes,
That they turn from gazing after and down the road,
And forthwith cipher and show me to a cent,
Exactly the value of one and exactly the value of two,
and which is ahead?

4

Trippers and askers surround me,
People I meet, the effect upon me of my early life or the
ward and city I live in, or the nation,
The latest dates, discoveries, inventions, societies,
authors old and new,
My dinner, dress, associates, looks, compliments, dues,

The real or fancied indifference of some man or woman I
    love,
The sickness of one of my folks or of myself, or ill-doing
    or loss or lack of money, or depressions or
    exaltations,
Battles, the horrors of fratricidal war, the fever of
    doubtful news, the fitful events;
These come to me days and nights and go from me again,
But they are not the Me myself.
Apart from the pulling and hauling stands what I am,
Stands amused, complacent, compassionating, idle,
    unitary,
Looks down, is erect, or bends an arm on an impalpable
    certain rest,
Looking with side-curved head curious what will come
    next,
Both in and out of the game and watching and wondering
    at it.

Backward I see in my own days where I sweated through
    fog with linguists and contenders,
I have no mockings or arguments, I witness and wait.

5

I believe in you my soul, the other I am must not abase
    itself to you,
And you must not be abased to the other.

Loafe with me on the grass, loose the stop from your
    throat,
Not words, not music or rhyme I want, not custom or
    lecture, not even the best,

Only the lull I like, the hum of your valvèd voice.

I mind how once we lay such a transparent summer
    morning,
How you settled your head athwart my hips and gently
    turn'd over upon me,
And parted the shirt from my bosom-bone, and plunged
    your tongue to my bare-stript heart,
And reach'd till you felt my beard, and reach'd till you
    held my feet.

Swiftly arose and spread around me the peace and
    knowledge that pass all the argument of the earth,
And I know that the hand of God is the promise of my
    own,
And I know that the spirit of God is the brother of my
    own,
And that all the men ever born are also my brothers, and
    the women my sisters and lovers,

And that a kelson of the creation is love,
And limitless are leaves stiff or drooping in the fields,
And brown ants in the little wells beneath them,
And mossy scabs of the worm fence, heap'd stones, elder,
    mullein and poke-weed.

6

A child said *What is the grass?* fetching it to me with full
    hands,
How could I answer the child? I do not know what it is
    any more than he.

I guess it must be the flag of my disposition, out of
    hopeful green stuff woven.

Or I guess it is the handkerchief of the Lord,
A scented gift and remembrancer designedly dropt,
Bearing the owner's name someway in the corners, that
    we may see and remark, and say *Whose?*

Or I guess the grass is itself a child, the produced babe of
    the vegetation.

Or I guess it is a uniform hieroglyphic,
And it means, Sprouting alike in broad zones and narrow
    zones,
Growing among black folks as among white,
Kanuck, Tuckahoe, Congressman, Cuff, I give them the
    same, I receive them the same.

And now it seems to me the beautiful uncut hair of
    graves.

Tenderly will I use you curling grass,
It may be you transpire from the breasts of young men,
It may be if I had known them I would have loved them,
It may be you are from old people, or from offspring
    taken soon out of their mothers' laps,
And here you are the mothers' laps.

This grass is very dark to be from the white heads of old
    mothers,
Darker than the colourless beards of old men,
Dark to come from under the faint red roofs of mouths.

O I perceive after all so many uttering tongues,
And I perceive they do not come from the roofs of mouths
    for nothing.

I wish I could translate the hints about the dead young
    men and women,
And the hints about old men and mothers, and the
    offspring taken soon out of their laps.

What do you think has become of the young and old men?
And what do you think has become of the women and
    children?

They are alive and well somewhere,
The smallest sprout shows there is really no death,
And if ever there was it led forward life, and does not
    wait at the end to arrest it,
And ceas'd the moment life appear'd.

All goes onward and outward, nothing collapses,
And to die is different from what any one supposed, and
    luckier.

7

Has any one supposed it lucky to be born?
I hasten to inform him or her it is just as lucky to die,
    and I know it.

I pass death with the dying and birth with the new-
    wash'd babe, and am not contain'd between my hat
    and boots,
And peruse manifold objects, no two alike and every one
    good,
The earth good and the stars good, and their adjuncts all
    good.

I am not an earth nor an adjunct of an earth,
I am the mate and companion of people, all just as
    immortal and fathomless as myself,
(They do not know how immortal, but I know.)

Every kind for itself and its own, for me mine male and
    female,
For me those that have been boys and that love women,
For me the man that is proud and feels how it stings to
    be slighted,
For me the sweet-heart and the old maid, for me mothers
    and the mothers of mothers,
For me lips that have smiled, eyes that have shed tears,
For me children and the begetters of children.

Undrape! you are not guilty to me, nor stale nor
    discarded,
I see through the broadcloth and gingham whether or no,
And am around, tenacious, acquisitive, tireless, and
    cannot be shaken away.

8

The little one sleeps in its cradle,
I lift the gauze and look a long time, and silently brush
    away flies with my hand.

The youngster and the red-faced girl turn aside up the
    bushy hill,
I peeringly view them from the top.

The suicide sprawls on the bloody floor of the bedroom,
I witness the corpse with its dabbled hair, I note where
    the pistol has fallen.

The blab of the pave, tires of carts, sluff of boot-soles,
    talk of the promenaders,
The heavy omnibus, the driver with his interrogating
    thumb, the clank of the shod horses on the granite
    floor,
The snow-sleighs, clinking, shouted jokes, pelts of
    snowballs,

The hurrahs for popular favorites, the fury of rous'd
    mobs,
The flap of the curtain'd litter, a sick man inside borne to
    the hospital,
The meeting of enemies, the sudden oath, the blows and
    fall,
The excited crowd, the policeman with his star quickly
    working his passage to the centre of the crowd,
The impassive stones that receive and return so many
    echoes,
What groans of over-fed or half-starv'd who fall sunstruck
    or in fits,
What exclamations of women taken suddenly who hurry
    home and give birth to babes,
What living and buried speech is always vibrating here,
    what howls restrain'd by decorum,
Arrests of criminals, slights, adulterous offers made,
    acceptances, rejections with convex lips,
I mind them or the show or resonance of them – I come
    and I depart.

9

The big doors of the country barn stand open and ready,
The dried grass of the harvest-time loads the slow-drawn
    wagon,
The clear light plays on the brown gray and green
    intertinged,
The armfuls are pack'd to the sagging mow.

I am there, I help, I came stretch'd atop of the load,
I felt its soft jolts, one leg reclined on the other,
I jump from the cross-beams and seize the clover and
    timothy,
And roll head over heels and tangle my hair full of wisps.

10

Alone far in the wilds and mountains I hunt,
Wandering amazed at my own lightness and glee,
In the late afternoon choosing a safe spot to pass the
    night,
Kindling a fire and broiling the fresh-kill'd game,
Falling asleep on the gather'd leaves with my dog and
    gun by my side.

The Yankee clipper is under her sky-sails, she cuts the
    sparkle and scud,
My eyes settle the land, I bend at her prow or shout
    joyously from the deck.

The boatmen and clam-diggers arose early and stopt for
    me,
I tuck'd my trowser-ends in my boots and went and had a
    good time;
You should have been with us that day round the
    chowder-kettle.

I saw the marriage of the trapper in the open air in the
    far west, the bride was a red girl,
Her father and his friends sat near cross-legged and
    dumbly smoking, they had moccasins to their feet
    and large thick blankets hanging from their
    shoulders,
On a bank lounged the trapper, he was drest mostly in
    skins, his luxuriant beard and curls protected his
    neck, he held his bride by the hand,
She had long eyelashes, her head was bare, her coarse
    straight locks descended upon her voluptuous limbs
    and reach'd to her feet.

The runaway slave came to my house and stopt outside,
I heard his motions crackling the twigs of the woodpile,

Through the swung half-door of the kitchen I saw him
    limpsy and weak,
And went where he sat on a log and led him in and
    assured him,
And brought water and fill'd a tub for his sweated body
    and bruis'd feet,
And gave him a room that enter'd from my own, and
    gave him some coarse clean clothes,
And remember perfectly well his revolving eyes and his
    awkwardness,
And remember putting plasters on the galls of his neck
    and ankles;
He staid with me a week before he was recuperated and
    pass'd north,
I had him sit next me at table, my fire-lock lean'd in the
    corner.

11

Twenty-eight young men bathe by the shore,
Twenty-eight young men and all so friendly;
Twenty-eight years of womanly life and all so lonesome.

She owns the fine house by the rise of the bank,
She hides handsome and richly drest aft the blinds of the
    window.
Which of the young men does she like the best?
Ah the homeliest of them is beautiful to her.

Where are you off to, lady? for I see you,
You splash in the water there, yet stay stock still in your
    room.

Dancing and laughing along the beach came the twenty-
    ninth bather,
The rest did not see her, but she saw them and loved
    them.

The beards of the young men glisten'd with wet, it ran
    from their long hair,
Little streams pass'd all over their bodies.

An unseen hand also pass'd over their bodies,
It descended tremblingly from their temples and ribs.

The young men float on their backs, their white bellies
    bulge to the sun, they do not ask who seizes fast to
    them,
They do not know who puffs and declines with pendant
    and bending arch,
They do not think whom they souse with spray.

12

The butcher-boy puts off his killing-clothes, or sharpens
    his knife at the stall in the market,
I loiter enjoying his repartee and his shuffle and
    breakdown.

Blacksmiths with grimed and hairy chests environ the
    anvil,
Each has his main-sledge, they are all out, there is a
    great heat in the fire.

From the cinder-strew'd threshold I follow their
    movements,
The lithe sheer of their waists plays even with their
    massive arms,
Overhand the hammers swing, overhand so slow,
    overhand so sure,
They do not hasten, each man hits in his place.

13

The negro holds firmly the reins of his four horses, the
 block swags underneath on its tied-over chain,
The negro that drives the long dray of the stone-yard,
 steady and tall he stands pois'd on one leg on the
 string-piece,
His blue shirt exposes his ample neck and breast and
 loosens over his hip-band,
His glance is calm and commanding, he tosses the slouch
 of his hat away from his forehead,
The sun falls on his crispy hair and mustache, falls on
 the black of his polish'd and perfect limbs.

I behold the picturesque giant and love him, and I do not
 stop there,
I go with the team also.

In me the caresser of life wherever moving, backward as
 well as forward sluing,
To niches aside and junior bending, not a person or object
 missing,
Absorbing all to myself and for this song.

Oxen that rattle the yoke and chain or halt in the leafy
 shade, what is that you express in your eyes?
It seems to me more than all the print I have read in my
 life.

My tread scares the wood-drake and wood-duck on my
 distant and day-long ramble,
They rise together, they slowly circle around.

I believe in those wing'd purposes,
And acknowledge red, yellow, white, playing within me,
And consider green and violet and the tufted crown
 intentional,

And do not call the tortoise unworthy because she is not
    something else,
And the jay in the woods never studied the gamut, yet
    trills pretty well to me,
And the look of the bay mare shames silliness out of
    me.

14

The wild gander leads his flock through the cool night,
Ya-honk he says, and sounds it down to me like an
    invitation,
The pert may suppose it meaningless, but I listening
    close,
Find its purpose and place up there toward the wintry
    sky.

The sharp-hoof'd moose of the north, the cat on the
    house-sill, the chickadee, the prairie-dog,
The litter of the grunting sow as they tug at her teats,
The brood of the turkey-hen and she with her half-spread
    wings,
I see in them and myself the same old law.

The press of my foot to the earth springs a hundred
    affections,
They scorn the best I can do to relate them.

I am enamour'd of growing out-doors,
Of men that live among cattle or taste of the ocean or
    woods,
Of the builders and steerers of ships and the wielders of
    axes and mauls, and the drivers of horses,
I can eat and sleep with them week in and week out.

What is commonest, cheapest, nearest, easiest, is Me,
Me going in for my chances, spending for vast returns,

Adorning myself to bestow myself on the first that will
    take me,
Not asking the sky to come down to my good will,
Scattering it freely forever.

15

The pure contralto sings in the organ loft,
The carpenter dresses his plank, the tongue of his
    foreplane whistles its wild ascending lisp,
The married and unmarried children ride home to their
    Thanksgiving dinner,
The pilot seizes the king-pin, he heaves down with a
    strong arm,
The mate stands braced in the whale-boat, lance and
    harpoon are ready,
The duck-shooter walks by silent and cautious stretches,
The deacons are ordain'd with cross'd hands at the altar,
The spinning-girl retreats and advances to the hum of
    the big wheel,
The farmer stops by the bars as he walks on a First-day
    loafe, and looks at the oats and rye,
The lunatic is carried at last to the asylum a confirm'd
    case,
(He will never sleep any more as he did in the cot in his
    mother's bedroom;)
The jour printer with gray head and gaunt jaws works at
    his case,
He turns his quid of tobacco while his eyes blurr with the
    manuscript;
The malform'd limbs are tied to the surgeon's table,
What is removed drops horribly in a pail;
The quadroon girls sold at the auction-stand, the
    drunkard nods by the bar-room stove,
The machinist rolls up his sleeves, the policeman travels
    his beat, the gate-keeper marks who pass,

The young fellow drives the express-wagon, (I love him, though I do not know him;)

The half-breed straps on his light boots to compete in the race,

The western turkey-shooting draws old and young, some lean on their rifles, some sit on logs,

Out from the crowd steps the marksman, takes his position, levels his piece;

The groups of newly-come immigrants cover the wharf or levee,

As the woolly-pates hoe in the sugar-field, the overseer views them from his saddle,

The bugle calls in the ball-room, the gentlemen run for their partners, the dancers bow to each other,

The youth lies awake in he cedar-roof'd garret and harks to the musical rain,

The Wolverine sets traps on the creek that helps fill the Huron,

The squaw wrapt in her yellow-hemm'd cloth is offering moccasins and bead-bags for sale,

The connoisseur peers along the exhibition-gallery with half-shut eyes bent sideways,

As the deck-hands make fast the steamboat the plank is thrown for the shore-going passengers,

The young sister holds out the skein while the elder sister winds it off in a ball, and stops now and then for the knots,

The one-year wife is recovering and happy having a week ago borne her first child,

The clean-hair'd Yankee girl works with her sewing-machine or in the factory or mill,

The paving-man leans on his two-handed rammer, the reporter's lead flies swiftly over the note-book, the sign-painter is lettering with blue and gold,

The canal boy trots on the tow-path, the book-keeper counts at his desk, the shoemaker waxes his thread,

The conductor beats time for the band and all the
    performers follow him,
The child is baptized, the convert is making his first
    professions,
The regatta is spread on the bay, the race is begun, (how
    the white sails sparkle!)
The drover watching his drove sings out to them that
    would stray,
The pedler sweats with his pack on his back, (the
    purchaser higgling about the odd cent;)
The bride unrumples her white dress, the minute-hand of
    the clock moves slowly,
The opium-eater reclines with rigid head and just-open'd
    lips,
The prostitute draggles her shawl, her bonnet bobs on
    her tipsy and pimpled neck,
The crowd laugh at her blackguard oaths, the men jeer
    and wink to each other,
(Miserable! I do not laugh at your oaths nor jeer you;)
The President holding a cabinet council is surrounded by
    the great Secretaries,
On the piazza walk three matrons stately and friendly
    with twined arms,
The crew of the fish-smack pack repeated layers of
    halibut in the hold,
The Missourian crosses the plains toting his wares and
    his cattle,
As the fare-collector goes through the train he gives
    notice by the jingling of loose change,
The floor-men are laying the floor, the tinners are tinning
    the roof, the masons are calling for mortar,
In single file each shouldering his hod pass onward the
    laborers;
Seasons pursuing each other the indescribable crowd is
    gather'd, it is the fourth of Seventh-month, (what
    salutes of cannon and small arms!)

Seasons pursuing each other the plougher ploughs, the
mower mows, and the winter-grain falls in the
ground;
Off on the lakes the pike-fisher watches and waits by the
hole in the frozen surface,
The stumps stand thick round the clearing, the squatter
strikes deep with his axe,
Flatboatmen make fast towards dusk near the cotton-
wood or pecan-trees,
Coon-seekers go through the regions of the Red river or
through those drain'd by the Tennessee, or through
those of the Arkansas,
Torches shine in the dark that hangs on the
Chattahooche or Altamahaw,
Patriarchs sit at supper with sons and grandsons and
great-grandsons around them,
In walls of adobie, in canvas tents, rest hunters and
trappers after their day's sport,
The city sleeps and the country sleeps,
The living sleep for their time, the dead sleep for their
time,
The old husband sleeps by his wife and the young
husband sleeps by his wife;
And these tend inward to me, and I tend outward to
them,
And such as it is to be of these more or less I am,
And of these one and all I weave the song of myself.

16

I am of old and young, of the foolish as much as the wise,
Regardless of others, ever regardful of others,
Maternal as well as paternal, a child as well as a man,
Stuff'd with the stuff that is coarse and stuff'd with the
stuff that is fine,
One of the Nation of many nations, the smallest the same
and the largest the same,

A Southerner soon as a Northerner, a planter nonchalant
and hospitable down by the Oconee I live,
A Yankee bound my own way ready for trade, my joints
the limberest joints on earth and the sternest joints
on earth,
A Kentuckian walking the vale of the Elkhorn in my
deerskin leggings, a Louisianian or Georgian,
A boatman over lakes or bays or along coasts, a Hoosier,
Badger, Buck-eye;
At home on Kanadian snow-shoes or up in the bush, or
with fishermen off Newfoundland,
At home in the fleet of ice-boats, sailing with the rest and
tacking,
At home on the hills of Vermont or in the woods of
Maine, or the Texan ranch,
Comrade of Californians, comrade of free North-
Westerners, (loving their big proportions,)
Comrade of raftsmen and coalmen, comrade of all who
shake hands and welcome to drink and meat,
A learner with the simplest, a teacher of the
thoughtfullest,
A novice beginning yet experient of myriads of seasons,
Of every hue and caste am I, of every rank and religion,
A farmer, mechanic, artist, gentleman, sailor, quaker,
Prisoner, fancy-man, rowdy, lawyer, physician, priest.

I resist any thing better than my own diversity,
Breathe the air but leave plenty after me,
And am not stuck up, and am in my place.

(The moth and the fish-eggs are in their place,
The bright suns I see and the dark suns I cannot see are
in their place,
The palpable is in its place and the impalpable is in its
place.)

17

These are really the thoughts of all men in all ages and
    lands, they are not original with me,
If they are not yours as much as mine they are nothing,
    or next to nothing,
If they are not the riddle and the untying of the riddle
    they are nothing,
If they are not just as close as they are distant they are
    nothing.

This is the grass that grows wherever the land is and the
    water is,
This the common air that bathes the globe.

18

With music strong I come, with my cornets and my
    drums,
I play not marches for accepted victors only, I play
    marches for conquer'd and slain persons.

Have you heard that it was good to gain the day?
I also say it is good to fall, battles are lost in the same
    spirit in which they are won.

I beat and pound for the dead,
I blow through my embouchures my loudest and gayest
    for them.

Vivas to those who have fail'd!
And to those whose war-vessels sank in the sea!
And to those themselves who sank in the sea!
And to all generals that lost engagements, and all
    overcome heroes!
And the numberless unknown heroes equal to the
    greatest heroes known!

19

This is the meal equally set, this the meat for natural
    hunger,
It is for the wicked just the same as the righteous, I
    make appointments with all,
I will not have a single person slighted or left away,
The kept-woman, sponger, thief, are hereby invited,
The heavy-lipp'd slave is invited, the venerealee is
    invited;
There shall be no difference between them and the rest.

This is the press of a bashful hand, this the float and odor
    of hair,
This the touch of my lips to yours, this the murmur of
    yearning,
This the far-off depth and height reflecting my own face,
This the thoughtful merge of myself, and the outlet
    again.

Do you guess I have some intricate purpose?
Well I have, for the Fourth-month showers have, and the
    mica on the side of a rock has.

Do you take it I would astonish?
Does the daylight astonish? does the early redstart
    twittering through the woods?
Do I astonish more than they?

This hour I tell things in confidence,
I might not tell everybody, but I will tell you.

20

Who goes there? hankering, gross, mystical, nude;
How is it I extract strength from the beef I eat?

What is a man anyhow? what am I? what are you?
All I mark as my own you shall offset it with your own,
Else it were time lost listening to me.

I do not snivel that snivel the world over,
That months are vacuums and the ground but wallow
    and filth.

Whimpering and truckling fold with powders for invalids,
    conformity goes to the fourth-remov'd,
I wear my hat as I please indoors or out.

Why should I pray? why should I venerate and be
    ceremonious?

Having pried through the strata, analyzed to a hair,
    counsel'd with doctors and calculated close,
I find no sweeter fat than sticks to my own bones.

In all people I see myself, none more and not one a
    barley-corn less,
And the good or bad I say of myself I say of them.

I know I am solid and sound,
To me the converging objects of the universe perpetually
    flow,
All are written to me, and I must get what the writing
    means.

I know I am deathless,
I know this orbit of mine cannot be swept by a
    carpenter's compass,
I know I shall not pass like a child's carlacue cut with a
    burnt stick at night.

I know I am august,
I do not trouble my spirit to vindicate itself or be
    understood,
I see that the elementary laws never apologize,
(I reckon I behave no prouder than the level I plant my
    house by, after all.)
I exist as I am, that is enough,
If no other in the world be aware I sit content,
And if each and all be aware I sit content.

One world is aware and by far the largest to me, and that
    is myself,
And whether I come to my own to-day or in ten thousand
    or ten million years,
I can cheerfully take it now, or with equal cheerfulness I
    can wait.

My foothold is tenon'd and mortis'd in granite,
I laugh at what you call dissolution,
And I know the amplitude of time.

21

I am the poet of the Body and I am the poet of the Soul,
The pleasures of heaven are with me and the pains of
    hell are with me,
The first I graft and increase upon myself, the latter I
    translate into a new tongue.

I am the poet of the woman the same as the man,
And I say it is as great to be a woman as to be a man,
And I say there is nothing greater than the mother of
    men.

I chant the chant of dilation or pride,
We have had ducking and deprecating about enough,
I show that size is only development.

Have you outstript the rest? are you the President?
It is a trifle, they will more than arrive there every one,
    and still pass on.

I am he that walks with the tender and growing night,
I call to the earth and sea half-held by the night.

Press close bare-bosom'd night – press close magnetic
    nourishing night!
Night of south winds – night of the large few stars!
Still nodding night – mad naked summer night.

Smile O voluptuous cool-breath'd earth!
Earth of the slumbering and liquid trees!
Earth of departed sunset – earth of the mountains
    misty-topt!
Earth of the vitreous pour of the full moon just tinged
    with blue!
Earth of shine and dark mottling the tide of the river!
Earth of the limpid gray of clouds brighter and clearer
    for my sake!
Far-swooping elbow'd earth – rich apple-blossom'd earth!
Smile, for your lover comes.
Prodigal, you have given me love – therefore I to you
    give love!
O unspeakable passionate love.

22

You sea! I resign myself to you also – I guess what you
    mean,
I behold from the beach your crooked inviting fingers,
I believe you refuse to go back without feeling of me,
We must have a turn together, I undress, hurry me out of
    sight of the land,
Cushion me soft, rock me in billowy drowse,
Dash me with amorous wet, I can repay you.

Sea of stretch'd ground-swells,
Sea breathing broad and convulsive breaths,
Sea of the brine of life and of unshovell'd yet always-
    ready graves,
Howler and scooper of storms, capricious and dainty sea,
I am integral with you, I too am of one phase and of all
    phases.

Partaker of influx and efflux, I, extoller of hate and
    conciliation,
Extoller of amies and those that sleep in each others'
    arms.

I am he attesting sympathy,
(Shall I make my list of things in the house and skip the
    house that supports them?)

I am not the poet of goodness only, I do not decline to be
    the poet of wickedness also.

What blurt is this about virtue and about vice?
Evil propels me and reform of evil propels me, I stand
    indifferent,
My gait is no fault-finder's or rejecter's gait,
I moisten the roots of all that has grown.

Did you fear some scrofula out of the unflagging
    pregnancy?
Did you guess the celestial laws are yet to be work'd over
    and rectified?

I find one side a balance and the antipodal side a balance,
Soft doctrine as steady help as stable doctrine,
Thoughts and deeds of the present our rouse and early
    start.

This minute that comes to me over the past decillions,
There is no better than it and now.

What behaved well in the past or behaves well to-day is
    not such a wonder,
The wonder is always and always how there can be a
    mean man or an infidel.

23

Endless unfolding of words of ages!
And mine a word of the modern, the word En-Masse.

A word of the faith that never balks,
Here or henceforward it is all the same to me, I accept
    Time absolutely.

It alone is without flaw, it alone rounds and completes
    all,
That mystic baffling wonder alone completes all.

I accept Reality and dare not question it,
Materialism first and last imbuing.

Hurrah for positive science! long live exact
    demonstration!
Fetch stonecrop mixt with cedar and branches of lilac,
This is the lexicographer, this the chemist, this made a
    grammar of the old cartouches,
These mariners put the ship through dangerous unknown
    seas,
This is the geologist, this works with the scalpel, and this
    is a mathematician.

Gentlemen, to you the first honors always!
Your facts are useful, and yet they are not my dwelling,
I but enter by them to an area of my dwelling.

Less the reminders of properties told my words,
And more the reminders they of life untold, and of
    freedom and extrication,
And make short account of neuters and geldings, and
    favor men and women fully equipt,
And beat the gong of revolt, and stop with fugitives and
    them that plot and conspire.

24

Walt Whitman, a kosmos, of Manhattan the son,
Turbulent, fleshy, sensual, eating, drinking and breeding,
No sentimentalist, no stander above men and women or
    apart from them,
No more modest than immodest.

Unscrew the locks from the doors!
Unscrew the doors themselves from their jambs!

Whoever degrades another degrades me,
And whatever is done or said returns at last to me.

Through me the afflatus surging and surging, through
    me the current and index.

I speak the pass-word primeval, I give the sign of
    democracy,
By God! I will accept nothing which all cannot have their
    counterpart of on the same terms.

Through me many long dumb voices,
Voices of the interminable generation of prisoners and
    slaves,
Voices of the diseas'd and despairing and of thieves and
    dwarfs,
Voices of cycles of preparation and accretion,

And of the threads that connect the stars, and of wombs
    and of the father-stuff,
And of the rights of them the others are down upon,
Of the deform'd, trivial, flat, foolish, despised,
Fog in the air, beetles rolling balls of dung.

Through me forbidden voices,
Voices of sexes and lusts, voices veil'd and I remove the
    veil,
Voices indecent by me clarified and transfigur'd.

I do not press my fingers across my mouth,
I keep as delicate around the bowels as around the head
    and heart,
Copulation is no more rank to me than death is.

I believe in the flesh and the appetites,
Seeing, hearing, feeling, are miracles, and each part and
    tag of me is a miracle.

Divine am I inside and out, and I make holy whatever I
    touch or am touch'd from,
The scent of these arm-pits aroma finer than prayer,
This head more than churches, bibles, and all the creeds.

If I worship one thing more than another it shall be the
    spread of my own body, or any part of it,
Translucent mould of me it shall be you!
Shaded ledges and rests it shall be you!
Firm masculine colter it shall be you!
Whatever goes to the tilth of me it shall be you!
You my rich blood! your milky stream pale strippings of
    my life!
Breast that presses against other breasts it shall be you!
My brain it shall be your occult convolutions!

Root of wash'd sweet-flag! timorous pond-snipe! nest of
    guarded duplicate eggs! it shall be you!
Mix'd tussled hay of head, beard, brawn, it shall be you!
Trickling sap of maple, fibre of manly wheat, it shall be
    you!
Sun so generous it shall be you!
Vapors lighting and shading my face it shall be you!

You sweaty brooks and dews it shall be you!
Winds whose soft-tickling genitals rub against me it shall
    be you!
Broad muscular fields, branches of live oak, loving
    lounger in my winding paths, it shall be you!
Hands I have taken, face I have kiss'd, mortal I have
    ever touch'd, it shall be you.

I dote on myself, there is that lot of me and all so
    luscious,
Each moment and whatever happens thrills me with joy,
I cannot tell how my ankles bend, nor whence the cause
    of my faintest wish,
Nor the cause of the friendship I emit, nor the cause of
    the friendship I take again.

That I walk up my stoop, I pause to consider if it really
    be,
A morning-glory at my window satisfies me more than
    the metaphysics of books.

To behold the day-break!
The little light fades the immense and diaphanous
    shadows,
The air tastes good to my palate.

Hefts of the moving world at innocent gambols silently
    rising, freshly exuding,
Scooting obliquely high and low.

Something I cannot see puts forward libidinous prongs,
Seas of bright juice suffuse heaven.

The earth by the sky staid with, the daily close of their
    junction,
The heav'd challenge from the east that moment over my
    head,
The mocking taunt, See then whether you shall be
    master!

25

Dazzling and tremendous how quick the sun-rise would
    kill me,
If I could not now and always send sun-rise out of me.

We also ascend dazzling and tremendous as the sun,
We found our own O my soul in the calm and cool of the
    day-break.

My voice goes after what my eyes cannot reach,
With the twirl of my tongue I encompass worlds and
    volumes of worlds.

Speech is the twin of my vision, it is unequal to measure
    itself,
It provokes me forever, it says sarcastically,
Walt you contain enough, why don't you let it out then?

Come now I will not be tantalized you conceive too much
    of articulation,
Do you not know O speech how the buds beneath you are
    folded?

Waiting in gloom, protected by frost,
The dirt receding before my prophetical screams,
I underlying causes to balance them at last,
My knowledge my live parts, it keeping tally with the
    meaning of all things,
Happiness, (which whoever hears me let him or her set
    out in search of this day.)

My final merit I refuse you, I refuse putting from me
    what I really am,
Encompass worlds, but never try to encompass me,
I crowd your sleekest and best by simply looking toward
    you.

Writing and talk do not prove me,
I carry the plenum of proof and every thing else in my
    face,
With the hush of my lips I wholly confound the skeptic.

26

Now I will do nothing but listen,
To accrue what I hear into this song, to let sounds
    contribute toward it.

I hear bravuras of birds, bustle of growing wheat, gossip
    of flames, clack of sticks cooking my meals,
I hear the sound I love, the sound of the human voice,
I hear all sounds running together, combined, fused or
    following,
Sounds of the city and sounds out of the city, sounds of
    the day and night,
Talkative young ones to those that like them, the loud
    laugh of work-people at their meals,
The angry base of disjointed friendship, the faint tones of
    the sick,

The judge with hands tight to the desk, his pallid lips
    pronouncing a death-sentence,
The heav'e'yo of stevedores unlading ships by the
    wharves, the refrain of the anchor-lifters,
The ring of alarm-bells, the cry of fire, the whirr of swift-
    streaking engines and hose-carts with premonitory
    tinkles and color'd lights,
The steam-whistle, the solid roll of the train of
    approaching cars,
The slow march play'd at the head of the association
    marching two and two,
(They go to guard some corpse, the flag-tops are draped
    with black muslin.)
I hear the violoncello, ('tis the young man's heart's
    complaint,)
I hear the key'd cornet, it glides quickly in through my
    ears,
It shakes mad-sweet pangs through my belly and breast.

I hear the chorus, it is a grand opera,
Ah this indeed is music – this suits me.

A tenor large and fresh as the creation fills me,
The orbic flex of his mouth is pouring and filling me full.

I hear the train'd soprano (what work with hers is this?)
The orchestra whirls me wider than Uranus flies,
It wrenches such ardors from me I did not know I
    possess'd them,
It sails me, I dab with bare feet, they are lick'd by the
    indolent waves,
I am cut by bitter and angry hail, I lose my breath,
Steep'd amid honey'd morphine, my windpipe throttled in
    fakes of death,
At length let up again to feel the puzzle of puzzles,
And that we call Being.

27

To be in any form, what is that?
(Round and round we go, all of us, and ever come back
    thither,)
If nothing lay more develop'd the quahaug in its callous
    shell were enough.

Mine is no callous shell,
I have instant conductors all over me whether I pass or
    stop,
They seize every object and lead it harmlessly through
    me.

I merely stir, press, feel with my fingers, and am happy,
To touch my person to some one else's is about as much
    as I can stand.

28

Is this then a touch? quivering me to a new identity,
Flames and ether making a rush for my veins,
Treacherous tip of me reaching and crowding to help
    them,
My flesh and blood playing out lightning to strike what is
    hardly different from myself,
On all sides prurient provokers stiffening my limbs,
Straining the udder of my heart for its withheld drip,
Behaving licentious toward me, taking no denial,
Depriving me of my best as for a purpose,
Unbuttoning my clothes, holding me by the bare waist,
Deluding my confusion with the calm of the sunlight and
    pasture-fields,
Immodestly sliding the fellow-senses away,
They bribed to swap off with touch and go and graze at
    the edges of me,
No consideration, no regard for my draining strength or
    my anger,

Fetching the rest of the herd around to enjoy them a
    while,
Then all uniting to stand on a headland and worry me.

The sentries desert every other part of me,
They have left me helpless to a red marauder,
They all come to the headland to witness and assist
    against me.

I am given up by traitors,
I talk wildly, I have lost my wits, I and nobody else am
    the greatest traitor,
I went myself first to the headland, my own hands
    carried me there.

You villain touch! what are you doing? my breath is tight
    in its throat,
Unclench your floodgates, you are too much for me.

29

Blind loving wrestling touch, sheath'd hooded sharp-
    tooth'd touch!
Did it make you ache so, leaving me?

Parting track'd by arriving, perpetual payment of
    perpetual loan,
Rich showering rain, and recompense richer afterward.

Sprouts take and accumulate, stand by the curb prolific
    and vital,
Landscapes projected masculine, full-sized and golden.

30

All truths wait in all things,
They neither hasten their own delivery nor resist it,
They do not need the obstetric forceps of the surgeon,

The insignificant is as big to me as any,
(What is less or more than a touch?)

Logic and sermons never convince,
The damp of the night drives deeper into my soul.

(Only what proves itself to every man and woman is so,
Only what nobody denies is so.)

A minute and a drop of me settle my brain,
I believe the soggy clods shall become lovers and lamps,
And a compend of compends is the meat of a man or
	woman,
And a summit and flower there is the feeling they have
	for each other,
And they are to branch boundlessly out of that lesson
	until it becomes omnific,
And until one and all shall delight us, and we them.

31

I believe a leaf of grass is no less than the journey-work
	of the stars,
And the pismire is equally perfect, and a grain of sand,
	and the egg of the wren,
And the tree-toad is a chef-d'œuvre for the highest,
And the running blackberry would adorn the parlors of
	heaven,
And the narrowest hinge in my hand puts to scorn all
	machinery,
And the cow crunching with depress'd head surpasses any
	statue,
And a mouse is miracle enough to stagger sextillions of
	infidels.

I find I incorporate gneiss, coal, long-threaded moss,
	fruits, grains, esculent roots,

And am stucco'd with quadrupeds and birds all over,
And have distanced what is behind me for good reasons,
But call any thing back again when I desire it.

In vain the speeding or shyness,
In vain the plutonic rocks send their old heat against my
    approach,
In vain the mastodon retreats beneath its own powder'd
    bones,
In vain objects stand leagues off and assume manifold
    shapes,
In vain the ocean setting in hollows and the great
    monsters lying low,
In vain the buzzard houses herself with the sky,
In vain the snake slides through the creepers and logs,
In vain the elk takes to the inner passes of the woods,
In vain the razor-bill'd auk sails far north to Labrador,
I follow quickly, I ascend to the nest in the fissure of the
    cliff.

32

I think I could turn and live with animals, they're so
    placid and self-contain'd,
I stand and look at them long and long.

They do not sweat and whine about their condition,
They do not lie awake in the dark and weep for their
    sins,
They do not make me sick discussing their duty to God,
Not one is dissatisfied, not one is demented with the
    mania of owning things,
Not one kneels to another, or to his kind that lived
    thousands of years ago,
Not one is respectable or unhappy over the whole earth.

So they show their relations to me and I accept them,
They bring me tokens of myself, they evince them plainly
    in their possession.

I wonder where they get those tokens,
Did I pass that way huge times ago and negligently drop
    them?

Myself moving forward then and now and forever,
Gathering and showing more always and with velocity,
Infinite and omnigenous, and the like of these among
    them,
Not too exclusive toward the reachers of my
    remembrancers,
Picking out here one that I love, and now go with him on
    brotherly terms.

A gigantic beauty of a stallion, fresh and responsive to
    my caresses,
Head high in the forehead, wide between the ears,
Limbs glossy and supple, tail dusting the ground,
Eyes full of sparkling wickedness, ears finely cut, flexibly
    moving.

His nostrils dilate as my heels embrace him,
His well-built limbs tremble with pleasure as we race
    around and return.
I but use you a minute, then I resign you, stallion,
Why do I need your paces when I myself out-gallop them?
Even as I stand or sit passing faster than you.

33

Space and Time! now I see it is true, what I guess'd at,
What I guess'd when I loaf'd on the grass,
What I guess'd while I lay alone in my bed,

And again as I walk'd the beach under the paling stars of
the morning.

My ties and ballasts leave me, my elbows rest in
sea-gaps,
I skirt sierras, my palms cover continents,
I am afoot with my vision.

By the city's quadrangular houses – in log huts, camping
with lumbermen,
Along the ruts of the turnpike, along the dry gulch and
rivulet bed,
Weeding my onion-patch or hoeing rows of carrots and
parsnips, crossing savannas, trailing in forests,
Prospecting, gold-digging, girdling the trees of a new
purchase,
Scorch'd ankle-deep by the hot sand, hauling my boat
down the shallow river,
Where the panther walks to and fro on a limb overhead,
where the buck turns furiously at the hunter,
Where the rattlesnake suns his flabby length on a rock,
where the otter is feeding on fish,
Where the alligator in his tough pimples sleeps by the
bayou,
Where the black bear is searching for roots or honey,
where the beaver pats the mud with his paddle-
shaped tail;
Over the growing sugar, over the yellow-flower'd cotton
plant, over the rice in its low moist field,
Over the sharp-peak'd farm house, with its scallop'd scum
and slender shoots from the gutters,
Over the western persimmon, over the long-leav'd corn,
over the delicate blue-flower flax,
Over the white and brown buckwheat, a hummer and
buzzer there with the rest,

Over the dusky green of the rye as it ripples and shades
    in the breeze;
Scaling mountains, pulling myself cautiously up, holding
    on by low scragged limbs,
Walking the path worn in the grass and beat through the
    leaves of the brush,
Where the quail is whistling betwixt the woods and the
    wheat-lot,
Where the bat flies in the Seventh-month eve, where the
    great gold-bug drops through the dark,
Where the brook puts out of the roots of the old tree and
    flows to the meadow,
Where cattle stand and shake away flies with the
    tremulous shuddering of their hides,
Where the cheese-cloth hangs in the kitchen, where
    andirons straddle the hearth-slab, where cobwebs fall
    in festoons from the rafters;
Where trip-hammers crash, where the press is whirling
    its cylinders,
Where the human heart beats with terrible throes under
    its ribs,
Where the pear-shaped balloon is floating aloft, (floating
    in it myself and looking composedly down,)
Where the life-car is drawn on the slip-noose, where the
    heat hatches pale-green eggs in the dented sand,
Where the she-whale swims with her calf and never
    forsakes it,
Where the steam-ship trails hind-ways its long pennant
    of smoke,
Where the fin of the shark cuts like a black chip out of
    the water,
Where the half-burn'd brig is riding on unknown
    currents,
Where shells grow to her slimy deck, where the dead are
    corrupting below;

Where the dense-starr'd flag is borne at the head of the
regiments,
Approaching Manhattan up by the long-stretching island,
Under Niagara, the cataract falling like a veil over my
countenance,
Upon a door-step, upon the horse-block of hard wood
outside,
Upon the race-course, or enjoying picnics or jigs or a good
game of base-ball,
At he-festivals, with blackguard gibes, ironical license,
bull-dances, drinking, laughter,
At the cider-mill tasting the sweets of the brown mash,
sucking the juice through a straw,
At apple-peelings wanting kisses for all the red fruit I
find,
At musters, beach-parties, friendly bees, huskings,
house-raisings;
Where the mocking-bird sounds his delicious gurgles,
cackles, screams, weeps,
Where the hay-rick stands in the barn-yard, where the
drystalks are scatter'd, where the brood-cow waits in
the hovel,
Where the bull advances to do his masculine work, where
the stud to the mare, where the cock is treading the
hen,
Where the heifers browse, where geese nip their food
with short jerks,
Where sun-down shadows lengthen over the limitless and
lonesome prairie,
Where herds of buffalo make a crawling spread of the
square miles far and near,
Where the humming-bird shimmers, where the neck of
the long-lived swan is curving and winding,
Where the laughing-gull scoots by the shore, where she
laughs her near-human laugh,

Where bee-hives range on a gray bench in the garden
    half hid by the high weeds,
Where band-neck'd partridges roost in a ring on the
    ground with their heads out,
Where burial coaches enter the arch'd gates of a
    cemetery,
Where winter wolves bark amid wastes of snow and
    icicled trees,
Where the yellow-crown'd heron comes to the edge of the
    marsh at night and feeds upon small crabs,
Where the splash of swimmers and divers cools the warm
    noon,
Where the katy-did works her chromatic reed on the
    walnut-tree over the wall,
Through patches of citrons and cucumbers with silver-
    wired leaves,
Through the salt-lick or orange glade, or under conical
    firs,
Through the gymnasium, through the curtain'd saloon,
    through the office or public hall;
Pleas'd with the native and pleas'd with the foreign,
    pleas'd with the new and old,
Pleas'd with the homely woman as well as the handsome,
Pleas'd with the quakeress as she puts off her bonnet and
    talks melodiously,
Pleas'd with the tune of the choir of the whitewash'd
    church,
Pleas'd with the earnest words of the sweating Methodist
    preacher, impress'd seriously at the camp-meeting;
Looking in at the shop-windows of Broadway the whole
    forenoon, flatting the flesh of my nose on the thick
    plate glass,
Wandering the same afternoon with my face turn'd up to
    the clouds, or down a lane or along the beach,
My right and left arms round the sides of two friends,
    and I in the middle;

Coming home with the silent and dark-cheek'd bush-boy,
    (behind me he rides at the drape of the day,)
Far from the settlements studying the print of animals'
    feet, or the moccasin print,
By the cot in the hospital reaching lemonade to a
    feverish patient,
Nigh the coffin'd corpse when all is still, examining with
    a candle;
Voyaging to every port to dicker and adventure,
Hurrying with the modern crowd as eager and fickle as
    any,
Hot toward one I hate, ready in my madness to knife
    him,
Solitary at midnight in my back yard, my thoughts gone
    from me a long while,
Walking the old hills of Judæa with the beautiful gentle
    God by my side,
Speeding through space, speeding through heaven and
    the stars,
Speeding amid the seven satellites and the broad ring,
    and the diameter of eighty thousand miles,
Speeding with tail'd meteors, throwing fire-balls like the
    rest,
Carrying the crescent child that carries its own full
    mother in its belly,
Storming, enjoying, planning, loving, cautioning,
Backing and filling, appearing and disappearing,
I tread day and night such roads.

I visit the orchards of spheres and look at the product,
And look at quintillions ripen'd and look at quintillions
    green.

I fly those flights of a fluid and swallowing soul,
My course runs below the soundings of plummets.

I help myself to material and immaterial,
No guard can shut me off, no law prevent me.

I anchor my ship for a little while only,
My messengers continually cruise away or bring their
    returns to me.

I go hunting polar furs and the seal, leaping chasms with
    a pike-pointed staff, clinging to topples of brittle and
    blue.

I ascend to the foretruck,
I take my place late at night in the crow's-nest,
We sail the arctic sea, it is plenty light enough,
Through the clear atmosphere I stretch around on the
    wonderful beauty,
The enormous masses of ice pass me and I pass them, the
    scenery is plain in all directions,
The white-topt mountains show in the distance, I fling
    out my fancies toward them,
We are approaching some great battle-field in which we
    are soon to be engaged,
We pass the colossal outposts of the encampment, we pass
    with still feet and caution,
Or we are entering by the suburbs some vast and ruin'd
    city,
The blocks and fallen architecture more than all the
    living cities of the globe.
I am a free companion, I bivouac by invading watchfires,
I turn the bridegroom out of bed and stay with the bride
    myself,
I tighten her all night to my thighs and lips.

My voice is the wife's voice, the screech by the rail of the
    stairs,
They fetch my man's body up dripping and drown'd.

I understand the large hearts of heroes,
The courage of present times and all times,
How the skipper saw the crowded and rudderless wreck
    of the steamship, and Death chasing it up and down
    the storm,
How he knuckled tight and gave not back an inch, and
    was faithful of days and faithful of nights,
And chalk'd in large letters on a board, *Be of good cheer,
    we will not desert you*;
How he follow'd with them and tack'd with them three
    days and would not give it up,
How he saved the drifting company at last,
How the lank loose-gown'd women look'd when boated
    from the side of their prepared graves,
How the silent old-faced infants and the lifted sick, and
    the sharp-lipp'd unshaved men;
All this I swallow, it tastes good, I like it well, it becomes
    mine,
I am the man, I suffer'd, I was there.

The disdain and calmness of martyrs,
The mother of old, condemn'd for a witch, burnt with dry
    wood, her children gazing on,
The hounded slave that flags in the race, leans by the
    fence, blowing, cover'd with sweat,
The twinges that sting like needles his legs and neck, the
    murderous buckshot and the bullets,
All these I feel or am.

I am the hounded slave, I wince at the bite of the dogs,
Hell and despair are upon me, crack and again crack the
    marksmen,
I clutch the rails of the fence, my gore dribs, thinn'd with
    the ooze of my skin,
I fall on the weeds and stones,
The riders spur their unwilling horses, haul close,

Taunt my dizzy ears and beat me violently over the head
    with whip-stocks.

Agonies are one of my changes of garments,
I do not ask the wounded person how he feels, I myself
    become the wounded person,
My hurts turn livid upon me as I lean on a cane and
    observe.
I am the mash'd fireman with breast-bone broken,
Tumbling walls buried me in their debris,
Heat and smoke I inspired, I heard the yelling shouts of
    my comrades,
I heard the distant click of their picks and shovels,
They have clear'd the beams away, they tenderly lift me
    forth.

I lie in the night air in my red shirt, the pervading hush
    is for my sake,
Painless after all I lie exhausted but not so unhappy,
White and beautiful are the faces around me, the heads
    are bared of their fire-caps,
The kneeling crowd fades with the light of the torches.

Distant and dead resuscitate,
They show as the dial or move as the hands of me, I am
    the clock myself.

I am an old artillerist, I tell of my fort's bombardment,
I am there again.

Again the long roll of the drummers,
Again the attacking cannon, mortars,
Again to my listening ears the cannon responsive.

I take part, I see and hear the whole,
The cries, curses, roar, the plaudits for well-aim'd shots,
The ambulanza slowly passing trailing its red drip,
Workmen searching after damages, making indispensable
    repairs,
The fall of grenades through the rent roof, the fan-shaped
    explosion,
The whizz of limbs, heads, stone, wood, iron, high in the
    air.

Again gurgles the mouth of my dying general, he
    furiously waves with his hand,
He gasps through the clot *Mind not me – mind – the
    entrenchments.*

34

Now I tell what I knew in Texas in my early youth,
(I tell not the fall of Alamo,
Not one escaped to tell the fall of Alamo,
The hundred and fifty are dumb yet at Alamo,)
Tis the tale of the murder in cold blood of four hundred
    and twelve young men.

Retreating they had form'd in a hollow square with their
    baggage for breastworks,
Nine hundred lives out of the surrounding enemy's, nine
    times their number, was the price they took in
    advance,
Their colonel was wounded and their ammunition gone,
They treated for an honorable capitulation, receiv'd
    writing and seal, gave up their arms and march'd
    back prisoners of war.

They were the glory of the race of rangers,
Matchless with horse, rifle, song, supper, courtship,
Large, turbulent, generous, handsome, proud, and
    affectionate,
Bearded, sunburnt, drest in the free costume of hunters,
Not a single one over thirty years of age.

The second First-day morning they were brought out in
    squads and massacred, it was beautiful early
    summer,
The work commenced about five o'clock and was over by
    eight.

None obey'd the command to kneel,
Some made a mad and helpless rush, some stood stark
    and straight,
A few fell at once, shot in the temple or heart, the living
    and dead lay together,
The maim'd and mangled dug in the dirt, the new-comers
    saw them there,
Some half-kill'd attempted to crawl away,
These were despatch'd with bayonets or batter'd with the
    blunts of muskets.
A youth not seventeen years old seiz'd his assassin till
    two more came to release him,
The three were all torn and cover'd with the boy's blood.

At eleven o'clock began the burning of the bodies;
That is the tale of the murder of the four hundred and
    twelve young men.

35

Would you hear of an old-time sea-fight?
Would you learn who won by the light of the moon and
    stars?

List to the yarn, as my grandmother's father the sailor
    told it to me.

Our foe was no skulk in his ship I tell you, (said he,)
His was the surly English pluck, and there is no tougher
    or truer, and never was, and never will be;
Along the lower'd eve he came horribly raking us.

We closed with him, the yards entangled, the cannon
    touch'd,
My captain lash'd fast with his own hands.

We had receiv'd some eighteen pound shots under the
    water,
On our lower-gun-deck two large pieces had burst at the
    first fire, killing all around and blowing up overhead.

Fighting at sun-down, fighting at dark,
Ten o'clock at night, the full moon well up, our leaks on
    the gain, and five feet of water reported,
The master-at-arms loosing the prisoners confined in the
    after-hold to give them a chance for themselves.

The transit to and from the magazine is now stopt by the
    sentinels,
They see so many strange faces they do not know whom
    to trust.

Our frigate takes fire,
The other asks if we demand quarter?
If our colors are struck and the fighting done?

Now I laugh content, for I hear the voice of my little
    captain,
We have not struck, he composedly cries, *we have just
    begun our part of the fighting.*

Only three guns are in use,
One is directed by the captain himself against the
    enemy's main-mast,
Two well serv'd with grape and canister silence his
    musketry and clear his decks.

The tops alone second the fire of this little battery,
    especially the main-top,
They hold out bravely during the whole of the action.

Not a moment's cease,
The leaks gain fast on the pumps, the fire eats toward
    the powder-magazine.

One of the pumps has been shot away, it is generally
    thought we are sinking.

Serene stands the little captain,
He is not hurried, his voice is neither high nor low,
His eyes give more light to us than our battle-lanterns.

Toward twelve there in the beams of the moon they
    surrender to us.

36

Stretch'd and still lies the midnight,
Two great hulls motionless on the breast of the darkness,
Our vessel riddled and slowly sinking, preparations to
    pass to the one we have conquer'd,
The captain on the quarter-deck coldly giving his orders
    through a countenance white as a sheet,
Near by the corpse of the child that serv'd in the cabin,
The dead face of an old salt with long white hair and
    carefully curl'd whiskers,

The flames spite of all that can be done flickering aloft
and below,
The husky voices of the two or three officers yet fit for
duty,
Formless stacks of bodies and bodies by themselves, dabs
of flesh upon the masts and spars,
Cut of cordage, dangle of rigging, slight shock of the
soothe of waves,
Black and impassive guns, litter of powder-parcels, strong
scent,
A few large stars overhead, silent and mournful shining,
Delicate sniffs of sea-breeze, smells of sedgy grass and
fields by the shore, death-messages given in charge
to survivors,
The hiss of the surgeon's knife, the gnawing teeth of his
saw,
Wheeze, cluck, swash of falling blood, short wild scream,
and long, dull, tapering groan,
These so, these irretrievable.

37

You laggards there on guard! look to your arms!
In at the conquer'd doors they crowd! I am possess'd!
Embody all presences outlaw'd or suffering,
See myself in prison shaped like another man,
And feel the dull unintermitted pain,
For me the keepers of convicts shoulder their carbines
and keep watch,
It is I let out in the morning and barr'd at night.

Not a mutineer walks handcuff'd to jail but I am
handcuff'd to him and walk by his side,
(I am less the jolly one there, and more the silent one
with sweat on my twitching lips.)

Not a youngster is taken for larceny but I go up too, and
am tried and sentenced.

Not a cholera patient lies at the last gasp but I also lie at
the last gasp,
My face is ash-color'd, my sinews gnarl, away from me
people retreat.

Askers embody themselves in me and I am embodied in
them,
I project my hat, sit shame-faced, and beg.

38

Enough! enough! enough!
Somehow I have been stunn'd. Stand back!
Give me a little time beyond my cuff'd head, slumbers,
dreams, gaping,
I discover myself on the verge of a usual mistake.

That I could forget the mockers and insults!
That I could forget the trickling tears and the blows of
the bludgeons and hammers!
That I could look with a separate look on my own
crucifixion and bloody crowning!

I remember now,
I resume the overstaid fraction,
The grave of rock multiplies what has been confided to it,
or to any graves,
Corpses rise, gashes heal, fastenings roll from me.

I troop forth replenish'd with supreme power, one of an
average unending procession,
Inland and sea-coast we go, and pass all boundary lines,
Our swift ordinances on their way over the whole earth,

The blossoms we wear in our hats the growth of
thousands of years.

Eleves, I salute you! come forward!
Continue your annotations, continue your questionings.

39

The friendly and flowing savage, who is he?
Is he waiting for civilization, or past it and mastering it?

Is he some Southwesterner rais'd out-doors? is he
Kanadian?
Is he from the Mississippi country? Iowa, Oregon,
California?
The mountains? prairie-life, bush-life? or sailor from the
sea?

Wherever he goes men and women accept and desire him,
They desire he should like them, touch them, speak to
them, stay with them.

Behavior lawless as snow-flakes, words simple as grass,
uncomb'd head, laughter, and naivetè,
Slow-stepping feet, common features, common modes and
emanations,
They descend in new forms from the tips of his fingers,
They are wafted with the odor of his body or breath, they
fly out of the glance of his eyes.

40

Flaunt of the sunshine I need not your bask – lie over!
You light surfaces only, I force surfaces and depths also.

Earth! you seem to look for something at my hands,
Say, old top-knot, what do you want?

Man or woman, I might tell how I like you, but cannot,
And might tell what it is in me and what it is in you, but
    cannot,
And might tell that pining I have, that pulse of my
    nights and days.

Behold, I do not give lectures or a little charity,
When I give I give myself.

You there, impotent, loose in the knees,
Open your scarf'd chops till I blow grit within you,
Spread your palms and lift the flaps of your pockets,
I am not to be denied, I compel, I have stores plenty and
    to spare,
And any thing I have I bestow.

I do not ask who you are, that is not important to me,
You can do nothing and be nothing but what I will infold
    you.

To cotton-field drudge or cleaner of privies I lean,
On his right cheek I put the family kiss,
And in my soul I swear I never will deny him.

On women fit for conception I start bigger and nimbler
    babes,
(This day I am jetting the stuff of far more arrogant
    republics.)

To any one dying, thither I speed and twist the knob of
    the door,
Turn the bed-clothes toward the foot of the bed,
Let the physician and the priest go home.

I seize the descending man and raise him with resistless
    will,
O despairer, here is my neck,
By God, you shall not go down! hang your whole weight
    upon me.

I dilate you with tremendous breath, I buoy you up,
Every room of the house do I fill with an arm'd force,
Lovers of me, bafflers of graves.

Sleep – I and they keep guard all night,
Not doubt, not disease shall dare to lay finger upon you,
I have embraced you, and henceforth possess you to
    myself,
And when you rise in the morning you will find what I
    tell you is so.

41

I am he bringing help for the sick as they pant on their
    backs,
And for strong upright men I bring yet more needed help.

I heard what was said of the universe,
Heard it and heard it of several thousand years;
It is middling well as far as it goes – but is that all?

Magnifying and applying come I,
Outbidding at the start the old cautious hucksters,
Taking myself the exact dimensions of Jehovah,
Lithographing Kronos, Zeus his son, and Hercules his
    grandson,
Buying drafts of Osiris, Isis, Belus, Brahma, Buddha,
In my portfolio placing Manito loose, Allah on a leaf, the
    crucifix engraved,
With Odin and the hideous-faced Mexitli and every idol
    and image,

Taking them all for what they are worth and not a cent
more,
Admitting they were alive and did the work of their days,
(They bore mites as for unfledg'd birds who have now to
rise and fly and sing for themselves,)
Accepting the rough deific sketches to fill out better in
myself, bestowing them freely on each man and
woman I see,
Discovering as much or more in a framer framing a
house,
Putting higher claims for him there with his roll'd-up
sleeves driving the mallet and chisel,
Not objecting to special revelations, considering a curl of
smoke or a hair on the back of my hand just as
curious as any revelation,
Lads ahold of fire-engines and hook-and-ladder ropes no
less to me than the gods of the antique wars,
Minding their voices peal through the crash of
destruction,
Their brawny limbs passing safe over charr'd laths, their
white foreheads whole and unhurt out of the flames;
By the mechanic's wife with her babe at her nipple
interceding for every person born,
Three scythes at harvest whizzing in a row from three
lusty angels with shirts bagg'd out at their waists,
The snag-tooth'd hostler with red hair redeeming sins
past and to come,
Selling all he possesses, traveling on foot to fee lawyers
for his brothers and sit by him while he is tried for
forgery;
What was strewn in the amplest strewing the square rod
about me, and not filling the square rod then,
The bull and the bug never worshipp'd half enough,
Dung and dirt more admirable than was dream'd,
The supernatural of no account, myself waiting my time
to be one of the supremes,

The day getting ready for me when I shall do as much
  good as the best, and be as prodigious;
By my life-lumps! becoming already a creator,
Putting myself here and now to the ambush'd womb of
  the shadows.

42

A call in the midst of the crowd,
My own voice, orotund sweeping and final.
Come my children,
Come my boys and girls, my women, household and
  intimates,
Now the performer launches his nerve, he has pass'd his
  prelude on the reeds within.

Easily written loose-finger'd chords – I feel the thrum of
  your climax and close.

My head slues round on my neck,
Music rolls, but not from the organ,
Folks are around me, but they are no household of mine.

Ever the hard unsunk ground,
Ever the eaters and drinkers, ever the upward and
  downward sun, ever the air and the ceaseless tides,
Ever myself and my neighbors, refreshing, wicked, real,
Ever the old inexplicable query, ever that thorn'd thumb,
  that breath of itches and thirsts,
Ever the vexer's *hoot! hoot!* till we find where the sly one
  hides and bring him forth,
Ever love, ever the sobbing liquid of life,
Ever the bandage under the chin, ever the trestles of
  death.

Here and there with dimes on the eyes walking,
To feed the greed of the belly the brains liberally
    spooning,
Tickets buying, taking, selling, but in to the feast never
    once going,
Many sweating, ploughing, thrashing, and then the chaff
    for payment receiving,
A few idly owning, and they the wheat continually
    claiming.
This is the city and I am one of the citizens,
Whatever interests the rest interests me, politics, wars,
    markets, newspapers, schools,
The mayor and councils, banks, tariffs, steamships,
    factories, stocks, stores, real estate and personal
    estate.

The little plentiful manikins skipping around in collars
    and tail'd coats,
I am aware who they are, (they are positively not worms
    or fleas,)
I acknowledge the duplicates of myself, the weakest and
    shallowest is deathless with me,
What I do and say the same waits for them,
Every thought that flounders in me the same flounders in
    them.

I know perfectly well my own egotism,
Know my omnivorous lines and must not write any less,
And would fetch you whoever you are flush with myself.

Not words of routine this song of mine,
But abruptly to question, to leap beyond yet nearer bring;
This printed and bound book – but the printer and the
    printing-office boy?
The well-taken photographs – but your wife or friend
    close and soild in your arms?

The black ship mail'd with iron, her mighty guns in her
    turrets – but the pluck of the captain and engineers?
In the houses the dishes and fare and furniture – but the
    host and hostess, and the look out of their eyes?
The sky up there – yet here or next door, or across the
    way?
The saints and sages in history – but you yourself?
Sermons, creeds, theology – but the fathomless human
    brain,
And what is reason? and what is love? and what is life?

43

I do not despise you priests, all time, the world over,
My faith is the greatest of faiths and the least of faiths,
Enclosing worship ancient and modern and all between
    ancient and modern,
Believing I shall come again upon the earth after five
    thousand years,
Waiting responses from oracles, honoring the gods,
    saluting the sun,
Making a fetich of the first rock or stump, powowing with
    sticks in the circle of obis,
Helping the llama or brahmin as he trims the lamps of
    the idols,
Dancing yet through the streets in a phallic procession,
    rapt and austere in the woods a gymnosophist,
Drinking mead from the skull-cup, to Shastas and Vedas
    admirant, minding the Koran,
Walking the teokallis, spotted with gore from the stone
    and knife, beating the serpent-skin drum,
Accepting the Gospels, accepting him that was crucified,
    knowing assuredly that he is divine,
To the mass kneeling or the puritan's prayer rising, or
    sitting patiently in a pew,
Ranting and frothing in my insane crisis, or waiting
    dead-like till my spirit arouses me,

Looking forth on pavement and land, or outside of
 pavement and land,
Belonging to the winders of the circuit of circuits.

One of that centripetal and centrifugal gang I turn and
 talk like a man leaving charges before a journey.

Down-hearted doubters dull and excluded,
Frivolous, sullen, moping, angry, affected, dishearten'd,
 atheistical,
I know every one of you, I know the sea of torment,
 doubt, despair and unbelief.

How the flukes splash!
How they contort rapid as lightning, with spasms and
 spouts of blood!

Be at peace bloody flukes of doubters and sullen mopers,
I take my place among you as much as among any,
The past is the push of you, me, all, precisely the same,
And what is yet untried and afterward is for you, me, all,
 precisely the same.

I do not know what is untried and afterward,
But I know it will in its turn prove sufficient, and cannot
 fail.

Each who passes is consider'd, each who stops is
 consider'd, not a single one can it fail.

It cannot fail the young man who died and was buried,
Nor the young woman who died and was put by his side,
Nor the little child that peep'd in at the door, and then
 drew back and was never seen again,
Nor the old man who has lived without purpose, and feels
 it with bitterness worse than gall,

Nor him in the poor house tubercled by rum and the bad
    disorder,
Nor the numberless slaughter'd and wreck'd, nor the
    brutish koboo call'd the ordure of humanity,
Nor the sacs merely floating with open mouths for food to
    slip in,
Nor any thing in the earth, or down in the oldest graves
    of the earth,
Nor any thing in the myriads of spheres, nor the myriads
    of myriads that inhabit them,
Nor the present, nor the least wisp that is known.

44

It is time to explain myself – let us stand up.

What is known I strip away,
I launch all men and women forward with me into the
    Unknown.

The clock indicates the moment – but what does eternity
    indicate?

We have thus far exhausted trillions of winters and
    summers,
There are trillions ahead, and trillions ahead of them.

Births have brought us richness and variety,
And other births will bring us richness and variety.

I do not call one greater and one smaller,
That which fills its period and place is equal to any.

Were mankind murderous or jealous upon you, my
    brother, my sister?
I am sorry for you, they are not murderous or jealous
    upon me,

All has been gentle with me, I keep no account with
 lamentation,
(What have I to do with lamentation?)
I am an acme of things accomplish'd, and I an encloser of
 things to be.

My feet strike an apex of the apices of the stairs,
On every step bunches of ages, and larger bunches
 between the steps,
All below duly travel'd, and still I mount and mount.

Rise after rise bow the phantoms behind me,
Afar down I see the huge first Nothing, I know I was
 even there,
I waited unseen and always, and slept through the
 lethargic mist,
And took my time, and took no hurt from the fetid
 carbon.

Long I was hugg'd close – long and long.

Immense have been the preparations for me,
Faithful and friendly the arms that have help'd me.

Cycles ferried my cradle, rowing and rowing like cheerful
 boatmen,
For room to me stars kept aside in their own rings,
They sent influences to look after what was to hold me.

Before I was born out of my mother generations guided
 me,
My embryo has never been torpid, nothing could overlay
 it.

For it the nebula cohered to an orb,
The long slow strata piled to rest it on,
Vast vegetables gave it sustenance,
Monstrous sauroids transported it in their mouths and
    deposited it with care

All forces have been steadily employ'd to complete and
    delight me,
Now on this spot I stand with my robust soul.

45

O span of youth! ever-push'd elasticity!
O manhood, balanced, florid and full.

My lovers suffocate me,
Crowding my lips, thick in the pores of my skin,
Jostling me through streets and public halls, coming
    naked to me at night,
Crying by day *Ahoy!* from the rocks of the river,
    swinging and chirping over my head,
Calling my name from flower-beds, vines, tangled
    underbrush,
Lighting on every moment of my life,
Bussing my body with soft balsamic busses,
Noiselessly passing handfuls out of their hearts and
    giving them to be mine.

Old age superbly rising! O welcome, ineffable grace of
    dying days!

Every condition promulges not only itself, it promulges
    what grows after and out of itself,
And the dark hush promulges as much as any.

I open my scuttle at night and see the far-sprinkled
    systems,
And all I see multiplied as high as I can cipher edge but
    the rim of the farther systems.

Wider and wider they spread, expanding, always
    expanding,
Outward and outward and forever outward.

My sun has his sun and round him obediently wheels,
He joins with his partners a group of superior circuit,
And greater sets follow, making specks of the greatest
    inside them.

There is no stoppage and never can be stoppage,
If I, you, and the worlds, and all beneath or upon their
    surfaces, were this moment reduced back to a pallid
    float, it would not avail in the long run,
We should surely bring up again where we now stand,
And surely go as much farther, and then farther and
    farther.

A few quadrillions of eras, a few octillions of cubic
    leagues, do not hazard the span or make it impatient,
They are but parts, any thing is but a part.

See ever so far, there is limitless space outside of that,
Count ever so much, there is limitless time around that.

My rendezvous is appointed, it is certain,
The Lord will be there and wait till I come on perfect
    terms,
The great Camerado, the lover true for whom I pine will
    be there.

46

I know I have the best of time and space, and was never
    measured and never will be measured.

I tramp a perpetual journey, (come listen all!)
My signs are a rain-proof coat, good shoes, and a staff cut
    from the woods,
No friend of mine takes his ease in my chair,
I have no chair, no church, no philosophy,
I lead no man to a dinner-table, library, exchange,
But each man and each woman of you I lead upon a
    knoll,
My left hand hooking you round the waist,
My right hand pointing to landscapes of continents and
    the public road.

Not I, not any one else can travel that road for you,
You must travel it for yourself.

It is not far, it is within reach,
Perhaps you have been on it since you were born and did
    not know,
Perhaps it is everywhere on water and on land.

Shoulder your duds dear son, and I will mine, and let us
    hasten forth,
Wonderful cities and free nations we shall fetch as we go.

If you tire, give me both burdens, and rest the chuff of
    your hand on my hip,
And in due time you shall repay the same service to me,
For after we start we never lie by again.

This day before dawn I ascended a hill and look'd at the
    crowded heaven,
And I said to my spirit *When we become the enfolders of*
    those orbs, and the pleasure and knowledge of every
    thing in them, shall we be fill'd and satisfied then?
And my spirit said *No, we but level that lift to pass and*
    continue beyond.

You are also asking me questions and I hear you,
I answer that I cannot answer, you must find out for
    yourself.

Sit a while dear son,
Here are biscuits to eat and here is milk to drink,
But as soon as you sleep and renew yourself in sweet
    clothes, I kiss you with a good-by kiss and open the
    gate for your egress hence.

Long enough have you dream'd contemptible dreams,
Now I wash the gum from your eyes,
You must habit yourself to the dazzle of the light and of
    every moment of your life.

Long have you timidly waded holding a plank by the
    shore,
Now I will you to be a bold swimmer,
To jump off in the midst of the sea, rise again, nod to me,
    shout, and laughingly dash with your hair.

47

I am the teacher of athletes,
He that by me spreads a wider breast than my own
    proves the width of my own,
He most honors my style who learns under it to destroy
    the teacher.

The boy I love, the same becomes a man not through
    derived power, but in his own right,
Wicked rather than virtuous out of conformity or fear,
Fond of his sweetheart, relishing well his steak,
Unrequited love or a slight cutting him worse than sharp
    steel cuts,
First-rate to ride, to fight, to hit the bull's eye, to sail a
    skiff, to sing a song or play on the banjo,
Preferring scars and the beard and faces pitted with
    smallpox over all latherers,
And those well-tann'd to those that keep out of the sun.

I teach straying from me, yet who can stray from me?
I follow you whoever you are from the present hour,
My words itch at your ears till you understand them.

I do not say these things for a dollar or to fill up the time
    while I wait for a boat,
(It is you talking just as much as myself, I act as the
    tongue of you,
Tied in your mouth, in mine it begins to be loosen'd.)

I swear I will never again mention love or death inside a
    house,
And I swear I will never translate myself at all, only to
    him or her who privately stays with me in the open
    air.

If you would understand me go to the heights or
    water-shore,
The nearest gnat is an explanation, and a drop or motion
    of waves a key,
The maul, the oar, the hand-saw, second my words.

No shutter'd room or school can commune with me,
But roughs and little children better than they.

The young mechanic is closest to me, he knows me well,
The woodman that takes his axe and jug with him shall
    take me with him all day,
The farm-boy ploughing in the field feels good at the
    sound of my voice,
In vessels that sail my words sail, I go with fishermen
    and seamen and love them.

The soldier camp'd or upon the march is mine,
On the night ere the pending battle many seek me, and I
    do not fail them,
On that solemn night (it may be their last) those that
    know me seek me.

My face rubs to the hunter's face when he lies down
    alone in his blanket,
The driver thinking of me does not mind the jolt of his
    wagon,
The young mother and old mother comprehend me,
The girl and the wife rest the needle a moment and
    forget where they are,
They and all would resume what I have told them.

48

I have said that the soul is not more than the body,
And I have said that the body is not more than the soul,
And nothing, not God, is greater to one than one's self is,
And whoever walks a furlong without sympathy walks to
    his own funeral drest in his shroud,
And I or you pocketless of a dime may purchase the pick
    of the earth,
And to glance with an eye or show a bean in its pod
    confounds the learning of all times,
And there is no trade or employment but the young man
    following it may become a hero,

And there is no object so soft but it makes a hub for the
    wheel'd universe,
And I say to any man or woman, Let your soul stand cool
    and composed before a million universes.

And I say to mankind, Be not curious about God,
For I who am curious about each am not curious about
    God,
(No array of terms can say how much I am at peace
    about God and about death.)

I hear and behold God in every object, yet understand
    God not in the least,
Nor do I understand who there can be more wonderful
    than myself.

Why should I wish to see God better than this day?
I see something of God each hour of the twenty-four, and
    each moment then,
In the faces of men and women I see God, and in my own
    face in the glass,
I find letters from God dropt in the street, and every one
    is sign'd by God's name,
And I leave them where they are, for I know that
    wheresoe'er I go,
Others will punctually come for ever and ever.

49

And as to you Death, and you bitter hug of mortality, it
    is idle to try to alarm me.

To his work without flinching the accoucheur comes,
I see the elder-hand pressing receiving supporting,
I recline by the sills of the exquisite flexible doors,
And mark the outlet, and mark the relief and escape.

And as to you Corpse I think you are good manure, but
    that does not offend me,
I smell the white roses sweet-scented and growing,
I reach to the leafy lips, I reach to the polish'd breasts of
    melons.

And as to you Life I reckon you are the leavings of many
    deaths,
(No doubt I have died myself ten thousand times before.)

I hear you whispering there O stars of heaven,
O suns – O grass of graves – O perpetual transfers and
    promotions,
If you do not say any thing how can I say any thing?

Of the turbid pool that lies in the autumn forest,
Of the moon that descends the steeps of the soughing
    twilight,
Toss, sparkles of day and dusk – toss on the black stems
    that decay in the muck,
Toss to the moaning gibberish of the dry limbs.

I ascend from the moon, I ascend from the night,
I perceive that the ghastly glimmer is noonday sunbeams
    reflected,
And debouch to the steady and central from the offspring
    great or small.

50

There is that in me – I do not know what it is – but I
    know it is in me.

Wrench'd and sweaty – calm and cool then my body
    becomes,
I sleep – I sleep long.

I do not know it – it is without name – it is a word
    unsaid,
It is not in any dictionary, utterance, symbol.

Something it swings on more than the earth I swing on,
To it the creation is the friend whose embracing awakes
    me.

Perhaps I might tell more. Outlines! I plead for my
    brothers and sisters.

Do you see O my brothers and sisters?
It is not chaos or death – it is form, union, plan – it is
    eternal life – it is Happiness.

51

The past and present wilt – I have fill'd them, emptied
    them,
And proceed to fill my next fold of the future.

Listener up there! what have you to confide to me?
Look in my face while I snuff the sidle of evening,
(Talk honestly, no one else hears you, and I stay only a
    minute longer.)

Do I contradict myself?
Very well then I contradict myself,
(I am large, I contain multitudes.)

I concentrate toward them that are nigh, I wait on the
    door-slab.

Who has done his day's work? who will soonest be
    through with his supper?
Who wishes to walk with me?

Will you speak before I am gone? will you prove already
   too late?

52

The spotted hawk swoops by and accuses me, he
   complains of my gab and my loitering.

I too am not a bit tamed, I too am untranslatable,
I sound my barbaric yawp over the roofs of the world.

The last scud of day holds back for me,
It flings my likeness after the rest and true as any on the
   shadow'd wilds,
It coaxes me to the vapor and the dusk.

I depart as air, I shake my white locks at the runaway
   sun,
I effuse my flesh in eddies, and drift it in lacy jags.

I bequeath myself to the dirt to grow from the grass I
   love,
If you want me again look for me under your boot-soles.

You will hardly know who I am or what I mean,
But I shall be good health to you nevertheless,
And filter and fibre your blood.

Failing to fetch me at first keep encouraged,
Missing me one place search another,
I stop somewhere waiting for you.

Once I Pass'd Through a Populous City

Once I pass'd through a populous city imprinting my
　　brain for future use with its shows, architecture,
　　customs, traditions,
Yet now of all that city I remember only a woman I
　　casually met there who detain'd me for love of me,
Day by day and night by night we were together — all
　　else has long been forgotten by me,
I remember I say only that woman who passionately
　　clung to me,
Again we wander, we love, we separate again,
Again she holds me by the hand, I must not go,
I see her close beside me with silent lips sad and
　　tremulous.

I Heard You Solemn-Sweet Pipes of the Organ

I heard you solemn-sweet pipes of the organ as last
　　Sunday morn I pass'd the church,
Winds of autumn, as I walk'd the woods at dusk I heard
　　your long-stretch'd sighs up above so mournful,
I heard the perfect Italian tenor singing at the opera, I
　　heard the soprano in the midst of the quartet
　　singing;
Heart of my love! you too I heard murmuring low
　　through one of the wrists around my head,
Heard the pulse of you when all was still ringing little
　　bells last night under my ear.

In Paths Untrodden

In paths untrodden,
In the growths by margins of pond-waters,
Escaped from the life that exhibits itself,
From all the standards hitherto publish'd, from the
    pleasures, profits, conformities,
Which too long I was offering to feed my soul,
Clear to me now standards not yet publish'd, clear to me
    that my soul,
That the soul of the man I speak for rejoices in comrades,
Here by myself away from the clank of the world,
Tallying and talk'd to here by tongues aromatic,
No longer abash'd, (for in this secluded spot I can respond
    as I would not dare elsewhere,)
Strong upon me the life that does not exhibit itself, yet
    contains all the rest,
Resolv'd to sing no songs to-day but those of manly
    attachment,
Projecting them along that substantial life,
Bequeathing hence types of athletic love,
Afternoon this delicious Ninth-month in my forty-first
    year,
I proceed for all who are or have been young men,
To tell the secret of my nights and days,
To celebrate the need of comrades.

When I Heard at the Close
of the Day

When I heard at the close of the day how my name had
    been receiv'd with plaudits in the capitol, still it was
    not a happy night for me that follow'd,
And else when I carous'd, or when my plans were
    accomplish'd, still I was not happy,

But the day when I rose at dawn from the bed of perfect
   health, refresh'd, singing, inhaling the ripe breath of
   autumn,
When I saw the full moon in the west grow pale and
   disappear in the morning light,
When I wander'd alone over the beach, and undressing
   bathed, laughing with the cool waters, and saw the
   sun rise,
And when I thought how my dear friend my lover was on
   his way coming, O then I was happy,
O then each breath tasted sweeter, and all that day my
   food nourish'd me more, and the beautiful day pass'd
   well,
And the next came with equal joy, and with the next at
   evening came my friend,
And that night while all was still I heard the waters roll
   slowly continually up the shores,
I heard the hissing rustle of the liquid and sands as
   directed to me whispering to congratulate me,
For the one I love most lay sleeping by me under the
   same cover in the cool night,
In the stillness in the autumn moonbeams his face was
   inclined toward me,
And his arm lay lightly around my breast – and that
   night I was happy.

I Saw in Louisiana a Live-Oak
Growing

I saw in Louisiana a live-oak growing,
All alone stood it and the moss hung down from the
   branches,
Without any companion it grew there uttering joyous
   leaves of dark green,

And its look, rude, unbending, lusty, made me think of
    myself,
But I wonder'd how it could utter joyous leaves standing
    alone there without its friend near, for I knew I could
    not,
And I broke off a twig with a certain number of leaves
    upon it, and twined around it a little moss,
And brought it away, and I have placed it in sight, in my
    room,
It is not needed to remind me as of my own dear friends,
(For I believe lately I think of little else than of them,)
Yet it remains to me a curious token, it makes me think
    of manly love;
For all that, and though the live-oak glistens there in
    Louisiana solitary in a wide flat space,
Uttering joyous leaves all its life without a friend a lover
    near,
I know very well I could not.

A Glimpse

A glimpse through an interstice caught,
Of a crowd of workmen and drivers in a bar-room around
    the stove late of a winter night, and I unremark'd
    seated in a corner,
Of a youth who loves me and whom I love, silently
    approaching and seating himself near, that he may
    hold me by the hand,
A long while amid the noises of coming and going, of
    drinking and oath and smutty jest,
There we two, content, happy in being together, speaking
    little, perhaps not a word.

Out of the Cradle Endlessly
Rocking

Out of the cradle endlessly rocking,
Out of the mocking-bird's throat, the musical shuttle,
Out of the Ninth-month midnight,
Over the sterile sands and the fields beyond, where the
    child leaving his bed wander'd alone, bareheaded,
    barefoot,
Down from the shower'd halo,
Up from the mystic play of shadows twining and twisting
    as if they were alive,
Out from the patches of briers and blackberries,
From the memories of the bird that chanted to me,
From your memories sad brother, from the fitful risings
    and fallings I heard,
From under that yellow half-moon late-risen and swollen
    as if with tears,
From those beginning notes of yearning and love there in
    the mist,
From the thousand responses of my heart never to cease,
From the myriad thence-arous'd words,
From the word stronger and more delicious than any,
From such as now they start the scene revisiting,
As a flock, twittering, rising, or overhead passing,
Borne hither, ere all eludes me, hurriedly,
A man, yet by these tears a little boy again,
Throwing myself on the sand, confronting the waves,
I, chanter of pains and joys, uniter of here and hereafter,
Taking all hints to use them, but swiftly leaping beyond
    them,
A reminiscence sing.

Once Paumanok,
When the lilac-scent was in the air and Fifth-month
    grass was growing,
Up this seashore in some briers,

Two feather'd guests from Alabama, two together,
And their nest, and four light-green eggs spotted with
brown,
And every day the he-bird to and fro near at hand,
And every day the she-bird crouch'd on her nest, silent,
with bright eyes,
And every day I, a curious boy, never too close, never
disturbing them,
Cautiously peering, absorbing, translating.

Shine! shine! shine!
Pour down your warmth, great sun!
While we bask, we two together.

Two together!
Winds blow south, or winds blow north,
Day come white, or night come black,
Home, or rivers and mountains from home,
Singing all time, minding no time,
While we two keep together.

Till of a sudden,
May-be kill'd, unknown to her mate,
One forenoon the she-bird crouch'd not on the nest,
Nor return'd that afternoon, nor the next,
Nor ever appear'd again.

And thenceforward all summer in the sound of the sea,
And at night under the full of the moon in calmer
weather,
Over the hoarse surging of the sea,
Or flitting from brier to brier by day,
I saw, I heard at intervals the remaining one, the
he-bird,
The solitary guest from Alabama.

Blow! blow! blow!
Blow up sea-winds along Paumanok's shore;
I wait and I wait till you blow my mate to me.

Yes, when the stars glisten'd,
All night long on the prong of a moss-scallop'd stake,
Down almost amid the slapping waves,
Sat the lone singer wonderful causing tears.

He call'd on his mate,
He pour'd forth the meanings which I of all men know.

Yes my brother I know,
The rest might not, but I have treasur'd every note,
For more than once dimly down to the beach gliding,
Silent, avoiding the moonbeams, blending myself with
    the shadows,
Recalling now the obscure shapes, the echoes, the sounds
    and sights after their sorts,
The white arms out in the breakers tirelessly tossing,
I, with bare feet, a child, the wind wafting my hair,
Listen'd long and long.

Listen'd to keep, to sing, now translating the notes,
Following you my brother.

Soothe! soothe! soothe!
Close on its wave soothes the wave behind,
And again another behind embracing and lapping, every
    one close,
But my love soothes not me, not me.

Low hangs the moon, it rose late,
It is lagging – O I think it is heavy with love, with love.

O madly the sea pushes upon the land,
With love, with love.

O night! do I not see my love fluttering out among the
*   breakers?*
What is that little black thing I see there in the white?

Loud! loud! loud!
Loud I call to you, my love!
High and clear I shoot my voice over the waves,
Surely you must know who is here, is here,
You must know who I am, my love.

Low-hanging moon!
What is that dusky spot in your brown yellow?
O it is the shape, the shape of my mate!
O moon do not keep her from me any longer.

Land! land! O land!
Whichever way I turn, O I think you could give me my
*   mate back again if you only would,*
For I am almost sure I see her dimly whichever way I
*   look.*

O rising stars!
Perhaps the one I want so much will rise, will rise with
*   some of you.*

O throat! O trembling throat!
Sound clearer through the atmosphere!
Pierce the woods, the earth,
Somewhere listening to catch you must be the one I want.

Shake out carols!
Solitary here, the night's carols!
Carols of lonesome love! death's carols!

Carols under that lagging, yellow, waning moon!
O under that moon where she droops almost down into the
    sea!
O reckless despairing carols.

But soft! sink low!
Soft! let me just murmur,
And do you wait a moment you husky-nois'd sea,
For somewhere I believe I heard my mate responding to
    me,
So faint, I must be still, be still to listen,
But not altogether still, for then she might not come
    immediately to me.

Hither my love!
Here I am! here!
With this just-sustain'd note I announce myself to you,
This gentle call is for you my love, for you.

Do not be decoy'd elsewhere,
That is the whistle of the wind, it is not my voice,
That is the fluttering, the fluttering of the spray,
Those are the shadows of leaves.

O darkness! O in vain!
O I am very sick and sorrowful.

O brown halo in the sky near the moon, drooping upon the
    sea!
O troubled reflection in the sea!
O throat! O throbbing heart!
And I singing uselessly, uselessly all the night.

O past! O happy life! O songs of joy!
In the air, in the woods, over fields,
Loved! loved! loved! loved! loved!
But my mate no more, no more with me!
We two together no more.

The aria sinking,
All else continuing, the stars shining,
The winds blowing, the notes of the bird continuous
    echoing,
With angry moans the fierce old mother incessantly
    moaning,
On the sands of Paumanok's shore gray and rustling,
The yellow half-moon enlarged, sagging down, drooping,
    the face of the sea almost touching,
The boy ecstatic, with his bare feet the waves, with his
    hair the atmosphere dallying,
The love in the heart long pent, now loose, now at last
    tumultuously bursting,
The aria's meaning, the ears, the soul, swiftly depositing,
The strange tears down the cheeks coursing,
The colloquy there, the trio, each uttering,
The undertone, the savage old mother incessantly crying,
To the boy's soul's questions sullenly timing, some
    drown'd secret hissing,
To the outsetting bard.

Demon or bird! (said the boy's soul,)
Is it indeed toward your mate you sing? or is it really to
    me?
For I, that was a child, my tongue's use sleeping, now I
    have heard you,
Now in a moment I know what I am for, I awake,
And already a thousand singers, a thousand songs,
    clearer, louder and more sorrowful than yours,

A thousand warbling echoes have started to life within
    me, never to die.

O you singer solitary, singing by yourself, projecting me,
O solitary me listening, never more shall I cease
    perpetuating you,
Never more shall I escape, never more the
    reverberations,
Never more the cries of unsatisfied love be absent from
    me,
Never again leave me to be the peaceful child I was
    before what there in the night,
By the sea under the yellow and sagging moon,
The messenger there arous'd, the fire, the sweet hell
    within,
The unknown want, the destiny of me.

O give me the clew! (it lurks in the night here
    somewhere,)
O if I am to have so much, let me have more!

A word then, (for I will conquer it,)
The word final, superior to all,
Subtle, sent up – what is it? – I listen;
Are you whispering it, and have been all the time, you
    sea waves?
Is that it from your liquid rims and wet sands?

Whereto answering, the sea,
Delaying not, hurrying not,
Whisper'd me through the night, and very plainly before
    daybreak,
Lisp'd to me the low and delicious word death,
And again death, death, death, death,
Hissing melodious, neither like the bird nor like my
    arous'd child's heart,

But edging near as privately for me rustling at my feet,
Creeping thence steadily up to my ears and laving me
    softly all over,
Death, death, death, death, death.

Which I do not forget,
But fuse the song of my dusky demon and brother,
That he sang to me in the moonlight on Paumanok's gray
    beach,
With the thousand responsive songs at random,
My own songs awaked from that hour,
And with them the key, the word up from the waves,
The word of the sweetest song and all songs,
That strong and delicious word which, creeping to my
    feet,
(Or like some old crone rocking the cradle, swathed in
    sweet garments, bending aside,)
The sea whisper'd me.

When Lilacs Last in the Dooryard Bloom'd

1

When lilacs last in the dooryard bloom'd,
And the great star early droop'd in the western sky in
    the night,
I mourn'd, and yet shall mourn with ever-returning
    spring.

Ever-returning spring, trinity sure to me you bring,
Lilac blooming perennial and drooping star in the west,
And thought of him I love.

2

O powerful western fallen star!
O shades of night – O moody, tearful night!
O great star disappear'd – O the black murk that hides
    the star!
O cruel hands that hold me powerless – O helpless soul of
    me!
O harsh surrounding cloud that will not free my soul.

3

In the dooryard fronting an old farm-house near the
    whitewash'd palings,
Stands the lilac-bush tall-growing with heart-shaped
    leaves of rich green,
With many a pointed blossom rising delicate, with the
    perfume strong I love,
With every leaf a miracle – and from this bush in the
    dooryard,
With delicate-color'd blossoms and heart-shaped leaves of
    rich green,
A sprig with its flower I break.

4

In the swamp in secluded recesses,
A shy and hidden bird is warbling a song.

Solitary the thrush,
The hermit withdrawn to himself, avoiding the
    settlements,
Sings by himself a song.

Song of the bleeding throat,
Death's outlet song of life, (for well dear brother I know,
If thou wast not granted to sing thou would'st surely die.)

5

Over the breast of the spring, the land, amid cities,
Amid lanes and through old woods, where lately the
    violets peep'd from the ground, spotting the gray
    debris,
Amid the grass in the fields each side of the lanes,
    passing the endless grass,
Passing the yellow-spear'd wheat, every grain from its
    shroud in the dark-brown fields uprisen,
Passing the apple-tree blows of white and pink in the
    orchards,
Carrying a corpse to where it shall rest in the grave,
Night and day journeys a coffin.

6

Coffin that passes through lanes and streets,
Through day and night with the great cloud darkening
    the land,
With the pomp of the inloop'd flags with the cities draped
    in black,
With the show of the States themselves as of crape-veil'd
    women standing,
With processions long and winding and the flambeaus of
    the night,
With the countless torches lit, with the silent sea of faces
    and the unbared heads,
With the waiting depot, the arriving coffin, and the
    sombre faces,
With dirges through the night, with the thousand voices
    rising strong and solemn,
With all the mournful voices of the dirges pour'd around
    the coffin,
The dim-lit churches and the shuddering organs – where
    amid these you journey,
With the tolling tolling bells' perpetual clang,

Here, coffin that slowly passes,
I give you my sprig of lilac.

7

(Nor for you, for one alone,
Blossoms and branches green to coffins all I bring,
For fresh as the morning, thus would I chant a song for
    you O sane and sacred death.

All over bouquets of roses,
O death, I cover you over with roses and early lilies,
But mostly and now the lilac that blooms the first,
Copious I break, I break the sprigs from the bushes,
With loaded arms I come, pouring for you,
For you and the coffins all of you O death.)

8

O western orb sailing the heaven,
Now I know what you must have meant as a month since
    I walk'd,
As I walk'd in silence the transparent shadowy night,
As I saw you had something to tell as you bent to me
    night after night,
As you drooped from the sky low down as if to my side,
    (while the other stars all look'd on,)
As we wander'd together the solemn night, (for
    something I know not what kept me from sleep,)
As the night advanced, and I saw on the rim of the west
    how full you were of woe,
As I stood on the rising ground in the breeze in the cool
    transparent night,
As I watch'd where you pass'd and was lost in the
    netherward black of the night,
As my soul in its trouble dissatisfied sank, as where you
    sad orb,
Concluded, dropt in the night, and was gone.

9

Sing on there in the swamp,
O singer bashful and tender, I hear your notes, I hear
    your call,
I hear, I come presently, I understand you,
But a moment I linger, for the lustrous star has detain'd
    me,
The star my departing comrade holds and detains me.

10

O how shall I warble myself for the dead one there I
    loved?
And how shall I deck my song for the large sweet soul
    that has gone?
And what shall my perfume be for the grave of him I
    love?

Sea-winds blown from east and west,
Blown from the Eastern sea and blown from the Western
    sea, till there on the prairies meeting,
These and with these and the breath of my chant,
I'll perfume the grave of him I love.

11

O what shall I hang on the chamber walls?
And what shall the pictures be that I hang on the walls,
To adorn the burial-house of him I love?

Pictures of growing spring and farms and homes,
With the Fourth-month eve at sundown, and the gray
    smoke lucid and bright,
With floods of the yellow gold of the gorgeous, indolent,
    sinking sun, burning, expanding the air,
With the fresh sweet herbage under foot, and the pale
    green leaves of the trees prolific,

In the distance the flowing glaze, the breast of the river,
    with a wind-dapple here and there,
With ranging hills on the banks, with many a line
    against the sky, and shadows,
And the city at hand with dwellings so dense, and stacks
    of chimneys,
And all the scenes of life and the workshops, and the
    workmen homeward returning.

12

Lo, body and soul – this land,
My own Manhattan with spires, and the sparkling and
    hurrying tides, and the ships,
The varied and ample land, the South and the North in
    the light, Ohio's shores and flashing Missouri,
And ever the far-spreading prairies cover'd with grass
    and corn.

Lo, the most excellent sun so calm and haughty,
The violet and purple morn with just-felt breezes,
The gentle soft-born measureless light,
The miracle spreading bathing all, the fulfill'd noon,
The coming eve delicious, the welcome night and the
    stars,
Over my cities shining all, enveloping man and land.

13

Sing on, sing on you gray-brown bird,
Sing from the swamps, the recesses, pour your chant from
    the bushes,
Limitless out of the dusk, out of the cedars and pines.

Sing on dearest brother, warble your reedy song,
Loud human song, with voice of uttermost woe.

O liquid and free and tender!
O wild and loose to my soul – O wondrous singer!
You only I hear – yet the star holds me, (but will soon
    depart,)
Yet the lilac with mastering odor holds me.

14

Now while I sat in the day and look'd forth,
In the close of the day with its light and the fields of
    spring, and the farmers preparing their crops,
In the large unconscious scenery of my land with its
    lakes and forests,
In the heavenly aerial beauty, (after the perturb'd winds
    and the storms,)
Under the arching heavens of the afternoon swift
    passing, and the voices of children and women,
The many-moving sea-tides, and I saw the ships how they
    sail'd,
And the summer approaching with richness, and the
    fields all busy with labor,
And the infinite separate houses, how they all went on,
    each with its meals and minutia of daily usages,
And the streets how their throbbings throbb'd, and the
    cities pent – lo, then and there,
Falling upon them all and among them all, enveloping
    me with the rest,
Appear'd the cloud, appear'd the long black trail,
And I knew death, its thought, and the sacred knowledge
    of death.

Then with the knowledge of death as walking one side of
    me,
And the thought of death close-walking the other side of
    me,
And I in the middle as with companions, and as holding
    the hands of companions,

I fled forth to the hiding receiving night that talks not,
Down to the shores of the water, the path by the swamp
   in the dimness,
To the solemn shadowy cedars and ghostly pines so still.

And the singer so shy to the rest receiv'd me,
The gray-brown bird I know receiv'd us comrades three,
And he sang the carol of death, and a verse for him I
   love.

From deep secluded recesses,
From the fragrant cedars and the ghostly pines so still,
Came the carol of the bird.

And the charm of the carol rapt me,
As I held as if by their hands my comrades in the night,
And the voice of my spirit tallied the song of the bird.

Come lovely and soothing death,
Undulate round the world, serenely arriving, arriving,
In the day, in the night, to all, to each,
Sooner or later delicate death.

Prais'd be the fathomless universe,
For life and joy, and for objects and knowledge curious,
And for love, sweet love – but praise! praise! praise!
For the sure-enwinding arms of cool-enfolding death.

Dark mother always gliding near with soft feet,
Have none chanted for thee a chant of fullest welcome?
Then I chant it for thee, I glorify thee above all,
I bring thee a song that when thou must indeed come,
*   come unfalteringly.*

Approach strong deliveress,
When it is so, when thou hast taken them I joyously sing
  the dead,
Lost in the loving floating ocean of thee,
Laved in the flood of thy bliss O death.

From me to thee glad serenades,
Dances for thee I propose saluting thee, adornments and
  feastings for thee,
And the sights of the open landscape and the high-spread
  sky are fitting,
And life and the fields, and the huge and thoughtful
  night.

The night in silence under many a star,
The ocean shore and the husky whispering wave whose
  voice I know,
And the soul turning to thee O vast and well-veil'd death,
And the body gratefully nestling close to thee.

Over the tree-tops I float thee a song,
Over the rising and sinking waves, over the myriad fields
  and the prairies wide,
Over the dense-pack'd cities all and the teeming wharves
  and ways,
I float this carol with joy, with joy to thee O death.

15

To the tally of my soul,
Loud and strong kept up the gray-brown bird,
With pure deliberate notes spreading filling the night.
Loud in the pines and cedars dim,
Clear in the freshness moist and the swamp-perfume,
And I with my comrades there in the night.

While my sight that was bound in my eyes unclosed,
As to long panoramas of visions.

And I saw askant the armies,
I saw as in noiseless dreams hundreds of battle-flags,
Borne through the smoke of the battles and pierc'd with
    missiles I saw them,
And carried hither and yon through the smoke, and torn
    and bloody,
And at last but a few shreds left on the staffs, (and all in
    silence,)
And the staffs all splinter'd and broken.

I saw battle-corpses, myriads of them,
And the white skeletons of young men, I saw them,
I saw the debris and debris of all the slain soldiers of the
    war,
But I saw they were not as was thought,
They themselves were fully at rest, they suffer'd not,
The living remain'd and suffer'd, the mother suffer'd,
And the wife and the child and the musing comrade
    suffer'd,
And the armies that remain'd suffer'd.

16

Passing the visions, passing the night,
Passing, unloosing the hold of my comrades' hands,
Passing the song of the hermit bird and the tallying song
    of my soul,
Victorious song, death's outlet song, yet varying ever-
    altering song,
As low and wailing, yet clear the notes, rising and
    falling, flooding the night,
Sadly sinking and fainting, as warning and warning, and
    yet again bursting with joy,
Covering the earth and filling the spread of the heaven,

As that powerful psalm in the night I heard from
    recesses,
Passing, I leave thee lilac with heart-shaped leaves,
I leave thee there in the door-yard, blooming, returning
    with spring.

I cease from my song for thee,
From my gaze on thee in the west, fronting the west,
    communing with thee,
O comrade lustrous with silver face in the night.

Yet each to keep and all, retrievements out of the night,
The song, the wondrous chant of the gray-brown bird,
And the tallying chant, the echo arous'd in my soul,
With the lustrous and drooping star with the
    countenance full of woe,
With the holders holding my hand nearing the call of the
    bird,
Comrades mine and I in the midst, and their memory
    ever to keep, for the dead I loved so well,
For the sweetest, wisest soul of all my days and lands –
    and this for his dear sake,
Lilac and star and bird twined with the chant of my soul,
There in the fragrant pines and the cedars dusk and dim.

A Boston Ballad

To get betimes in Boston town I rose this morning early,
Here's a good place at the corner, I must stand and see
    the show.

Clear the way there Jonathan!
Way for the President's marshal – way for the
    government cannon!

Way for the Federal foot and dragoons, (and the
    apparitions copiously tumbling.)

I love to look on the Stars and Stripes, I hope the fifes
    will play Yankee Doodle.
How bright shine the cutlasses of the foremost troops!
Every man holds his revolver, marching stiff through
    Boston town.

A fog follows, antiques of the same come limping,
Some appear wooden-legged, and some appear bandaged
    and bloodless.
Why this is indeed a show – it has called the dead out of
    the earth!
The old graveyards of the hills have hurried to see!

Phantoms! phantoms countless by flank and rear!
Cock'd hats of mothy mould – crutches made of mist!
Arms in slings – old men leaning on young men's
    shoulders.

What troubles you Yankee phantoms? What is all this
    chattering of bare gums?
Does the ague convulse your limbs? do you mistake your
    crutches for firelocks and level them?

If you blind your eyes with tears you will not see the
    President's marshal,
If you groan such groans you might balk the government
    cannon.

For shame old maniacs – bring down those toss'd arms,
    and let your white hair be,
Here gape your great grandsons, their wives gaze at
    them from the windows,

See how well dress'd, see how orderly they conduct
    themselves.

Worse and worse – can't you stand it? are you retreating?
Is this hour with the living too dead for you?

Retreat then – pell-mell!
To your graves – back – back to the hills old limpers!
I do not think you belong here anyhow.

But there is one thing that belongs here – shall I tell you
    what it is, gentlemen of Boston?

I will whisper it to the Mayor, he shall send a committee
    to England,
They shall get a grant from the Parliament, go with a
    cart to the royal vault,
Dig out King George's coffin, unwrap him quick from the
    grave-clothes, box up his bones for a journey,
Find a swift Yankee clipper – here is freight for you,
    black-bellied clipper,
Up with your anchor – shake out your sails – steer
    straight toward Boston bay.

Now call for the President's marshal again, bring out the
    government cannon,
Fetch home the roarers from Congress, make another
    procession, guard it with foot and dragoons.

This centre-piece for them;
Look, all orderly citizens – look from the windows,
    women!

The committee open the box, set up the regal ribs, glue
    those that will not stay,
Clap the skull on top of the ribs, and clap a crown on top
    of the skull.

You have got your revenge, old buster – the crown is
    come to its own, and more than its own.

Stick your hands in your pockets, Jonathan – you are a
    made man from this day,
You are mighty cute – and here is one of your bargains.

Good-bye My Fancy!

Good-bye my Fancy!
Farewell dear mate, dear love!
I'm going away, I know not where,
Or to what fortune, or whether I may ever see you again,
So Good-bye my Fancy.

Now for my last – let me look back a moment;
The slower fainter ticking of the clock is in me,
Exit, nightfall, and soon the heart-thud stopping.

Long have we lived, joy'd, caress'd together;
Delightful! – now separation – Good-bye my Fancy.

Yet let me not be too hasty,
Long indeed have we lived, slept, filter'd, become really
    blended into one;
Then if we die we die together, (yes, we'll remain one,)
If we go anywhere we'll go together to meet what
    happens,
May-be we'll be better off and blither, and learn
    something,

May-be it is yourself now really ushering me to the true
    songs, (who knows?)
May-be it is you the mortal knob really undoing, turning
    – so now finally,
Good-bye – and hail! my Fancy.

I Hear America Singing

I hear America singing, the varied carols I hear,
Those of mechanics, each one singing his as it should be
    blithe and strong,
The carpenter singing his as he measures his plank or
    beam,
The mason singing his as he makes ready for work, or
    leaves off work,
The boatman singing what belongs to him in his boat,
    the deckhand singing on the steamboat deck,
The shoemaker singing as he sits on his bench, the hatter
    singing as he stands,
The wood-cutter's song, the ploughboy's on his way in the
    morning, or at noon intermission or at sundown,
The delicious singing of the mother, or of the young wife
    at work, or of the girl sewing or washing,
Each singing what belongs to him or her and to none
    else,
The day what belongs to the day – at night the party of
    young fellows, robust, friendly,
Singing with open mouths their strong melodious songs.

WALT WHITMAN

Pioneers! O Pioneers!

Come my tan-faced children,
Follow well in order, get your weapons ready,
Have you your pistols? have you your sharp-edged axes?
    Pioneers! O pioneers!

For we cannot tarry here,
We must march my darlings, we must bear the brunt of
    danger,
We the youthful sinewy races, all the rest on us depend,
    Pioneers! O pioneers!

O you youths, Western youths,
So impatient, full of action, full of manly pride and
    friendship,
Plain I see you Western youths, see you tramping with
    the foremost,
    Pioneers! O pioneers!

Have the elder races halted?
Do they droop and end their lesson, wearied over there
    beyond the seas?
We take up the task eternal, and the burden and the
    lesson,
    Pioneers! O pioneers!

All the past we leave behind,
We debouch upon a newer mightier world, varied world,
Fresh and strong the world we seize, world of labor and
    the march,
    Pioneers! O pioneers!

We detachments steady throwing,
Down the edges, through the passes, up the mountains
    steep,

Conquering, holding, daring, venturing as we go the
　　unknown ways,
　　　　Pioneers! O pioneers!

　　We primeval forests felling,
We the rivers stemming, vexing we and piercing deep the
　　mines within,
We the surface broad surveying, we the virgin soil
　　upheaving,
　　　　Pioneers! O pioneers!

　　Colorado men are we,
From the peaks gigantic, from the great sierras and the
　　high plateaus,
From the mine and from the gully, from the hunting trail
　　we come,
　　　　Pioneers! O pioneers!

　　From Nebraska, from Arkansas,
Central inland race are we, from Missouri, with the
　　continental blood intervein'd,
All the hands of comrades clasping, all the Southern, all
　　the Northern,
　　　　Pioneers! O pioneers!

　　O resistless restless race!
O beloved race in all! O my breast aches with tender love
　　for all!
O I mourn and yet exult, I am rapt with love for all,
　　　　Pioneers! O pioneers!

　　Raise the mighty mother mistress,
Waving high the delicate mistress, over all the starry
　　mistress, (bend your heads all,)

Raise the fang'd and warlike mistress, stern, impassive,
    weapon'd mistress,
        Pioneers! O pioneers!

     . See my children, resolute children,
By those swarms upon our rear we must never yield or
    falter,
Ages back in ghostly millions frowning there behind us
    urging,
        Pioneers! O pioneers!

      On and on the compact ranks,
With accessions ever waiting, with the places of the dead
    quickly fill'd,
Through the battle, through defeat, moving yet and never
    stopping,
        Pioneers! O pioneers!

      O to die advancing on!
Are there some of us to droop and die? Has the hour
    come?
Then upon the march we fittest die, soon and sure the
    gap is fill'd,
        Pioneers! O pioneers!

      All the pulses of the world,
Falling in they beat for us, with the Western movement
    beat,
Holding single or together, steady moving to the front, all
    for us,
        Pioneers! O pioneers!

      Life's involv'd and varied pageants,
All the forms and shows, all the workmen at their work,

All the seamen and the landsmen, all the masters with
    their slaves,
        Pioneers! O pioneers!

        All the hapless silent lovers,
All the prisoners in the prisons, all the righteous and the
    wicked,
All the joyous, all the sorrowing, all the living, all the
    dying,
        Pioneers! O pioneers!

        I too with my soul and body,
We, a curious trio, picking, wandering on our way,
Through these shores amid the shadows, with the
    apparitions pressing,
        Pioneers! O pioneers!

        Lo, the darting bowling orb!
Lo, the brother orbs around, all the clustering suns and
    planets,
All the dazzling days, all the mystic nights with dreams,
        Pioneers! O pioneers!

        These are of us, they are with us,
All for primal needed work, while the followers there in
    embryo wait behind,
We today's procession heading, we the route for travel
    clearing,
        Pioneers! O pioneers!

        O you daughters of the West!
O you young and elder daughters! O you mothers and you
    wives!
Never must you be divided, in our ranks you move
    united,
        Pioneers! O pioneers!

Not for delectations sweet,
Not the cushion and the slipper, not the peaceful and the
    studious,
Not the riches safe and palling, not for us the tame
    enjoyment,
        Pioneers! O pioneers!

Do the feasters gluttonous feast?
Do the corpulent sleepers sleep? have they lock'd and
    bolted doors?
Still be ours the diet hard, and the blanket on the
    ground,
        Pioneers! O pioneers!

Has the night descended?
Was the road of late so toilsome? did we stop discouraged
    nodding on our way?
Yet a passing hour I yield you in your tracks to pause
    oblivious,
        Pioneers! O pioneers!

Till with sound of trumpet,
Far, far off the daybreak call – hark! how loud and clear
    I hear it wind,
Swift! to the head of the army! – swift! spring to your
    places,
        Pioneers! O pioneers!

On the Beach at Night

On the beach at night,
Stands a child with her father,
Watching the east, the autumn sky.

Up through the darkness,
While ravening clouds, the burial clouds, in black masses
    spreading,
Lower sullen and fast athwart and down the sky,
Amid a transparent clear belt of ether yet left in the east,
Ascends large and calm the lord-star Jupiter,
And nigh at hand, only a very little above,
Swim the delicate sisters the Pleiades.
From the beach the child holding the hand of her father,
Those burial clouds that lower victorious soon to devour
    all,
Watching, silently weeps.

Weep not, child,
Weep not, my darling,
With these kisses let me remove your tears,
The ravening clouds shall not long be victorious;
They shall not long possess the sky, they devour the stars
    only in apparition,
Jupiter shall emerge, be patient, watch again another
    night, the Pleiades shall emerge,
They are immortal, all those stars both silvery and
    golden shall shine out again,
The great stars and the little ones shall shine out again,
    they endure,
The vast immortal suns and the long-enduring pensive
    moons shall again shine.

Then dearest child mournest thou only for Jupiter?
Considerest thou alone the burial of the stars?

Something there is,
(With my lips soothing thee, adding I whisper,
I give thee the first suggestion, the problem and
    indirection,)
Something there is more immortal even than the stars,

(Many the burials, many the days and nights, passing
    away,)
Something that shall endure longer even than lustrous
    Jupiter,
Longer than sun or any revolving satellite,
Or the radiant sisters the Pleiades.

One's-Self I Sing

One's-Self I sing, a simple separate person,
Yet utter the word Democratic, the word En-Masse.

Of physiology from top to toe I sing,
Not physiognomy alone nor brain alone is worthy for the
    Muse, I say the Form complete is worthier far,
The Female equally with the Male I sing.

Of Life immense in passion, pulse, and power,
Cheerful, for freest action form'd under the laws divine,
The Modern Man I sing.

To a Stranger

Passing stranger! you do not know how longingly I look
    upon you,
You must be he I was seeking, or she I was seeking, (it
    comes to me as of a dream,)
I have somewhere surely lived a life of joy with you,
All is recall'd as we flit by each other, fluid, affectionate,
    chaste, matured,
You grew up with me, were a boy with me or a girl with
    me,
I ate with you and slept with you, your body has become
    not yours only nor left my body mine only,

You give me the pleasure of your eyes, face, flesh, as we
    pass, you take of my beard, breast, hands, in return,
I am not to speak to you, I am to think of you when I sit
    alone or wake at night alone,
I am to wait, I do not doubt I am to meet you again,
I am to see to it that I do not lose you.

A Noiseless Patient Spider

A noiseless patient spider,
I mark'd where on a little promontory it stood isolated,
Mark'd how to explore the vacant vast surrounding,
It launch'd forth filament, filament, filament, out of itself,
Ever unreeling them, ever tirelessly speeding them.

And you O my soul where you stand,
Surrounded, detached, in measureless oceans of space,
Ceaselessly musing, venturing, throwing, seeking the
    spheres to connect them,
Till the bridge you will need be form'd, till the ductile
    anchor hold,
Till the gossamer thread you fling catch somewhere, O
    my soul.

EMILY DICKINSON
1830-1886

Emily Dickinson was the daughter of a prominent lawyer in Amherst, Mass. where she spent most of her uneventful life. After a few unsuccessful attempts at publication, she wrote secretly, guarding her work even from the eyes of her family, but after her death over 1000 brief lyrics were discovered among her papers.

None of the following were published during Emily Dickinson's lifetime or with her permission, but are taken from *Poems* (1890), *Poems: Second Series* (1891), *Poems: Third Series* (1896) and *The Single Hound* (1914).

I never hear the word 'escape'
Without a quicker blood,
A sudden expectation,
A flying attitude!

I never hear of prisons broad
By soldiers battered down,
But I tug childish at my bars
Only to fail again!

I'm Nobody! Who are you?
Are you – Nobody – Too?
Then there's a pair of us?
Don't tell! they'd advertise – you know!

How dreary – to be – Somebody!
How public – like a Frog—
To tell one's name – the livelong June—
To an admiring Bog!

She dealt her pretty words like Blades—
How glittering they shone—
And every One unbared a Nerve
Or wantoned with a Bone—

She never deemed – she hurt—
That – is not Steel's Affair—
A vulgar grimace in the Flesh—
How ill the Creatures bear—

To Ache is human – not polite—
The Film upon the eye
Mortality's old Custom—
Just locking up – to Die.

I could not drink it, Sweet,
Till You had tasted first,
Though cooler than the Water was
The Thoughtfulness of Thirst.

We'll pass without the parting
So to spare
Certificate of Absence—
Deeming where

I left Her I could find Her
If I tried—
This way, I keep from missing
Those that died.

The last Night that She lived
It was a Common Night
Except the Dying – this to Us
Made Nature different

We noticed smallest things—
Things overlooked before
By this great light upon our Minds
Italicized – as 'twere.

As We went out and in
Between Her final Room
And Rooms where Those to be alive
Tomorrow were, a Blame

That Others could exist
While She must finish quite
A Jealousy for Her arose
So nearly infinite—

We waited while She passed—
It was a narrow time—
Too jostled were Our Souls to speak
At length the notice came.

She mentioned, and forgot—
Then lightly as a Reed
Bent to the Water, struggled scarce—
Consented, and was dead—

And We – We placed the Hair—
And drew the Head erect—
And then an awful leisure was
Belief to regulate—

God made no act without a cause,
  Nor heart without an aim,
Our inference is premature,
  Our premises to blame.

The most triumphant Bird I ever knew or met
Embarked upon a twig today
And till Dominion set
I famish to behold so eminent a sight
And sang for nothing scrutable
But intimate Delight.
Retired, and resumed his transitive Estate—
To what delicious Accident
Does finest Glory fit!

Is Heaven a Physician?
They say that He can heal—
But Medicine Posthumous
Is unavailable—
Is Heaven an Exchequer?
They speak of what we owe—
But that negotiation
I'm not a Party to—

To make a prairie it takes a clover and one bee,
One clover, and a bee,
And revery.
The revery alone will do,
If bees are few.

My life closed twice before its close;
  It yet remains to see
If Immortality unveil
  A third event to me,

So huge, so hopeless to conceive,
  As these that twice befell.
Parting is all we know of heaven,
  And all we need of hell.

I taste a liquor never brewed,
From tankards scooped in pearl;
Not all the vats upon the Rhine
Yield such an alcohol!

Inebriate of air am I,
And debauchee of dew,
Reeling, through endless summer days,
From inns of molten blue.

When landlords turn the drunken bee
Out of the foxglove's door,
When butterflies renounce their drams,
I shall but drink the more!

Till seraphs swing their snowy hats,
And saints to windows run,
To see the little tippler
Leaning against the sun!

The soul selects her own society,
Then shuts the door;
On her divine majority
Obtrude no more.

Unmoved, she notes the chariot's pausing
At her low gate;
Unmoved, an emperor is kneeling
Upon her mat.

I've known her from an ample nation
Choose one;
Then close the valves of her attention
Like stone.

I like a look of agony,
Because I know it's true;
Men do not sham convulsion,
Nor simulate a throe.

The eyes glaze once, and that is death.
Impossible to feign
The beads upon the forehead
By homely anguish strung.

Because I could not stop for Death,
He kindly stopped for me;
The carriage held but just ourselves
And Immortality.

We slowly drove, he knew no haste,
And I had put away
My labor, and my leisure too,
For his civility.

We passed the school where children played
Their lessons scarcely done;
We passed the fields of gazing grain,
We passed the setting sun.

We paused before a house that seemed
A swelling of the ground;
The roof was scarcely visible,
The cornice but a mound.

Since then 'tis centuries; but each
Feels shorter than the day
I first surmised the horses' heads
Were toward eternity.

A bird came down the walk:
He did not know I saw;
He bit an angle-worm in halves
And ate the fellow, raw.

And then he drank a dew
From a convenient grass,
And then hopped sidewise to the wall
To let a beetle pass.

He glanced with rapid eyes
That hurried all abroad,—
They looked like frightened beads, I thought
He stirred his velvet head

Like one in danger; cautious,
I offered him a crumb,
And he unrolled his feathers
And rowed him softer home

Then oars divide the ocean,
Too silver for a seam,
Or butterflies, off banks of noon,
Leap, plashless, as they swim.

I like to see it lap the miles,
And lick the valleys up,
And stop to feed itself at tanks;
And then, prodigious, step

Around a pile of mountains,
And, supercilious, peer
In shanties by the sides of roads;
And then a quarry pare

To fit its sides, and crawl between,
Complaining all the while
In horrid, hooting stanza;
Then chase itself down hill

And neigh like Boanerges;
Then, punctual as a star,
Stop – docile and omnipotent—
At its own stable door.

I heard a fly buzz when I died;
  The stillness round my form
Was like the stillness in the air
  Between the heaves of storm.

The eyes beside had wrung them dry,
  And breaths were gathering sure
For that last onset, when the king
  Be witnessed in his power.

I willed my keepsakes, signed away
  What portion of me I
Could make assignable, – and then
  There interposed a fly,

With blue, uncertain, stumbling buzz,
  Between the light and me;
And then the windows failed, and then
  I could not see to see.

There's been a death in the opposite house
  As lately as today.
I know it by the numb look
  Such houses have alway.

The neighbours rustle in and out,
  The doctor drives away.
A window opens like a pod,
  Abrupt, mechanically;

Somebody flings a mattress out,—
  The children hurry by;
They wonder if It died on that,—
  I used to when a boy.

The minister goes stiffly in
 As if the house were his,
And he owned all the mourners now,
 And little boys besides;

And then the milliner, and the man
 Of the appalling trade,
To take the measure of the house.
 There'll be that dark parade

Of tassels and of coaches soon;
 It's easy as a sign,—
The intuition of the news
 In just a country town.

I cannot live with You—
It would be Life—
And Life is over there—
Behind the Shelf

The Sexton keeps the Key to—
Putting up
Our Life – His Porcelain—
Like a Cup—

Discarded of the Housewife—
Quaint – or Broke—
A newer Sevres pleases—
Old Ones crack—

I could not die – with You—
For One must wait
To shut the Other's Gaze down—
You – could not—

And I – Could I stand by
And see You – freeze—
Without my Right of Frost—
Death's privilege?

Nor could I rise – with You—
Because Your Face
Would put out Jesus'—
That New Grace

Glow plain – and foreign
On my homesick Eye—
Except that You than He
Shone closer by—

They'd judge Us – How—
For You – served Heaven – You know,
Or sought to—
I could not—

Because You saturated Sight—
And I had no more Eyes
For sordid excellence
As Paradise

And were You lost, I would be—
Though My Name
Rang loudest
On the Heavenly fame—

And were You – saved—
And I – condemned to be
Where You were not—
That self – were Hell to Me—

So We must meet apart—
You there – I – here—
With just the Door ajar
That Oceans are – and Prayer—
And that White Sustenance—
Despair—

SIDNEY LANIER
1842-1881

Born in Macon, Ga., Sidney Lanier served in the
Confederate Army during the Civil War and
contracted consumption in a Union prison. After the
war, finding himself still in bad health and with little
money, he abandoned his career as a 'third-rate
struggling lawyer' and turned to writing, supporting
himself by playing the flute. In time he became a
lecturer in English literature at Johns Hopkins
University and published an important volume of
theoretical prosody entitled *The Science of English Verse*.

'The Raven Days' was written in 1868, 'The
Marshes of Glynn' and 'Struggle' between 1877 and
1880. All were collected in *Poems* of 1884.

The Raven Days

Our hearths are gone out, and our hearts are broken,
  And but the ghosts of homes to us remain,
And ghostly eyes and hollow sighs give token
  From friend to friend of an unspoken pain.

O, Raven Days, dark Raven Days of sorrow,
  Bring to us, in your whetted ivory beaks,
Some sign out of the far land of To-morrow,
  Some strip of sea-green dawn, some orange streaks.

Ye float in dusky files, forever croaking—
  Ye chill our manhood with your dreary shade.
Pale, in the dark, not even God invoking,
  We lie in chains, too weak to be afraid.

O Raven Days, dark Raven Days of sorrow,
  Will ever any warm light come again?
Will ever the lit mountains of To-morrow
  Begin to gleam across the mournful plain?

Struggle

My Soul is like the oar that momently
  Dies in a desperate stress beneath the wave,
Then glitters out again and sweeps the sea:
  Each second I'm new-born from some new grave.

Thar's More in the Man Than Thar Is in the Land

I knowed a man, which he lived in Jones,
Which Jones is a county of red hills and stones,
And he lived pretty much by gittin' of loans,
And his mules was nuthin' but skin and bones,

And his hogs was flat as his corn-bread pones,
And he had 'bout a thousand acres o' land.

This man – which his name it was also Jones—
He swore that he'd leave them old red hills and stones,
Fur he couldn't make nuthin' but yallerish cotton,
And little o' *that*, and his fences was rotten,
And what little corn he had, *hit* was boughten,
And dinged ef a livin' was in the land.

And the longer he swore the madder he got,
And he riz and he walked to the stable lot,
And he hollered to Tom to come thar and hitch,
Fur to emigrate somewhar whar land was rich,
And to quit rasin' cock-burrs, thistles and sich,
And a wastin' ther time on the cussed land.

So him and Tom they hitched up the mules,
Pertestin' that folks was mighty big fools
That 'ud stay in Georgy ther lifetime out,
Jest scratchin' a livin' when all of 'em mought
Git places in Texas whar cotton would sprout
By the time you could plant it in the land.

And he driv by a house whar a man named Brown
Was a livin', not fur from the edge o' town,
And he bantered Brown fur to buy his place,
And said that bein' as money was skace,
And bein' as sheriffs was hard to face,
Two dollars an acre would git the land.

They closed at a dollar and fifty cents,
And Jones he bought him a waggin and tents,
And loaded his corn, and his wimmin, and truck,
And moved to Texas, which it tuck
His entire pile, with the best of luck,
To git thar and git him a little land.

But Brown moved out on the old Jones farm,
And he rolled up his breeches and bared his arm,
And he picked all the rocks from off'n the groun',
And he rooted it up and he plowed it down,
Then he sowed his corn and his wheat in the land.

Five years glid by, and Brown, one day
(Which he'd got so fat that he wouldn't weigh),
Was a settin' down, sorter lazily,
To the bulliest dinner you ever see,
When one o' the children jumped on his knee
And says, 'Yan's Jones, which you bought his land.'

And thar was Jones, standin' out at the fence,
And he hadn't no waggin, nor mules, nor tents,
Fur he had left Texas afoot and cum
To Georgy to see if he couldn't git sum
Employment, and he was a lookin' as hum-
Ble as ef he had never owned any land.

But Brown he axed him in, and he sot
Him down to his vittles smokin' hot,
And when he had filled hisself and the floor
Brown looked at him sharp and riz and swore
That, 'whether men's land was rich or poor
Thar was more in the *man* than thar was in the *land*.'

Corn

Today the woods are trembling through and through
With shimmering forms, that flash before my view,
Then melt in green as dawn-stars melt in blue.
    The leaves that wave against my cheek caress
    Like women's hands; the embracing boughs express
      A subtlety of mighty tenderness;

The copse-depths into little noises start,
That sound anon like beatings of a heart,
Anon like talk 'twixt lips not far apart.
    The beech dreams balm, as a dreamer hums a song;
    Through that vague wafture, expirations strong
    Throb from young hickories breathing deep and long
With stress and urgence bold of prisoned spring
        And ecstasy of burgeoning.

    Now, since the dew-plashed road of morn is dry,
    Forth venture odors of more quality
    And heavenlier giving. Like Jove's locks awry,
        Long muscadines
Rich-wreathe the spacious foreheads of great pines,
And breathe ambrosial passion from their vines.
    I pray with mosses, ferns and flowers shy
    That hide like gentle nuns from human eye
    To lift adoring perfumes to the sky.
I hear faint bridal-sighs of brown and green
Dying to silent hints of kisses keen
As far lights fringe into a pleasant sheen.
    I start at fragmentary whispers, blown
    From undertalks of leafy souls unknown,
    Vague purports sweet, of inarticulate tone.

Dreaming of gods, men, nuns and brides, between
Old companies of oaks that inward lean
To join their radiant amplitudes of green
    I slowly move, with ranging looks that pass
    Up from the matted miracles of grass
Into yon veined complex of space
Where sky and leafage interlace
    So close, the heaven of blue is seen
    Inwoven with a heaven of green.

I wander to the zigzag-cornered fence
Where sassafras, intrenched in brambles dense,
Contests with solid vehemence
        The march of culture, setting limb and thorn
        As pikes against the army of the corn.

There, while I pause, my fieldward-faring eyes
Take harvests, where there the stately corn-ranks rise,
                Of inward dignities
And large benignities and insights wise,
                Graces and modest majesties.
Thus, without theft, I reap another's field;
Thus, without tilth, I house a wondrous yield,
And heap my heart with quintuple crops concealed.

Look, out of line one tall corn-captain stands
Advanced beyond the foremost of his bands,
        And waves his blades upon the very edge
        And hottest thicket of the battling hedge.
Thou lustrous stalk, that ne'er mayst walk nor talk,
        Still shalt thou type the poet-soul sublime
        That leads the vanward of his timid time
        And sings up cowards with commanding rhyme—
Soul calm, like thee, yet fain, like thee, to grow
By double increment, above, below;
        Soul homely, as thou art, yet rich in grace like thee,
        Teaching the yeomen selfless chivalry
        That moves in gentle curves of courtesy;
Soul filled like thy long veins with sweetness tense,
                By every godlike sense
Transmuted from the four wild elements.
                Drawn to high plans,
        Thou lift'st more stature than a mortal man's,
Yet ever piercest downwards in the mould
                And keepest hold

Upon the reverend and steadfast earth
    That gave thee birth;
Yea, standest smiling in thy future grave,
    Serene and brave,
With unremitting breath
Inhaling life from death,
Thine epitaph writ fair in fruitage eloquent
    Thyself thy monument.

    As poets should,
Thou hast built up thy hardihood
With universal food,
    Drawn in select proportion fair
    From honest mould and vagabond air;
From darkness of the dreadful night,
    And joyful light;
    From antique ashes, whose departed flame
    In thee has finer life and longer fame;
From wounds and balms,
From storms and calms,
From potsherds and dry bones
    And ruin-stones.

Into thy vigorous substance thou hast wrought
Whate'er the hand of Circumstance hath brought;
    Yea, into cool solacing green hast spun
    White radiance hot from out the sun.
So thou dost mutually leaven
Strength of earth with grace of heaven;
    So thou dost marry new and old
    Into a one of higher mould;
    So thou dost reconcile the hot and cold,
    The dark and bright,
And many a heart-perplexing opposite,
    And so,
    Akin by blood to high and low,

Fitly thou playest out thy poet's part,
Richly expending thy much-bruisèd heart
   In equal care to nourish lord in hall
     Or beast in stall:
   Thou took'st from all that thou might'st give to all.

O steadfast dweller on the selfsame spot
Where thou wast born, that still repinest not—
Type of the home-fond heart, the happy lot!—
   Deeply thy mild content rebukes the land
   Whose flimsy homes, built on the shifting sand
Of trade, for ever rise and fall
With alternation whimsical,
   Enduring scarce a day,
   Then swept away
By swift engulfments of incalculable tides
Whereon capricious Commerce rides.

Look, thou substantial spirit of content!
Across this little vale, thy continent,
   To where, beyond the mouldering mill,
   Yon old deserted Georgian hill
Bares to the sun his piteous aged crest
     And seamy breast,
   By restless-hearted children left to lie
   Untended there beneath the heedless sky,
   As barbarous folk expose their old to die.

Upon that generous-rounding side,
     With gullies scarified
   Where keen Neglect his lash hath plied,
Dwelt one I knew of old, who played at toil,
And gave to coquette Cotton soul and soil.
   Scorning the slow reward of patient grain,
   He sowed his heart with hopes of swifter gain,
   Then sat him down and waited for the rain.

He sailed in borrowed ships of usury—
A foolish Jason on a treacherous sea,
Seeking the Fleece and finding misery.
    Lulled by smooth-rippling loans, in idle trance
    He lay content that unthrift Circumstance
    Should plough for him the stony field of Chance.
Yea, gathering crops whose worth no man might tell,
He staked his life on games of Buy-and-Sell,
And turned each field into a gambler's hell.
    Aye, as each year began,
    My farmer to the neighboring city ran;
Passed with a mournful anxious face
Into the banker's inner place;
Parleyed, excused, pleaded for longer grace;
    Railed at the drought, the worm, the rust, the grass;
    Protested ne'er again 'twould come to pass;
    With many an *oh* and *if* and *but alas*
Parried or swallowed searching questions rude,
And kissed the dust to soften Dives's mood.
At last, small loans by pledges great renewed,
    He issues smiling from the fatal door,
    And buys with lavish hand his yearly store
    Till his small borrowings will yield no more.
Aye, as each year declined,
With bitter heart and ever-brooding mind
He mourned his fate unkind.
    In dust, in rain, with might and main,
    He nursed his cotton, cursed his grain,
    Fretted for news that made him fret again,
Snatched at each telegram of Future Sale,
And thrilled with Bulls' or Bears' alternate wail—
In hope or fear alike for ever pale.
    And thus from year to year, through hope and fear,
    With many a curse and many a secret tear,
    Striving in vain his cloud of debt to clear,
        At last

He woke to find his foolish dreaming past,
    And all his best-of-life the easy prey
    Of squandering scamps and quacks that lined his
        way
        With vile array,
From rascal statesman down to petty knave;
Himself, at best, for all his bragging brave,
A gamester's catspaw and a banker's slave.
    Then, worn and gray, and sick with deep unrest,
    He fled away into the oblivious West,
        Unmourned, unblest.

Old hill! old hill! thou gashed and hairy Lear
Whom the divine Cordelia of the year,
E'en pitying Spring, will vainly strive to cheer—
    King, that no subject man nor beast may own,
    Discrowned, undaughtered and alone—
Yet shall the great God turn thy fate,
And bring thee back into thy monarch state
        And majesty immaculate.
Lo, through hot waverings of the August morn,
    Thou givest from thy vasty sides forlorn
    Visions of golden treasuries of corn—
Ripe largesse lingering for some bolder heart
That manfully shall take thy part,
        And tend thee,
        And defend thee,
With antique sinew and with modern art.

Evening Song

Look off, dear Love, across the sallow sands,
   And mark yon meeting of the sun and sea,
How long they kiss in sight of all the lands.
   Ah! longer, longer, we.

Now in the sea's red vintage melts the sun,
  As Egypt's pearl dissolved in rosy wine,
And Cleopatra night drinks all. 'Tis done,
  Love, lay thine hand in mine.

Come forth, sweet stars, and comfort heaven's heart;
  Glimmer, ye waves, round else unlighted sands.
O night! divorce our sun and sky apart,
  Never our lips, our hands.

The Marshes of Glynn

Glooms of the live-oaks, beautiful-braided and woven
With intricate shades of the vines that myriad-cloven
    Clamber the forks of the multiform boughs,—
        Emerald twilights,—
        Virginal shy lights,
Wrought of the leaves to allure to the whisper of vows,
When lovers pace timidly down through the green
            colonnades
    Of the dim sweet woods, of the dear dark woods,
        Of the heavenly woods and glades,
    That run to the radiant marginal sand-beach within
        The wide sea-marshes of Glynn;—

    Beautiful glooms, soft dusks in the noon-day fire,—
    Wildwood privacies, closets of lone desire,
Chamber from chamber parted with wavering arras of
            leaves,—
Cells for the passionate pleasure of prayer to the soul
            that grieves,
    Pure with a sense of the passing of saints through
            the wood,
    Cool for the dutiful weighing of ill with good;—

O braided dusks of the oak and woven shades of the vine.
While the riotous noon-day sun of the June-day long did
    shine,
Ye held me fast in your heart and I held you fast in
    mine;
  But now when the noon is no more, and riot is rest,
  And the sun is a-wait at the ponderous gate of the
    West,
    And the slant yellow beam down the wood-aisle
     doth seem
    Like a lane into heaven that leads from a
     dream,—
Ay, now, when my soul all day hath drunken the soul of
    the oak,
And my heart is at ease from men, and the wearisome
    sound of the stroke
  Of the scythe of time and the trowel of trade is low,
  And belief overmasters doubt, and I know that I
    know,
  And my spirit is grown to a lordly great compass
    within,
  That the length and the breadth and the sweep of the
    marshes of Glynn
  Will work me no fear like the fear they have
    wrought me of yore
    When length was fatigue, and when breadth was
    but bitterness sore,
    And when terror and shrinking and dreary
    unnamable pain
Drew over me out of the merciless miles of the plain,—
  Oh, now, unafraid, I am fain to face
    The vast sweet visage of space.
  To the edge of the wood I am drawn, I am drawn,
  Where the gray beach glimmering runs, as a belt of
    the dawn,

For a mete and a mark
To the forest-dark:—
　　So:
Affable live-oak, leaning low,—
Thus – with your favor – soft, with a reverent hand,
(Not lightly touching your person, Lord of the land!)
Bending your beauty aside, with a step I stand
　　On the firm-packed sand,
　　　　Free
　　By a world of marsh that borders a world of sea.
Sinuous southward and sinuous northward the
　　　shimmering band
Of the sand-beach fastens the fringe of the marsh to
　　the folds of the land.
Inward and outward to northward and southward the
　　　beach-lines linger and curl
As a silver-wrought garment that clings to and follows
　　the firm sweet limbs of a girl.
Vanishing, swerving, evermore curving again into sight,
Softly the sand-beach wavers away to a dim gray looping
　　　of light.
And what if behind me to westward the wall of the woods
　　stands high?
The world lies east: how ample, the marsh and the sea
　　and the sky!
A league and a league of marsh-grass, waist-high,
　　broad in the blade,
Green, and all of a height, and unflecked with a light
　　or a shade,
　　Stretch leisurely off, in a pleasant plain
　　To the terminal blue of the main.

Oh, what is abroad in the marsh and the terminal
　　sea?
Somehow my soul seems suddenly free

From the weighing of fate and the sad discussion of
    sin,
By the length and the breadth and the sweep of the
    marshes of Glynn.
Ye marshes, how candid and simple and nothing-
    withholding and free
Ye publish yourselves to the sky and offer yourselves to
    the sea!
Tolerant plains, that suffer the sea and the rains and the
    sun,
Ye spread and span like the catholic man who hath
    mightily won
God out of knowledge and good out of infinite pain
And sight out of blindness and purity out of a stain.

As the marsh-hen secretly builds on the watery sod,
Behold I will build me a nest on the greatness of
    God:
I will fly in the greatness of God as the marsh-hen
    flies
In the freedom that fills all the space 'twixt the
    marsh and the skies:
By so many roots as the marsh-grass sends in the sod
I will heartily lay me a-hold on the greatness of God:
Oh, like to the greatness of God is the greatness
    within
The range of the marshes, the liberal marshes of
    Glynn.

And the sea lends large, as the marsh: lo, out of his
    plenty the sea
Pours fast: full soon the time of the flood-tide must
    be:
Look how the grace of the sea doth go
About and about through the intricate channels that
    flow

Here and there,
Everywhere,
Till his waters have flooded the uttermost creeks and the
low-lying lanes,
And the marsh is meshed with a million veins,
That like as with rosy and silvery essences flow
In the rose-and-silver evening glow.
Farewell, my lord Sun!
The creeks overflow: a thousand rivulets run
'Twixt the roots of the sod; the blades of the marsh-
grass stir;
Passeth a hurrying sound of wings that westward whirr;
Passeth, and all is still; and the currents cease to run;
And the sea and the marsh are one.
How still the plains of the waters be!
The tide is in his ecstasy.
The tide is at his highest height:
And it is night.

And now from the Vast of the Lord will the waters of
sleep
Roll in on the souls of men,
But who will reveal to our waking ken
The forms that swim and the shapes that creep
Under the waters of sleep?
And I would I could know what swimmeth below when
the tide comes in
On the length and the breadth of the marvellous
marshes of Glynn.

Song of the Chattahoochee

Out of the hills of Habersham,
   Down the valleys of Hall,
I hurry amain to reach the plain,
Run the rapid and leap the fall,
Split at the rock and together again,
Accept my bed, or narrow or wide,
And flee from folly on every side
With a lover's pain to attain the plain
     Far from the hills of Habersham,
     Far from the valleys of Hall.

All down the hills of Habersham,
   All through the valleys of Hall,
The rushes cried *Abide, abide,*
The willful waterweeds held me thrall,
The laving laurel turned my tide,
The ferns and the fondling grass said *Stay,*
The dewberry dipped for to work delay,
And the little reeds sighed *Abide, abide,*
     Here in the hills of Habersham,
     Here in the valleys of Hall.

High o'er the hills of Habersham,
   Veiling the valleys of Hall,
The hickory told me manifold
Fair tales of shade, the poplar tall
Wrought me her shadowy self to hold,
The chestnut, the oak, the walnut, the pine,
Overleaning, with flickering meaning and sign,
Said, *Pass not, so cold, these manifold*
     Deep shades of the hills of Habersham,
     These glades in the valleys of Hall.
     And oft in the hills of Habersham,
     And oft in the valleys of Hall,

The white quartz shone, and the smooth brook-stone
Did bar me of passage with friendly brawl,
And many a luminous jewel lone
—Crystals clear or a-cloud with mist,
Ruby, garnet and amethyst—
Made lures with the lights of streaming stone
    In the clefts of the hills of Habersham,
    In the beds of the valleys of Hall.

    But oh, not the hills of Habersham,
    And oh, not the valleys of Hall
Avail: I am fain for to water the plain.
Downward the voices of Duty call—
Downward, to toil and be mixed with the main,
The dry fields burn, and the mills are to turn,
And a myriad flowers mortally yearn,
And the lordly main from beyond the plain
    Calls o'er the hills of Habersham,
    Calls through the valleys of Hall.

Opposition

Of fret, of dark, of thorn, of chill,
    Complain no more; for these, O heart,
Direct the random of the will
    As rhymes direct the rage of art.

The lute's fixt fret, that runs athwart
    The strain and purpose of the string,
For governance and nice consort
    Doth bar his wilful wavering.

The dark hath many dear avails;
    The dark distils divinest dews;
The dark is rich with nightingales,
    With dreams, and with the heavenly Muse.

Bleeding with thorns of petty strife,
  I'll ease (as lovers do) my smart
With sonnets to my lady Life
  Writ red in issues from the heart.

What grace may lie within the chill
  Of favor frozen fast in scorn!
When Good's a-freeze, we call it Ill!
  This rosy Time is glacier-born.

Of fret, of dark, of thorn, of chill,
  Complain thou not, O heart; for these
Bank-in the current of the will
  To uses, arts, and charities.

The Stirrup-Cup

Death, thou'rt a cordial old and rare:
Look how compounded, with what care!
Time got his wrinkles reaping thee
Sweet herbs from all antiquity.

David to thy distillage went,
Keats, and Gotama excellent,
Omar Khayyam, and Chaucer bright,
And Shakspere for a king-delight.

Then, Time, let not a drop be spilt:
Hand me the cup whene'er thou wilt;
'Tis thy rich stirrup-cup to me;
I'll drink it down right smilingly.

Marsh Song – At Sunset

Over the monstrous shambling sea,
  Over the Caliban sea,
Bright Ariel-cloud, thou lingerest:
Oh wait, oh wait, in the warm red West,—
  Thy Prospero I'll be.

Over the humped and fishy sea,
  Over the Caliban sea,
O cloud in the West, like a thought in the heart
Of pardon, loose thy wing and start,
  And do a grace for me.

Over the huge and huddling sea,
  Over the Caliban sea,
Bring hither my brother Antonio, – Man,—
My injurer: night breaks the ban;
  Brother, I pardon thee.

ROBERT FROST
1874-1963

Born in San Francisco, Robert Frost returned with his family to their original home of New England at the age of ten. After a long spell as a farmer, he moved to England where he published his first book of poems. On his return to the United States, Robert Frost settled on a New Hampshire farm and carved out a reputation as a major American poet with a series of distinguished, Pulitzer Prize-winning collections, exploring the New England countryside.

The poems which follow are taken from *A Boy's Will* (1913), *North of Boston* (1914), *Mountain Interval* (1916) and *New Hampshire* (1923).

The Pasture

I'm going out to clean the pasture spring;
I'll only stop to rake the leaves away
(And wait to watch the water clear, I may):
I sha'n't be gone long. — You come too.

I'm going out to fetch the little calf
That's standing by the mother. It's so young
It totters when she licks it with her tongue.
I sha'n't be gone long. — You come too.

Mowing

There was never a sound beside the wood but one,
And that was my long scythe whispering to the ground.
What was it it whispered? I knew not well myself;
Perhaps it was something about the heat of the sun,
Something, perhaps, about the lack of sound—
And that was why it whispered and did not speak.

It was no dream of the gift of idle hours,
Or easy gold at the hand of fay or elf:
Anything more than the truth would have seemed too
    weak
To the earnest love that laid the swale in rows,
Not without feeble-pointed spikes of flowers
(Pale orchises), and scared a bright green snake.
The fact is the sweetest dream that labor knows.
My long scythe whispered and left the hay to make.

Meeting and Passing

As I went down the hill along the wall
There was a gate I had leaned at for the view
And had just turned from when I first saw you
As you came up the hill. We met. But all
We did that day was mingle great and small
Footprints in summer dust as if we drew
The figure of our being less than two
But more than one as yet. Your parasol
Pointed the decimal off with one deep thrust.
And all the time we talked you seemed to see
Something down there to smile at in the dust.
(Oh, it was without prejudice to me!)
Afterward I went past what you had passed
Before we met and you what I had passed.

Design

I found a dimpled spider, fat and white,
On a white heal-all, holding up a moth
Like a white piece of rigid satin cloth—
Assorted characters of death and blight
Mixed ready to begin the morning right,
Like the ingedients of a witches' broth—
A snow-drop spider, a flower like froth,
And dead wings carried like a paper kite.

What had that flower to do with being white,
The wayside blue and innocent heal-all?
What brought the kindred spider to that height,
Then steered the white moth thither in the night?
What but design of darkness to appall?—
If design govern in a thing so small.

Fire and Ice

Some say the world will end in fire,
Some say in ice.
From what I've tasted of desire
I hold with those who favor fire.
But if it had to perish twice,
I think I know enough of hate
To say that for destruction ice
Is also great
And would suffice.

The Road Not Taken

Two roads diverged in a yellow wood,
And sorry I could not travel both
And be one traveler, long I stood
And looked down one as far as I could
To where it bent in the undergrowth;

Then took the other, as just as fair,
And having perhaps the better claim,
Because it was grassy and wanted wear;
Though as for that the passing there
Had worn them really about the same,

And both that morning equally lay
In leaves no step had trodden black.
Oh, I kept the first for another day!
Yet knowing how way leads on to way,
I doubted if I should ever come back.

I shall be telling this with a sigh
Somewhere ages and ages hence:
Two roads diverged in a wood, and I—
I took the one less traveled by,
And that has made all the difference.

WALLACE STEVENS
1879-1955

Born in Pennsylvania, educated at Harvard and New York University Law School, Wallace Stevens became known as the 'Insurance Man' of American poetry. Much of his early work he destroyed and most of the surviving work he wrote after the age of fifty but it is all characterized by elegant wit, bizarre images and rich musicality.

The following poems are taken from *Harmonium* (1931), *Ideas of Order* (1935), *Parts of a World* (1942) and *Transport to Summer* (1947).

The Emperor of Ice-Cream

Call the roller of big cigars,
The muscular one, and bid him whip
In kitchen cups concupiscent curds.
Let the wenches dawdle in such dress
As they are used to wear, and let the boys
Bring flowers in last month's newspapers.
Let be be finale of seem.
The only emperor is the emperor of ice-cream.

Take from the dresser of deal,
Lacking the three glass knobs, that sheet
On which she embroidered fantails once
And spread it so as to cover her face.
If her horny feet protrude, they come
To show how cold she is, and dumb.
Let the lamp affix its beam.
The only emperor is the emperor of ice-cream.

Disillusionment of Ten O'Clock

The houses are haunted
By white night-gowns.
None are green,
Or purple with green rings,
Or green with yellow rings,
Or yellow with blue rings.
None of them are strange,
With socks of lace
And beaded ceintures.
People are not going
To dream of baboons and periwinkles.
Only, here and there, an old sailor,
Drunk and asleep in his boots,
Catches tigers
In red weather.

Anecdote of the Jar

I placed a jar in Tennessee,
And round it was, upon a hill.
It made the slovenly wilderness
Surround that hill.

The wilderness rose up to it,
And sprawled around, no longer wild.
The jar was round upon the ground
And tall and of a port in air.

It took dominion everywhere.
The jar was gray and bare.
It did not give of bird or bush,
Like nothing else in Tennessee.

Sad Strains of a Gay Waltz

The truth is that there comes a time
When we can mourn no more over music
That is so much motionless sound.

There comes a time when the waltz
Is no longer a mode of desire, a mode
Of revealing desire and is empty of shadows.

Too many waltzes have ended. And then
There's that mountain-minded Hoon,
For whom desire was never that of the waltz,

Who found all form and order in solitude,
For whom the shapes were never the figures of men.
Now, for him, his forms have vanished.

There is order in neither sea nor sun.
The shapes have lost their glistening.
There are these sudden mobs of men,

These sudden clouds of faces and arms,
An immense suppression, freed,
These voices crying without knowing for what,

Except to be happy, without knowing how,
Imposing forms they cannot describe,
Requiring order beyond their speech.

Too many waltzes have ended. Yet the shapes
For which the voices cry, these, too, may be
Modes of desire, modes of revealing desire.

Too many waltzes – The epic of disbelief
Blares oftener and soon, will soon be constant.
Some harmonious skeptic soon in a skeptical music

Will unite these figures of men and their shapes
Will glisten again with motion, the music
Will be motion and full of shadows.

Poetry Is a Destructive Force

That's what misery is,
Nothing to have at heart.
It is to have or nothing.

It is a thing to have,
A lion, an ox in his breast,
To feel it breathing there.

Corazon, stout dog,
Young ox, bow-legged bear,
He tastes its blood, not spit.

He is like a man
In the body of a violent beast.
Its muscles are his own ...

The lion sleeps in the sun.
Its nose is on its paws.
It can kill a man.

Holiday in Reality

1

It was something to see that their white was different,
Sharp as white paint in the January sun;

Something to feel that they needed another yellow,
Less Aix than Stockholm, hardly a yellow at all,

A vibrancy not to be taken for granted, from
A sun in an almost colorless, cold heaven.

They had known that there was not even a common
    speech,
Palabra of a common man who did not exist.

Why should they not know they had everything of their
    own
As each had a particular woman and her touch?

After all, they knew that to be real each had
To find for himself his earth, his sky, his sea.

And the words for them and the colors that they
    possessed.
It was impossible to breathe at Durand-Ruel's.

2

The flowering Judas grows from the belly or not at all.
The breast is covered with violets. It is a green leaf.

Spring is umbilical or else it is not spring.
Spring is the truth of spring or nothing, a waste, a fake.

These trees and their argentines, their dark-spiced
    branches,
Grow out of the spirit or they are fantastic dust.

The bud of the apple is desire, the down-falling gold,
The catbird's gobble in the morning half-awake—

These are real only if I make them so. Whistle
For me, grow green for me and, as you whistle and grow
    green,

Intangible arrows quiver and stick in the skin
And I taste at the root of the tongue the unreal of what is
    real.

EZRA POUND
1885-1972

Ezra Pound, poet and critic, was a writer of esoteric sources and immense influence. Steeped in medieval and Eastern literature, he became the leader of the Imagist poets in the 1920s and sponsored such modern figures as T.S. Eliot, James Joyce, Tagore and the sculptor Gaudier-Brzeska while his poetic masterwork *Cantos* had a tremendous effect on such major modern poetry as *The Wasteland* and *The Bridge*.

The following poems are taken from the early collections, *Personae, Ripostes* and *Lustra*.

A Pact

I make a pact with you, Walt Whitman—
I have detested you long enough.
I come to you as a grown child
Who has had a pig-headed father;
I am old enough now to make friends.
It was you that broke the new wood,
Now is a time for carving.
We have one sap and one root—
Let there be commerce between us.

Dance Figure
For The Marriage in Cana of Galilee

Dark eyed,
O woman of my dreams,
Ivory sandaled,
There is none like thee among the dancers,
None with swift feet.

I have not found thee in the tents,
In the broken darkness.
I have not found thee at the well-head
Among the women with pitchers.

Thine arms are as a young sapling under the bark;
Thy face as a river with lights.
White as an almond are thy shoulders;
As new almonds stripped from the husk.
They guard thee not with eunuchs;
Not with bars of copper.

Gilt turquoise and silver are in the place of thy rest.
A brown robe, with threads of gold woven in patterns,
    hast thou gathered about thee,
O Nathat-Ikanaie, 'Tree-at-the-river.'

As a rillet among the sedge are thy hands upon me;
Thy fingers a frosted stream.

Thy maidens are white like pebbles;
Their music about thee!

There is none like thee among the dancers;
None with swift feet.

Sestina: Altaforte

Loquitur: En Bertrans de Born. Dante Alighieri put this
    man in hell for that he was a stirrer up of strife.
    Eccovi! Judge ye! Have I dug him up again? The
    scene is at his castle, Altaforte. 'Papiols' is his
    jongleur. 'The Leopard,' the *device* of Richard Cœur
    de Lion.

1

Damn it all! all this our South stinks peace.
You whoreson dog, Papiols, come! Let's to music!
I have no life save when the swords clash.
But ah! when I see the standards gold, vair, purple,
    opposing
And the broad fields beneath them turn crimson,
Then howl I my heart nigh mad with rejoicing.

2

In hot summer have I great rejoicing
When the tempests kill the earth's foul peace,
And the lightnings from black heav'n flash crimson,

And the fierce thunders roar me their music
And the winds shriek through the clouds mad, opposing,
And through all the riven skies God's swords clash.

3

Hell grant soon we hear again the swords clash!
And the shrill neighs of destriers in battle rejoicing,
Spiked breast to spiked breast opposing!
Better one hour's stour than a year's peace
With fat boards, bawds, wine and frail music!
Bah! there's no wine like the blood's crimson!

4

And I love to see the sun rise blood-crimson.
And I watch his spears through the dark clash
And it fills all my heart with rejoicing
And pries wide my mouth with fast music
When I see him so scorn and defy peace,
His lone might 'gainst all darkness opposing.

5

The man who fears war and squats opposing
My words for stour, hath no blood of crimson
But is fit only to rot in womanish peace
Far from where worth's won and the swords clash
For the death of such sluts I go rejoicing;
Yea, I fill all the air with my music.

6

Papiols, Papiols, to the music!
There's no sound like to swords swords opposing,
No cry like the battle's rejoicing
When our elbows and swords drip the crimson
And our charges 'gainst 'The Leopard's' rush clash.
May God damn for ever all who cry 'Peace!'

7

And let the music of the swords make them crimson!
Hell grant soon we hear again the swords clash!
Hell blot black for alway the thought 'Peace'!

Cino

Italian Campagna 1309, the open road

Bah! I have sung women in three cities,
But it is all the same;
And I will sing of the sun.

Lips, words, and you snare them,
Dreams, words, and they are as jewels,
Strange spells of old deity,
Ravens, nights, allurement:
And they are not;
Having become the souls of song.

Eyes, dreams, lips, and the night goes.
Being upon the road once more,
They are not.
Forgetful in their towers of our tuneing
Once for wind-runeing
They dream us-toward and
Sighing, say, "Would Cino,
Passionate Cino, of the wrinkling eyes,
Gay Cino, of quick laughter,
Cino, of the dare, the jibe.
Frail Cino, strongest of his tribe
That tramp old ways beneath the sun-light,
Would Cino of the Luth were here!'

Once, twice, a year—
Vaguely thus word they:

    'Cino?' 'Oh, eh, Cino Polnesi
    The singer is't you mean?'
    'Ah yes, passed once our way,
    A saucy fellow, but ...

    (Oh they are all one these vagabonds),
    Peste! 'tis his own songs?
    Or some other's that he sings?
    But *you*, My Lord, how with your city?'

But you 'My Lord,' God's pity!
And all I knew were out, My Lord, you
Were Lack-land Cino, e'en as I am,
O Sinistro.

I have sung women in three cities.
But it is all one.
I will sing of the sun.
... eh? ... they mostly had grey eyes,
But it is all one, I will sing of the sun.

    ''Pollo Phoibee, old tin pan, you
    Glory to Zeus' aegis-day,
    Shield o' steel-blue, th' heaven o'er us
    Hath for boss thy lustre gay!

    'Pollo Phoibee, to our way-fare
    Make thy laugh our wander-lied;
    Bid thy 'fulgence bear away care.
    Cloud and rain-tears pass they fleet!

    Seeking e'er the new-laid rast-way
    To the gardens of the sun ...

I have sung women in three cities.
But it is all one.

I will sing of the white birds
In the blue waters of heaven,
The clouds that are spray to its sea.'

The Tea Shop

The girl in the tea shop
    Is not so beautiful as she was,
The August has worn against her.
She does not get up the stairs so eagerly;
Yes, she also will turn middle-aged,
And the glow of youth that she spread about us
    As she brought us our muffins
Will be spread about us no longer,
    She also will turn middle-aged.

The Lake Isle

O God, O Venus, O Mercury, patron of thieves,
Give me in due time, I beseech you, a little tobacco-shop,
With the little bright boxes
    piled up neatly upon the shelves
And the loose fragrant cavendish
    and the shag,
And the bright Virginia
    loose under the bright glass cases,
And a pair of scales not too greasy,
And the whores dropping in for a word or two in passing,
For a flip word, and to tidy their hair a bit.
O God, O Venus, O Mercury, patron of thieves,
Lend me a little tobacco-shop,

or install me in any profession
Save this damn'd profession of writing,
    where one needs one's brains all the time.

Epitaphs

Fu I
Fu I loved the high cloud and the hill,
Alas, he died of alcohol.

Li Po
And Li Po also died drunk.
He tried to embrace a moon
In the Yellow River.

In a Station of the Metro

The apparition of these faces in the crowd;
Petals on a wet, black bough.

Alba

As cool as the pale wet leaves
        of lily-of-the-valley
She lay beside me in the dawn.

Praise of Ysolt

In vain have I striven, to teach my heart to bow;
In vain have I said to him
'There be many singers greater than thou.'

But his answer cometh, as winds and as lutany,
As a vague crying upon the night
That leaveth me no rest, saying ever,
      'Song, a song.'

Their echoes play upon each other in the twilight
Seeking ever a song.
Lo, I am worn with travail
And the wandering of many roads hath made my eyes
As dark red circles filled with dust.
Yet there is a trembling upon me in the twilight,
    And little red elf words crying 'A song,'
    Little grey elf words crying for a song,
    Little brown leaf words crying 'A song,'
    Little green leaf words crying for a song.
The words are as leaves, old brown leaves in the spring
    time
Blowing they know not whither, seeking a song.

White words as snow flakes but they are cold,
Moss words, lips words, words of slow streams.

In vain have I striven to teach my soul to bow,
In vain have I pled with him:
    'There be greater souls than thou.'

For in the morn of my years there came a woman
As moon light calling,
As the moon calleth the tides,
    'Song, a song.'
Wherefore I made her a song and she went from me
As the moon doth from the sea,
But still came the leaf words, little brown elf words
Saying "The soul sendeth us."
    'A song, a song!'

And in vain I cried unto them 'I have no song
For she I sang of hath gone from me.'

But my soul sent a woman, a woman of the wonderfolk,
A woman as fire upon the pine woods
    crying 'Song, a song.'
As the flame crieth into the sap.
My song was ablaze with her and she went from me
As flame leaveth the embers so went she unto new forests
And the words were with me
    crying ever 'Song, a song.'

And I "I have no song,"
Till my soul sent a woman as the sun:
Yea as the sun calleth to the seed,
As the spring upon the bough
So is she that cometh, the mother of songs,
She that holdeth the wonder words within her eyes
The words, little elf words
    that call ever unto me
      'Song, a song.'

Grace Before Song

Lord God of heaven that with mercy dight
Th'alternate prayer-wheel of the night and light
Eternal hast to thee, and in whose sight
Our days as rain drops in the sea surge fall,

As bright white drops upon a leaden sea
Grant so my songs to this grey folk may be:

As drops that dream and gleam and falling catch the sun,
Evanescent mirrors every opal one
Of such his splendour as their compass is,
Be bold, My Songs, to seek such death as this.

Envoi

In vain have I striven with my soul
   to teach my soul to bow
What soul boweth
   while in his heart art thou?

In Durance

I am homesick after mine own kind,
Oh I know that there are folk about me, friendly faces,
But I am homesick after mine own kind.

'These sell our pictures'! Oh well,
They reach me not, touch me some edge or that,
But reach me not and all my life's become
One flame, that reaches not beyond
My heart's own hearth,
Or hides among the ashes there for thee.
'Thee'? Oh, 'Thee' is who cometh first
Out of mine own soul-kin,
For I am homesick after mine own kind
And ordinary people touch me not.
                And I am homesick
After mine own kind that know, and feel
And have some breath for beauty and the arts.

Aye, I am wistful for my kin of the spirit
And have none about me save in the shadows
When come *they*, surging of power, 'DAEMON,'
'Quasi KALOUN.' S.T. says Beauty is most that, a "calling
    to the soul."
Well then, so call they, the swirlers out of the mist of my
    soul,
They that come mewards, bearing old magic.

But for all that, I am homesick after mine own kind
And would meet kindred even as I am,
Flesh-shrouded bearing the secret.
'All they that with strange sadness'
Have the earth in mockery, and are kind to all,
My fellows, aye I know the glory
Of th'unbounded ones, but ye, that hide
As I hide most the while
And burst forth to the windows only whiles or whiles
For love, or hope, or beauty or for power,
Then smoulder, with the lids half closed
And are untouched by echoes of the world.

Oh ye, my fellows: with the seas between us some be,
Purple and sapphire for the silver shafts
Of sun and spray all shattered at the bows;
And some the hills hold off,
The little hills to east us, though here we
Have damp and plain to be our shutting in.

And yet my soul sings 'Up!' and we are one.
Yea thou, and Thou, and THOU, and all my kin
To whom my breast and arms are ever warm,
For that I love ye as the wind the trees
That holds their blossoms and their leaves in cure
And calls the utmost singing from the boughs
That 'thout him, save the aspen, were as dumb

Still shade, and bade no whisper speak the birds of how
'Beyond, beyond, beyond, there lies...'

And Thus in Nineveh

'Aye! I am a poet and upon my tomb
Shall maidens scatter rose leaves
And men myrtles, ere the night
Slays day with her dark sword.

"Lo! this thing is not mine
Nor thine to hinder,
For the custom is full old,
And here in Nineveh have I beheld
Many a singer pass and take his place
In those dim halls where no man troubleth
His sleep or song.
And many a one hath sung his songs
More craftily, more subtle-souled than I;
And many a one now doth surpass
My wave-worn beauty with his wind of flowers,
Yet am I poet, and upon my tomb
Shall all men scatter rose leaves
Ere the night slay light
With her blue sword.

"It is not, Raana, that my song rings highest
Or more sweet in tone than any, but that I
Am here a Poet, that doth drink of life
As lesser men drink wine.'

Aux Belles de Londres

I am aweary with the utter and beautiful weariness
And with the ultimate wisdom and with things terrene,
I am aweary with your smiles and your laughter,
And the sun and the winds again
Reclaim their booty and the heart o' me.

Francesca

You came in out of the night
And there were flowers in your hands,
Now you will come out of a confusion of people,
Out of a turmoil of speech about you.

I who have seen you amid the primal things
Was angry when they spoke your name
In ordinary places.
I would that the cool waves might flow over my mind,
And that the world should dry as a dead leaf,
Or as a dandelion seed-pod and be swept away,
So that I might find you again,
Alone.

Planh
Of White Thoughts he saw in a Forest

Heavy with dreams,
Thou who art wiser than love,
Though I am hungry for their lips
        When I see them a-hiding
And a-passing out and in through the shadows
        In the pine wood,
And they are white, like the clouds in the sky's forest
Ere the stars arise to their hunting;

O White Poppy, who art wiser than love,
I am come for peace, yea from the hunting
Am I come to thee for peace.
Out of a new sorrow it is,
That my hunting hath brought me.

White Poppy, heavy with dreams,
Though I am hungry for their lips
        When I see them a-hiding
And a-passing out and in through the shadows
—And it is white they are—
But if one should look at me with the old hunger in her
        eyes,
How will I be answering her eyes?
For I have followed the white folk of the forest.

Aye! It's a long hunting
And it's a deep hunger I have when I see them a-gliding
And a-flickering there, where the trees stand apart.

But oh, it is sorrow and sorrow
When love dies-down in the heart.

Silet

When I behold how black, immortal ink
Drips from my deathless pen—ah, well-away!
Why should we stop at all for what I think?
There is enough in what I chance to say.

It is enough that we once came together;
What is the use of setting it to rime?
When it is autumn do we get spring weather,
Or gather may of harsh northwindish time?

It is enough that we once came together;
What if the wind have turned against the rain?
It is enough that we once came together;
Time has seen this, and will not turn again;

And who are we, who know that last intent,
To plague tomorrow with a testament!

In Exitum Cuiusdam
On a certain one's departure

'Time's bitter flood'! Oh, that's all very well,
But where's the old friend hasn't fallen off,
Or slacked his hand-grip when you first gripped fame?

I know your circle and can fairly tell
What you have kept and what you've left behind:
I know my circle and know very well
How many faces I'd have out of mind.

Portrait d'une Femme

Your mind and you are our Sargasso Sea,
London has swept about you this score years
And bright ships left you this or that in fee:
Ideals, old gossip, oddments of all things,
Strange spars of knowledge and dimmed wares of price.
Great minds have sought you—lacking someone else.
You have been second always. Tragical?
No. You preferred it to the usual thing:
One dull man, dulling and uxorious,
One average mind—with one thought less, each year.

Oh, you are patient, I have seen you sit
Hours, where something might have floated up.
And now you pay one. Yes, you richly pay.
You are a person of some interest, one comes to you
And takes strange gain away:
Trophies fished up; some curious suggestion;
Fact that leads nowhere; and a tale for two,
Pregnant with mandrakes, or with something else
That might prove useful and yet never proves,
That never fits a corner or shows use,
Or finds its hour upon the loom of days:
The tarnished, gaudy, wonderful old work;
Idols and ambergris and rare inlays,
These are your riches, your great store; and yet
For all this sea-hoard of deciduous things,
Strange woods half sodden, and new brighter stuff:
In the slow float of differing light and deep,
No! there is nothing! In the whole and all,
Nothing that's quite your own.
       Yet this is you.

N.Y.

My City, my beloved, my white! Ah, slender,
Listen! Listen to me, and I will breathe into thee a soul.
Delicately upon the reed, attend me!

Now do I know that I am mad,
For here are a million people surly with traffic;
This is no maid.
Neither could I play upon any reed if I had one.

My City, my beloved,
Thou art a maid with no breasts,
Thou art slender as a silver reed.

Listen to me, attend me!
And I will breathe into thee a soul,
And thou shalt live for ever.

A Girl

The tree has entered my hands,
The sap has ascended my arms,
The tree has grown in my breast—
Downward,
The branches grow out of me, like arms.

Tree you are,
Moss you are,
You are violets with wind above them.
A child—*so* high—you are,
And all this is folly to the world.

Plunge

I would bathe myself in strangeness:
These comforts heaped upon me, smother me!
I burn, I scald so for the new,
New friends, new faces,
Places!
Oh to be out of this,
This that is all I wanted
        —save the new.

And you,
Love, you the much, the more desired!
Do I not loathe all walls, streets, stones,
All mire, mist, all fog,

All ways of traffic?
You, I would have flow over me like water,
Oh, but far out of this!
Grass, and low fields, and hills,
And sun,
Oh, sun enough!
Out, and alone, among some
Alien people!

A Virginal

No, no! Go from me. I have left her lately.
I will not spoil my sheath with lesser brightness,
For my surrounding air hath a new lightness;
Slight are her arms, yet they have bound me straitly
And left me cloaked as with a gauze of æther;
As with sweet leaves; as with a subtle clearness.
Oh, I have picked up magic in her nearness
To sheathe me half in half the things that sheathe her.

No, no! Go from me. I have still the flavour,
Soft as spring wind that's come from birchen bowers.
Green come the shoots, aye April in the branches,
As winter's wound with her sleight hand she staunches,
Hath of the trees a likeness of the savour:
As white their bark, so white this lady's hours.

An Immorality

Sing we for love and idleness,
Naught else is worth the having.

Though I have been in many a land,
There is naught else in living.

And I would rather have my sweet,
Though rose-leaves die of grieving,

Than do high deeds in Hungary
To pass all men's believing.

MARIANNE MOORE
1887-1972

After graduating from Bryn Mawr and Carlisle
Commercial College, Marianne Moore taught for a
period and then moved to New York City where she
became editor of the magazine *The Dial*. She did not
publish a book until her mid-thirties but *Poems* of 1921
was followed by an infrequent series of collections
including *The Pangolin and Other Verse* (1936), *Collected
Poems* (1951, Pulitzer Prize) and *O To Be a Dragon*
(1959).

Moore described poetry as 'imaginary gardens
with real toads in them'. Her own work is illuminated
by precise and pleasingly unexpected metaphors based
on her knowledge of biology and interest in zoos.

The Steeple-Jack
Revised, 1961

Dürer would have seen a reason for living
   in a town like this, with eight stranded whales
to look at; with the sweet sea air coming into your house
on a fine day, from water etched
   with waves as formal as the scales
on a fish.

One by one in two's and three's, the seagulls keep
   flying back and forth over the town clock,
or sailing around the lighthouse without moving their
     wings—
rising steadily with a slight
   quiver of the body – or flock
mewing where

a sea the purple of the peacock's neck is
   paled to greenish azure as Dürer changed
the pine green of the Tyrol to peacock blue and guinea
gray. You can see a twenty-five-
   pound lobster; and fish nets arranged
to dry. The

whirlwind fife-and-drum of the storm bends the salt
   marsh grass, disturbs stars in the sky and the
star on the steeple; it is a privilege to see so
much confusion. Disguised by what
   might seem the opposite, the sea-
side flowers and

trees are favored by the fog so that you have
   the tropics at first hand: the trumpet vine,
foxglove, giant snapdragon, a salpiglossis that has
spots and stripes; morning-glories, gourds,

or moon-vines trained on fishing twine
at the back door:

cattails, flags, blueberries and spiderwort,
    striped grass, lichens, sunflowers, asters, daisies—
yellow and crab-claw ragged sailors with green bracts –
        toad-plant,
petunias, ferns; pink lilies, blue
    ones, tigers; poppies; black sweet-peas.
The climate

is not right for the banyan, frangipani, or
    jack-fruit trees; or for exotic serpent
life. Ring lizard and snakeskin for the foot, if you see fit;
but here they've cats, not cobras, to
    keep down the rats. The diffident
little newt

with white pin-dots on black horizontal spaced-
    out bands lives here; yet there is nothing that
ambition can buy or take away. The college student
named Ambrose sits on the hillside
    with his not-native books and hat
and sees boats

at sea progress white and rigid as if in
    a groove. Liking an elegance of which
the source is not bravado, he knows by heart the antique
sugar-bowl shaped summerhouse of
    interlacing slats, and the pitch
of the church

spire, not true, from which a man in scarlet lets
    down a rope as a spider spins a thread;
he might be part of a novel, but on the sidewalk a
sign says C. J. Poole, Steeple-Jack,

in black and white; and one in red
and white says

Danger. The church portico has four fluted
   columns, each a single piece of stone, made
modester by whitewash. This would be a fit haven for
waifs, children, animals, prisoners,
   and presidents who have repaid
sin-driven

senators by not thinking about them. The
   place has a schoolhouse, a post-office in a
store, fish-houses, hen-houses, a three-masted
   schooner on
the stocks. The hero, the student,
   the steeple-jack, each in his way,
is at home.

It could not be dangerous to be living
   in a town like this, of simple people,
who have a steeple-jack placing danger signs by the
     church
while he is gilding the solid-
   pointed star, which on a steeple
stands for hope.

The Jerboa
Too Much

A Roman had an
artist, a freedman,
   contrive a cone – pine cone
   or fir cone – with holes for a fountain. Placed on
     the Prison of St Angelo, this cone
     of the Pompeys which is known

now as the Popes', passed
for art. A huge cast
  bronze, dwarfing the peacock
  statue in the garden of the Vatican,
    it looks like a work of art made to give
    to a Pompey, or native

of Thebes. Others could
build, and understood
  making colossi and
  how to use slaves, and kept crocodiles and put
    baboons on the necks of giraffes to pick
    fruit, and used serpent magic.

They had their men tie
hippopotami
  and bring out dappled dog-
  cats to course antelopes, dikdik, and ibex;
    or used small eagles. They looked on as theirs,
    impalas and onigers,

the wild ostrich herd
with hard feet and bird
  necks rearing back in the
  dust like a serpent preparing to strike, cranes,
    mongooses, storks, anoas, Nile geese;
    and there were gardens for these—

combining planes, dates,
limes, and pomegranates,
  in avenues – with square
  pools of pink flowers, tame fish, and small frogs.
    Besides
    yarns dyed with indigo, and red cotton,
    they had a flax which they spun

into fine linen
cordage for yachtsmen.
  These people liked small things;
  they gave to boys little paired playthings such as
    nests of eggs, ichneumon and snake, paddle
    and raft, badger and camel;

and made toys for them-
selves: the royal totem;
  and toilet boxes marked
  with the contents. Lords and ladies put goose-grease
    paint in round bone boxes – the pivoting
    lid incised with a duck-wing

or reverted duck-
head; kept in a buck
  or rhinoceros horn,
  the ground horn; and locust oil in stone locusts.
    It was a picture with a fine distance;
    of drought, and of assistance

in time, from the Nile
rising slowly, while
  the pig-tailed monkey on
  slab hands, with arched-up slack-slung gait, and the
    brown
    dandy looked at the jasmine two-leafed twig
    and bud, cactus pads, and fig.

Dwarfs here and there, lent
to an evident
  poetry of frog grays,
  duck-egg greens, and eggplant blues, a fantasy
    and a verisimilitude that were
    right to those with, everywhere,

power over the poor.
The bees' food is your
  food. Those who tended flower-
    beds and stables were like the king's cane in the
      form of a hand, or the folding bedroom
      made for his mother of whom

he was fond. Princes
clad in queens' dresses,
  calla or petunia
    white, that trembled at the edge, and queens in a
      king's underskirt of fine-twilled thread like silk-
      worm gut, as bee-man and milk-

maid, kept divine cows
and bees; limestone brows,
  and gold-foil wings. They made
    basalt serpents and portraits of beetles; the
      king gave his name to them and he was named
      for them. He feared snakes, and tamed

Pharaoh's rat, the rust-
backed mongoose. No bust
  of it was made, but there
    was pleasure for the rat. Its restlessness was
      its excellence; it was praised for its wit;
      and the jerboa, like it,

a small desert rat,
and not famous, that
  lives without water, has
    happiness. Abroad seeking food, or at home
      in its burrow, the Sahara fieldmouse
      has a shining silver house

of sand. O rest and
joy, the boundless sand,
  the stupendous sandspout,
    no water, no palm trees, no ivory bed,
      tiny cactus; but one would not be he
      who has nothing but plenty.

The Fish

wade
through black jade.
  Of the crow-blue mussel shells, one keeps
  adjusting the ash heaps;
    opening and shutting itself like

an
injured fan.
  The barnacles which encrust the side
  of the wave, cannot hide
    there for the submerged shafts of the

sun,
split like spun
  glass, move themselves with spotlight swiftness
  into the crevices—
    in and out, illuminating

the
turquoise sea
  of bodies. The water drives a wedge
  of iron through the iron edge
    of the cliff; whereupon the stars,

pink
rice-grains, ink-
   bespattered jellyfish, crabs like green
   lilies, and submarine
      toadstools, slide each on the other.

All
external
   marks of abuse are present on this
   defiant edifice—
      all the physical features of

ac-
cident – lack
   of cornice, dynamite grooves, burns, and
   hatchet strokes, these things stand
      out on it; the chasm side is

dead.
Repeated
   evidence has proved that it can live
   on what can not revive
      its youth. The sea grows old in it.

Poetry
Original version

I, too, dislike it: there are things that are important
                              beyond all this fiddle.
   Reading it, however, with a perfect contempt for it, one
                           discovers in
      it after all, a place for the genuine.
         Hands that can grasp, eyes
         that can dilate, hair that can rise
            if it must, these things are important not because a

high-sounding interpretation can be put upon them but
because they are
useful. When they become so derivative as to become
unintelligible,
the same thing may be said for all of us, that we
do not admire what
we cannot understand: the bat
holding on upside down or in quest of something to

eat, elephants pushing, a wild horse taking a roll, a
tireless wolf under
a tree, the immovable critic twitching his skin like a
horse that feels a flea, the
base-
ball fan, the statistician
nor is it valid
to discriminate against 'business documents and

school-books'; all these phenomena are important. One
must make a distinction
however: when dragged into prominence by half poets,
the result is not poetry,
nor till the poets among us can be
'literalists of
the imagination' – above
insolence and triviality and can present

for inspection, 'imaginary gardens with real toads in
them,' shall we have
it. In the meantime, if you demand on the one hand,
the raw material of poetry in
all its rawness and
that which is on the other hand
genuine, you are interested in poetry.

Silence

My father used to say,
'Superior people never make long visits,
have to be shown Longfellow's grave
or the glass flowers at Harvard.
Self-reliant like the cat—
that takes its prey to privacy,
the mouse's limp tail hanging like a shoelace from its
    mouth—
they sometimes enjoy solitude,
and can be robbed of speech
by speech which has delighted them.
The deepest feeling always shows itself in silence;
not in silence, but restraint.'
Nor was he insincere in saying, 'Make my house your
    inn.'
Inns are not residences.

The Pangolin

Another armored animal – scale
    lapping scale with spruce-cone regularity until they
form the uninterrupted central
    tail-row! This near artichoke with head and legs and
                 grit-equipped gizzard,
  the night miniature artist engineer is,
    yes, Leonardo da Vinci's replica—
      impressive animal and toiler of whom we seldom
         hear.
    Armor seems extra. But for him,
      the closing ear-ridge—
        or bare ear lacking even this small
        eminence and similarly safe

contracting nose and eye apertures
    impenetrably closable, are not; a true ant-eater,
not cockroach-eater, who endures
    exhausting solitary trips through unfamiliar ground at
                night,
    returning before sunrise; stepping in the moonlight,
      on the moonlight peculiarly, that the outside
        edges of his hands may bear the weight and save
             the claws
    for digging. Serpentined about
      the tree, he draws
        away from danger unpugnaciously,
        with no sound but a harmless hiss; keeping

the fragile grace of the Thomas-
    of-Leighton Buzzard Westminster Abbey wrought-
              iron vine, or
rolls himself into a ball that has
    power to defy all effort to unroll it; strongly intailed,
              neat
    head for core, and neck not breaking off, with curled-in
              feet.
    Nevertheless he has sting-proof scales; and nest
      of rocks closed with earth from inside, which he
             can thus darken.
    Sun and moon and day and night and man and
             beast
      each with a splendor
        which man in all his vileness cannot
        set aside; each with an excellence!

'Fearful yet to be feared', the armored
    ant-eater met by the driver-ant does not turn back,
             but

engulfs what he can, the flattened sword-
　　edged leafpoints on the tail and artichoke set leg- and
　　　　　　　　body-plates
quivering violently when it retaliates
　　and swarms on him. Compact like the furled
　　　　　　　　fringed frill
　　on the hat-brim of Gargallo's hollow iron head of
　　　　　　　　a
　　matador, he will drop and will
　　　then walk away
　　　　unhurt, although if unintruded on,
　　　he cautiously works down the tree, helped

by his tail. The giant-pangolin-
　　tail, graceful tool, as prop or hand or broom or ax,
　　　　　　　　tipped like
an elephant's trunk with special skin,
　　is not lost on this ant- and stone-swallowing
　　　　　　　　uninjurable
artichoke which simpletons thought a living fable
　　whom the stones had nourished, whereas ants had
　　　　　　　　done
　　so. Pangolins are not aggressive animals;
　　　　　　　　between
　　dusk and day they have the not unchain-like
　　　　　　　　machine-like
　　　form and frictionless creep of a thing
　　　made graceful by adversities, con-

versities. To explain grace requires
　　a curious hand. If that which is at all were not
　　　　　　　　forever,
why would those who graced the spires
　　with animals and gathered there to rest, on cold
　　　　　　　　luxurious

low stone seats – a monk and monk and monk –
> between the thus
ingenious roof supports, have slaved to confuse
> grace with a kindly manner, time in which to
> > pay a debt,
the cure for sins, a graceful use
> of what are yet
> > approved stone mullions branching out across
> > the perpendiculars? A sailboat

was the first machine. Pangolins, made
> for moving quietly also, are models of exactness,
on four legs; on hind feet plantigrade,
> with certain postures of a man. Beneath sun and moon,
> > man slaving
to make his life more sweet, leaves half the flowers
> > worth having,
> needing to choose wisely how to use his strength;
> a paper-maker like the wasp; a tractor of
> > foodstuffs,
> like the ant; spidering a length
> of web from bluffs
> > above a stream; in fighting, mechanicked
> > like the pangolin; capsized in

disheartenment. Bedizened or stark
> naked, man, the self, the being we call human,
> > writing-
master to this world, griffons a dark
> 'Like does not like like that is obnoxious'; and writes
> > error with four
r's. Among animals, *one* has a sense of humor.
> Humor saves a few steps, it saves years.
> > Unignorant,
> modest and unemotional, and all emotion,
> he has everlasting vigor,

power to grow,
      though there are few creatures who can make
                              one
      breathe faster and make one erecter.

Not afraid of anything is he,
      and then goes cowering forth, tread paced to meet an
                              obstacle
at every step. Consistent with the
   formula – warm blood, no gills, two pairs of hands and
                        a few hairs – that
   is a mammal; there he sits in his own habitat,
      serge-clad, strong-shod. The prey of fear, he,
                              always
      curtailed, extinguished, thwarted by the dusk,
                        work partly done,
      says to the alternating blaze,
         'Again the sun!
            anew each day; and new and new and new,
            that comes into and steadies my soul.'

E. E. CUMMINGS
1894-1962

Born in Cambridge, Mass., Edward Estlin Cummings worked as a volunteer in the Ambulance Corps in France during World War One and was imprisoned in a French concentration camp for several months on a charge of treasonable correspondence. This provided the inspiration for his first book in 1923 and his first poetry appeared one year later. From then on he continued to publish experimental poetry, prose and drama, characterized by faith in the individual and an idiosyncratic use of words and structure.

The following poems are drawn from *Tulips and Chimneys* (1923), *Is* (1926) and *1 x 1* (1944).

*'it is at moments after
i have dreamed'*

it is at moments after i have dreamed
of the rare entertainment of your eyes,
when (being fool to fancy) i have deemed

with your peculiar mouth my heart made wise;
at moments when the glassy darkness holds

the genuine apparition of your smile
(it was through tears always) and silence moulds
such strangeness as was mine a little while;

moments when my once more illustrious arms
are filled with fascination, when my breast
wears the intolerant brightness of your charms:

one pierced moment whiter than the rest

– turning from the tremendous lie of sleep
i watch the roses of the day grow deep.

'the Cambridge ladies'

the Cambridge ladies who live in furnished souls
are unbeautiful and have comfortable minds
(also, with the church's protestant blessings
daughters, unscented shapeless spirited)
they believe in Christ and Longfellow, both dead,
are invariably interested in so many things—
at the present writing one still finds
delighted fingers knitting for the is it Poles?
perhaps. While permanent faces coyly bandy
scandal of Mrs N and Professor D

.... the Cambridge ladies do not care, above
Cambridge if sometimes in its box of
sky lavender and cornerless, the
moon rattles like a fragment of angry candy

*'a man who had fallen
among thieves'*

a man who had fallen among thieves
lay by the roadside on his back
dressed in fifteenthrate ideas
wearing a round jeer for a hat

fate per a somewhat more than less
emancipated evening
had in return for consciousness
endowed him with a changeless grin

whereon a dozen staunch and leal
citizens did graze at pause
then fired by hypercivic zeal
sought newer pastures or because

swaddled with a frozen brook
of pinkest vomit out of eyes
which noticed nobody he looked
as if he did not care to rise

one hand did nothing on the vest
its wideflung friend clenched weakly dirt
while the mute trouserfly confessed
a button solemnly inert.

Brushing from whom the stiffened puke
i put him all into my arms
and staggered banged with terror through
a million billion trillion stars

'next to of course god'

'next to of course god america i
love you land of the pilgrims' and so forth oh
say can you see by the dawn's early my
country 'tis of centuries come and go
and are no more what of it we should worry
in every language even deafanddumb
thy sons acclaim your glorious name by gorry
by jingo by gee by gosh by gum
why talk of beauty what could be more beaut-
iful than these heroic happy dead
who rushed like lions to the roaring slaughter
they did not stop to think they died instead
then shall the voice of liberty be mute?'

He spoke. And drank rapidly a glass of water

'my sweet old etcetera'

my sweet old etcetera
aunt lucy during the recent

war could and what
is more did tell you just
what everybody was fighting

for,
my sister

isabel created hundreds
(and
hundreds) of socks not to
mention shirts fleaproof earwarmers

etcetera wristers etcetera, my

mother hoped that

i would die etcetera
bravely of course my father used
to become hoarse talking about how it was
a privilege and if only he
could meanwhile my

self etcetera lay quietly
in the deep mud et

cetera
(dreaming,
et
    cetera, of
Your smile
eyes knees and of your Etcetera)

'what if a much of a which
of a wind'

what if a much of a which of a wind
gives the truth to summer's lie;
bloodies with dizzying leaves the sun
and yanks immortal stars awry?
Blow king to beggar and queen to seem
(blow friend to fiend:blow space to time)
– when skies are hanged and oceans drowned,
the single secret will still be man

what if a keen of a lean wind flays
screaming hills with sleet and snow:
strangles valleys by ropes of thing
and stifles forests in white ago?
Blow hope to terror; blow seeing to blind
(blow pity to envy and soul to mind)
– whose hearts are mountains, roots are trees,
it's they shall cry hello to the spring

what if a dawn of a doom of a dream
bites this universe in two,
peels forever out of his grave
and sprinkles nowhere with me and you?
Blow soon to never and never to twice
(blow life to isn't:blow death to was)
– all nothing's only our hugest home;
the most who die, the more we live

LANGSTON HUGHES
1902-1967

Born in Missouri, Langston Hughes was a major figure
in the Harlem Renaissance of New York in the 1920s.
He began his literary career with *The Weary Blues*
(1926), a collection of poems on black themes in jazz
rhythms and idioms, and went on to write novels,
plays, short stories, autobiography and political
writings. His work is distinguished by its social
consciousness, being primarily concerned with his race,
mainly in an urban setting. He remains best known for
his poetry.

The Weary Blues

Droning a drowsy syncopated tune,
Rocking back and forth to a mellow croon,
    I heard a Negro play.
Down on Lenox Avenue the other night
By the pale dull pallor of an old gas light
    He did a lazy sway....
    He did a lazy sway....
To the tune o' those Weary Blues.
With his ebony hands on each ivory key
He made that poor piano moan with melody.
    O Blues!
Swaying to and fro on his rickety stool
He played that sad raggy tune like a musical fool.
    Sweet Blues!
Coming from a black man's soul.
    O Blues!
In a deep song voice with a melancholy tone
I heard that Negro sing, that old piano moan—
    'Ain't got nobody in all this world,
    Ain't got nobody but ma self.
    I's gwine to quit ma frownin'
    And put ma troubles on the shelf.'
Thump, thump, thump, went his foot on the floor.
He played a few chords then he sang some more—
    'I got the Weary Blues
    And I can't be satisfied.
    Got the Weary Blues
    And can't be satisfied—
    I ain't happy no mo'
    And I wish that I had died.'
And far into the night he crooned that tune.
The stars went out and so did the moon.
The singer stopped playing and went to bed
While the Weary Blues echoed through his head.
He slept like a rock or a man that's dead.

Stony Lonesome

They done took Cordelia
Out to stony lonesome ground.
Done took Cordelia
To stony lonesome,
Laid her down.
They done put Cordelia
Underneath that
Grassless mound.

   Ay-Lord!
     Ay-Lord!
       Ay-Lord!
She done left po' Buddy
To struggle by his self.
Po' Buddy Jones,
Yes, he's done been left.
She's out in stony lonesome,
Lordy! Sleepin' by herself.
  Cordelia's
    In stony
      Lonesome
        Ground!

Ballad of the Landlord

Landlord, landlord,
My roof has sprung a leak.
Don't you 'member I told you about it
Way last week?

Landlord, landlord,
These steps is broken down.
When you come up yourself
It's a wonder you don't fall down.

Ten Bucks you say I owe you?
Ten Bucks you say is due?
Well, that's Ten Bucks more'n I'll pay you
Till you fix this house up new.

What? You gonna get eviction orders?
You gonna cut off my heat?
You gonna take my furniture and
Throw it in the street?

Um-huh! You talking high and mighty.
Talk on – till you get through.
You ain't gonna be able to say a word
If I land my fist on you.

Police! Police!
Come and get that man!
He's trying to ruin the government
And overturn the land!

Copper's whistle!
Patrol bell!
Arrest.

Precinct Station.
Iron cell.
Headlines in press:

MAN THREATENS LANDLORD

TENANT HELD NO BAIL

JUDGE GIVES NEGRO 90 DAYS IN COUNTY JAIL

Madam and the Minister

Reverend Butler came by
My house last week.
He said, Have you got
A little time to speak?

He said, I am interested
In your soul.
Has it been saved,
Or is your heart stone-cold?

I said, Reverend,
I'll have you know
I was baptized
Long ago.

He said, What have you
Done since then?
I said, None of your
Business, friend.

He said, Sister
Have you back-slid?
I said, It felt good—
If I did!

He said, Sister,
Come time to die,
The Lord will surely
Ask you why!
I'm gonna pray
For you!
Goodbye!

I felt kinder sorry
I talked that way
After Rev. Butler
Went away—
So I ain't in no mood
For sin today.

Preference

I likes a woman
six or eight and ten years older'n myself.
I don't fool with these young girls.
Young girl'll say,
> *Daddy, I want so-and-so.*
> *I needs this, that, and the other.*
But a old woman'll say,
> *Honey, what does YOU need?*
> *I just drawed my money tonight*
> *and it's all your'n.*
That's why I likes a older woman
who can appreciate me:
When she conversations you
it ain't forever, *Gimme!*

The Negro

I am a Negro:
  Black as the night is black,
  Black like the depths of my Africa.

I've been a slave:
  Caesar told me to keep his door-steps clean.
  I brushed the boots of Washington.

I've been a worker:
    Under my hand the pyramids arose.
    I made mortar for the Woolworth Building.

I've been a singer:
    All the way from Africa to Georgia I carried my sorrow
        songs.
    I made ragtime.

I've been a victim:
    The Belgians cut off my hands in the Congo.
    They lynch me now in Texas.

I am a Negro:
    Black as the night is black,
    Black like the depths of my Africa.

Acknowledgements

The Publishers wish to thank the following for permission to reprint previously published material. Every effort has been made to locate all persons having any rights in the poems appearing in this book, but appropriate acknowledgement may have been omitted in some cases through lack of information. Such omissions will be corrected in future printings of the book upon written notification to the Publishers.

Henry Holt and Company, Inc for *The Pasture, Fire and Ice, Meeting and Passing, The Road Not Taken* and *Design* from THE POETRY OF ROBERT FROST edited by Edward Canery Lathem. Copyright © 1969 by Holt Rinehart and Winston, Inc. Copyright © 1962 by Robert Frost. Copyright © 1975 by Lesley Frost Ballantine.

Alfred A. Knopf Inc for *The Emperor of Ice Cream, Disillusionment of Ten O'Clock* and *Anecdote of the Jar* © 1923 and renewed 1951 by Wallace Stevens; *Sad Strains of a Gay Waltz* © 1936 by Wallace Stevens and renewed 1964 by Holly Stevens; *Poetry is a Destructive Force* 1942 and renewed 1970 by Holly Stevens; *Holiday in Reality* © 1947 Wallace Stevens. All these were reprinted from THE COLLECTED POEMS OF WALLACE STEVENS.

Viking Penguin Inc for *The Steeple Jack, The Jerboa, The Fish, Poetry, Silence, The Pangolin* from THE COLLECTED POEMS OF MARIANNE MOORE © 1951.

Liveright Publishing Corporation for *it is at moments after i have dreamed* and *the cambridge ladies* from TULIPS AND CHIMNEYS by E.E. Cummings, edited by George James Firmage, © 1923, 1925 and renewed 1951, 1953 by E.E. Cummings. Copyright © 1973, 1976 by the Trustees for the E.E. Cummings Trust. Copyright © 1973, 1976 by George James Firmage; *a man who had fallen among thieves, next to of course god america i, my sweet old etcetera* from IS 5 poems by E.E. Cummings, edited by George James Firmage. Copyright © 1985 by E.E. Cummings Trust. Copyright 1926 by Horace Liveright. Copyright © 1954 by E.E. Cummings. Copyright © 1985 by George James Firmage. *what if a much of a which of a wind* from COMPLETE POEMS 1913-1962 by E.E. Cummings. Copyright © 1923, 1925, 1931, 1938, 1939, 1940, 1944, 1945, 1946, 1947, 1948, 1949, 1950, 1951, 1952, 1953, 1954, 1955, 1956, 1957, 1958, 1959, 1960, 1961, 1962, by the trustees for the E.E. Cummings Trust. Copyright © 1961, 1963, 1968 by Marion Morehouse Cummings.

Alfred A. Knopf Inc. for *The Weary Blues* copyright 1926 by Alfred A. Knopf, Inc. and renewed 1954 by Langston Hughes; *Stony Lonesome* copyright 1942 by Alfred A. Knopf, Inc.; *Madam and the Minister* copyright 1948 by Alfred A. Knopf, Inc. from SELECTED POEMS OF LANGSTON HUGHES.

David Higham Associates for *Ballad of the Landlord, Preference* and *The Negro* from SELECTED POEMS.